ADVANCE PRAISE FOR JON BELL'S BOOK!

"The bite-sized exercises are easy to follow, and move so smoothly from beginner to advanced that you'll be shocked at what you've created in such a short time."

—Michele Bousquet
Author of 3D Studio Max R2 *and* 3D Studio Max: Tutorials From the Masters

"This book offers the most insight into the various ways you can use 3DMAX to create any scene you could possibly want. An instant classic!"

—Greg Gleason
MIS Manager for the Phoenix Suns and 3D Animator

"This book is nothing less than the instructional *tour de force* for using 3D Studio MAX to create completely professional Hollywood-style animation effects. For those looking to move up to professional film work, *3D Studio Max R2.5 f/x and design* is a necessary resource leading to the mastery of those often-encountered Hollywood staples: Spaceships, lasers, and the dim underwater world."

—Alex Kiriako
Associate Editor, 3D Artist *magazine*

"I was amazed at what was possible with MAX after reading this book. The included CD-ROM comes with the cinemas created in the tutorials, along with many texture maps and other goodies. You will gain valuable MAX skills that can be applied to many scenes besides just space and underwater effects. You'll have fun with this book!!"

—Ben Horne
3D graphic artist, Bonehead Software

"Die-hard Internet junkies may recognize Jon Bell's name from the 3D Studio mail lists and newsgroups, and already know that he is funny, helpful, and incredibly knowledgeable about 3D Studio. For those who haven't seen him anywhere on the Internet, you're in for a treat. Jon covers lasers, outer space effects, warp, explosions, shields, underwater caustic effects, and more.

This book will help anyone who has mastered the basics of MAX make ordinary scenes look incredible. Lighting and scene layout are given thorough treatment throughout the text, giving you the foundational elements for doing serious 3D scene work.

The CD that accompanies the book contains the models, textures, and animations used in the book , and some to spare. A final plus is the addition of numerous Internet resources containing information about 3D Studio Max."

—Rick Spaulding
DesignCAD Solutions Group

Creative PROFESSIONALS PRESS™

3D STUDIO MAX R2.5

f/x
and design

JON A. BELL

with **James Green, Ken Allen Robertson, Michael Spaw, and Scot Tumlin**
Plug-ins by **Harry Denholm and Tom Hudson**

The Coriolis Group, Inc.
An International Thomson Publishing Company
14455 N. Hayden Road, Suite 220
Scottsdale, Arizona 85260

602/483-0192
FAX 602/483-0193
http://www.coriolis.com

Library of Congress Cataloging-In-Publication Data
Bell, Jon A. (Jon Allen), 1961-
   3D Studio MAX release 2.5 f/x and design / by Jon Bell.
     p. cm
   Includes index.
   ISBN 1-56604-770-6
   1. Computer animation. 2. 3D studio. 3. Computer graphics.
I. Title.
TR897.7.B47   1998
006.6'93--DC21
                      97-43401
                       CIP

Printed in the United States of America
10 9 8 7 6 5 4 3 2

Publisher
Keith Weiskamp

Acquisitions
Stephanie Wall

Project Editor
Michelle Stroup

Production Coordinator
Jon Gabriel

Cover Design
Anthony Stock

Layout Design
April Nielsen

CD-ROM Development
Robert Clarfield

an International Thomson Publishing company

Albany, NY • Belmont, CA • Bonn • Boston • Cincinnati • Detroit • Johannesburg
London • Madrid • Melbourne • Mexico City • New York • Paris • Singapore
Tokyo • Toronto • Washington

DEDICATION

This book is dedicated to my beautiful and talented wife Joan Gale Frank—
"Instant Guts!" author, adventurer, risk-taker, and best friend.

"I will follow you, as you will follow me…"

…ad astra per terra.

3D STUDIO
MAX R2.5
F/X AND DESIGN

ABOUT THE AUTHOR

Jon A. Bell is a writer and 3D computer graphics artist who has used 3D Studio since Version 1 (for MS-DOS). After working 10 years as an editor and writer in the computer magazine industry, Jon changed careers to concentrate full time on producing 3D computer graphics and animation for television, films, computer games multimedia, and print. He provided animation for the films *Exorcist III: Legion*, *Terminator 2: Judgment Day*, and *Honey, I Blew Up the Kid*. His video work includes Autodesk's/Kinetix's 1991, 1994, and 1997 SIGGRAPH reels, their 1993 and 1996 NAB (National Association of Broadcasters) reels, and consulting work for Digital Phenomena and Matte World Digital. His multimedia and game industry work includes architectural models and animation for the Oracle Systems *Athenia* CD-ROM, model designs and animation for LucasArt's Entertainment's *X-Wing* and *Rebel Assault*, Sega of America's *Jurassic Park* and *Wild Woody* CD-ROMS, and Gametek's *Robotech* and *Wheel of Fortune*. In addition, he provides 3D graphics as a volunteer for Hawkes Ocean Technologies, Pt. Richmond, CA, the builders of the experimental minisub Deep Flight I.

You can reach Jon at 74124.276@compuserve.com.

About the Guest Contributors

Scot Tumlin is a San Francisco Bay Area 3D artist and animator with over seven years' experience in creating digital content. Scot has worked with several game developers, including Acclaim Coin-Op Entertainment, Maxis, Sega of America and Spectrum Holobyte. He currently works at GameTek, a leading developer of console and PC-based games. In his spare time he writes "how to" articles for 3D Design Magazine, and provides 3D graphics support for Hawkes Ocean Technologies.

You can reach Scot at scottumlin@aol.com.

Michael Spaw is a 2D illustrator and 3D artist with Gametek, Inc., of Sausalito, CA. Michael's projects include the content for Autodesk's Texture Universe CD-ROM, the Xeno-1 CD-ROM, and shots for Autodesk's 1995 SIGGRAPH reel and the Kinetix 1996 NAB (National Association of Broadcasters) MAX Release 1 reel. In addition, he has provided documentation for Digimation's Chameleon and Pandora plug-ins.

You can reach Michael at eclipse@scc.net.

Ken Allen Robertson began his career as an actor/director for theatre and film, and has appeared in numerous productions. He's created graphics and animations the 1996 Summer Olympics, and for such companies as Mattel, Velocity, Intel, and AT&T. For the past three years he's focused on next-generation real-time 3D for gaming platforms and Internet environments. Ken holds an MFA from the National Theatre Conservatory. Currently, he works in the computer games industry, teaches 3D Studio Max special effects at the Computer Arts Institute in San Francisco, and also teaches cinematography at Pixar.

You can reach Ken at aceallen@hooked.net.

Harry Denholm (founder of Ishani Graphics) stumbled into the MAX scene in 1997 while working with a games company, and began working with MAX's SDK almost immediately. Unfortunately, he had to return to school and was left suddenly with only a fraction of free time to pursue his fascination with graphics programming and 3D. This proved not to be a problem, however, as he realized that doing no school work whatsoever provided a significant boost in spare time to learn and experiment with 3D Studio. (His teachers and tutors at school took a less-than-ecstatic view that Harry chose to build a MAX cloud material rather than write an English essay.)

After (miraculously) passing his final exams, Harry left school and now works for Autodesk Ltd., Kinetix division, as a technical consultant supporting MAX developers worldwide. He currently lives in Guildford, UK.

You can reach Harry at harry.denholm@eur.autodesk.com.

Tom Hudson is one of the original developers of 3D Studio/DOS (along with Dan Silva) and has worked on every version of 3D Studio/DOS and 3D Studio MAX. As an independent software developer, Tom has created numerous 2D and 3D graphics packages, including DEGAS, DEGAS Elite, CAD-3D and CyberSculpt for the Atari ST; 3D Studio/DOS Releases 1-4, IPAS plug-ins such as the Starfield generator, MAX Release 1 and 2, and several MAX plug-ins, such as Starfield. His contribution to this book is Greeble 1.0, a procedural detailing object modifier plug-in.

You can reach Tom at hudson-oconnell@aol.com.

James Green is a 3D graphics artist and recovering physics major who's returned to a profession that allows him to play with cool toys that don't involve keVs and high vacuum systems. The first computer he worked with was a Timex-Sinclair Z80. In discovering that he could get the computer to do graphics, it was a short journey from the Timex-Sinclair to an Amiga, where he honed many of his 2D skills on the Amiga platform. James jumped from the Amiga to doing 3D on the IBM PC, using 3D Studio R1 and POV-Ray. His work has appeared in magazines, corporate videos, and product demo reels. Currently, he's a 3D animator with Gametek, Inc., Sausalito, California, where he uses 3D Studio MAX, Softimage, and NinGen.

You can reach James at jamesg01@hotmail.com.

3D STUDIO

MAX R2.5

F/X AND DESIGN

3D STUDIO
MAX R2.5
F/X AND DESIGN

ACKNOWLEDGMENTS

In 1996, I wrote *3D Studio MAX f/x: Creating Hollywood-Style Special Effects*. It was my first book, and a bunch of people helped me give birth to it (a very painful event, even metaphorically).

Once again, at the risk of sounding like an Academy Awards speech, the following people need public thanks and acknowledgment for providing advice, encouragement and inspiration to me for this second book:

- My Ventana publisher Neweleen Trebnick, Acquisitions Editor Chris Grahms, Editors Paul Cory and Amy Hayworth; Coriolis Editor Michelle Stroup, Art Director Anthony Stock, CD-ROM Developer Robert Clarfield, Production Coordinator Jon Gabriel, and Designer April Nielsen.

- My technical editors, friends and fellow authors Andy and Stephanie Reese, for their friendship, moral and editorial support, and legal advice.

- Gametek's Tom Reuterdahl, Mimi Doggett and Clifford Lau for their encouragement, support and understanding of this second (crazy) endeavor.

- My contributors and co-conspirators James Green, Ken Allen Robertson, Michael Spaw, and Scot Tumlin; I (literally!) couldn't have done this book without your help.

- Special thanks to John Wainwright, author of MAXScript, for his invaluable assistance on the scripting chapters of this book.

- The amazing folks at Hawkes Ocean Technologies: Graham, Karen and Oliver Hawkes, Bob Whiteaker, Eric Hobson, and Howard Konvalin, the builders of the experimental minisub Deep Flight I; thanks for letting me be a part of your dream.

- The magical 3D mutants at Digital Phenomena (www.dph.com): Jamie Clay and Jeannie O'lone (who are so overwhelmingly nice they make Barney the Dinosaur look like a Klingon barbarian), Kevin O'lone, Peter Clay (thanks for the particle stuff!), Karl, Jonah, Kim, Lance, and Laurel; thanks for your pointers and for letting me steal cycles from your rendering farm.

- Industrial Light and Magic Effects Supervisors John Knoll and Bill George, Model Shop Supervisor John Goodson, and "Star Trek" model-maker extraordinaire Ed Miarecki, who've provided expert advice to me over the years on both CGI and traditional cinematic effects.

- Hollywood Production Artist Ron Cobb, an immensely talented artist and wonderful human being whose work has inspired me for 20 years.

- Doug Fake and Jeff Johnson at Intrada, San Francisco; thanks for all the music (even if my soundtrack purchases are helping put Doug's daughters through college).

- 3D Studio/DOS and 3D Studio MAX developers Gary Yost, Jack Powell, Tom Hudson, Dan Silva, Don Brittain, Rolf Berteig, and Eric and Audrey Peterson.

- And again, my parents Jim and Bonnie Thomas; now you have another incomprehensible computer book from your son (but it's suitably thick, so you might at least be able to crack walnuts with it).

Foreword

During the first six months of 1996, I wrote my first book, entitled *3D Studio MAX f/x: Creating Hollywood-style Special Effects*. It was an amazingly difficult task—dictating, writing, and editing a 500-page MAX book, while simultaneously learning and testing the (then-beta) MAX Release 1 software—and without a finished manual until the software shipped in April! On top of that, I had to create all the scene files, models, animations and texture maps for the CD-ROM—as well as produce over 200 still renderings, screen grabs and the rendering for the book's cover. (The latter was a first for Ventana; I, in a coin-toss between naivete and artistic temperament, had always assumed I would create the cover of my own book.)

Concurrent with this activity, I produced a 40-second shot for Kinetix's first MAX NAB (National Association of Broadcasters) reel, worked part-time in the computer games industry, and planned a whirlwind, 33-day round-the-world trip with my wife Joan. The trip was to take place the entire month of July, therefore, the book *had* to be done in late June to meet its press date, and be available at the 1996 SIGGRAPH in New Orleans.

To get all this insanity accomplished, I worked long hours, dictated most of the tutorials (and later edited dozens of transcript pages), lived on lattes and cinnamon rolls, and played non-stop film scores (while editing, not dictating) to give me the fortitude to carry on.

I almost went crazy, and vowed I would never do it again.

Right.

Anyway, I succeeded in finishing the book, shipped it off to Ventana, and retained (at least the appearance of) my sanity. Joan and I went on our trip, had a fantastic experience (a story for another day), we returned in time for SIGGRAPH, and I saw my first book debut at Digimation's booth. It was a heady experience seeing new MAX users, hungry for information, snatch it up—and it was really strange signing their copies, as if I were Stephen King or John Grisham. (Actually, these guys are welcome to their fame, but if I could just get a *tenth* of their royalties…)

Since then, I've received dozens of positive emails from MAX users letting me know that *3D Studio MAX f/x* was fun, inspirational, and informative, and was well worth their time and money.

Sigh. Oh well…

As you've probably noticed, in 1997-1998, I decided that writing another MAX book was worth my time again, too. Only this time, I decide to share the wealth—for this book, I've farmed out 10 chapters to my talented friends Scot Tumlin, Ken Robertson, Michael Spaw, and James Green, and commissioned MAX Release 2.5 plug-ins from Harry Denholm and Tom Hudson. Their MAX expertise helps make this a better book, as they cover material that I have neither the time nor the specific knowledge to address.

I said I'd never do it again. Guess I lied.

Hope you don't mind.

Jon A. Bell
Sonoma, CA

TABLE OF CONTENTS

3D STUDIO MAX R2.5

F/X AND DESIGN

"ONCE MORE UNTO THE BREACH, DEAR FRIENDS..."

1

...In which the author tells the tale of both the genesis of 3D Studio MAX, and his first MAX f/x book, while quoting Shakespeare's Henry V...

When I was writing *3D Studio MAX f/x: Creating Hollywood-Style Special Effects* (Ventana, 1996), Gary Yost and his team were still putting the finishing touches on what has now become a milestone in the 3D graphics software field. In April 1996, at the National Association of Broadcasters (NAB) show in Las Vegas, the new Autodesk multimedia subsidiary, Kinetix, took the wraps off 3D Studio MAX and changed the face of desktop 3D graphics once again.

3D Studio MAX was a radical departure from its predecessor, 3D Studio Release 4. It was not a port of its MS-DOS-based ancestor; instead, 3D Studio MAX was, and is, a completely reworked application that takes full advantage of its Windows NT environment. With its elegant GUI, open architecture, and "core components" technology, 3D Studio MAX has blazed a path that others—including its competitors—are being forced to follow.

In addition, every copy of MAX that is sold now includes MAX source code and the software development kit (SDK), which has enabled MAX users with C++ programming expertise to develop their own plug-ins. The anticipated effect came to pass, but perhaps more quickly than any of us realized. In short order, both professional software development companies and individual MAX users began writing dozens of plug-ins. Many of the latter group, such as Peter Watje, Harry Denholm, Blur Studio's Steven Blackmon, and others, seemed to regard it as a contest: who could write the most cool MAX plug-ins the fastest—and better yet, make them available for download—for *free!*

By bringing market forces to bear, Kinetix and The Yost Group have succeeded in their goal of making MAX a true "3D graphics operating environment"—with an ever-increasing arsenal of features that seems to grow virtually every day. This metaphor is being copied by other 3D graphics software developers, both PC- and workstation-based, and is a real indicator of where the 3D visualization industry is heading. Concurrent with this software development are the incredible increases in CPU speeds, graphics accelerators, and other hardware that make everyone wonder: What new marvel could be next?

Well, one of those marvels is here: 3D Studio MAX Release 2 and 2.5. The second release of MAX features over 1,000 new and improved features, including:

- NURBS modeling capability
- Ray-traced rendering, materials, and map types
- Digimation's LenZFX (now called simply Lens Effects) optical effects package

- Enhanced Track View and Material Editor menus and dialogs

- Advanced particle systems

- A new inverse kinematics (IK) controller

- Object dynamics for real-world physical simulations

...and a wealth of other features.

In addition, many new features that were available as third-party plug-ins for MAX Release 1.x have now been incorporated into the core feature set of MAX Release 2 and 2.5. This array of new features and functionality gives MAX users even greater ability to produce eye-popping, award-winning graphics.

As this book's contributors and I (all MAX Release 2 beta testers) were working on this book, we had witnessed the first 18 months in the life of MAX Release 1, which grew to an installed base of 35,000 copies. In August 1997, we attended the SIGGRAPH computer graphics show in Los Angeles and watched the reactions to MAX Release 2's introduction. The audience's reaction during the demos bordered on ecstatic, to put it mildly. The reel that Kinetix played at its booth showcased a staggering variety of MAX 3D animations for multimedia, film, and television. And now, with the release of MAX's second incarnation, and its update R2.5, tens of thousands of new MAX artists all over the world are not only envisioning new worlds, but creating them as well. It will be an awesome experience to see what new worlds they take us to.

I hope that this book, like *3D Studio MAX f/x* before it, can help MAX users bring their dreams into reality—or at least capture them as 24-bit color "paintings of light" on film, on tape, or in print.

The Original Book Vs. The Sequel

As previously mentioned, I spent the first half of 1996 writing *3D Studio MAX f/x*, the predecessor to this book. In the first book, I mentioned that its emphasis derived from my interests in outer space and underwater environments. These interests, in turn, came from a childhood spent watching 1960s television. Shows such as the original *Star Trek*, *Voyage to the Bottom of the Sea*, *The Time Tunnel*, and *Land of the Giants*, as well as *Wild Kingdom*, Jacques Cousteau specials, and shows about the Apollo space program, fueled my youthful imagination. My interest in the unusual continues to this day; indeed, my wife has remarked that I'm "more interested in what *isn't*, than in what *is*."

The first *3D Studio MAX f/x* book introduced readers to techniques for creating Hollywood-style special visual effects using 3D Studio MAX Release 1 only—additional plug-ins weren't required. (No plug-ins existed for MAX at the time, anyway.) The book covered techniques for creating believable outer space and underwater environments and all of the elements therein, such as planets, laser beams, nebulas, force fields, explosions, solar flares, bubbles, plankton, water caustics, and so on. It also covered MAX's unique parametric Object Modifiers, its rendering features (such as environmental mapping, volumetric fog, and lighting), and advanced texture-mapping techniques.

Figure 1.1 My first 3D Studio MAX book, *3D Studio MAX f/x: Creating Hollywood-Style Special Effects*, describes how to create a wide variety of outer space and underwater special effects.

Although in this book I continue to focus on the extraordinary rather than the mundane, I also present a "grab bag" of effects techniques that are feature-related rather than genre-related. The contributors and I will cover all-new special effects techniques such as:

- Creating complex materials using custom Diffuse, Shininess, Shininess Strength, and Specular maps and new maps such as Falloff, Cellular, and Raytrace

- Creating organic shapes with NURBS (see Figure 1.2)

- Using Object- and World-Space Modifiers

- Using the improved particle systems

- Raytracing and Dynamics

- Expressions and Scripting

...and more!

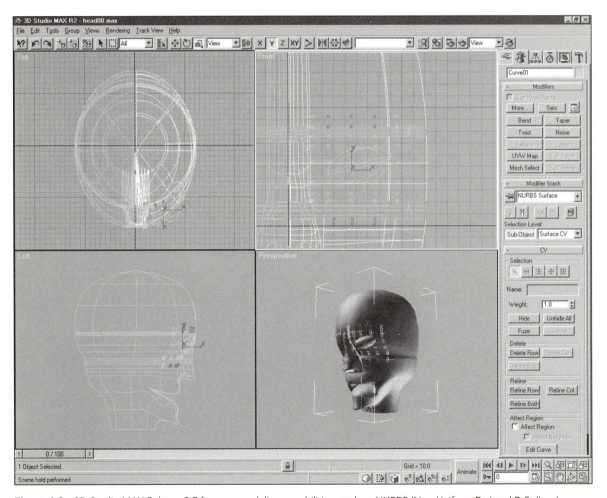

Figure 1.2 3D Studio MAX Release 2.5 features modeling capabilities, such as NURBS (Non-Uniform Rational B-Splines).

In addition to material that is native to MAX Release 2.5, this book presents general 3D effects techniques, such as suggestions for improving your lighting and creating realistic materials. It also discusses how you can augment your MAX work with third-party tools, such as Adobe Photoshop. Finally, you'll see how you can use MAX Release 2.5 plug-ins—some developed exclusively for this book—to create cool new effects.

3D Studio MAX R2.5 f/x and design: The Guest Cast

With virtually all complex creative endeavors, there's no such thing as a one-man show. Although I wrote the first *3D Studio MAX f/x* book myself, for this one, I decided to farm out some of the writing and effects to jazz up the mix. (It also helped me preserve my sanity while covering the huge number of new MAX features.)

So, assisting me on *3D Studio MAX R2.5 f/x and design* are:

- Harry Denholm of Ishani Graphics, a noted developer of excellent shareware MAX plug-ins and now working as with Kinetix Technical Support

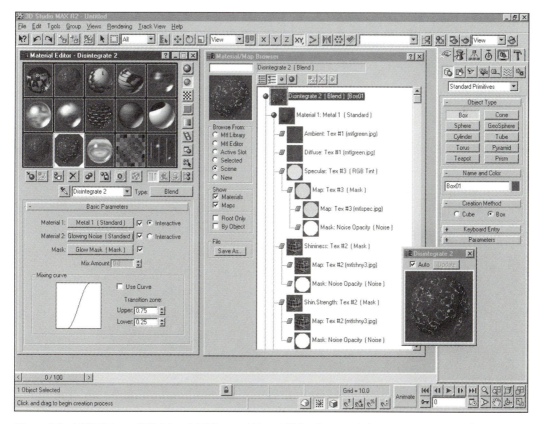

Figure 1.3   MAX Release 2.5's Material Editor and Material/Map Browser help you navigate around your maps and materials quickly.

- James Green, a longtime friend and computer-graphics problem-solver who braved the trenches with me at Antic Computing
- Tom Hudson, one of the primary programmers on 3D Studio/DOS and 3D Studio MAX
- Ken Robertson, a MAX artist who has worked in the games industry and is also a 3D graphics instructor for San Francisco State University
- Michael Spaw, a 3D artist and MAX Release 1 and Release 2 beta tester who produced the images for Autodesk's Texture Universe CD-ROM and Digimation's Xeno-1 CD-ROM
- And Scot Tumlin, another longtime friend, computer-graphics firefighter, and Antic survivor

Ken, Scot, James, and Mike have contributed chapters; Harry and Tom have contributed custom plug-ins for this book's companion CD-ROM.

In this book's Color Studio, you'll see my work in addition to the work of many other 3D Studio MAX users, ranging from talented students to professional 3D artists working on theatrical films, multimedia, and broadcast video.

About This Book

This book will teach you effects you may have seen in various Hollywood movies and TV shows, such as *Star Wars*, the *Star Trek* films and TV series, and *Babylon 5*. In addition, we cover various "cartoony" or fantasy-style effects such as those in *The Mask*.

Therefore, this book is geared primarily toward those MAX users who have an interest in special visual effects, particularly the unusual and otherworldly. It is *not* intended to be an exhaustive tutorial on every capability found in MAX. (For that, you can rely on MAX's own tutorials, online help from MAX users, and other MAX books. These and other MAX resources are covered in the appendices at the end of this book.) Nor is this book

intended specifically for architects or forensic animators, although certain techniques discussed here may be useful to them.

This book is designed for 3D Studio MAX Release 1 users and newcomers to MAX Release 2 and 2.5. (Note that *some* of the techniques described here may also be created in 3D Studio MAX Release 1, although you may have to do some creative workarounds or use third-party R1 plug-ins to produce the same effects.)

To get the most from this book, you need to complete the tutorials included with 3D Studio MAX R2 and R2.5. In addition, it is very helpful to have solid experience with 3D Studio MAX Release 1 and some of its plug-ins.

Core Feature Tutorials Vs. Plug-ins

This book concentrates on how to make the most of MAX Release 2 and 2.5's new features and covers topics not included in the first *3D Studio MAX f/x* book. The material includes such topics as using Lens Effects, organic modeling with NURBS and MeshSmooth, and third-party plug-ins. (At the time I wrote *3D Studio MAX f/x*, none of the third-party plug-ins existed, so I confined that book's effects tutorials to techniques that users could accomplish with just the core MAX Release 1 program.)

Since then, there has been a veritable flood of MAX plug-ins, both commercial and shareware, or freeware. In a one-year period (from MAX Release 1's ship date in April 1996 to April 1997), there were more than 150 plug-ins released; fully *half* were freeware or shareware, and the rest averaged $150 in price. As of the shipping date of MAX R2 (October 1997), there were more than 400 plug-ins available—again, with half of that number representing freeware or shareware.

However, covering commercial plug-ins presents a vexing challenge from a book tutorial standpoint.

MAX users who've purchased these plug-ins often want additional information and tips beyond those presented in the plug-in documentation.

On the other hand, in discussions with MAX users, I've heard that many want to explore the interesting effects achievable using just the core features of the program. Some 3D Studio/DOS and MAX tutorial books are criticized by readers who are resentful of tutorials that require specific plug-ins.

Although it's impossible to please everyone, this book focuses on how you can create a wide variety of effects with just MAX Release 2.5's core feature set and the plug-ins included on this book's companion CD-ROM. Note that I have included a chapter on using Adobe Photoshop; it's a widely used application that should be part of any professional 3D artist's toolbox.

Free Inside This Book!

While we're on the subject of plug-ins, the companion CD-ROM contains numerous shareware MAX plug-ins for Release 1, Release 2, and Release 2.5. I've included almost two dozen plug-ins written by Tom Hudson and Harry Denholm.

Greeble 1.0 is a procedural object creator written by Tom Hudson, one of the main developers of 3D Studio/DOS and 3D Studio MAX. Greeble builds industrial detail consisting of beveled plates with additional "widget" details on top. These parametric building blocks are excellent for creating futuristic cities and other man-made (or alien-made) topography. Although inspired by both Mayan architecture and art deco designs of the 1930s, you could use it in a pinch to create surfaces similar to the *Deathstar* from *Star Wars* and *Return of the Jedi*. Note that this plug-in isn't available anywhere else!

Harry Denholm has provided the rest of the plug-ins, which offer some fun (and useful) new

capabilities for MAX Release 2 and 2.5. The remaining plug-ins are:

- Ambient
- Bulge
- Crunch
- Decay
- Electrolize
- Frenetic
- GhostMatte
- Gradynt
- Lossy
- Melt
- Mix
- Outline
- Pinch
- Rock
- Softspot
- Spin
- Stacker
- Stratus
- Wiremap

Bulge, Decay, Melt, Pinch, and Spin are object modifiers; Electrolize, Frenetic, GhostMatte, Gradynt, Mix, Stacker, Softspot, Stratus, and Wiremap are map types. Rock is an "Ishani Primitive" and re-creates procedural rocks, or boulders. Ambient, Crunch, Lossy, and Outline are Video Post filters. Use them in good health!

Moving On

The next chapter includes a brief look at how you can get the most out of this book, the breakdown of its chapters and CD-ROM contents, and the effects covered. In addition, you'll learn about some basic MAX resource information that can be found in print, on video, and on the Internet.

HOW TO USE
THIS BOOK

2

In this chapter, you'll see how to get the most out of this book and its companion CD-ROM, and you'll get a preview of some of the goodies contained herein.

This book is divided into five sections. Each section covers a different category of MAX Release 2.5 features:

- Lighting and materials
- Modeling techniques
- "Moving parts" (space warps and object modifiers)
- MAX plug-ins and third-party functionality
- "Techie stuff" (expressions and scripting)

In each section, a series of rendered scenes illustrates the effects. Each chapter includes step-by-step tutorials on how to create the various effects and presents suggestions for customizing the techniques.

A standard ISO 9660-format CD-ROM accompanies this book; it is located in a sleeve on the inside back cover. This companion CD-ROM contains all of the example animations and images contained in the book, as well as scene files, models, material libraries, and the Photoshop 4.0 ATN batch files that I used to create the effects described here. The CD-ROM also includes more than 300MB of original texture maps, distributed royalty-free and available immediately for your personal use.

Demonstration animations for the chapter tutorials are on the CD-ROM as AVI files rendered at 320×240 resolution. Various figures from each chapter are included in the \FIGURES subdirectories within each chapter's directory. As you follow along with the instructions in each chapter, you will be either viewing or loading pertinent images and mesh and/or scene files from the CD-ROM.

As you read in the previous chapter, the companion CD-ROM contains almost two dozen MAX Release 2.5 plug-ins. First is Tom Hudson's Greeble 1.0, which was developed exclusively for this book. In addition, there are a large number of Harry Denholm's Ishani plug-ins: object modifiers, custom materials, utilities, and Video Post filters. (As I was writing this chapter, Harry was still giving me last-minute plug-ins to throw on the CD, so copy them from the \PLUGINS directory and see what's there.)

My intention is to present a series of interesting yet relatively easy-to-create effects from which you, as a 3D Studio MAX user, can learn and that also serve as inspiration for your own experimentation. Have fun!

Getting The Most From This Book

Most of the special-effects techniques in this book require only 3D Studio MAX Release 2 or Release 2.5 and the plug-ins included on the companion CD-ROM. To get the most out of this book, however, it's helpful to have a few other programs in your 3D toolbox.

For instance, virtually every 3D animator today owns a paint and/or image compositing program (many people have several different types) that produces 24-bit images with an added alpha channel. Programs such as Autodesk Animator Studio, Adobe Photoshop, Hi-res QFX, Fractal Design Painter, and Adobe AfterEffects are absolutely necessary for creating and retouching texture maps and manipulating final rendered 3D scenes. The layering features of these 24-bit programs are invaluable for compositing prerendered 3D imagery, especially for print. Although you can use 8-bit programs such as Autodesk Animator Pro to create simple maps, for photo-realistic textures, 24-bit images are the way to go.

However, even good ol' Animator Pro still has many uses, such as creating flic files for animated materials, grayscale masks, and for Bump, Shininess, and Opacity maps. It's also fun to take a flic file, change its palette to 256 levels of gray, and then force a bizarrely colored palette to it. This can produce striking effects, including liquid crystal photography, thermographs, and *Predator*-style "alien vision."

On the hardware side, because you're running 3D Studio MAX, you should also have the most powerful PC you can afford. For Release 2.5 of MAX, Kinetix recommends the following:

- A Pentium (or Pentium-equivalent) PC with a minimum speed of 120MHz
- A minimum of 48MB of RAM
- A 1GB or larger hard disk drive
- A CD-ROM drive
- A 24-bit video display card (preferably one with 2 to 4MB of onboard video memory)

As with Release 1 and Release 2, of course, 3D Studio MAX Release 2.5 (running under Windows NT 4.0 and above) takes advantage of symmetric multiprocessing (SMP) via multithreading; that is, MAX can use multiple CPUs to perform its tasks. If you can afford a multiple-CPU computer or motherboard upgrade, you'll see a noticeable increase in both rendering speed and screen redraws in the user interface.

And, speaking of screen redraws, another nifty piece of hardware that MAX can use is a graphics accelerator card. MAX Release 2.5 uses Autodesk's custom Heidi drivers as well as the industry-standard OpenGL. A large number of cards from such vendors as Diamond Multimedia, Dynamic Pictures, and ELSA Technologies are available to speed up your MAX PC interaction so that it rivals that of a Silicon Graphics workstation. For more information, see Appendix B.

3D Studio MAX References

Here is a collection of important books, magazines, and online hotspots that are excellent 3D Studio MAX resources.

Books

Besides 3D Studio MAX's reference manuals, there are some excellent third-party books to help you produce better animations. Being a good computer animator means that you should also be a good *filmmaker* in general. Too often, the near-instant gratification of being able to create their own desktop movies seduces computer animators. They then go on to create animations that ignore the cinematic language that filmmakers have developed over the last 100 years.

Consequently, a good place to start is in the film, theater, and video reference section of a good bookstore or your local library. Books on classical animation techniques, set design, cinematography, direction, lighting, and editing are all useful for 3D animators. (And, of course, nothing prevents you from checking out the latest in computer graphics books, too.) The manuals for your existing 3D and 2D software tools are useful, as are "how-to" software books available in the computer section of your local bookstore.

The following books are among the excellent resources available for MAX (note that every MAX book currently available is not listed here; for more information, see Appendix B):

- *Inside 3D Studio MAX Release 2, Volume 1*, by Dave Espinosa-Aguilar and Mark Williamson (New Riders Publishing, 1998, ISBN 1-56205-857-6. $59.99 U.S., $84.95 Canada. 1250 pages, black and white/color, with CD-ROM). The bible for MAX owners. As with Steven Elliot and Phillip Miller's earlier *Inside 3D Studio Release 4* and *Inside 3D Studio MAX* (Release 1), this is an exhaustive reference, and it covers virtually everything you'll ever want to know about MAX. Note, however, that Volume I is *not* a tutorial book; the later Volumes II and III cover specific MAX effects techniques in greater depth.

- *Inside 3D Studio MAX Release 2, Volume 2: Advanced Modeling and Materials*, by Ted Boardman, Jeremy Hubbell, and others (New Riders Publishing, 1998, ISBN 1-56205-864-9. $59.99 U.S., $84.95 Canada. 800 pages, black and white/color, with CD-ROM).

- *Inside 3D Studio MAX Release 2, Volume 3: Animation*, by Ralph Frantz, Angie Jones, and others (New Riders Publishing, 1998, ISBN 1-56205-865-7. $59.99 U.S., $84.95 Canada. 800 pages, black and white/color, with CD-ROM).

- *Character Animation With 3D Studio MAX*, by Stephanie Reese (Coriolis Group Books, 1996, ISBN 1-57610-054-5. $39.99 U.S. 500 pages, black and white/color, with CD-ROM). The first half of this book deals with anatomy, physical characteristics of humans and nonhuman characters, and general character animation. The second half features tutorials on creating character animation in MAX using Kinetix's Character Studio and Digimation's Bones Pro MAX. The Tips section on integrating these two programs is worth the price of the book. A follow-up book covering Release 2 is scheduled for release in 1998.

- *Digital Character Animation*, by George Maestri (New Riders Publishing, 1997, ISBN 1-56205-559-3. $55.00 U.S., $77.95 Canada. 370 pages, black and white/color, with CD-ROM). This book uses MAX and Softimage examples to cover 3D character animation in depth. However, the topics covered (posing, walk and run cycles, lip sync, facial animation) are also valid across other 3D software and hardware platforms.

- *3D Studio Max Plug-Ins Guide*, by Stephanie Reese and Andrew Reese (Coriolis Group Books, 1997, ISBN 1-57610-134-7. $49.99 U.S. 552 pages, black and white/color, with CD-ROM). A handy guide to the enormous number of MAX plug-ins, both commercial and shareware.

And, lest you think I forgot, here's a plug for another book that you might find useful, if you don't already have it: *3D Studio MAX f/x: Creating Hollywood-Style Special Effects*, by Jon A. Bell (Ventana, 1996, ISBN 1-56604-427-8. $49.99 U.S., $69.99 Canada. 500 pages, color/black and white, with CD-ROM). Written by yours truly, the predecessor to the book you're now reading tells you how to create many different types of science-fiction-style effects. The effects include laser beams, planets, nebulas, "photon" torpedoes, asteroids, and explosions. It also covers underwater effects such as water surfaces, plankton, bubbles, a swimming shark, volumetric light beams, and water caustics (using Noise and projector spotlights). You can create all of these effects without using any third-party plug-ins.

Its companion CD-ROM contains all the models, texture maps, and scene files used to create the animations, as well as over three dozen demonstration AVI files illustrating the effects. In addition, the CD-ROM features several different spaceship models, a 688-class submarine, the Viewpoint DataLabs hammerhead shark, the Diving Bell from *Voyage to the Bottom of the Sea* (built from the original 20th-Century Fox blueprints), and a huge number of original texture maps—more than 800 in all. (Some of these maps—but by no means all—are included with this book's companion CD-ROM.) So, if you enjoy the book you're now reading and you don't have the previous volume, I (ahem) suggest that you might want to complete your MAX f/x collection.

Finally, note that even older 3D Studio Release 4 books or general 3D graphics software books may include CD-ROMs with texture maps that you can employ in your 3D Studio MAX animations.

Computer Graphics And Visual Effects

There is an increasing number of magazines devoted to computer graphics in film and video production. Such magazines as *Computer Graphics World* (*CGW*), *3D Design*, *3D Artist*, *Digital Artist*, *NT Studio*, *Computer Artist,* and *Digital Imaging* all cover CGI. You can find these magazines at a good newsstand or perhaps at your local library. All of them also offer subscriptions, some free to qualified individuals. (If you attend the annual SIGGRAPH computer graphics trade show, you can often find booths where

subscriptions to these magazines are free of charge. Just fill out the necessary forms, swipe your registration card through their reader if necessary, and you're all set.)

Several good publications cater to filmmakers with an interest in special-effects techniques. Magazines such as *Cinefex*, *Cinefantastique*, and *American Cinematographer* offer behind-the-scenes looks at films that have special visual effects. The in-depth coverage in *Cinefex*, for example, is absolutely invaluable to special-effects artists.

For more information, check out Appendix B and Appendix C at the end of this book.

3D Studio MAX Forums Online

Another excellent way to get firsthand information on 3D Studio MAX is by using online services. There are several newsgroups that discuss computer graphics and animation; you can also find newsgroups, such as comp.graphics.packages.3dstudio, and Web pages devoted specifically to 3D Studio/DOS and 3D Studio MAX. (For more information, use the Search features of your newsreader software or your Web browser. Just type "3D STUDIO MAX" and see what's out there.) The newsgroups feature ongoing discussion and debate about their particular topics and are also a good resource if you have questions about 3D Studio/DOS, 3D Studio MAX, and related software and hardware.

The number-one place to find MAX information on the Internet is Kinetix's own Web site at www.ktx.com, of course. Other excellent sources of info include:

- www.max3d.com (news, links, tutorials, and plug-in information)

- www.3dartist.com (the Web site for *3D Artist Magazine*; also features links to many MAX-related hardware and software vendors as well as The MAX Page, a MAX-specific resources page)

- www.3dsite.com (a great source for 3D models and freeware and shareware plug-ins)
- www.3dcafe.com (another excellent source for 3D models and plug-ins)

Probably the best source for 3D Studio MAX information is the Kinetix Forum on the CompuServe Information Service. Technical support personnel from Autodesk's Kinetix subsidiary frequent the forum regularly and are available to answer questions. In addition, third-party vendors who provide supplemental tools for 3D Studio also have a strong presence on the forum. Programmers, animators, and hardware experts are always available to help you with your 3D Studio needs. (At press time, Kinetix was considering moving much of its support from CompuServe to a Web-based service; check the www.ktx.com Web site for further updates.)

To find the forum, just type "Go Kinetix" at any CompuServe prompt (for your 3D Studio/DOS needs, type "Go Ammedia").

The Companion CD-ROM

In the back of this book is a CD-ROM that contains the MAX scene files, texture maps, and meshes used to create all of the special effects described here. The companion CD-ROM contains animation files in 24-bit AVI format for the demonstration animations. The files for the particular effects are in separate directories and correspond to each chapter of this book.

You do not need to install the MAX files from the companion CD-ROM onto your hard drive. If you load the MAX files directly into 3D Studio MAX, the program will automatically add the proper CD-ROM directories to the MAX Map Paths list. Because of the size of the demo animation files, however, you may want to copy them into your 3DSMAX\IMAGES directory and play them back from your hard drive to get better playback speed.

A large assortment of still and animated texture maps from my personal collection is also on the companion CD-ROM, as well as some maps provided by vendors such as Digimation, Visual Concepts Engineering, and Artbeats. Some of these maps are featured on the various models used in this book, of course. Many of them started life as scanned photos of real-world industrial textures, which I then manipulated in Adobe Photoshop. I created many of the textures with an eye toward the industrial; they can serve to decorate your own spaceships, futuristic factory walls, robot bodies, and so on (even though the source material often originated from photos of dumpsters and earth-moving equipment).

The majority of the textures are 24-bit color, lossless JPG files at 640×480 pixel resolution; the textures also span a wide variety of colors. These images are designed to serve as a "kit" that you can alter and manipulate endlessly to create new materials. (For instance, if you wish to place a wide red stripe down the body of a spaceship, you might select a strip of the red CLEMBOX1.TGA material, which you then paste across ALUMINM6.TGA.) Other textures have been included at varying resolutions; you can use many of these textures as Bump, Shininess, Opacity, Alpha, and Reflection maps.

The texture maps are all found in the \MAPS directory, although many of them are found in the respective companion CD-ROM chapter directories as well. Note that although you can use the textures in your own projects, you may not resell or distribute them. A sampling of some of the maps is shown in the Color Gallery section in the middle of this book.

Getting Started: The Directories

The companion CD-ROM contains the following directories:

- \ARTBEATS contains 53 digitized explosion images, courtesy of Artbeats Software (www.artbeats.com).

- \CHAP_03 through \CHAP_22 correspond to the tutorials presented in Chapters 3 through 23. They contain the MAX scene files, textures, and other files required for each chapter's tutorial.

- \DIGIMATN contains demo versions of the Digimation plug-ins Bones Pro, Clay Studio Pro, Shag: Fur, Lightning, Sandblaster, Tree Factory, and Splash! In addition, there are several demonstration .AVIs and image files to preview. Each demo is a self-installing executable file; to install, copy it to a temporary directory on your hard drive, then double-click on the file in Windows Explorer, or use the Start|Run feature of Windows 95 or Windows NT. The file will launch and install the demo on your hard drive; just follow the instructions on your screen.

- \INFOGRAF contains two subdirectories: \PLUGINS and MODELS. The \PLUGINS directory contains compressed (ZIP format) demonstration versions of REM Infografica's MetaREYES, DirtyREYES, ClothREYES, JetaREYES, and CartoonREYES. To use these plug-ins, copy them to a temporary directory on your hard drive, then use an uncompression utility, such as PK-Zip from PK-Ware, or WinZIP, from Niko-Mak Computing, to unzip the files. Then, double-click on each program's SETUP.EXE file in Windows Explorer, or use the Start|Run feature of Windows 95 or Windows NT. The file will launch and install the demo on your hard drive; just follow the instructions on your screen. The \MODELS directory contains another subdirectory called \KAMOV; in it, you'll find an incredibly detailed version of a Russian Kamov-type helicopter, complete with texture maps. These plug-ins and the model were kindly furnished by REM Infografica, a leading distributor and creator of MAX plug-ins and models. (For more information on its products, contact it online at www.infografica.com.)

- \MAPS contains all the maps used in the book, along with additional maps.

- \MATLIBS contains the MAXFX2.MAT Material Library, which includes all of the materials used in the book's .MAX scene files, as well as some cool additional materials. (Note that you can learn a lot about creating cool materials—especially the new Raytrace

SETTING UP YOUR MAP PATHS

All of the maps you need for the tutorials are contained in their respective chapter directories and in the \MAPS directory of your companion CD-ROM.

To make sure you have access to all the maps on the CD-ROM, load 3D Studio MAX Release 2.5, select File|Configure Paths, and manually add the companion CD-ROM \MAPS directory to your map paths.

materials and maps—by loading some of these pre-built versions, then examining their settings.)

- \PLUGINS contains duplicates of the plug-ins in \CHAP_18 (for those of you who need a quick reminder of where to find all this stuff). This directory contains Tom Hudson's Greeble 1.0 plug-in, and Harry Denholm's Ishani plug-ins (about 20 in all!)

- \PYROMANI contains several image sequences adapted from Visual Concept Engineering's Pyromania CD-ROM series (used by permission from VCE). I've processed the original versions of these images in Photoshop 4.0, and they're suitable for many colorful optical effects. (You can order the originals from VCE and from various 3D software dealers; for more information, see Appendix B and check the various Internet URLs.)

- \SCENES contains two files: the Deep Flight I mini-submarine, built by Scot Tumlin and book author/editor Jon A. Bell, and the Japanese *anime*-style robot featured in Chapter 3, built exclusively for this book. (Feel free to animate it using MAX's inverse kinematics.)

Moving On

In the next two chapters, contributor Michael Spaw discusses some basics of lighting and shows you how to create realistic materials in 3D Studio MAX. Although these tutorials aren't specific to Release 2.5, Mike presents important information that's useful for both MAX users and 3D artists in general.

Then, in Chapters 5, 6, 7, and 8, I'll take the helm again and show you how to create some cool metal materials and animated optical effects using some of Release 2.5's new features.

So, let's get started. Let's take our computers where they haven't gone before.

PART I

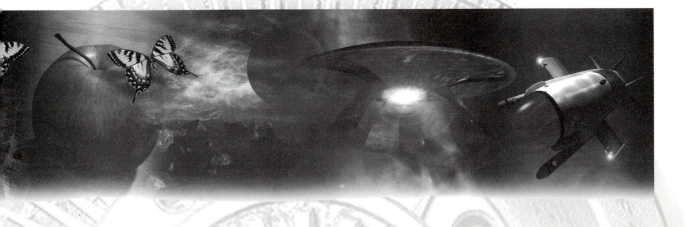

LIGHTING AND MATERIALS

Lux Aeterna

3

By

Michael Spaw

In this chapter, you'll find some general thoughts on creating realistic lighting techniques for CG scenes. You'll learn about some of the lighting features found in MAX Release 2.5 and see some examples that show how you can build lighting from the "ground up" for different 3D scenes.

You may rarely think about how light works in the real world. Yet, it often takes a great deal of thought and experimentation to achieve the look you want when you create lighting in the computer graphics world. Computer graphics offer nearly endless options for lighting a scene, without the constraints found in nature. Unfortunately, this freedom to create any type of lighting you can dream up can also make it difficult to produce a realistic look in your finished image. Although digital lighting provides you with new tools that are unavailable with traditional lighting design, you can improve your CG work dramatically if you know traditional techniques.

Lighting: The Basics

Light and its interaction in the real world is so complex that, because of the physics involved, any reasonable discussion of it would fill this book.

Fortunately for us, it's not necessary to go to that level of detail. Instead, you'll learn about some of the important attributes that light possesses and what you can do to re-create those attributes in MAX. Some of the concepts presented here may sound familiar, or even obvious, but it's often helpful to revert to the basics when it's difficult to light a particular scene.

First, every time you're ready to light a MAX scene, you should ask yourself these questions:

What kind of environment is this scene in?
One way to break this problem down is to try to fit your scene into one of three basic groups. Lighting can often be categorized into natural lighting, artificial lighting, and a combination of the two.

Natural lighting typically refers to lighting from the sun, whether the scene is outdoors or in an enclosed environment that is solely illuminated by the sun from windows and other openings. There are several additional issues to consider when using natural lighting: What time of day is it? Is it bright or overcast? And how much light will be bouncing around in the environment?

Figure 3.1 shows a prehistoric outdoor scene created by Dreamworks Interactive for "The Lost World: Jurassic Park" CD-ROM game. In this image, the volumetric shafts of sunlight shining through the trees provide a contrasting, pastoral feeling to an otherwise frightening encounter.

Artificial lighting can be almost anything. Any type of environment lit by electric light, firelight, or both can be considered artificial; a photo-

Image courtesy of Kinetix, Inc.

Figure 3.1 A tyrannosaur chases a stegosaurus in a primeval forest setting.

studio light setup is a good example. Artificial lighting is probably the most common of the three types.

Once again, you need to consider where the light will come from and what its qualities are. If there are several sources, which one is the main source? With artificial light, it's also important to determine whether or not there will be a colorcast to the lights. Colorcast refers to the tint color of the light. Almost all light sources have a color tint instead of being pure white.

The last type of lighting is a combination of natural and artificial lighting. Even in brightly lit outdoor shots for films, the cameraman and lighting technicians may use reflectors or supplemental lights to mitigate harsh shadows.

What's the objective of the lighting?
In other words, what is the mood or atmosphere of the scene? Conveying a mood in the lighting can be critical to selling the overall look of the image. In some cases, the only goal is to see the object or objects clearly. More often than not, though, the goal is more complex.

Lighting can help convey an emotion or direct the viewer's eye to a particular point. It can also give greater depth and richness to a scene. Many of these considerations reflect the use of lighting as a storytelling element; this is particularly true in cinematic lighting. The use of pools of light in Figure 3.2 conveys a sense of mystery in the empty castle setting.

Figure 3.2 The pools of light in this otherwise dark castle courtyard help create a sense of mystery and loneliness.

These same considerations are important when you are lighting a still image. Studio photographers can spend enormous amounts of time creating appropriate and captivating lighting. Consequently, when you are lighting a scene, you may ask yourself, what mood am I trying to convey? Is there a story to this scene, and does the lighting I've created enhance it? (For further reference, check out books on stage, film, and studio lighting. There are hundreds of books on studio photography alone.)

Are there special lighting effects that take place in the scene, and if so, should they be created with lights or by other means?
Besides the normal light types, MAX offers many additional effect possibilities in the form of glows, volume lights, lens flares, and special material attributes. Although some are not strictly light types, they often add to the appearance of visible light effects in the scene. A simple example of this is a flare or glow from a visible light source. Because these effects are not produced automatically in 3D (as they are in nature), you need to specifically include them in your renderings and give some thought to their look and prominence. Lightning, beacons, neon, and other light-producing sources all have their own special considerations.

You can also take into account the actual qualities of the objects that you are "photographing," or rendering. Figure 3.3 shows a highly

©1997, Johnny Ow–johnny@ywd.com; http://www.ywd.com/jow

Image courtesy of Johnny Ow.

Figure 3.3 A shiny sports car is illuminated by practical scene lights and the reflections of the environment itself.

reflective sports car in a futuristic garage; the glowing light panels in the garage convey the overall lighting scheme. However, the reflections of the environment itself (especially the ceiling light panels) help accentuate the extremely reflective vehicle surface.

Do I have reference material to draw from?

When you're creating realistic 3D lighting scenarios, it's helpful to get into the habit of working from actual photo and film references. Clippings from magazines and other sources can provide an excellent source of visual reference. Likewise, good reference materials can provide subtle clues to how certain objects and environments look at various times of day or under specific conditions.

By carefully analyzing the position of highlights and shadows in a photo, you can often reconstruct the basic position and intensities of the lights that contributed to the image. You can also learn a lot by using an existing source to re-create a lighting setup because the artist who originally created it probably worked out some of the problems that you may otherwise encounter.

Quite often, you will have a general idea of how a scene should look, but without reference, you will be working solely from your visual memory. Sometimes the end result will be less than you hoped for. Much like when you draw or paint, you can often accomplish a good lighting approximation for 3D scenes solely from memory, but the end result often turns out better when you can work from real life. This is especially true when you need to light a scene that is easily recognizable, but you can't quite remember what it *really* looks like.

Basic Light Types

After considering all of the questions in the preceding section, it's time to get to work lighting a MAX scene. Although the number and types of lights and their individual attributes will change from scene to scene, there's a general process you can follow that will give you better results than if you merely create several lights and adjust their parameters and positions in no particular order.

The first step in this process is to consider the type of lighting that your scene requires—then you can begin to list the various light sources that you'll need. Often, you'll find similarities from scene to scene in the basic number of lights and their relative positions. Unfortunately, there is no single lighting setup that will work for every scene, but there are three basic types of lights that reappear consistently and that you can use to start: a key light, a fill light, and a kicker (see Figure 3.4).

Figure 3.4 A standard three-light setup showing a key light, a fill light, and a kicker.

The Key Light

The main light in a scene is often referred to as the *key light*. The key light is not necessarily just one light, but it's always the primary source of illumination. Likewise, the key light is not always localized like a spotlight; it can cover an extended area in a scene.

Even though the key light is often placed at a three-quarter position (usually, an angle of 45 degrees from the object's front, and 45 degrees above the centerline), it doesn't have to be in this location—it could even come from behind or below the subject, or from any other position. However, the key light is often the first light a photographer or 3D artist places, and he or she usually uses it to create preliminary light in the scene.

Although this initial placement provides a good way to see the object, the result is typically a flat, uninteresting image. If you use a key light alone as shown in Figure 3.5, shadows are generally harsh and very pronounced. Likewise, the scene will almost always appear too dark because there is no natural ambient light to brighten the shadow areas. This look can be useful in some occasions—a nighttime scene, for example—but it's rarely adequate for most scenes.

Figure 3.5   In this image, only the key light is used; it provides strong illumination from the three-quarter top and side angles.

The Fill Light

Fill lights round out the dark and shadow areas of the scene. The key light may be the most noticeable source in the scene, but it's up to fill lights to give the scene depth and a sense of reality.

Fill lights can be broken down into two groups. The first and most important group results from natural diffuse interreflections, or *radiosity*. This type of lighting is often called *ambient light*. Ambient light is light that, once emitted from the source, bounces around the scene until it's fully absorbed by the objects in the scene. This effect occurs automatically in nature, but it is one of the components that is missed the most when it comes to rendering in the CG world.

For a moment, take a good look around the room you're now in. Although some of the surfaces are directly illuminated by specific light sources, there are other surfaces that are indirectly illuminated. In fact, most environments contain a large number of surfaces that are not directly illuminated.

Unfortunately, most 3D rendering software (save specific radiosity rendering software, which I'll discuss later) ignores the contribution of indirect illumination. Part of the reason this type of light is so important is that it brings up the level of illumination throughout the scene, but it is not necessarily consistent across all objects. MAX's renderer, along with most other renderers, simulates the ambient component of fill light with a global ambient amount.

MAX's ambient light is applied uniformly throughout the scene with no apparent source. This additional "bump-up" in illumination decreases the overall darkness in a scene, but it tends to wash out the range of possible values. It also fails to provide any modeling of light and shadow on the objects it illuminates, which is the main reason a scene appears unrealistic.

1. Start 3D Studio MAX, then open up the Environment dialog box located on the Rendering menu. Click on the Ambient color swatch to bring up the Color Selector. If you haven't changed the MAX Release 2.5 default values, you'll notice that the Ambient value is set to 11.

    Although this doesn't add a significant amount of light to the scene, some artists prefer to have no ambient light added to the scene at all, which allows for a full range of values in the final rendering.

Better Ambient Lighting Techniques

A better way to simulate ambient light is to place low-intensity spot and Omni lights in logical locations throughout your scene. Basically, your goal is to simulate the light that's bounced from the light's initial point of contact. This type of secondary illumination should decrease the shadow areas and provide some light to the underside and corners not hit directly by the key light. If you set up fill lights with care, the whole scene can take on a "radiosity-like" quality.

In addition to the natural diffuse or ambient light in the scene, photographers use fill lights for both studio photography and cinema to brighten areas that are too dark or to emphasize some aspect of the scene. These additional sources sometimes come in the form of bounce cards (or reflectors) that merely reflect existing light from other sources. Bounce cards can be placed close to the base of objects to lighten the underside, or they can be placed opposite the key light to soften shadows.

In lighting for the CG environment, the difference between the aforementioned ambient light and other fill lights is vague because all

---

A NOTE ON AMBIENT LIGHTING

John Knoll, coauthor of Photoshop and a visual effects supervisor at Industrial Light and Magic, suggests that, for optimum realism, 3D artists should use *no* ambient light in their scenes whatsoever. Although it may increase your rendering times, Knoll suggests you use shadow-casting lights for all aspects of your scene—including "fill" lighting.

secondary light is created by hand. What you need to determine is how much your lights will influence the scene and whether or not the additional fill lights will cast shadows. Typically, the natural diffuse/ambient light is soft enough that it will not cast a discernible shadow. Other fill lights from practical sources are often strong enough to cast shadows, as shown in Figure 3.6.

Figure 3.6   Through the use of a second spot placed to the front and opposite of the key light, fill lighting gives some shading to the shadow areas.

The Kicker

In this case, *the kicker* isn't a football term; it's a light that provides backlighting to an object in the scene. Also known as rim light or backlight, the kicker's job is to help separate the target objects from the background by illuminating the object's edge (see Figure 3.7).

The kicker is often placed directly opposite the three-quarter key light. This works very well if you want a stylized, "studio photography" look. However, this effect also happens in nature. Both sunrise and sunset have what is known as "a magic hour." It's during this time that the sun acts as a rim light and can produce an unreal glow around objects as you look toward the sun.

Backlighting also tends to catch edges of objects, causing small specular highlights. If the models in your 3D scene are constructed with small radiused edges, this highlighting can lend believability to the scene.

Other Types Of Lights

Practical lights are those sources of illumination that actually appear in the scene. Table lamps, car headlights, lightning, and open

BACKLIGHTING ADDS TO REALISM

Bill George, Effects Art Director at Industrial Light and Magic (*Star Trek Generations*, *Star Trek: First Contact*, *Deep Impact*), recommends that CG artists remember a lighting rule for shooting miniature sets—when appropriate, try to backlight your "miniature," or the models in your 3D scene. It tends to make the models look larger or more imposing and can heighten their realism.

Figure 3.7 When it is placed high and opposite the key light, the kicker helps to separate the objects from the background, as well as produce nice highlights along the edges.

flames are all potential light sources that can end up in your rendered frames.

When lights exist in the frame, they're quite often fairly localized in effect. It's critical to use attenuation to simulate these types of lights. To the human observer and the camera, bright lights and surfaces also have the tendency to look as if they are flaring or blooming. In MAX Release 2.5, you can simulate these effects easily by using the Lens Effects Glow or Highlight filter in Video Post.

Sample Scenes: A Simple Three-light Setup

Now that you know what the basic types of lights are, it's time to actually see them in action. To do this, you'll load a scene that has all three of the main light types and look at what each one does in turn:

1. Start 3D Studio MAX Release 2.5, or save your current work and reset the program.

2. Select File|Open, and load LIGHT_1.MAX from the \CHAP_03 directory of this book's companion CD-ROM.

   When the file opens, you'll see that it consists of basic studio-photography-style objects and lighting setup (it's the same scene you saw in the previous example images). Although this setup will not be exactly what you need for every MAX scene, it shows the three main types of lights that appear most often. At the moment, only the key light is turned on.

3. With the Camera view selected, render the scene.

As you can see from the finished rendering, all of the light is currently coming from the upper right. The overall image, including the shadow areas, is very dark. Likewise, the background sweep goes to black in the areas that the light misses.

Now that you know what the key light looks like, it's time to move on to the fill light.

4. Press the H key to bring up the Select By Name menu, select the Key light, and click on OK. Next, go to the Modify tab to bring up the Light attributes. At the top of the General Parameters section, uncheck the On button to turn the light off.

5. Bring up the Select By Name menu again, select the Fill light, and click on OK. Go back to the Modify tab, check the light on, and re-render the scene.

    The first thing you'll notice is that the fill light is very low in intensity and coming from the lower-left side. The main job of fill lights is to lessen the dark and shadow areas.

6. Using the Select By Name menu and the Modify panel, turn off the Fill light, select the Kicker light and turn it on, then render the scene again. This time, you'll see that all the light is coming from above and opposite the key light. The kicker or backlight not only highlights the top edges of the objects, it also separates the objects from the background sweep.

7. Finally, turn on all three of the lights and render the scene. Your screen should look like Figure 3.8.

Figure 3.8   The finished image combines all the lights and reproduces a full studio-lighting setup.

With all three lights in place, your scene now looks very much like a studio shot.

Although this is a good start, there's room for improvement. What's missing is the subtle bounce light found in reality. To produce it, you would create additional fill lights. You'll see how in the next example.

Lighting An Interior Environment

Many 3D scenes you create fall into the category of enclosed environments. When this is the case, it's critical that you pay close attention to the effects of radiosity or ambient lighting. As mentioned earlier, light will bounce around an environment until it's fully absorbed by the various surfaces. Unless you're using a true radiosity renderer, you need to give careful thought when re-creating these effects.

The following example demonstrates a more complex lighting arrangement. Here, I've created a total of eight lights to give this room a sunlit appearance with no practical lights visible. To help visualize the lighting process, the scene starts off with only the sun's contribution. To see the scene, follow these steps:

1. Start MAX, or save your current work and reset the program.

2. Select File|Open, and load ROOM_1.MAX from the \CHAP_03 directory of this book's companion CD-ROM. When the scene is loaded, render the Camera01 viewport. Your screen should look like Figure 3.9.

At this point, you will see only the effect of the sun and the small amount of global ambient light. Although the light streaming through

Figure 3.9   Only the strong directional lighting of the sun is produced, leaving no illumination in the rest of the room, save for the amount of shading given by the global ambient light.

the windows looks okay, the rest of the room is lacking any directed bounce light. The little bit of the room that you see is the result of the Global Ambient light set in the Environment dialog. If you increased the Ambient value, the room would be illuminated, but the result would be flat and unrealistic. What you need to do is employ several carefully placed lights to simulate the room's diffuse light.

Note that the sun isn't the only source of light from outside this room. General bounce light from outdoors also contributes to the light coming in the windows. To simulate this bluish sky light, I created three additional lights for this scene. I set up one light for each of the windows and one at the far end of the hall. You can see an example of this in the next MAX scene.

3. Select File|Open, and load ROOM_2.MAX from the \CHAP_03 directory of the companion CD-ROM. Render the Camera01 view; your screen should look something like Figure 3.10.

Figure 3.10 The widely scattered light from the sky helps to bring up the overall level of illumination. It acts like a fill light and begins to provide shading to the walls, ceiling, and objects in the room.

The three new light sources help lighten most of the surfaces in the room. Unlike the general ambient light, however, they don't illuminate every surface evenly. The corners of the room still provide shadow areas. Also, notice in your rendering the broad specular highlight on the floor with its blue tint.

4. Now that you've seen the two primary sources of illumination, it's time for the first set of bounce lights to be called into play. Select File|Open, load ROOM_3.MAX from the \CHAP_03 directory, and render the Camera01 viewport. Your screen should look like Figure 3.11.

ORDER OF OPERATIONS

One good method for setting up lights is to create and modify them in the order of least importance or brightness. When you first start, you may want to create the main key light, but before you get too comfortable with it, turn it off and decide which of the lights you need to create will have the most *subtle* influence. By doing so, you can clearly see the individual contributions of the various lights. This backward process can also help reduce the amount of time you'll spend going back and forth tweaking lights when you don't really know their net effect.

Figure 3.11 Two spotlights placed below the room simulate the bounce light produced when the sunlight reflects off the floor.

Take a close look at your rendering. When the sunlight from outside the room hits the floor, a portion of it will bounce up to illuminate the walls and ceiling.

To create this secondary light, I placed two additional spotlights below the floor and used the Exclusion list to set them to exclude the floor. Both lights have a warm yellow color to not only simulate the warmth of the sunlight, but also pick up the color of the floor.

This subtle attribute of radiosity is called *color bleeding*. Simply put, color bleeding takes place when light strikes a colored surface and then bounces to another surface. The first surface's color tends to influence the second surface's apparent color. The idea of color constancy in human perception works to counter this effect and is part of the reason you don't tend to notice color bleeding. Even though you may often not notice this effect in "the real world," if it's missing from your 3D renderings, the final result may appear wrong.

5. In this scene, take a moment to select one of the secondary spotlights and then click on the Modify tab and look over the light attributes. Although the light has a light yellow tint, its overall amount of illumination is low within the scene. The reason for this is that the light's Multiplier value is set to only 0.25, a quarter of the normal value. The Multiplier setting allows you to easily control the relative intensity of a light without changing its base color.

The final lighting attribute this scene needs is light that bounces from the ceiling back onto the floor and walls.

6. Load ROOM_4.MAX from the \CHAP_03 directory and render the Camera01 viewport. Your screen should look like Figure 3.12.

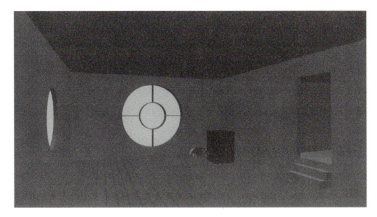

Figure 3.12 The last level of illumination comes from the light bouncing off the ceiling around the rest of the room. This is accomplished with two additional lights above the ceiling.

This time, I've placed two lights above the ceiling; I used the Exclusion list to exclude the ceiling so that only the walls and floors are lit.

7. Next, load ROOM_FNL.MAX from the \CHAP_03 directory and render the scene. Your screen should look like Figure 3.13.

Now that all of the lights have been turned on, you can see the final result. Notice that there is a great deal of subtlety in the luminance values of the walls and ceiling. These variations lend a credibility to the scene and look like the variations generated by a radiosity solution, but without the long radiosity rendering times.

It's also worth noting that, even though there are eight lights in this scene, only one is shadow casting, so the render time is not a problem. With the addition of some digitized texture maps and some fine-tuning, you can probably make this room rendering into a photorealistic representation. (You should try this out, as an exercise.)

Figure 3.13 The final image (when shown in color) has a richness in values and tonality that is very similar to an image produced with a radiosity renderer.

8. For an additional exercise, try changing the lighting to re-create different times of day or atmospheric conditions. You could also try to change the mood of the scene or add a practical light, like a floor lamp.

Note that you can use these same techniques for a variety of lighting situations. Although this scene differs in appearance from the studio example, it contains most of the same basic lighting types. In this case, the sun was the key light, and all the additional lights contributed to the effect of natural bounce light.

Lighting An *Anime*-Style Robot

As I mentioned previously, the goal of lighting is often not only to illuminate the object, but to lend focus to the scene or to create a particular mood.

In the next example, you'll load a complex scene featuring a Japanese *anime*-style robot built by Jon A. Bell. This robot scene is a good example of how the author has used lighting to create a stylized look to the objects in the environment. To view the scene, follow these steps:

1. Load 3D Studio MAX Release 2.5 or save your current work and reset the program.

2. Select File|Open, and load ROBOTFX2.MAX from the \CHAP_03 directory of the companion CD-ROM.

This scene consists of a custom-built giant robot model standing in a circular "hanger bay." Jon created the spiked details and ribbing on the walls by duplicating the original cylindrical shape for the room and then applying MAX Release 2.5's new Lattice modifier. Green industrial textures for the walls and custom robot textures (created from digitized photos and modified in Adobe Photoshop) complete this metallic behemoth.

3. Render the Camera01 view. Your screen should look like Figure 3.14.

Take a look at the effects of the colored lights in your rendering. Note how the colors give the robot a more menacing appearance. The lighting also "pulls" the robot out from the background.

The choice of color is also important. Notice how the warm red and orange colors of the rim- and backlights contrast with the overall blue color of the robot. The color also could be a reference to off-camera "warning" lights, giving an additional story element to the scene. If you were to animate this scene, you might pan these lights or pulse their intensity or colors to impart a sense of danger or impending movement.

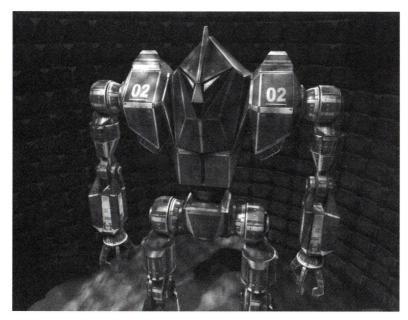

Figure 3.14   The varied lighting focuses on the robot and adds drama to the scene.

4. This scene also makes use of another not-so-evident lighting trick. Open the Select By Name menu, select Spot01, and click on OK. Go to the Modify panel and scroll down to the Spotlight Parameters rollup. Notice that there is a bitmap placed in the light and the Projector checkbox has been checked.

5. Select File|View File, select GRIDLITE.JPG from the \MAPS directory, and click on OK. The image is shown in Figure 3.15.

As you can see, the GRIDLITE map is a simple black-and-white grid that acts as a *gobo* in the scene. In traditional studio and film photography, gobos are used to mask out portions of a light, as well as provide

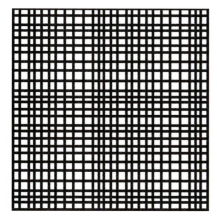

Figure 3.15   This simple grid bitmap, placed in a projector light, produces complex shadows within the scene and replicates a lighting effect known as a gobo.

READY FOR INVERSE KINEMATICS

Note that this robot model has linking already established on its joints and is suitable for animating with MAX Release 2.5's inverse kinematics (IK).

Colored Lights

Lights are almost never white. Both natural and artificial lights generally have some colorcast to them. We typically think of sunlight as being pure white light, but even it changes color with the time of day and the environment. Artificial lighting is also notorious for having a tint to it. Fluorescent lights generally have a green cast to them; halogen bulbs give off a blue-white light.

Truly color-corrected lighting environments are exceptionally rare. This fact should be used to your advantage when you are trying to reproduce specific lighting. You can add depth and richness to otherwise sterile-looking environments by giving slight variations to the color of lights in a scene. Tinting lights for artistic purposes can also be very effective for conveying a specific mood or atmosphere. In most cases, subtlety is wise; dramatic color in lighting can lead to refreshing but stylized-looking images.

additional shadow elements. These masks are sometimes simple card-board cutouts mounted on an additional stand in front of the light. In other situations, camouflage netting or tree branches are used to simulate the shadows produced in outdoor conditions. The net result typically lends a more complex and interesting look to the lighting, without the need to create additional elements that sit in between the light and the receiving objects.

In the case of the robot scene, the map takes the place of grating or an overhead gantry. In addition to making the lighting more interesting, gobos can give a sense of scale to the illuminated objects.

6. Take a moment and play with the lighting in the scene. If you look at the lights individually, you'll notice that most of them cast shadows and use exclusion lists. Excluding the background from the effects of the colored lights tends to isolate the robot from the background. Remove the exclusions and notice how the background becomes tied into the foreground elements. You could also apply attenuation to the lights to reach a compromise in these two looks.

7. Finally, you could also create your own gobo to insert in place of the GRIDLITE, or you could remove it altogether and see how this influences the scene.

Some Other Thoughts On Lighting

After you've set up lighting for your MAX scene, it's worthwhile to look back over your work and ask a few more questions.

Is my solution both simple and necessary?

Unlike real lighting, CG lighting requires overhead in terms of rendering time. Naturally, the more complex the lighting setup, the more time will be spent for the render and the more difficult the lighting management becomes. You should ask yourself if every light is necessary for the look that you are trying to achieve.

There is certainly a point of diminishing returns when it comes to adding lights. At some point, adding more lights will not add to the look of the scene, and it will become difficult to distinguish the worth of any additional light. If this becomes the case, try to look at each light independently to gauge its relative worth to the scene. If its contribution is questionable, get rid of it. If you follow the suggestion of creating the lighting based on the least noticeable light first and work your way up to the key light, you'll probably avoid creating redundancies.

Are the lights excluding objects that do not need to be lit? Are the lights using attenuation?

Make sure you've checked all your lights and objects to see that their properties match your expectations. By simply excluding an object from some lights, you can save time when it comes to rendering.

The same is true for shadow casting. It's rare that every light in the scene needs to cast shadows. Casting shadows can be very expensive (especially in the case of ray-traced shadows) and sometimes detrimental to the resultant image as well.

Have you simulated ambient light adequately?
As I pointed out earlier, using MAX's default ambient lighting is not the best way to simulate the subtle effects that diffuse lighting can provide. A little of the default ambient lighting may be okay, but it's worth the extra effort to place additional lights to compensate for ambient light's inherent lack of contrast.

Can any of the lighting be simulated with mapping effects instead of actual lights?
Building lights, illuminated displays, and other small, self-contained pools of light can sometimes be created with maps instead of actual light sources.

Other Options

One of the nicest aspects of MAX's design is its ability to accept plug-in components. This plug-in architecture extends not only into the realm of modeling and materials, but also into the renderer.

Several new plug-ins make it possible for MAX's rendering and shading to look more photorealistic. MAX Release 2.5 includes ray-traced materials and map types, which can greatly enhance the look of your scenes. (You'll find out more about MAX's raytracing features in Chapter 10.)

As I mentioned earlier, using radiosity is another way of producing photorealistic effects. Unlike the standard scanline render, a radiosity solution provides for diffuse light interaction in an environment. With radiosity, you do not need to cheat when you are trying to create the look of ambient light in a scene. Radiosity physically calculates the various bounces that light makes as it travels from the light source until all of the energy is absorbed in the environment. Although this type of rendering typically takes much more time to calculate than the standard MAX scanline render, it also easily re-creates one of the most difficult aspects of lighting to re-create.

Two programs—Lightscape, from Lightscape Technologies, and RadioRay, from Kinetix—give MAX users this powerful rendering option. Whereas Lightscape is a standalone rendering engine, it imports MAX scenes and materials directly. RadioRay is a plug-in radiosity renderer that integrates directly into MAX. Both programs can produce images of startling realism, as shown in Figure 3.16.

The other benefits of using a physically-based rendering engine like RadioRay is that you can specify real-world luminaire light types in the scene. This allows architects and lighting designers to simulate actual lighting scenarios prior to construction and to "previsualize" the finished look. Radiosity rendering is also finding its way into film usage because it can more accurately match lighting setups on location.

RadioRay allows for very quick raytracing internally; once the light solution has been calculated, it is view-independent, enabling real-time navigation through the environment. As the state of the art in rendering moves forward, radiosity will begin to play a greater roll because it allows users to create more photorealistic lighting scenarios almost automatically.

Moving On

In this chapter, you explored some of the basic concepts of lighting design. You walked through several examples to get a better understanding of how to approach lighting a scene, and you learned the importance of fill and ambient lighting.

Image courtesy of Kinetix.

Figure 3.16 An example image from RadioRay.

Finally, you explored new lighting features in MAX Release 2.5. With these concepts under your belt, you should be able to improve the lighting in your 3D scenes, whether they're realistic or fantasy-oriented.

In the next chapter, I'll discuss some of the general considerations for designing realistic materials, both organic and inorganic.

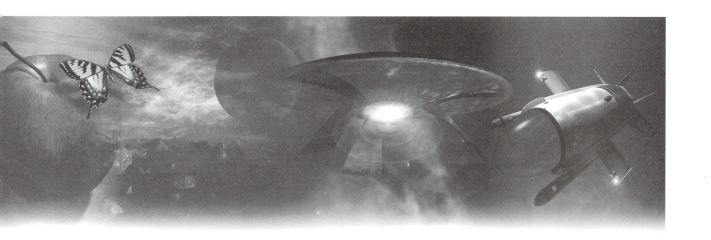

CREATING REALISTIC
MATERIALS

4

BY

MICHAEL SPAW

In this chapter, instead of re-creating specific materials by completing tutorials that take you step-by-step through the process, you'll learn a more generalized set of techniques that you can apply to many natural and man-made materials to make them realistic.

It can be tough to build believable natural materials that represent real-world surfaces. Not only do you need to have a keen eye and a reasonable understanding of how nature looks, but you also need a good deal of creativity. MAX's Material Editor enables you to create highly complex and convincing materials—if you have a clear idea of what you want to create and how to achieve a particular look.

The topics in this chapter include:

- The use of layered detail to produce dirt, grime, and natural weathering

- Determining the appropriate level of detail and realism

- Building maps from scratch with various paint programs

- Ways to modify existing maps for increased realism

- Materials for skin, eyes, and fur

What Does Reality Look Like?

For many 3D graphics artists, attaining photorealistic (or at least strongly believable) results is the Holy Grail of CG visualization. Unfortunately, even with the most powerful 3D tools, re-creating the exact look of reality can be elusive. There's a lot conspiring against this— reality is inherently complex, and re-creating it in the 3D world can be expensive, in both creation time and rendering time.

Thankfully, we don't need to model at the sub-pixel level or write physically-based reflectance shaders to create images that look stunningly real. The bulk of both realistic lighting and shading currently relies on clever cheats. Even with the cheats, however, re-creating real-looking images can be difficult.

Part of the problem of re-creating reality comes from the fact that we, as observers, are immersed in visually complex environments our entire lives and can determine immediately if something doesn't look "right." A large portion of our visual perception system is designed to do just that—detect differences and irregularities in what we see. (In terms of pattern recognition, humans can blow the most sophisticated computer out of the water any day of the week.) When we see something that looks "wrong," it tends to be glaringly apparent.

The real problem in creating a realistic CG environment is not just one of knowing when something looks wrong, but of analyzing what the problem is and figuring out what modifications are needed to correct the problem. As with most of the arts, success at re-creating reality requires practice and a keen eye. Understanding the attributes that most natural materials share is a good starting point for re-creating them in the 3D world.

Fortunately, 3D Studio MAX's Material Editor gives you a great deal of power in manipulating your material attributes. You can use additional maps (preferably real-world, digitized bitmap textures) in the various map channels or add modifications to the main Diffuse texture map. For any material, you can also use any of MAX's 11 map channels. Although you may end up creating complex material "trees" composed of multiple layers of maps and masks, you shouldn't consider it a burdensome task. You may literally spend days building your models and getting the details right. But when it's time to create the materials for the objects, you don't want to adopt a "hurry up and get it done" attitude. When it's time to create your textures, you need to spend as much time on your objects' "paint jobs" as you did creating the objects themselves.

Levels Of Complexity

To create the look of a particular material, all too often a 3D artist places a single texture map in the Diffuse channel, makes some modifications to the Shininess parameter, and proclaims it done. The result of this quick-and-dirty material creation resembles a sheet of contact paper that's been slapped on the object. Regardless of the quality of the texture map, the resulting material may lack the subtle complexities associated with most real-world surfaces.

The single most important quality of real objects and materials is that they are *complex*. Even a flat, white, painted wall will look complex when viewed at the right angle.

In 3D Studio MAX, select File|View File, and view the STUCCO.JPG image in the \CHAP_04 directory of this book's companion CD-ROM. This image is also shown in Figure 4.1.

Figure 4.1 A digitized photo of a white stucco wall texture; you could not only use this on a wall as a Bump map, but as a Diffuse map as well. (Note that this bitmap is included in both the \CHAP_04 and \MAPS directories of this book's companion CD-ROM as STUCCO.JPG.)

The Diffuse component of a material is typically the first one noticed by the observer, but it's not the only one. To add to the material's verisimilitude, you need to consider not just color, but also the amount of gloss, roughness, and wear and tear that most natural materials exhibit.

One of the best ways to create realistic materials for the objects in your scene is to consider their history. How old is the object in question? How often is it used and does that use impart a particular type of wear? How long has it been in its environment, and how has the environment affected it? Is it wet, dry, dusty, or cracked? This list could go on, but it's important to think of how the object has been affected so that you can re-create the appropriate look. Once you know what the effects are, you need to consider their placement; most types of degradation are not omnipresent over the surface of objects. Finally, you need to find good visual research from which to work—don't guess at the look of a surface when you can work from real life!

Color And Saturation

Take a quick look around and study the objects that surround you. The first thing you'll probably notice is an object's overall color. Under good lighting, if you squint, you can get a pretty good feel for what that color is. This said, it's important to realize that color isn't nearly as constant as you might think. Lighting plays a critical role in a material's perceived color. When the lighting changes, so does the apparent color.

When you replicate a material, it's a good idea to view whatever source you are working from in conditions that are as close to daylight as possible. This ensures that no unwanted color cast that alters the appearance of the base color is introduced. Usually, you'll want to build a material based upon this unmodified color. However, there may be situations in which you need to design a whole set of materials around a specific type of environmental lighting. You may want to create custom versions of materials for scenes with low-level lighting, add stylized or painterly effects to a material, or convey a particular mood.

Another common attribute of most natural real-world materials is that they rarely contain highly saturated colors. This is especially important when creating materials that replicate environments. The sky, ground cover, soil, and rocky surfaces rarely exhibit saturated colors, especially when viewed from a distance.

In 3D Studio MAX, select File|View File, and view the ROCKS.JPG image in the \CHAP_04 directory of the companion CD-ROM. This image is also shown in Figure 4.2.

Figure 4.2   A rocky surface.

This digitized photo of a rocky surface shows clear earth tones and shading, but none of the colors is particularly vibrant in the image on your screen.

Note that there are exceptions to the "saturated color" rule in nature. For example, many animals utilize vibrant colors for defensive and display purposes. Foliage, when viewed at close or medium range without much atmospheric attenuation, also can appear saturated. Wet surfaces also display increased saturation and overall darkening.

In 3D Studio MAX, select File|View File, and view the MUD_5.JPG image in the \CHAP_04 directory of the companion CD-ROM. This image is also shown in Figure 4.3.

Figure 4.3   A muddy patch of earth after a rainstorm.

Figure 4.3 shows a close-up of a wet, muddy surface taken near a parking lot after a hard rain. The bright sunlight accentuates shiny highlights in the mud. This texture is useful for (you guessed it) depicting a muddy, slimy surface, such as a wet field or even the bottom of the deep ocean.

It's often good practice to bring down the saturation of many materials to better help blend them into their environment. The real world is a dusty, dirty place, and dirt has a tendency to get on objects, which will naturally mute normally vibrant colors. Most texture maps that are either created from scanned images or acquired from a CD source can generally benefit from decreasing the saturation (using a paint package) 5 to 10 percent to help account for this.

A material's saturation can also suggest how new it is. Many materials' colors have a tendency to fade over time when exposed to sunlight. This bleaching effect is especially noticeable in man-made objects. Pigments often fade dramatically because of exposure to ultra-violet light. It's also important to note that all colors or pigments don't fade equally. Reds and yellows are notorious for fading. Printed material sitting in a store display window will probably be faded. Quite often, the only colors left are cyan and black. The magenta will have faded because of the bleaching action of the sun.

In 3D Studio MAX, select File|View File, and view the GRENELEC.JPG image in the \CHAP_04 directory of the companion CD-ROM. This image is also shown in Figure 4.4.

Figure 4.4   An electrical junction box with a faded surface.

This is a picture of the front of an industrial electrical junction box. As it sits outside exposed to the sun and rain, its painted surface becomes bleached and faded.

Saturation also plays an important role when you create materials for poorly lit or nighttime scenes. The rods and cones in the human eye control overall perception of color. The cones are adapted to detect variations in color during normal levels of illumination. When the level of illumination falls, as in the case of a darkened room or at night, the rods begin to take over and color vision disappears. The rods sense light achromatically; that is, they can only detect changes in the value of a color. The net result is that in low illumination, colors appear to become desaturated. To help account for this, you may want to alter your standard maps for the various objects in a dim scene and create textures with far less saturation.

Dirt, Grime, And Other Weathering

Nothing stays clean very long. It may sound pessimistic, but it's a useful fact to consider when you're replicating a natural-materials look. Virtually everything you come into contact with (especially outdoors) eventually acquires some form of weathering as a result of general use and exposure to the sun and the elements.

The effects of weathering can take many forms—typically, variances in coloration, texture, and shininess. When you create these texture effects, you need to consider the object's environment and the types of weathering that would be appropriate. Keep all effects understated unless their purpose is to attract attention.

The degradation of an object's "factory-new" surface can be the result of one or more of the following: bleaching or fading due to the sun; abrasions, dents, and scratches; stains due to splashes, dripping, and leaching; dust, soot, and other airborne particles; polishing due to wear; chipping, cracking, and peeling paint; and oxidizing and patination.

In 3D Studio MAX, select File|View File, and view the RUSTYCAR.JPG image in the \CHAP_04 directory of the companion CD-ROM. This image is also shown in Figure 4.5.

Figure 4.5   An old car door shows rust and paint cracks.

This image shows the door of an old junked car. Its paint has become cracked and is falling off; rust spreading over the metal underneath the paint is also accelerating the aging process. In the case of organic materials such as wood and leaves, surface changes may be the result of moss, mold, decomposition, and bacterial decay.

In the sections that follow, you'll find some of the approaches you might take to achieve various weathering effects on an object's surface.

Bleaching Or Fading

The most simple way to achieve the effect of bleaching or fading is to alter the saturation of the texture map in Photoshop or a similar program. Although it's not seen all the time, this modification to the basic material can help blend man-made objects into natural environments.

Look for areas on the object that may not have direct exposure to the sun—these areas could retain more of their original color and vibrancy. For example, a label or other object may cover a portion of the surface; the covered areas would most likely retain much of their original coloration.

Remember, not all colors fade equally. You could re-create this effect in Photoshop by utilizing the Curves function in the individual color channels of a bitmap to desaturate specific colors. As with all weathering effects, good reference is a must.

Abrasions, Dents, And Scratches

General wear and tear is apparent in almost every object that we come in contact with; thus, it's critical that objects in your 3D environment share these attributes.

The simplest way to achieve the effects of general wear and tear on a material is through the use of Bump and Shininess maps. A library of premade maps for this purpose can be a great time-saver.

In 3D Studio MAX, select File|View File, and view the GENBUMP1.JPG image in the \CHAP_04 directory of the companion CD-ROM. This image is also shown in Figure 4.6. I created this bump map in Photoshop to depict scratches for many surfaces.

If you have a graphics tablet, it's simple to create a fairly large grayscale image and fill it lightly with scratchlike markings of various sizes and intensities. It's often helpful to create a number of marks, slightly blur them using Gaussian Blur, and continue to make more. By repeating this process

Figure 4.6   A subtle bump map used for various surfaces.

several times, you can create a layered look that matches the effect that real objects receive from continuous exposure to scratching and burnishing through contact with other objects.

If you have access to a flatbed scanner, you can create bump maps via "analog" means. Just take a soft pencil or charcoal, draw marks on a sheet of plain white paper, and then scan it. You can smudge and soften these marks on the paper—or in a paint program after you've scanned them—to build up a complex layered appearance. In addition, charcoal rubbings from natural surfaces such as brick and concrete can provide all manner of textures that look pitted and abraded.

Stains: Splashes, Dripping, And Leaching

Any material that can absorb moisture has a tendency to become stained. These items include not only the obvious materials, such as fabrics, but also nonorganic porous surfaces, such as concrete and painted items. Parking lots and tabletops provide ample proof that relatively hard surfaces can also acquire stains.

The most straightforward way to create a stained look is, once again, via a paint program. In general, stains have the tendency to darken and saturate the receiving surface. By using airbrush tools, or Photoshop's Burn, Dodge, or Sponge tools, you can create the color changes that stains create. If the surface should appear wet or oily, you may also need to use the same Diffuse map you created as a Shininess map. Of course, you can also start from a real-world texture.

In 3D Studio MAX, select File|View File, and view the GRYSTREK.JPG image in the \CHAP_04 directory of the companion CD-ROM. This image is also shown in Figure 4.7.

Figure 4.7 Water stains and streaks on a painted surface.

Because stains usually occur from contact with water or other liquids, you should consider how and where the exposure will take place. Unless the receiving surface is flat and horizontal, liquids will flow, leave streaks, and concentrate in low spots. More viscous liquids such as oil will flow less and will tend to pool.

Another result of exposure to moisture and dirt is an accumulation of these materials in the recesses of an object. This effect is so critical to the appearance of large man-made objects that traditional model-makers have created a special weathering technique called a *wash*. In traditional modeling, artists may dilute small amounts of dark brown, gray, or black paint with thinner and allow it to flow into the recesses

CREATING CUSTOM WEATHERING MAPS

Creating a library of grayscale weathering maps can save a huge amount of time, rather than creating everything each time from scratch. Many details, such as dents, smudges, and water spots, can be used repeatedly on several objects in a scene, as long as they remain subtle and you place them carefully. Use a paint program (such as Fractal Design Painter or Adobe Photoshop) that allows you to layer several maps with varying degrees of blur and detail until you arrive at a result you like.

and cracks on a model. When they wipe away the excess wash, some of it remains in corners and along seams and panel lines and gives an increased sense of depth to the model.

You can simulate this effect in 3D with careful painting of object-specific maps. You can darken panel lines or recesses to re-create the accumulation of dirt, oil, and other grime. (For more information on this process, see Chapter 17.) There are also third-party MAX plug-ins, such as REM Infografica's DirtyREYES, that can simulate this effect automatically. An example is shown in Figure 4.8.

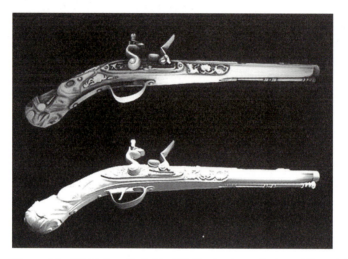

Figure 4.8 REM Infografica's DirtyREYES plug-in applied to a 3D model.

Dust, Soot, And Airborne Particles

As you just learned, recesses are best accentuated with dark shading. Flat or top surfaces of objects can acquire an accumulation of dust and other airborne particulate matter, which generally dulls the surface and decreases the saturation of the surface.

To create dust-accumulation effects in MAX, try using a Top/Bottom material. The top material should contain a Blend material; the bottom material represents the main material for the object. In the Blend material, Material1 should re-create the dust or particle covering. Material2 should be an Instance of the main body material that you used as the bottom material for the Top/Bottom. In the Mask: Map entry, use procedural Noise to simulate the collection and variation of dust covering. To see an example of this technique, follow these steps:

1. Select File|Load, and load the DUSTY.MAX file from the \CHAP_04 directory of this book's companion CD-ROM.

2. Open the Material Editor and take a look at the Dusty Top/Bottom material settings. The Top material consists of a Blend material, with a grayish surface blended with a blue surface using a Noise map as the mask. The Bottom material consists of the same blue surface as above (as an Instance copy), with the Top/Bottom settings further blending among all these material components. (Note that this material is saved in your MAX_FX_2.MAT Material Library. In addition, you'll explore the Top/Bottom material type later on in Chapter 12.)

3. Next, activate your Camera01 viewport and render a test image of this scene. As your rendering indicates, the top of the sphere looks as if it's accumulated a coating of dust, making its surface less shiny.

Polishing Caused By Wear

Objects that are handled often or are subject to abrasion exhibit either a shine or a dullness. These effects, which are critical to realism, show that the surface is not consistently smooth.

You can generate this look in MAX by using custom maps in the Shininess and Shininess Strength channels. The trick is in careful placement of the effects, as they will most often appear only in certain areas. You can use simple grayscale maps to enhance the perceived complexity of the material. (In the next two chapters, you'll see how to create complex metal materials using these techniques.)

Chipping, Cracking, And Peeling

Through the processes of heat expansion and contraction, cracks tend to form in both solid and coated surfaces. You can create simple representations of the effects of chipping, cracking, and peeling with both Diffuse and Bump maps.

If your objects are going to be viewed up close, you may want to create more complex geometry so the surface will self-shadow correctly. MAX's Object Modifiers, such as Noise or Displace, can create random surface displacements or custom topology on your objects.

Oxidizing And Patination

Metals and surfaces that are chemically active oxidize when exposed to oxygen and moisture. In nature, the process is known as oxidation. When this effect is created for artistic purposes, it's called a *patina*.

The most common example of metal oxidation is reddish rust on iron surfaces, of course. However, copper, brass, and bronze also demonstrate the reaction to oxygen and moisture—they tend to develop a powdery, greenish-blue coating of copper oxide when exposed to the elements. Bronze, if not fully oxidized, can take on a darker, mottled appearance with little or no green cast.

In 3D Studio MAX, select File|View File, and view the BRASS_1.JPG image in the \CHAP_04 directory of the companion CD-ROM. This image is also shown in Figure 4.9.

Figure 4.9 An image of a mottled brass metal surface with tarnished areas in the detail.

Aluminum also oxidizes, but to a lesser visual degree. You may represent this effect in MAX by softening your object's reflectivity and adding some dark gray or black specks to its Diffuse map to give it a dusty appearance. Silver blackens with oxidation, and other metals oxidize and acquire different appearances. Even when metal objects are polished frequently, the oxide tends to remain in recesses.

You can often re-create the look of many chemically active surfaces by acquiring existing digitized texture maps of metal materials via CD-ROM texture libraries such as Kinetix Texture Universe or Digimation's Xeno-1 collection. Check the appendices in this book for other sources.

Determining Levels Of Detail

Geometry and material detail go hand in hand. Sometimes, it is difficult to separate what should be modeled and what can be accomplished through the use of well-constructed textures. One way to approach this problem is to divide a model's surface characteristics into three separate levels: the macro level, the material level, and the sub-pixel level. I'll explain these here.

The Macro Level

The *macro* level describes gross features that you can't create with either materials or shading and that you need to add during the modeling phase. Some 3D artists create their models with the same level of overall detail and don't add appropriate complexity in certain areas. Certainly, not allowing for enough faces on curved surfaces is a noticeable flaw when dealing with polygon-based geometry.

Less obvious is the lack of radiuses, or "rounded-off" edges, on your models. Few objects, other than knife or razor blades, have absolutely straight, sharp edges where two surfaces meet. Most have at least a small radius on the edge.

Sharp edges on natural and man-made objects tend to be worn down through general use and abrasion and thereby create radiuses. Conversely, many manufactured objects have radiused edges, so they *won't* show wear, and because radius edges are safer and more appealing to interact with.

In the CG world, adding radiused edges (even tiny ones) to your objects will increase their complexity (and possibly your rendering time), but the result is increased realism. In any object with a degree of shininess, specular highlights will tend to show up on the radiused edges. The human visual system recognizes this, and we've come to expect that the highlights will be present.

Figure 4.10   By adding radiused edges to objects, you can pick up specular highlights.

Figure 4.10 shows two parametric MAX box objects. The left object has standard sharp edges with no radius on them. The right one has a slight edge, which I created with the Fillet modifier.

Notice how the box on the right has better specular highlights along its radiused edges. Tiny surface details like these, although subtle, can make your 3D objects much more aesthetically pleasing.

The Material Level

You control the next level of detail at the *material* level. When it comes to re-creating medium-scale texture, bump mapping is a must. Because few natural surfaces are as smooth as glass, very subtle bump mapping, using either procedural Noise or texture maps, lends to more interesting surfaces and takes away some of the flat or plastic look so prevalent in CGI. You should also use scratches, dents, and other surface defects in conjunction with the regular surface to indicate wear. Although very small bumps will most likely be filtered out when rendered at a distance, they should be present if the object will appear close to the camera during an animation.

As with all map and geometry details, consider how much time they will appear in the scene and at what distance. If the object is moving and has motion blur, it may negate the need for more subtle details. Sometimes you may want to create multiple versions of the same maps with different resolutions (using the Image|Image Size features of Photoshop) depending on the needs of your scene.

REAL OR STYLIZED RENDERING?

Although attention to detail is critical when you want to create a realistic scene, "reality" may not always be the goal. *Toy Story* provides an excellent example of "stylized reality." Regardless of the level of stylization, you should try to make the materials in your scene have a consistent look. This will have a unifying effect and give continuity to the various objects.

The Sub-pixel Level

The final level of surface detail can be thought of as occurring on the *sub-pixel* level. Very flat surfaces reflect light with less scattering and tend to be shiny; perfectly flat surfaces act as a mirror. However, because real surfaces are rarely perfectly smooth, this micro-scale roughness causes light to bounce around a localized area, which tends to further illuminate the surface.

You can see this effect on materials like flat paint or chalk, where the shadow areas tend to be less pronounced. You can also see it if you take a look at the full moon some clear night; you'll notice how there's little in the way of shading, even though Luna is basically a sphere lit from one source—the sun.

When you're creating objects with very dull surfaces, consider how light may be scattered across them and adjust your texture maps and material parameters accordingly.

Creating Good Texture Maps: The Basics

With the advent of Photoshop and Fractal Design Painter for the PC, you can create convincing MAX texture maps with relative ease if you know exactly what you're trying to reproduce. Once again, real-world photographic reference is critical. If you can go out and photograph the subject, do it. Otherwise, hit your local library or bookstore to find examples of the material. Magazines can provide excellent visual reference on a myriad of subjects. (You may yet find use for those copies of *National Geographic* that you just can't throw away.) For relatively simple materials, try the following basic techniques:

- Create a new map at a larger resolution than its intended final size, once you know what the material should look like. It's always better to start off larger than you think is necessary and crop it or scale it down later.

- Consider the type of mapping coordinates you're going to use with the map. If the mapping requires a particular aspect ratio, set the length and width of the bitmap appropriately. If you're using planar projection to apply the map, render an orthographic view of your geometry in MAX and use it to help determine the final aspect ratio.

- Determine if the map needs to be tilable. If so, you can use the Offset filter in Photoshop with the Wrap Around feature enabled. This will help you locate the map's seams and then paint them out.

Painting The Maps

If you have Photoshop or Fractal Design Painter, here are some quick steps to get you started on a plain Diffuse map for a MAX object:

1. Determine the base color of the map. If it's going to be an ivory-colored texture, you need to determine the correct RGB settings for the initial ivory color. You should then determine the RGB settings for lighter highlights and darker shadings of the ivory color.

2. In either Photoshop or Fractal Design Painter, create a new image of at least 640×480 resolution; then, fill the map with the most prominent base color.

   Note that very few materials are one solid, consistent color. Try to identify secondary colors within the material and create swatches for them in a palette or second file. By adding subtle color variations in the map, you can help remove a flat appearance, as shown in Figure 4.11. (You can also view this file in MAX or one of the paint programs; load IVORY.TGA from your \CHAP_04 or \MAPS directory.)

Figure 4.11 An ivory texture.

3. At this point, you may want to introduce some noise into the basic map. To produce some nice variations, apply Photoshop's Add Noise filter at a low amount with Monochromatic either checked or unchecked. (The latter depends on how much additional color variation you want to introduce into the original map.)

4. If the end result is too prominent, apply a small amount of Gaussian Blur over it. For a more layered look, you can repeat this combination several times, decreasing the amounts each time.

By using many filters in combination, you'll have a good starting point for more complex bitmaps. This is especially true when creating Bump maps. It's also useful to make several copies of your base map in case you want to create variations.

Analyzing The Map

Once you've painted a basic texture, you need to analyze the main details and see if you should replicate particularly effective areas. If the features are large in scale, you may want to find a second map that has similar features and clone and blend them into your new map. You can also use cloning to add subtle amounts of a color to other areas of the map.

If you like the look of one feature, clone it several times and modify the copies to hide their repetition. For best results (especially for high-resolution still images), try to keep the features random unless you specifically need to create a particular repeating pattern to the surface. Now, consider the extra details (such as dirt, dents, scuffs, and discoloration) you need to add to make the material convincing. One of Photoshop 4.0's most useful features is that it allows you to work in layers. Sometimes a modification of the base map can provide a starting point for the Bump or Shininess maps. You can add dusty spots and general grime by airbrushing lightly on a transparent layer on top of the finished texture.

You will also be able to see the exact placement of details if you create the maps in a layered format. Once all the layers are complete, you can save them individually and place them in their respective map slots.

The Apple Scene

For an example of convincing hand-painted texture maps created with the layering techniques you learned in the preceding section, take a look at this apple scene:

1. In 3D Studio MAX, load APPLE.MAX from the \CHAP_04 directory of the companion CD-ROM. When the file loads, you'll see a simple scene consisting of an apple sitting on a tabletop.

2. Activate the Camera01 viewport and render the scene; your rendering should look like Figure 4.12. To create the apple's surface, I painted two textures—a Diffuse map and a Bump map—in Photoshop.

Figure 4.12 Hand-painted Diffuse and Bump maps help create this convincing apple image.

3. To see the bitmaps, open the Material Editor and examine the Apple texture's Diffuse and Bump map slots, or choose File|View File and view the APPLESKN.JPG and APPLEBMP.JPG images in the \CHAP_04 directory of the companion CD-ROM. These images are also shown in Figures 4.13 and 4.14.

Figure 4.13   The Diffuse map for the apple.

Figure 4.14   The Bump map for the apple.

Using Preexisting Textures

If you feel you don't have the art skills to paint your own realistic texture maps, you might want to use existing bitmaps for your scenes. If you do, however, you should ask yourself several questions.

Is the map of high enough photographic quality and resolution for its intended purpose?

Quite often, maps that come on texture CDs are fairly small. If this is the only problem, you may tile or retouch the map to increase its size. If the map is much too small, you may be better off finding a replacement or trying to paint one from scratch. To determine if the map's resolution is high enough for your rendering, ask yourself if the object that uses the map will be rendered, at any point, at a larger resolution than the map itself (for still images, this may often be the case).

Is the scale of the texture correct for the scale that will be represented?

When you photograph surfaces, it can be especially difficult to keep the lighting consistent over large areas. Consequently, the map you want to use may be the right material but at the wrong scale. You can tile maps if there are few macro features that will betray the repeats, but it's usually best to create a larger map that has had these features removed or rearranged.

Does the map have intrinsic lighting clues in it that will contradict the lighting in the scene?

Sometimes maps that come from photographs include shadows and highlights because of the lighting in their environment when they were shot. These lighting artifacts will rarely correspond with your

HIDING A REPEATING BITMAP PATTERN

Here's an excellent trick to "hide" tiling bitmaps. Use a Blend material in MAX with the exact same bitmap in both Material #1's and #2's Diffuse slots. However, change the UV tiling of the Diffuse map in Material #2—for example, if the first is UV tiling at 1/1, tile the second at 2/2 or 3/3. Then load a procedural Noise texture as the mask between the maps. The subtle shades in the Noise will blend between the two textures and help "extend" the non-tiling areas of the maps.

scene's lighting. Your best bet is to use maps that are flatly lit, or create your own. If you have to use a map with shadows and highlights already in it, you can sometimes minimize them by using the Dodge and Burn tools in Photoshop. By decreasing the variance in luminance, you can hide some of these artifacts.

Is there a color cast to the map?
Photos from print film and scanned images sometimes acquire a color cast due to their original lighting. Use Photoshop's Curves tools to neutralize the color cast if possible. Also remember that overly saturated colors tend to be unrealistic.

Does the map need to be tilable?
Many of the better CD collections try to make their maps tile without visual discontinuities at the seams. If you are forced to make a map tile, use the Offset filter in Photoshop and be prepared to spend some time working on it. Retouching can take practice. This is especially true if the detail is macro or the seams are wildly different in content. Sometimes retouching isn't an option and the map is best replaced.

Will the map be used in more than one place in the scene?
If the answer is yes, consider making variations of the map. Slight variations of smudges, dents, stains, and so on, can make multiple instances of geometry appear more realistic. If you can't modify the map, consider changing its mapping to help conceal the repetition.

Organic Materials

Organic materials are some of the most difficult surfaces to reproduce faithfully with the current level of sophistication in CG. Often, these materials are not merely defined by their outermost surface.

Skin

Human skin in particular is difficult to reproduce because there are several layers to it and each layer has varying degrees of opacity, color, shininess, and texture. When you try to paint the net results of these effects, you'll typically produce a flat unrealistic surface.

Some of the components to keep in mind when you paint skin textures are variations in skin tone, blemishes, bruises, large and small wrinkle textures, hairs, oiliness, and subsurface features such as veins. To create an excellent reference from which to paint or clone, try scanning or photographing a representational-size image of real skin. Although human skin remains a real challenge to reproduce, various animal skins have been replicated to appear photo-realistic. Both in TV and in films such as *Jumanji*, animals like elephants, crocodiles, and dogs are showing up with greater regularity; a large part of their believability is due to accurate surface representation. Figure 4.15 shows a human skin example. While this image is fairly macro in scale, it should give you a good starting point to create object-specific skin maps.

Figure 4.15 The H_FLESH2.TGA map from the Xeno-1 texture CD is included on this book's companion CD-ROM in the \MAPS and CHAP_04 directories.

Eyes

Eyes make up another area that deserves some attention in character-material creation. We tend to get a lot of information from the movement and appearance of a character's eyes. Consequently, it's important to put enough detail into the eyes so that they appear realistic.

If the creature remains at a far enough distance from the camera, you can often incorporate the eyes into the overall body texture maps. In most other cases, though, you'll want to create independent maps and geometry for the eyes.

As with everything else, working from reference is a must when trying to replicate the fine detail within the eye. One problem with grabbing an eye image from an existing photo is that the extremely shiny, wet eye surface invariably produces unwanted highlights on the image. You can sometimes retouch these lighting artifacts out of the image. Unfortunately, eye images are often too small; you must either find close-up images to retouch or paint maps from scratch.

To alleviate some of these problems, this book's companion CD-ROM includes several animal and alien eye examples. You can use them in your own work or use them as reference for creating your own original eye texture maps. Figure 4.16 shows two sample eye maps from Digimation's Xeno-1 texture CD.

To see an example of one of these textures used in a MAX scene, follow these steps:

1. In MAX Release 2.5, load EYE.MAX from the \CHAP_04 directory of the companion CD-ROM. When the file loads, you'll see two hemispheres sitting inside a boxy room.

2. The smaller hemisphere serves as a cornea over the main eye surface. Open the Material Editor and you'll see that it has a ray-traced material applied to it. This provides a slight amount of spherical distortion to the eye bitmap and makes the final rendering more realistic.

3. To see an example of the spherical distortion, activate your Camera01 viewport and render the scene (it may take a few minutes because of the ray-traced material). When the scene appears, your screen should look like Figure 4.17.

Figure 4.17 The SHEEP_Y.TGA eye map as applied to a hemisphere; a second hemisphere with a ray-traced material provides spherical distortion.

Fur

There has been a lot of interest in the last few years in the simulation of fur for CGI. As with most developments in the field, the first examples of fur and hair came out of the research community.

Images courtesy of Digimation.

Figure 4.16 Some sample eye images from the Xeno-1 texture CD.

Not long after, proprietary software examples began to show up in both TV and film. Now, this same functionality has shown up on our desktops. Although MAX doesn't have a specific hair routine built into it, there are workarounds and new plug-ins that not only make the creation of fur and hair possible, but make them realistic looking as well.

One simple solution is to use MAX's Scatter compound object type to distribute simple hair geometry across the surface of your object. Figure 4.18 shows an example of how this technique was used by noted MAX artist Martin Foster.

Martin Foster 1997

Image courtesy of Martin Foster.

Figure 4.18 On its nighttime feeding flight, a bat chases after a moth.

You can also use shareware or commercial MAX plug-ins to create hair or fur on your MAX creatures. Plug-in developer Peter Watje has created a particle-system-based hair that enables users to create long, dense hairs on their creatures and base the coloration on the object's original texture mapping. It also allows for secondary motion-based dynamics.

Digimation's Shag: Fur plug-in produces ultrafast photo-realistic fur through the use of an atmospheric shader. Unlike the other options mentioned here, Shag produces no geometry, which allows you to create super dense coats of fur with little problem. It also allows you to set most all of its parameters via maps. This gives you solid visual control of where and how the fur will be created.

Regardless of which method you use, make sure to give some randomness to the hair and fur through various parameters. Variations in color and length will improve realism. Figure 4.19 shows an example created with the Shag: Fur plug-in.

Figure 4.19   An example created with Digimation's Shag: Fur plug-in.

Moving On

In this chapter, you explored some of the most important aspects of realistic material design, including materials for both organic and inorganic surfaces.

In the next few chapters, you'll learn how to create realistic metal materials and how to combine materials with glowing optical effects.

INDUSTRIAL MATERIALS, PART I

5

Now that you've learned the basics of creating natural materials in MAX, we'll move on to duplicate industrial materials—specifically, you'll learn how to create refined metal textures.

In this chapter, you'll create a Standard metal material in Release 2.5's Material Editor; then you'll build on this material through a series of layering techniques. These techniques include using a variety of custom bitmaps and using Blend materials to mix between Phong, Blinn, and Metal shaders to refine the results.

By employing a combination of maps, consisting of Diffuse, Ambient, RGB Tint, Specular, Shininess, Shininess Strength, and Reflection, you can create stunning metallic surfaces for your objects. (You can even simulate an effect known as *anisotropic specularity*, which I'll discuss later in this chapter.) These techniques are applicable to all sorts of objects, whether they be a present-day factory interior, a sleek sports car, or a futuristic space vehicle.

Finally, you'll take a look at Falloff, a new Map Type that you can use to produce excellent reflective surfaces, iridescent effects, and even "X-ray" imagery.

Setting Up The Test Scene

First, you'll create a simple scene consisting of a sphere, a camera, and a couple of spotlights. You'll use the sphere as a test object for most of these metallic textures. Follow these steps to set up the test scene:

1. Load 3D Studio MAX Release 2.5, or else save your current work and reset the program.

2. In your MAX Top viewport, create a sphere with a radius of 100 units. Set Segments to 60 to make the sphere nicely rounded. Make sure Smooth is checked, and also check the Generate Mapping Coordinates box.

3. In the Top viewport, zoom out somewhat from the sphere and create a Target Spotlight at approximate XYZ coordinates X -600, Y -400, Z 0. (You may want to activate 3D Snap Toggle to make this easier.) Drag the spotlight's target to the center of the Sphere. Then, activate the Left viewport, zoom out, and move the spotlight up on the Y axis approximately 400 units. The spotlight should be shining down on the sphere, from the left, at roughly a 45-degree angle.

4. Go to the Modify panel and change Spot01 to pure white, or RGB 255, 255, 255. Change its Multiplier to 1.5 so that the specular highlights on the sphere are much brighter—this will enhance the final metal effect. Turn Cast Shadows on.

5. In the Top viewport, press the Shift key and drag the spotlight you just created to the right to approximate XYZ coordinates

X 1200, Y 100, Z 0 to create a second light. (Make it a Copy, not an Instance.) Activate the Left viewport and drag Spot02 down the Y axis about 550 units. Go to the Modify Panel and change the spotlight's colors to RGB 12, 64, 196, or a medium-dark blue. This will be a shadow-casting fill light for the bottom of the sphere.

6. Go to Rendering|Environment and change the background color to a dark blue, or RGB 0, 0, 32. This will help the (soon-to-be) bright green sphere show up better in the test renderings.

7. Finally, create a Target Camera in the Top viewport at approximate XYZ coordinates X 0, Y -350, Z 0 and drag its target to the center of the sphere. In the Left viewport, drag Camera01 up the Y axis about 160 units. Activate the camera in the Perspective viewport and render the scene. Your screen should look somewhat like Figure 5.1 (note that I have Show Cone on the spotlights activated in this illustration).

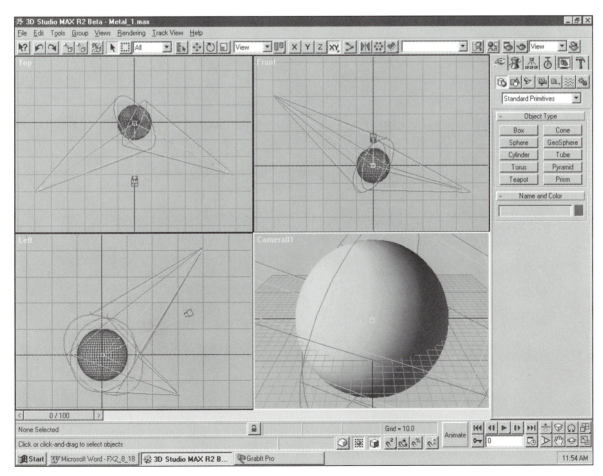

Figure 5.1   A simple test scene for creating your metal textures.

You'll use this basic scene for most of this chapter. (If you want, you can simply load the METAL_1.MAX scene file from the \CHAP_05 directory of the CD-ROM accompanying this book. You can then use this file for the next few tutorial examples.)

Heavy Metal

Now that you've created this simple test scene, it's time to create the first metal material for it:

1. Select the sphere and then open the Material Editor. Rename Material #1 to Metal 1 Single, change the Shading option from Blinn to Phong, and then apply it to the sphere, either by dragging it over to the sphere or by clicking on the Assign Material To Selection button. (You can experiment with the Blinn shading type later, if you want, and examine the differences in the sphere's shading.)

2. First, you want to change the Ambient and Diffuse colors, so change Ambient to RGB 8, 32, 48, or a dark, dusky blue.

3. Drag the Ambient color swatch down to Diffuse to copy it; then, change the Diffuse value to 64, 255, 255, or a light cyan. Change Specular to pure white, or 255, 255, 255 and then change Shininess to 0 and Shininess Strength to 100.

You may be wondering—why set Shininess to 0, but Shininess Strength to 100 percent? As you see in the Material Editor, you have a cyan object with a giant diffused specular highlight. Don't worry about that for now—in a moment you'll apply some bitmaps that will "clamp" the highlight to specific areas, yet still allow for shininess all over your test Sphere. These bitmaps will then "pump up" the Shininess value to create the proper specular highlight, even if the actual Shininess value is low.

4. Now, go down to the Maps section of the rollout, open it (if it's not already open), and click on the Diffuse/Ambient Map Lock button to unlock the mapping of these two attributes from one another.

It's usually better to *not* have these attributes locked when you're creating realistic materials. By unlocking them and adjusting the color settings and map levels individually, you can increase the contrast and realism inherent in your materials. (See the sidebar in this chapter, "Five Steps To Improve Your MAX Renderings," for a refresher on this.)

5. Click on the Ambient slot in the Maps rollout to bring up the new modeless Material/Map Browser. Under Browse From, select New, and then select Bitmap. When the Bitmap rollout appears,

click on the empty Bitmap name field. From the \CHAP_05 directory of the companion CD-ROM, select the file MTLGREEN.JPG, and click on View. The image is also shown here in Figure 5.2.

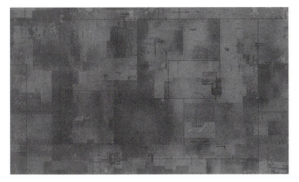

Figure 5.2 The MTLGREEN.JPG forms the basis for the primary Metal_1 texture.

The MTLGREEN.JPG image is an 800x400 bitmap of a mottled green metal surface. This texture began as a photograph of a large electrical junction box I found in a Silicon Valley industrial parking lot. The large metal box, once painted a uniform green, had irregular patterns where its hues had been bleached out by the sun. The accumulated scratches and scuff marks in its surface added to its usefulness as a realistic CGI texture map. I digitized the photograph on a flatbed scanner and then loaded it into Adobe Photoshop to tweak. I cut and pasted parts of the image and used the Offset filter to make it seamlessly tileable. I then drew on various light panel lines, and overlaid dark panel lines, which were derived from a separate Bump map (which you'll load in a moment). The 2:1 ratio of this bitmap makes it perfect for spherical mapping and our spherical test object.

6. Close the View window and click on OK to load the image into your Ambient bitmap slot. Under Tiling, change U and V to 2.0; then, click on the Go To Parent icon to return to the main Material Editor rollout. Drag this bitmap down to Diffuse and select Instance instead of Copy.

Making It From Scratch(es)

At the moment, the sample sphere in the Material Editor doesn't look like much—you still have to fix that shininess problem. You'll do that now:

1. Click on the Map slot next to Specular; when the Material/Map Browser appears, select RGB Tint. This map adjusts the value of the three color channels in an image. You'll use it to enhance the greenish tint of the specular highlights in the metal texture.

2. Click on the Red color swatch of the RGB Tint map; when the Color Selector appears, bring the Green color value up to 255 so the Red Tint is bright yellow instead of pure red. Now, click on the Green color swatch, and bring it down to 128. Leave the Blue color swatch as it is. The final settings for the Red swatch are 128, 255, 0. Close the Color Selector.

3. Click on the Map button, and select Bitmap from the Material/Map Browser. From the \CHAP_05 directory on the companion CD-ROM, select the file MTLSPEC.JPG and click on View.

The image shown on your screen and in Figure 5.3 is very simple: grayish, crisscrossing lines on a lighter background. I created this texture in Adobe Photoshop by applying a heavy layer of Noise to a

Figure 5.3 A crosshatched specular highlight pattern created in Adobe Photoshop.

new white background image. Next, I applied Motion Blur (approximately 25 pixels in length, at a 45-degree angle). This "streaked" the Noise pixels. I then copied the image, flipped it horizontally, and pasted the original image on top of the flipped one using Multiply. The result is a simple crosshatched pattern that resembles scratched metal. Close the View window and assign MTLSPEC.JPG as the bitmap for the RGB Tint map in the Specular slot.

4. Click on the Go To Parent Icon twice to return to the main Material Editor rollout, and click on the Shininess Map name slot. Select Bitmap from the Material/Map Browser and from the \CHAP_05 directory on the companion CD-ROM, select the file MTLSHNY3.JPG and view it.

   Figure 5.4 is a grayscale bitmap derived from the "panel lines" present in the MTLGREEN.JPG image. The thick white and gray lines and irregular specks against the dark background help clamp the highlights to specific areas.

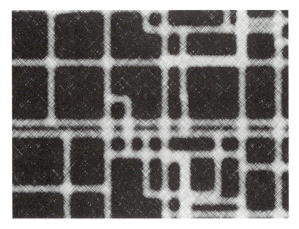

Figure 5.4   The MTLSHNY3.JPG image restricts the specular highlight to specific areas.

To create these Shininess/Shininess Strength textures, I inverted the MTLBMP.JPG Bump map image (which you'll load in a moment) in Photoshop. This produced white lines on a black background. I applied Gaussian Blur to the image, which created soft washes of gray along the original panel line areas. Then, I applied various other filters and added bitmaps on top of the image to produce several variants. If you want, take a moment to use MAX's File|View File feature to examine the other MTL*.JPG bitmaps in the \MAPS directory of the companion CD-ROM.

(For more information on how to create these custom textures, see Chapter 17.)

5. Change the U and V Tiling to 2.0 and then return to the main Material Editor rollout. Change the Shininess Map Amount to 50 and then drag the MTLSHNY3.JPG map down to the Shininess Strength map slot. Make it a Copy instead of an Instance, but leave the Shininess Strength Map amount at 100.

6. Open the Maps button next to Bump, select Bitmap from the Material/Map Browser, and load MTLBMP.JPG into the Bump map slot. By viewing the file, you can see that it's a network of black "panel lines" that correspond to the lines present in the MTLGREEN.JPG bitmap.

I used the MTLBMP.JPG image shown in Figure 5.5 to create the panel lines on the first MTLGREEN.JPG image. By pasting the former image onto the latter using Adobe Photoshop's Multiply option, I darkened the areas of the Diffuse and Ambient textures where the Bump map would appear later. This emphasizes the recessed panel lines scribed into the metal surface.

7. Change both the U and V tiling to 2.0 so the Bump map panel lines correspond to the other maps. To mitigate Bump map aliasing in the final rendering, set the Blur Offset to 0.003, then return to the main Material Editor rollout.

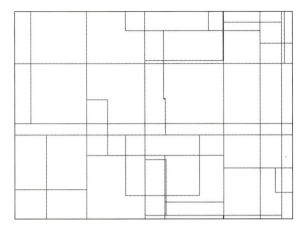

Figure 5.5   The MTLBMP.JPG Bump map.

Now it's time to finally render this scene.

8. Activate the Camera01 viewport and render a test image of at
    least 640×480 resolution. The image will appear on your screen,
    and it should look like Figure 5.6.

The final effect shows a green metallic sphere, looking vaguely reminiscent of the *Star Wars* Deathstar before all the windows were installed
and it was painted in Evil Empire Gray. (Now that I think about it, it
also looks kind of like Luke Skywalker's little training sphere that was
zapping him aboard the *Millenium Falcon* during his Jedi lightsaber
training.) Sorry, geeked out there for a moment. In your rendering,

Figure 5.6   The custom bitmap textures create specular highlights confined near
the panel lines of the object.

FIVE STEPS TO IMPROVE YOUR MAX RENDERINGS

Below are five easily-overlooked Material Editor and lighting parameters that can help improve the look of your MAX renderings dramatically.

Texture Blur

By default, Max applies Pyramidal filtering and a Blur of 1.0 to all texture maps. In some cases, these settings are inadequate. Textures with long lines, rendered near-horizontal or vertical, tend to show some aliasing when rendered with the default settings. Changing the Blur of 2.0—or better yet, using Summed Area with Blur set to 1.5—yields far better results.

Bump Maps and Supersampling

Max Release 2 has introduced supersampling to materials. This makes a significant reduction in aliasing along bright highlights, which typically occurs when you're using Bump maps. (Note that checking Supersampling will increase your rendering times somewhat.)

Absolute Shadow Bias

For shadow-mapped lights, MAX has Absolute Bias set to On by default. This is an essential feature if your scene is changing size over time or if objects are changing visibility over time, because "Regular" bias adapts for the scene size and may cause popping of your shadows. The downside of Absolute is that you must appropriately crank up the Bias value to reflect the size of your scene, sometimes orders of magnitude higher. If your Absolute Bias setting is too low, you will see moire patterns, "dirty" edges, and bleeding shadows.

Ambient/Diffuse Lock

One vital material consideration is the difference between the Ambient and Diffuse swatches. By default, Max assigns the same texture map to both the Ambient and Diffuse channels, yielding the same result as having both swatches the same color. If the Ambient swatch is not darker than the Diffuse one, shadows and dark areas lack depth.

Beginning animators often make this mistake; when the Ambient and Diffuse colors are the same, depending 100 percent on the lighting in the scene to create the range between the Diffuse and Ambient components. No matter how well the scene is lighted, that range often won't be large enough to provide the dynamics necessary to make an image look deep.

To fix this problem, do one of the following:

1. Make sure the Ambient and Diffuse color settings are not identical. Unlock the Lock icon, and use a modified version of the Diffuse texture in the Ambient swatch. A good rule of thumb is to make the Ambient color a much darker version of the Diffuse color. Use the same Hue and Saturation—just a different Luminance value. (The RGB Tint map provides an easy way to darken or tint the bitmap.) Note that for some special-case materials, the Ambient and Diffuse color settings make little or no difference in the final material appearance.

2. For an interesting "Maxfield Parrish" effect, make the Ambient color a complimentary color of the Diffuse color. This can produce some stunning results.

Note: Many of the default materials that ship with the 3D Studio MAX (and the 3DS/DOS) default Material Library have locked Ambient/Diffuse colors preset. Unlock those colors and follow one of the rules above to achieve better results.

Ropiness (Temporal Aliasing)

If you're rendering for video, be sure to apply either motion blur to frames, and/or render to fields and set an appropriate Pixel Size (usually 1.5 or higher). High-contrast edges that are near-horizontal or vertical tend to "crawl" as the objects (or camera) move through the scene. Pixel Size adjustments will minimize this artifact.

(Thanks and a tip o' the hat go to David J. Marks and Gary Yost, 3D Studio MAX Development Team leader, for providing these tips.)

notice how the bright green specular highlights run along the edges of the panel seams. Faint scratches also appear in the shiny areas—the specular highlights aren't simply shiny white patches. All these bitmaps, when combined, create the effect of scuffed or worn metal and create the illusion of bare metal showing through where the paint has worn off along the edges.

For a Phong shading type, the metal texture you've just created is pretty realistic. However, you can refine this effect further by using Blend materials to combine Phong, Blinn, and Metal shaders. These hybrid materials will enable you to further adjust the shininess and reflective qualities of your materials. (You'll explore this later in this chapter.)

You can use this metal effect in numerous ways, of course. You can apply these techniques to objects—from fighter planes and spaceships to weathered pickup trucks or construction equipment. You could also use it to create realistic galvanized tin or the metal siding of buildings.

The possibilities, if not endless, are at least varied enough to keep you going until the aliens land and whisk us all off to a transcendent utopia on Altair-4.

Blending The Shaders

Now, you'll improve this metal texture by creating a Blend material combining the attributes of the Phong shading type with the Metal shader. You'll create your new metal texture by expanding the existing Metal 1 Single material.

1. Return to the Material Editor. Under the Metal 1 Single material slot, click on the Standard button next to Type, and select Blend from the Material/Map Browser. When the Replace Material alert box appears, click on Keep Old Material As Sub-Material. The original Metal 1 Single material now appears in the Material #1 slot.

2. Before you go further, it's a good idea to change the names of your various materials to eliminate confusion as you edit the materials. (It also helps to give specific names to your various maps, too, rather than simply Tex. #1 and the like. That way, if you are browsing from your scene or the Material Editor, you can more easily pick out a specific map that you want to duplicate in another slot.) Highlight the Metal 1 Single name in the Material Editor and change it to Metal 2 Blend.

3. Next, click on the Name button for Material #1 and change its name to Metal 2 Phong. Go down to Ambient and change its settings to RGB 0, 64, 32, drag this color swatch down to Diffuse to copy it, and then change the Diffuse RGB settings to 0, 235, 128 (dragging the value up to around 235 will be close enough). Make sure Specular is set to pure white or RGB 255, 255, 255.

4. Right-click on the Shininess and Shininess Strength spinners to set them to 0; then, go to the Maps rollout. Click on the Ambient button to go to the Ambient map level and then click on Type: Bitmap to bring up the Material/Map Browser. Double-click on RGB Tint, and when the alert box appears, select Keep Old Map As Sub-Map. Click on the Red color swatch under Tint Parameters and change its parameters to RGB 64, 0, 0. Click on the Green color swatch and change it to RGB 0, 128, 0. Leave Blue as it is and close the Color Selector.

5. Click on the Go To Parent icon to return to the Metal 2 Phong rollout; then, click on the Go To Parent icon again to return to the Metal 2 Blend level of the material. Drag the Metal 1 Single material down to the Material #2 slot; in the Instance Material dialog box under Method, make sure Copy is checked rather than Instance. Then, open this new material

ANISOTROPIC SPECULARITY: COOL BUZZWORD, COOLER EFFECT

The scratch effect that you're seeing actually has a name: *anisotropic specularity*. Although this sounds like a *Star Trek* buzzword, it's the new rage for CGI users who want to create better-looking materials. Essentially, anisotropic specularity describes nonuniform specular highlights in shiny materials where the surface tends to break up the highlight or even produce multiple highlights.

There are many examples of this, both organic and man-made. The sheen of long human hair (just think of shampoo commercials or print ads) and glossy animal fur shows the effect of anisotropic specularity. Likewise, scratches in metallic surfaces (such as the faint lines you see in machined aluminum) display this effect. (A good example of this is the METAL7.JPG texture map included with the CD-ROM that ships with 3D Studio MAX.) In addition, a lacquered surface such as the surface on a well-waxed, newly washed car can also display multiple highlights. You'll often see a deep, soft highlight created by layers of paint (perhaps with metallic flakes) and then a hotter kicker on the top surface of the lacquer.

Although some 3D programs or plug-ins can produce this effect automatically, you have to custom-create it in MAX. That's not really a problem. With the multiple map channels available in the Material Editor, as well as Release 2.5's second set of UVW coordinates, you can tailor-make this specular effect for whatever object you need.

and change its name to Metal 2 Metal (which sounds like a new headbanger rock band).

6. Next, change Material #2 not just in word but in deed. To do this, select Metal under Shading Type. When you do, you see the Specular component of the Maps become grayed out. (You'll use the Diffuse attribute to provide the specular for the Metal material.) Change Ambient to RGB 0, 64, 0 and change Diffuse to pure white, or RGB 255, 255, 255. Change Shininess to 75 and Shininess Strength to 100.

7. Go to the Maps section, and drag the MTLGREEN.JPG Diffuse map up to Ambient to replace the existing RGB Tint map. (You can make this an Instance instead of a Copy.) Change the Ambient Map amount to 25 and the Diffuse amount to 50.

8. Click in the Shininess and Shininess Strength map checkboxes to turn them off—for this Blend material, we don't need the custom bitmaps as part of the Metal shader. Then, click on the Go To Parent icon to return to the Metal 2 Blend material level.

Masked Marvels

You now have a material that allows you to blend between a Phong and a Metal shading type, each with its own particular specular attributes.

Now, you'll apply the Metal 2 Blend material to the sphere and adjust the Blend between the two material components:

1. If you want to see what each material looks like individually, apply this new Metal 2 Blend texture to the Sphere01 object and adjust the Mix Amount. (If you set it at 0, only the Metal 2 Phong material shows up, of course.) For a new test rendering, crank it all the way up to 100 (so just the Metal 2 Metal material is present) and then activate your Camera01 viewport and render the object.

The image on your screen and in Figure 5.7 shows the effects of a pure Metal shader. Unfortunately, it's not particularly interesting; the large specular highlight and the extremely dark surface tend to drown out the Ambient and Diffuse map details. Here, it looks somewhat like a dark metallic soccer ball.

2. Adjust the Mix Amount to 50 so you're seeing a half-and-half blend of the Phong and Metal shading types, and re-render the scene.

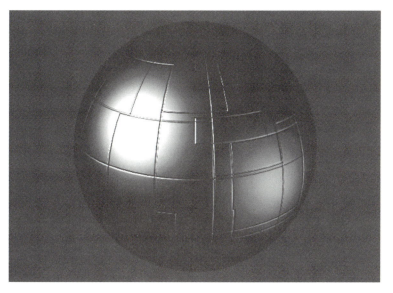

Figure 5.7 The Metal shader component of the Metal 2 Blend material shown at 100 percent.

As your rendering shows, this is a more interesting effect. The Phong shading of the first material provides an overall glossiness, yet you can begin to see the faint specular areas of the Metal shader.

3. Change the Mix Amount to 25 and rerender the scene. As a straight blend, this is a better compromise between the two materials. The Phong provides more Diffuse and Ambient detail, while you can still see Metal shading delineation.

Here's one final thing to try for this particular metal texture. Instead of simply mixing between the two materials, you'll load another custom bitmap as a mask to blend between the two.

4. Click on the Mask Name button to bring up the Material/Map Browser, select Bitmap, and from the \CHAP_05 directory on the companion CD-ROM, click on MTLSHNY6.JPG and view it.

The MTLSHNY6.JPG image, shown in Figure 5.8, is another bitmap derived from the Bump map you're using in the scene. As with the Shininess and Shininess Strength textures, I inverted the Bump map

---

MAX RELEASE 2.5'S LIGHTING ATTRIBUTES

For additional control over your metal materials, check out 3D Studio MAX Release 2.5's lighting attributes, such as Soften Diffuse Edge, Affect Diffuse, and Affect Specular. By setting different lights for the Diffuse and Specular components of your materials, you can produce striking results.

NAME YOUR MATERIALS!

When you're creating complex materials, give both the materials and each map within them specific names rather than the defaults. That way, if you are browsing for a new map or material from your scene or the Material Editor, you can more quickly pick out the items that you need.

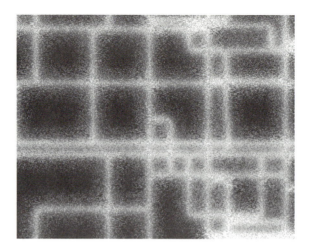

Figure 5.8 The MTLSHNY6.JPG image used as a mask between the Phong and Metal materials.

values in Adobe Photoshop and applied Gaussian Blur. I then combined this image with another inverted Bump map modified in good old Autodesk Animator Pro using Jumble ink. This broke up the white panel lines into a dusting of scattered pixels.

5. Click on OK to load it into the Material Editor; then, activate your Camera01 viewport again and render the scene; it should look like Figure 5.9.

Take a close look at the rendering on your screen. As you can see, the MTLSHNY6.JPG mask allows the Metal material to show through the

Figure 5.9 The final Metal Blend material.

Phong material only along the panel lines, with scratches and flecks fading out to the middle of each panel.

Also, note the appearance of the bright specular areas along the bump-mapped panel lines as contrasted with the matte appearance of the overall sphere. It looks as if the object started out with a satin painted finish (the Diffuse and Ambient maps of the Phong material). However, due to wear and tear, the edges of the panel appear as bare, scuffed metal. The combined qualities of the respective materials provide a better effect than the same materials used separately.

Variations On A Theme

If you like this effect, here are some variations to try:

- Change the UV tiling of all the bitmaps on one of the Blend materials (either the Phong or the Metal). Keep one set at 2.0 and change the others back to 1.0, 3.0, or whatever best appeals to you.

- Experiment with different Specular, Shininess, and Shininess Strength settings and bitmaps. (Explore the \CHAP_05 and the \MAPS directories of the companion CD-ROM for other textures.)

- Use procedural textures, such as Noise, as masks between the two materials. (For a really odd effect, you might even try animating the mask.)

- Use 3D Studio MAX Release 2.5's new ray-traced map type for any of the map channels. (This is covered in greater detail in Chapter 10.)

Note that two versions of this scene are saved in the \CHAP_05 directory of the companion CD-ROM as METAL_1.MAX and METAL_2.MAX. The materials described here are also included in the MAXFX2.MAT material library on the companion CD-ROM.

If you want, save your scene to your 3DSMAX\ SCENES directory for further experimentation. (You'll also be using it for the tutorials in the next chapter. Alternately, you can load the needed files from the companion CD-ROM.)

Moving On

In this chapter, you explored how to create good-looking metal textures using custom bitmaps and Blend materials. By applying multiple layers of bitmaps (or even procedural textures) in MAX's powerful Material Editor, you can produce texture effects both subtle and striking.

In the next chapter, you'll see how to refine your metal textures using Reflection maps and MAX Release 2.5's new Falloff material. In addition, you'll see how you can use Falloff to create iridescent or pearlescent effects, an interesting "retro-computer graphics" look, or even an X-ray look.

INDUSTRIAL MATERIALS, PART II

6

In this chapter, you'll expand on the techniques used in Chapter 5 to create metal textures with Custom bitmaps and Blend materials. You'll also see how to create other metal textures using Reflection maps and MAX Release 2.5's new Falloff material.

You can use the techniques shown in this chapter for any metallic objects in your scenes, whether they're spaceships, factory walls or '57 Chevys in need of body work. You'll also see how you can use Falloff to create iridescent or pearlescent effects, a retro-computer-graphics look, or even an X-rayed object.

Testing Your Metal Mettle

As I mentioned in the previous chapter, the depiction of anisotropic specularity—or nonuniform highlights—is an intriguing effect to create in MAX. In this tutorial, you'll create new anisotropic specular metal materials using Shininess, Shininess Strength, Bump and Reflection maps, and Release 2.5's new Falloff map.

For the first part of this tutorial, you don't need the test sphere you created in Chapter 5. Instead, you'll load an existing model from the companion CD-ROM and experiment with the new metal textures on it by following these steps:

1. Reset MAX, then load the METAL_3.MAX file from the \CHAP_06 directory of the companion CD-ROM. The file loads, and your screen should look like Figure 6.1.

This simple model is designed to resemble a NASA rocket thruster. In a moment, you'll modify some of MAX's reflective metal materials and apply them to this object. Then, you'll begin altering the materials to create a "machined aluminum" effect on the thruster.

2. Open the Material Editor. There are three different materials loaded: Chrome Blue Sky 2, Chrome Pearl Falloff, and Copper Anisotropic 2. (These are my variations of some similar materials that come with 3D Studio MAX Release 2.5.) Each has its own variations of Ambient and Diffuse colors.

3. If you open the Maps section of each material, you'll also see different Reflection bitmaps loaded, at different strengths, into each material. Fitted Cylindrical UVW mapping coordinates and the Chrome Blue Sky material have already been applied to the thruster model. Now, activate your Camera01 viewport and do a test rendering; it should resemble Figure 6.2.

As your rendering and Figure 6.2 indicate, the Chrome Blue Sky 2 material creates a very shiny object. For most purposes, MAX's reflection mapping (including automatic reflections and cubic environment maps) can provide many of the same effects as true raytracing, but without the rendering slowdown inherent in

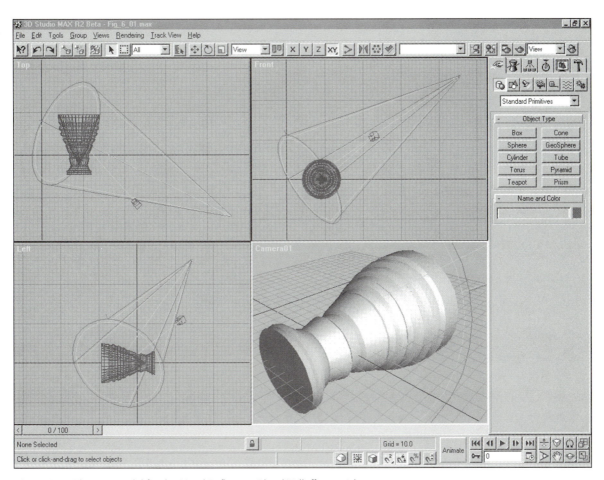

Figure 6.1   The test model for the Metal Reflection Blend/Falloff material type.

Figure 6.2   The rocket thruster model with the Chrome Blue Sky 2 material applied.

USE BLUR OFFSET

Always use at least a small amount of Blur Offset in your maps, particularly when using Bump and Reflection maps. This will help you avoid aliasing in your final renderings.

raytracing. (In Chapter 10, you'll see how to use Release 2.5's new ray-traced map type to create spectacular reflective and refractive effects.) In this chapter, you'll concentrate on using Reflection maps only to create these reflective metal surfaces.

4. Select the thruster model, return to the Material Editor, apply the Chrome Pearl 2 material, and render another test shot.

5. When you're finished looking at the image, apply the Copper 2 material and then render a third test.

Other than changes in color, the model looks similar in each rendering. Although the rendering looks like metal, the thruster model seems too bright and shiny—the lack of further surface detail, as well as the soft wash of color across its surface, tends to flatten the 3D object.

Sharpening The Reflection

To add more definition to the surface, follow these steps to sharpen the Reflection map:

1. Return to the Material Editor, change the name of the Chrome Blue Sky 2 material to Chrome Blue Sky 3, and then apply it to the thruster. Then, open this material's Reflection Map button, which contains the file SKY2.JPG. This is a modified version of the SKY.JPG bitmap that ships with Release 1. Under General Parameters, you'll note that the Blur is at 2.0 and the Blur Offset is at 0.064.

2. Change Blur to 1.0 and Blur Offset to 0.01. Then, activate your Camera01 viewport and render another test image.

As the image on your screen indicates, the whitish cloud shapes in the original SKY2.JPG image have placed additional reflective highlights on the object. The longitudinal detail of the map also helps better delineate the thruster's shape.

Scratching The Surface

Now you'll add some surface relief to the thruster via a Bump map. Then, you'll begin tweaking the Shininess and Reflection map settings. To start, follow these steps:

1. Click on the Bump Map button. In the Material/Map Browser, make New active, and select Bitmap.

2. From the \CHAP_06 directory of the companion CD-ROM, click on SCRATCH1.JPG and use File|View to examine it. As you see on your screen and in Figure 6.3, this 320×160 image consists of white and gray "scratches" and noise pixels on a black field.

Figure 6.3   The SCRATCH1.JPG, used as a Bump map, helps break up the surface of the thruster object.

3. Click on OK to load the image.

4. Now you want to change the U and V Tiling. (Otherwise, when this image is used as a Bump map, the low resolution will make the thruster look as if it were hammered out by a drunken blacksmith rather than machined by precision tooling.) Set U Tiling to 4.0, set V Tiling to 8.0, and then render another test image.

As the image on your screen indicates, the Bump map creates the appearance of slight scratches in the thruster surface. This texture is better, but you can refine it further by altering shininess settings and maps for the model.

5. Click on the Go To Parent icon to return to the main Material Editor rollout. Under General Parameters, change Shininess to 25 and Shininess Strength to 100.

6. Go back to the Maps section and drag-copy the SCRATCH1.JPG image from the Bump map slot up to the Shininess slot. (Make this a Copy, not an Instance, because you're going to change this bitmap's parameters in a moment.) Change the Shininess map's amount to 75; then, activate your Camera01 viewport and render another test image.

As your rendering shows, the Shininess bitmap adds a little more detail to the thruster. It looks more like a piece of machined aluminum, but the overall effect is still too bright.

7. Click on the Shininess Map button to open it, open the Output rollout, and click on Invert. Now, render another test image.

As you can see in Figure 6.4 and on your screen, the inverted SCRATCH1.JPG image has darkened the overall Reflection map, yet it has emphasized the "tooling marks" along the surface of the object. Note how the specular highlight is broken up further by the combination of Bump and Shininess maps—another example of the "anisotropic specularity" effect discussed in Chapter 5.

Figure 6.4 The inverted SCRATCH1.JPG image, used as a Shininess map, helps darken the overall Reflection map.

MAX Release 2.5's New Falloff Map

At this point, you should take a moment and reflect (so to speak) on the effect that you're trying to accomplish.

Although your Chrome Blue Sky 3 material is now more realistic than the original, it can still be improved. 3D Studio MAX's Reflection mapping sometimes produces reflective objects that look self-illuminated, especially when the map level is set high, and in 3D scenes with dim lighting conditions. Although we may tend to think of chrome objects as "bright," they don't have a high ambient value, as brightly colored or self-illuminated objects do.

One way to fix this is to knock down the levels of apparent illumination along the edges of a reflective object. By doing this, more of the reflection is visible in an object surface at an acute angle; at more oblique angles, the reflection appears to diminish in strength or brightness.

You can use Release 2.5's Falloff map to achieve this effect. Falloff enables you to create interesting transparency effects, or blend between different materials, based on the face normals of your geometry. You can adjust the effect and the angle of attack based on world coordinates, or based on the viewing direction relative to the object to which the map is assigned. (For more information on this map type, consult your 3D Studio MAX Release 2.5 manuals or the Release 2.5 Help file.)

Using The Falloff Map

Here, you'll modify your Reflection map with a Mix material, keep the SKY2.JPG image, and use Falloff to determine how the bitmap is masked on the thruster:

1. Go to the Material Editor and open the Reflection map for the Chrome Blue Sky 3 material. To replace this single bitmap with a Mix map, click on the Type: Bitmap button. From the Material/Map Browser, click on Mix, check Keep Old Map as Sub-Map, and click on OK.

2. In the Material Editor, you should see that the SKY2.JPG bitmap is placed in the Color #1 swatch by default. For the proper rendering results, you need this map in the Color #2 (default white) slot. Drag it down to the Color #2 swatch to copy it, and then drag the None Name button from Mix Amount back up to Color #1 to clear it. (You could simply click on Swap and then change the colors of the two swatches back to their defaults.)

   You should see on your Material Editor sample sphere that the effect of the Reflection map seems to have disappeared. This is because the Environment mapping coordinates of the copied SKY2.JPG bitmap have changed to Texture: Explicit UVW mapping coordinates.

3. Click on the SKY2.JPG button to go to the Color #2 rollout, change the mapping coordi-

nates from Texture to Environ: Spherical Environment. Then, return to the Mix Material rollout.

4. Now, click on the Map button next to Mix Amount, and then select Falloff from the Material/Map Browser. As the Falloff Parameters rollout appears, you see that the Falloff Type defaults to Perpendicular/Parallel. Again, this makes the SKY2.JPG appear to reflect more toward the viewing angle, and to diminish as the faces of the thruster retreat from the Camera01 view.

5. Activate your Camera01 viewport and render a test image.

   Notice in Figure 6.5 how the Falloff map has darkened the edges of the thruster reflection. You now get the benefits of the Reflection map, without washing out the object, which might cause it to look flat or self-illuminated.

6. When you're finished viewing the rendering, close your Camera01 VFB and click on the Go To Parent icon several times to return to the main Chrome Blue Sky 3 rollout. Now, save this scene to your local \SCENES directory; call it ROCKET1.MAX.

This scene is also saved in the \CHAP_06 directory of the companion CD-ROM as ROCKET1.MAX.

Falloff Effects With Different Metals

For this tutorial, you're going to load a more complex object and examine its appearance under the effects of different metal materials. Each of the materials uses a Reflection Mix map, with Falloff toning down the effects of the Color #2 Reflection bitmap. To start out, follow these steps:

1. From the \CHAP_06 directory of the companion CD-ROM, load ROCKET2.MAX. Your screen should look like Figure 6.6.

Figure 6.5 The Falloff map mixes the SKY2.JPG bitmap with a black "nonexistent" material.

This model resembles the business end of an old NASA Saturn rocket booster—four rocket thrusters, surrounded by fuel intermix tanks and piping, sitting on a baseplate. A primary white spotlight and a blue fill spotlight illuminate the geometry.

2. Before you continue, do a quick test rendering of this scene.

   As your screen indicates, the various model pieces have materials that are similar to the modified Blue Sky 3 material you created in the previous example.

3. If you open the Material Editor, you'll see three materials used in the scene: Chrome Anisotropic 1, Copper Anisotropic 3, and Chrome Pearl 2. The scratches in the surface of the various objects make the geometry resemble machined aluminum, copper, and pewter.

4. Now, take a look at the piping running between the thrusters. If you select it and go to the Modify panel, you'll see that it's actually a renderable Spline—a new feature of Release 2.5. (For further information on Release 2.5's new modeling features, check out Chapter 11. There, you'll see how you can use a renderable spline and a Noise modifier to create controllable electrical arcs, or lightning.)

5. To better see how each material looks on the model, select all the geometry in the scene (press the H key to bring up the Select By Name menu), apply one of the materials to the entire model, and then do a test rendering.

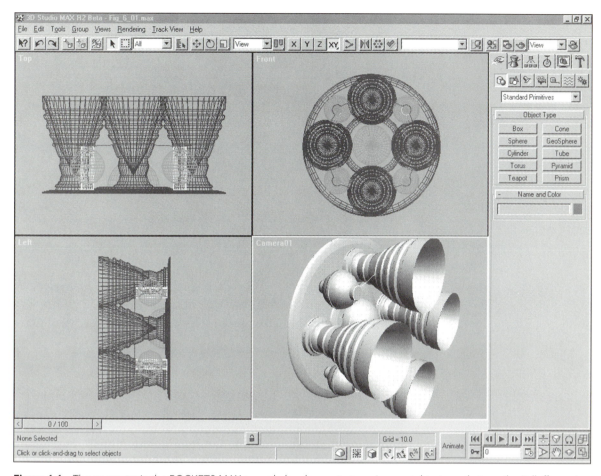

Figure 6.6 The geometry in the ROCKET2.MAX scene helps demonstrate various metal textures that use the Falloff map in a Mix map slot.

The Chrome Anisotropic 1 material gives the entire model a very shiny, almost liquid metal-like appearance. The deep scratches of the SCRATCH1.JPG Shininess and Bump maps are very evident on the baseplate.

6. Now, assign and render the remaining two materials.

The Copper Anisotropic 3 material is colorful, and the high tiling value of the Bump and Shininess map creates a rich, burnished surface. Finally, the Chrome Pearl 2 material creates a satiny surface that resembles dark pewter.

7. Close your Camera01 VFB.

Using Falloff For Iridescent Effects

Okay, that's enough scratchy metal textures for now. For the next tutorial, you're going to create some iridescent effects using the Falloff map to mix between two widely varying material colors.

Webster's New Collegiate Dictionary (12th edition) defines *iridescence* as "a play of colors producing rainbow effects (as in a soap bubble)." From an optical—and computer graphics—standpoint, an object displaying iridescence refracts or reflects various spectra of light differently. This can depend on the viewing angle of its surface (a beetle's carapace, scratched aluminum, or stainless steel) or chemical reactions occurring on the surface (the aforementioned soap bubble, oil on the surface of water, and so on).

You can also see this effect in some translucent objects. For example, if you examine the inner surface of an abalone shell, you see a whitish mother-of-pearl look, with layers of bright color that appear inside the surface as you rotate the shell.

For the tutorials in this chapter, you're going to create a simple iridescent material. You'll take a brief side trip into the land of retro-computer graphics and X-ray effects and then take a simple material and enhance it with various maps to create the abalone-shell effect.

Although it may seem like an odd choice of geometry, you can keep the existing rocket baseplate model to try out these textures. (If you want, you can load a different mesh or MAX scene and apply the materials to a mesh of your choice.) Whatever mesh or MAX scene you choose to work with, begin this way:

1. Go to the Material Editor, select an unused material slot, and change the Material Type from Standard to Blend. (You can discard the existing material if you want.) Click on the Material 1 slot, change the Ambient value to RGB 0, 16, 0, or dark green, and then drag-copy this color swatch down to Diffuse. Change the Diffuse value to RGB 0, 255, 0, or pure bright green. Change Shininess Strength to 100 and then change the material name to Green.

2. Click on the Go To Parent icon and open Material 2. Change its Ambient values to RGB 0, 0, 16, drag this color swatch down to Diffuse, and change it to RGB 0, 0, 128, or dark blue. Change Shininess Strength to 100, change the material name to Blue, and then click on the Go To Parent icon to return to the main Material slot. Change this material name to Iridescent 1.

3. Click on the Mask button, and select Falloff from the Material/Map Browser. As you do, you'll see the sample sphere (or other object) in the Material Editor change to a dark blue with a bright green halo around its edges.

4. Now, select the entire rocket geometry (either from your viewports or using the Select By Name menu) and assign the Iridescent 1 material to all of the pieces.

5. When you're finished, activate your Camera01 viewport and render the scene.

As you can see on your screen, the bright green material appears on the outer edges of the geometry, roughly parallel to your Camera01 viewpoint. The green material then blends into the dark blue material, which appears predominantly on the surfaces that are more perpendicular to your viewpoint.

This effect can be quite striking when applied to complex geometry and enhanced with different Diffuse, Bump, or Reflection maps. (You'll play with these techniques at the end of this chapter.)

"Retro CG" And "X-Ray" Materials

Now, here's a simple way to modify the material you've just created to produce a retro computer graphics or X-ray effect:

1. Go to the Material Editor and open the Green material component of the Iridescent 1

Figure 6.7   The Falloff map blends between two different material colors.

material. Change Ambient to RGB 0, 0, 32; leave Diffuse as it is. Change Shininess to 40 and Shininess Strength to 30. Change Self-Illumination to 100.

2. Open the Extended Parameters section. Verify that Falloff is set to In, set the Amount to 100, and change Falloff Type to Additive.

3. Click on the Go To Parent icon, drag the Green Material #1 down to the Blue Material #2 slot, make it a Copy, and then open this new material. Change its name from Green to Inner and then make Diffuse pure black, or RGB 0, 0, 0. Change Self-Illumination to 0.

4. Now, apply this material to the rocket thruster geometry (if it's not already applied), activate your Camera01 viewport, and render a test image, which should look like Figure 6.8.

You've undoubtedly seen this computer graphics look in some older movies and TV shows, where wireframe or edge-lit computer graphics illustrate technical data. (You'll see examples of this in the original *Star Wars* briefing scene, the *Nostromo* landing sequence in *Alien*, and Snake Plissken's flight by Manhattan skyscrapers in John Carpenter's film *Escape From New York*.)

I call this look "retro-CG." This type of 3D Studio MAX material could be very useful for showing off 3D imagery that's specifically intended to look synthetic or obviously computer-generated.

So, how else can we use this particular material? Well, as your last rendering indicates, you could use it to simulate an X-ray look. It

Figure 6.8 The modified Iridescent 1 material creates an old-fashioned computer-graphics look.

would be particularly effective used on a complex human skeleton mesh (especially if that mesh were itself inside another, properly proportioned human mesh object). By changing the green outer color to a bluish-white and adjusting the Shininess and Shininess Strength values, you could simulate the spaceport X-ray scanner scene in the movie *Total Recall*, for example.

Varying The Materials

Here are some other things you could try:

- Change the outer Green Material component to Wireframe.

- Apply an automatic Reflection map to just one of the materials. (This would work best on an object surrounded by other geometry and an Environment map, of course.)

- Use a ray-traced map type for one of the materials. (For more information on MAX Release 2.5's new raytracing capabilities, see Chapter 10.)

You should also experiment with the Falloff settings to create different material blending effects.

Good Abalone (At Far Less Than $40 A Pound)

For the final tutorial, you'll create a new iridescent material that resembles the mother-of-pearl abalone effect that I mentioned earlier.

This material uses Falloff maps to mix Reflection maps and Bump maps.

1. Return to the Material Editor and select (or create) a new Standard material (you don't need a Blend material for this example). Change Ambient to pure black, or RGB 0, 0, 0. Change Diffuse to RGB 16, 0, 32, or a dark purple. Don't worry about these colors being surprisingly dark for a "pearl" material; most of the bright colors for this material will come from the Reflection map Mix. Change Specular to pure white, or RGB 255, 255, 255.

2. Change Shininess to 50, and Shininess Strength to 100, then rename this material Abalone Iridescence. (Sounds kind of like a lipstick color...although marketing cosmetics named after giant sea snails might be challenging.)

Okay, bear with me here for these next few steps. This Abalone Iridescent material is going to get complicated as you create multilayered maps for Reflection and Bump.

3. Go to the Maps rollout for this material, and open the Reflection map slot. When the Material/Map Browser appears, select Mix.

4. In the Mix Parameters rollout, click on the Maps slot next to Color #1, and select Mask. In the Mask rollout, click on the Map button and then pick Bitmap. Now, click on the Bitmap Name button in the Bitmap Parameters rollout, and from the \CHAP_06 directory of the companion CD-ROM, click on the file COLRFOIL.JPG and view it.

COLRFOIL.JPG is a 1024×768 bitmap that I created in Autodesk Animator Pro. It began as a screen full of grayscale pixels, to which I then applied various enlargement and pixelation effects. I then forced a rainbow-hued color palette into the grayscale bitmap to produce this op-art

"REAL VIRTUALITY"

Although the graphics in 1981's *Escape From New York* appeared to be early computer graphics work, they were actually "simulated simulations." Instead of using early computer graphics, the film's effects technicians created the illusion of a wireframe cityscape by placing fluorescent pinstriping tape along the contours of matte-black miniature buildings. This miniature Manhattan was then bathed in heavy ultraviolet light and filmed with a snorkel camera rig.

Another interesting note: The effects supervisor in charge of this sequence was Jim Cameron, who has gone on to direct such groundbreaking effects films as *The Terminator* and *Terminator 2*, *Aliens*, *The Abyss*, *True Lies*, and *Titanic*.

image. It serves as a colorful Reflection map for your Abalone texture.

5. Click on OK in the Select Bitmap Image File dialog box to load the image into the Material Editor. Under Coordinates, make sure Environment: Spherical Environment is selected. Verify that Blur is 1.0, set Blur Offset to 0.05, and then open the Output section. Change the Output Amount to 2.0.

6. Click on the Go To Parent icon to return to the Mask map rollout. Click on the Mask button and then select Falloff from the Material/Map Browser. In the Falloff rollout, change Perpendicular Value to 0.5, and change Parallel Value to 0.0. This strengthens the COLRFOIL.JPG image along the edges of the object, yet clamps it toward the object's center.

7. Double-click on the Go To Parent icon to return to the main Reflection map rollout and then click on the Color #2 button. From the Material/Map Browser, select Bitmap; then, click on and view the ABALONE.JPG image from the \CHAP_06 directory of the companion CD-ROM.

This 400×400 pixel image began as a scanned photograph of a colorful Victorian house in San Francisco. (If you can still see a Haight-Ashbury house in this image, then the Summer of Love must've had a *really* long-term effect on you.)

Anyway, I loaded the image into Adobe Photoshop and used the Black Box 2.0 filters (now called Eye Candy) from Alien Skin Software to distort the original photo. The resultant image probably resembles the inside of my stomach eight hours after eating a box of Crayolas. (For more information on other Photoshop and MAX plug-ins, including ones that don't produce intestinal distress effects, see Appendix B.)

8. When you're finished viewing ABALONE.JPG, click on OK to load the image. Under Coordinates, make sure that Texture: Explicit UVW 1 is selected (the Diffuse map shouldn't use Environmental coordinates). Verify that Blur is 1.0 and set Blur Offset to 0.05; then, click on the Mix button and pick Falloff from the Material/Map Browser.

9. Leave the settings as they are and then click on the Go To Parent icon. Change this map name to Reflect Mask/Mix. Then, click on the Go To Parent icon again to return to the main Material Editor rollout.

10. Click on the Bump Map button and select Mix from the Material/Map Browser. Click on the Color #1 button and select Noise from the Material/Map Browser.

11. In the Noise rollout, change Noise Type to Fractal, Noise Size to 10.0, and then click on the Go To Parent icon to return to the Bump Mix rollout. Leave Color #2 as it is, click on the Mix button, and select the Falloff map again. Leave the settings at their defaults and return to the main Material Editor rollout.

12. Now, if you were to click on the Get Material button and use the "Active Slot" option of the new modeless Material/Map Browser, you would see the entire Material tree in the Browser (see Figure 6.9). By clicking on the various View icons, you can examine all the components that make up the Iridescent Abalone material.

13. Close the Browser, select all the geometry in your scene (if it's not already selected), and apply the Iridescent Abalone material to it. When you do, activate your Camera01 viewport and do a test rendering, as shown in Figure 6.10.

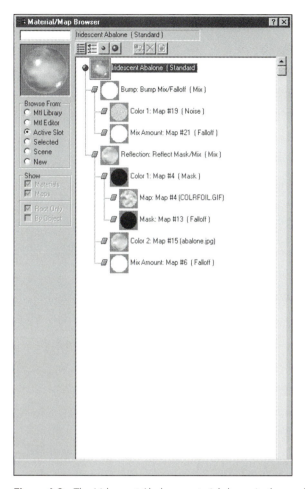

Figure 6.9   The Iridescent Abalone material shown in the modeless Material/Map Browser (View List + Icons selected).

As your rendering indicates, this complex mix of maps combined with the Falloff masking places bright reflected colors along the edges of the geometry, but leaves a bluish white pearly finish on the faces that are more perpendicular to the Camera01 view. The Bump map, using the Noise material and Falloff masking, creates slight variations in the surface and helps break up the specular highlights of the material.

Like the abalone shell inner surface, the material appears to have depth and complexity that belie its Standard material origins. Although an abalone shell isn't an industrial material, of course, this particular texture somewhat resembles a fine porcelain or translucent china and might be appropriate on a punch bowl, flower vase, or the like.

The Iridescent Abalone material that you've just created is also saved in the MAXFX2.MAT Material Library.

Figure 6.10 The Iridescent Abalone material creates a combination of bright edge colors with a lighter pearly texture.

Moving On

In the previous two chapters, you've seen how you could create a wide variety of complex "man-made" materials (plus one natural one) using various custom bitmaps, procedural textures, and the Falloff map.

In the next two chapters, you'll see how to create animated materials and you'll combine them with Video Post filters to create such science-fiction-style effects as disintegrations, plasma explosions, and an explosive shockwave ring. It's going to be a hot time in the old Material Editor tonight!

ANIMATED MATERIALS AND OPTICAL EFFECTS, PART I

Now that you've explored complex, non-animated materials, it's time to make them move. In this chapter, you'll see how to create colorful animated material effects and combine the materials with the new Video Post Lens Effects Glow filter to produce explosive results.

First, you'll create glowing, animated optical effects using Blend materials and masks to restrict the glowing effect to specific areas of your objects. You'll then add animated Opacity maps (via Noise or animated bitmap sequences) to make objects disintegrate in a burst of glowing lightning a la *Star Trek*.

In Part II, you'll learn how to create two different types of explosions: a glowing "plasma ball," using our old friend, the Falloff map, and the famous shockwave ring, popularized in *Star Trek VI: The Undiscovered Country*, *Stargate*, and the Special Editions of *Star Wars* and *Return of the Jedi*.

Making Glow Effects

In the many different incarnations of *Star Trek*—both the TV series and the film versions—you've probably seen a disintegration effect. In the original *Trek* series, for example, an alien beam weapon would often zap a red-shirted security guard. He'd then disintegrate into a glowing mess and disappear with nary a residual smudge (or a residual royalty agreement from the producers, for that matter). Space cruisers, locked doors, and naughty robots would also get blasted, with similar results.

It's easy to create this effect in MAX with Blend materials. To kick it off, you'll work on creating the glowing lightning effect. Then, you'll proceed to the actual disintegration. To create a glow effect, follow these steps:

1. Load DISINTG1.MAX from the \CHAP_07 directory of the companion CD-ROM. You'll see that it's a simple sphere sitting on a flat Quad Patch, as shown in Figure 7.1. A targeted spotlight and a camera complete the scene.

2. Open the Material Editor and take a look at the materials in the scene. The sphere and the ground plane are both mapped with the Metal 1 texture from Chapter 5. Since you're going to modify the Metal 1 texture for the sphere, drag the Metal 1 texture over to the second material sample slot. Rename this material Metal 2, select the Quad Patch ground object, and apply this second material to it. (For this tutorial, you'll disintegrate only the sphere, not the ground upon which it's sitting.)

3. Select the original Metal 1 material to activate it and click on the Type: Standard button to bring up the Material/Map Browser. Select New and then choose Blend. When the alert box appears, select Keep Old Material As Sub-Material. The Blend texture loads, and you'll see the Metal 1 material loaded into the Material 1 slot. Name this new Blend material Disintegrate 1.

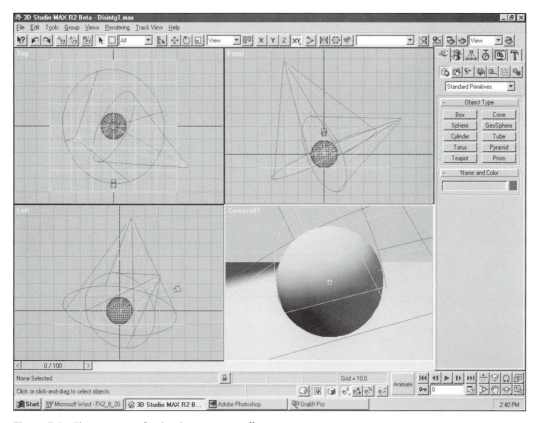

Figure 7.1 The test scene for the disintegration effect.

4. Next, click on the Material 2 button. Change the name of this material to Glowing Lightning. This material will create the crackling energy effect that crawls over the surface of the sphere.

5. Before you continue, click on the Material Effects Channel icon and select Channel 1. The Video Post Lens Effects Glow filter will affect the second material only. An additional Noise map will then mask this material.

6. Change both the Shininess and Shininess Strength values to 0. Change Self-Illumination to 100, and then open the Maps rollout.

7. Click on the Diffuse Map button, and choose Noise from the Material/Map Browser. When the Noise Parameters rollout appears, change Noise Type to Fractal and Size to 10.0. Click on the black Color #1 swatch, and change its

RGB values to 128, 128, 255, or a bright blue. Leave Color #1 as white and click twice on the Go To Parent icon to return to the main Disintegrate 1 Blend material rollout.

8. Click on the Mask button under Basic Parameters and select Cellular from the Material/Map Browser.

The Cellular map type is one of 3D Studio MAX Release 2.5's new procedural textures. It is an extremely useful map that can produce very "organic" imagery, including realistic ocean surfaces, cracked rock or mud, and even scaly dragon skin. By tweaking some of its values, you can also produce convincing lightning effects, as you'll soon see.

9. When the Cellular map rollout appears, change the map name to Cellular Mask, then make the following changes: Under

SIMPLIFYING THE EFFECT

You don't have to use a Noise Diffuse map for the Glowing Noise material. By making material #2 self-illuminated and then changing the Ambient and Diffuse colors to the desired shade, you can produce similar (although simpler) results.

Coordinates, change Tiling to 0.5 on X, Y, and Z; under Cell Color, change the color swatch to pure black, or RGB 0, 0, 0; under Division Colors, make the first color pure white (or RGB 255, 255, 255) and the second color pure black (you can drag the color swatch from the Cell Color down to this third swatch to copy it).

10. Under Cell Characteristics, select Circular, set Size to 25, and set Spread to 0.5. Check the Fractal box to activate it.

11. To produce the thin fractal lightning patterns, you need to change the Thresholds. Set Low to 0.475, keep Mid at 0.5, and set High to 0.525. This will restrict the white Division color to thin fractal lines. Finally, to make the Glowing Noise material appear brighter, open the Output section and change Output Amount from 1.0 to 2.0. Click on the Go To Parent icon to return to the main Blend material level.

12. Because this is a "hot" material in your scene, activate your Camera01 viewport and do a test rendering to see the effects of this new material without the glow effect.

As your rendering and Figure 7.2 show, the Cellular Mask has restricted the blue-white Glowing Noise to thin fractal "worms" on the surface of the first Metal 1 material.

Glow Worms?

Now, to keep the second material true to its name, you need to add a glow effect to it. To do so, follow these steps:

Figure 7.2 The Disintegrate 1 Blend material (without Glow) on the sample sphere.

1. Click on Rendering|Video Post to open the Video Post menu. Click on the Add Scene Event icon and pick Camera01. Then, click on the Add Image Filter Event icon and from your list of filters, pick Lens Effects Glow.

As I mentioned earlier, 3D Studio MAX Release 2.5 incorporates Digimation's Lens Effects plug-in (formerly LenZFX), which produces superior glow effects as well as lens flares, fractal explosions, and depth-of-field. For this tutorial, you'll play with some basic Lens Effects Glow settings.

2. Click on the Lens Effects Glow Setup button. The Lens Effects Glow setup menu appears, as shown in Figure 7.3. (Note that the Preview window has been activated for this figure.)

3. Click on the Preview button to display the Lens Effects Glow defaults, which are shown in the image window at the top of the menu. You'll be making some basic changes to the default settings, so make sure the Properties

tab is active. Select Material ID under Source and set it to 1 so it will affect only the Cellular "glowing worms" effect.

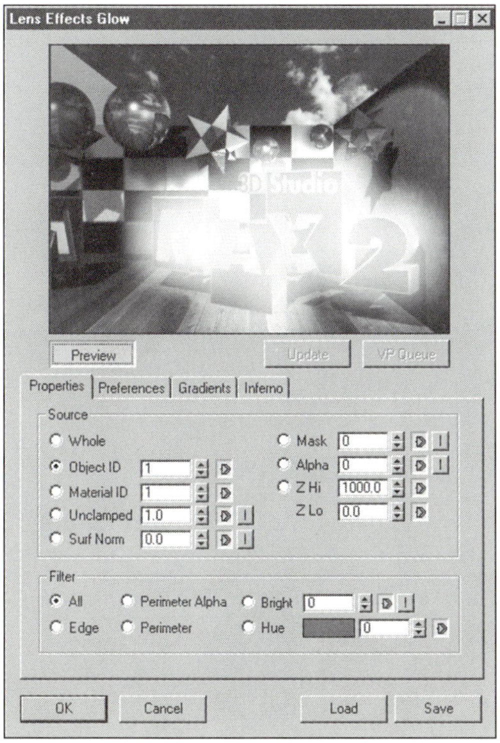

4. Click on the Preferences tab. Under Effect, change Size to 2.5, and under Color, change Intensity to 50.0. As you make these changes, you'll see the glow effect in the Preview window change to match the new settings.

5. Click on OK to return to the Video Post menu. Next, click on the Execute Sequence icon, select Single, and render a 640×480 image of the scene, which should resemble Figure 7.4.

As your rendering indicates, the Lens Effects Glow filter is operating only on the second material (the masked Glowing Noise texture). It has no effect on the first Metal 1 texture, which retains its metallic Diffuse characteristics.

There are many other uses for this technique. If you load a bitmap mask with rows of square or round pixels, for example, you can produce glowing windows on a distant building or on a vehicle such as a large luxury liner or a spaceship. This type of Blend material can be more flexible and

Figure 7.3 The Lens Effects Glow setup menu.

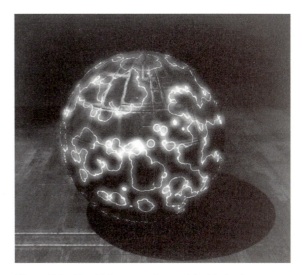

Figure 7.4 The Disintegrate 1 material with the Lens Effects Glow applied.

controllable and provide better results than a Standard material that uses separate Diffuse and Self-Illumination maps.

As mentioned earlier, you don't have to load a Noise map into the Diffuse slot of the Glowing Noise material. However, if an additional texture is revealed by the Noise Mask, you can create—and animate—subtle or dramatic color variations in the glowing lightning itself.

Crawling Glow Worms?

I promised earlier that you would create animated glowing textures, so here's how:

1. Click on the Animate button, drag the Frame slider to 100, then return to the Material Editor. Click on the Cellular Mask button to open the Cellular Mask map. Under Coordinates, change the Z Offset value to 100.0. You'll see the lightning change position on the sample object in the Material #1 slot. Under Cell Characteristics, change the Roughness value to 0.1 and then turn off the Animate button.

2. If you have a minute or two, click on the Make Preview icon in the Material Editor to create an animated thumbnail of this lightning effect, sans Glow. If you'd rather not wait, choose File|View File, and from the \CHAP_07 directory on the companion CD-ROM, click on DISINTG1.AVI to view the final effect, with the Video Post Lens Effects Glow added.

The animated Cellular Mask creates a "crawling lightning" effect over the surface of the sphere, and the Glow accentuates the effect.

3. After you've viewed the animation, close the preview window(s).

Making The Sphere Disintegrate

Now that you've seen the basic effect of the glowing lightning, you can combine it with animated Opacity maps to make it look as if the sphere is being "eaten away" while the lightning sparkles on the disappearing pieces.

The first step is to add an animated Opacity map to Material #1 and then use this same Opacity map as a submap in a masked Mask material.

Uh—what?!

Yes, I know this sounds confusing. However, I've already figured it out, which is the hard part; all you have to do is follow along, and you'll see how it works.

The first step is to create a new material. You'll use the Disintegrate 1 material to start:

1. In the Material Editor, drag the Disintegrate 1 material over to a free material slot to copy it. Name the duplicated material Disintegrate 2 and drag it to the sphere in the scene to apply it.

2. Open the Material 1: Metal 1 (Standard) material of Disintegrate 2. Change the Shininess value to 75 and then go to the Maps section. Click on the Opacity map button, select New, and select Noise from the Material/Map Browser. (You'll see the sample sphere in the Material Editor become "ghosted" as the soft Noise texture wipes out some of the Diffuse map.) Change the name of the Noise map to Noise Opacity—this is important because this specific name will help you pick this material later from the Material/Map Browser.

3. Under Noise Parameters, change Type to Fractal, and under Noise Threshold, change High to 0.005. Keep Low at 0.0. By clamping the High Noise threshold so close to Color #2, or pure white, you'll create a solid Opacity map (the sample sphere turns solid again). Then, by animating the threshold, you can create the effect of the Opacity map

"eating away" the Diffuse Metal material on the sphere.

4. Click on the Animate button, go to frame 100, and in the Material Editor, change the Noise Opacity Threshold settings so that High is 1.0 and Low is 0.995. In the Material Editor, the sample sphere disappears, leaving just the Cellular lightning and the shininess maps hanging around, like the smile of Alice's Cheshire Cat (you'll fix them in a moment).

5. Turn off the Animate button, but keep the Time slider at frame 100—this will help you see the effects of the copied maps better. Click the Go To Parent icon to return to the Metal 1 material level of the Disintegrate 2 material.

Wiping The Smile Off The Cheshire Cat

Next, you'll use the Opacity Noise map to mask the Shininess and Shininess Strength maps of the Metal 1 material so there isn't an unwanted (and unrealistic) specular "ghost" of the original sphere still present:

1. First, check 2-Sided, then in the Maps rollout, open the Specular map, which now has RGB Tint loaded. Click on the Map button (now loaded with the MTLSPEC.JPG bitmap) and then click on the Bitmap button next to Type. Select Mask from the Material/Map Browser. When the Replace Map button appears, click on Keep Old Map As Sub-Map and then click on OK.

2. Under the Mask Parameters rollout, the MTLSPEC.JPG image is now loaded as the Map, and nothing (None) is loaded into Mask. Click on the Mask button, and when the Material/Map Browser appears, click on Browse From: Mtl Editor. In the Browser window, double-click on the Noise Opacity map, load it as an Instance (not a Copy), and click

on OK. This will mask the specular highlight as it also masks the Diffuse map.

3. Click on the Go To Parent icon until you're back at the Metal 1 material level, then click on the Shininess Map button. Click on the Bitmap button next to Type, select New in the Material/Map Browser, and select Mask again. When the Replace Map button appears, click on Keep Old Map As Sub-Map and click on OK.

4. As you did with the Specular map, click on the Mask button and select the Noise Opacity map from the Material Editor to load it as the Shininess Mask.

5. Click the Go To Parent icon and drag the Shininess Mask map down to the Shininess Strength slot to copy it (you can make it an Instance, not a Copy).

Masking The Lightning

At this point, you should see only the Cellular lightning effect on frame 100 in the Material Editor sample slot. As you did in the preceding section, you can mask this lightning so that, as the sphere disintegrates, the electrical arcs only crawl over the (disappearing) surface—not across empty space. To do so, follow these steps:

1. Click on the Go To Parent icon to return to the Disintegrate 2 material level, and then click on the Mask: Cellular button. Click on the Type: Cellular button and select Mask from the Material/Map Browser (Browse From New). Keep the Cellular map as a submap, and click on the Mask button (below the Cellular map).

2. Under Browse From: Mtl Editor in the Material/Map Browser, select Noise Opacity, make it an Instance, and click the Go To Parent icon several times to return to the main Disintegrate 2 material level.

In the same way you used the Specular, Shininess, and Shininess maps in Material #1: Metal 1, you'll use the Opacity Noise map to mask the Cellular texture, which is itself masking the self-illuminated Material #2: Glowing Noise material. The end result is that, at frame 100, the sample sphere in the Material Editor should be completely invisible—or disintegrated.

3. Open the Glowing Noise material, select Material Effects Channel, and change the channel from 0 to 1 (it reset to 0 when you made the copy of the initial Disintegrate 1 texture).

4. Before you render a test scene, select Spotlight01, open the Modify Panel, and go down to Shadow Parameters. Under Cast Shadows, you'll see that Use Ray-Traced Shadows is checked (Spotlight02, the blue fill light, uses shadow mapping instead of raytracing.) The ray-traced Spotlight01 will cast shadows "through" the holes created by the sphere's Opacity maps; as the sphere disintegrates, its shadow disappears as well.

5. Click on Render|Video Post, click on the Execute Sequence button, and select Single under Time Output. Change the frame number to 50, set Output Size to 640×480, and click on Render.

   As your rendering and Figure 7.5 show, the sphere on frame 50 is being "eaten away" by the animated Opacity Noise map while the glowing cellular lightning crackles across its surface.

6. You can return to the Material Editor and render your own preview of the Disintegrate 2 material, but to speed up matters, choose File|View File, select DISINTG2.AVI from the /CHAP_07 directory on the companion CD-ROM, and view it.

Figure 7.5   The disintegrating sphere with glowing Cellular lightning applied.

You'll see how the sphere appears to be completely eaten away by the lightning (much like one of those hapless, red-shirted security guards from *Star Trek: The Original Series* I mentioned earlier).

Again, if you want to save these scenes and materials to your local hard drive and play with them later, feel free to do so. The scene files (DISINTG1.MAX, DISINTG2.MAX) and materials are on this book's companion CD-ROM in the \CHAP_07 directory and MAXFX2.MAT Material Library, respectively.

Hole-y Opacity Maps, Batman!

In this chapter, you've seen how to create an animated Opacity map by using the procedural Noise texture. However, what if you want to create custom animated opacity bitmaps so you have greater control over the final disintegration effect?

There are a couple of ways you can do this. First, determine how long you want your finished disintegration effect to be. Then, paint an incremental series of bitmaps (using a program such as Kinetix Animator Pro/Studio, Adobe Photoshop, or the like) with the holes growing larger on each incremental frame. The advantage of this technique is that you can determine precisely where you want your openings, or translucent areas, to appear. The drawback, of course, is that this is extremely tedious, especially for a long sequence.

You can automate the process by building two simple objects, animating them, and using an orthographic rendering to produce the effect of holes appearing and growing in your image. This is a much faster process than, say, painting an incremental series of bitmaps entirely by hand. Once the bitmaps are rendered, you can then load them into a paint program and tweak them by hand, if necessary.

Here's an easy way to create such imagery:

1. In MAX, save your current work and reset the program. Press the S key to activate 3D Snap Toggle. Go to the Command Panel and select Create|Patch Grids|Quad Patch. In the Top viewport, create a patch grid roughly 240 units long and 320 units wide.

2. In either the Left or Front viewport Shift-clone the QuadPatch01 object downward vertically 10 units to duplicate it. Make it a Copy, not an Instance, and then turn off 3D Snap.

3. Go to the Modify panel, and change both the Length and Width Segments settings of QuadPatch02 to 20, which will produce a dense mesh object.

4. Now, from the Modify panel, apply a Noise modifier to the QuadPatch02 object. Check the Fractal box, and under Strength, change Z to 25. The Quad Patch object distorts into a sort of terrain shape.

5. Open the Material Editor and change Material #1's Ambient and Diffuse colors to pure black, or RGB 0, 0, 0. Change the Shininess and Shininess Strength settings to 0, then apply this material to the selected QuadPatch02.

6. Change Material #2's Ambient and Diffuse colors to RGB 255, 255, 255, or pure white. Change the Shininess and Shininess Strength settings to 0, change Self-Illumination to 100, select QuadPatch01, and apply this material to it.

7. Next, click on the Animate button, go to frame 100, and in the Left or Front viewport, drag the top QuadPatch01 object down on the Y axis until it's just below the solid black QuadPatch02 object. (Alternately, you can drag the bottom QuadPatch02 object up until it covers the entire top object.) Turn off the Animate button.

8. Activate the Top viewport and zoom into the Quad Patches until they fill the frame. (You may want to activate the Safe Frame option to help determine when the edges of the objects are just outside the field of view.) Then, go to frame 35 and render a test image at 640×480 resolution.

   As your rendering and Figure 7.6 indicate, the intersecting geometry creates the effect of holes appearing in the top, flat-white Quad Patch.

9. Choose File|View File, select OPACITY.AVI from the \CHAP_07 directory of the companion CD-ROM, and play it.

As this animation shows, when the moving geometry is rendered from the Top viewport, it reveals the patches that appear to grow and devour the white field.

As with virtually all computer graphics techniques, there are many ways to vary this effect. Try these:

• Render this imagery at whatever resolution is necessary for your final animated Opacity map (either as a bitmap sequence or an animation such as an AVI or FLC file). By changing the Quad Patch dimensions, your rendering resolution/aspect ratio, or both, you

Figure 7.6 The intersecting geometry creates the effect of dark patches eating away the white field.

can create an animated sequence tailored to your particular needs.

- Change the overall frame rate to whatever length you need.

- Adjust the number of Quad Patch segments or Noise parameters to produce holes that are either relatively smooth or sharp and jagged.

- By applying a Bend or Taper modifier to either of the Quad Patches (producing a "hill" or "valley"), you can restrict the growing black holes to specific areas, such as the center of the white field. This may be useful for creating a transparency effect that emerges from a specific spot, such as the middle of a door that's being disintegrated by a laser beam.

Note that the file you've just created is saved in the \CHAP_07 directory on the companion CD-ROM as OPACITY.MAX.

Variations Of Disintegrations

As with the previous tutorials, you should play around with the techniques presented in this chapter and vary them according to your needs. A particularly striking application might be to depict the outer hull of a damaged spacecraft being burned away to reveal the framework and super-structure underneath.

However, you don't have to use these techniques only for disintegration effects. As I mentioned earlier, by applying a glow effect to only one material in a Blend, you can create glowing windows on office buildings, the sides of ocean liners, in aerial shots of distant cityscapes, and so on. But if your heart is set on destroying things, here are some additional effects you can try:

- Change the Cellular lightning texture parameters (use Chips instead of Circular, for example) and animate the Roughness more for a jittery lightning effect.

- Animate the Glowing Noise parameters or change the map's color.

- Use different Noise types for the Opacity maps. You should also try using different procedural textures or even prerendered opacity bitmaps.

- Explore the various options available in Lens Effects (including Inferno) and animate the glow effect.

Finally, I'd like to thank Ron Lussier, MAX artist extraordinaire, who originally pointed me in the right direction (shortly after the release of MAX 1.0) on how to create the Noise Opacity/Glow Blend technique. Since then, Ron has used his own variations of this technique with spectacular results in a variety of 3D projects.

Moving On

In this chapter, you saw how to use layers of materials, Opacity maps, ray-traced spotlights, and Video Post filters to produce the illusion of a disintegrating object.

In the next chapter, you'll continue to explore animated materials and pyrotechnics by examining two explosion techniques, both created with simple geometry, animated textures, and MAX Release 2.5's new Lens Effects Glow routine.

ANIMATED MATERIALS
AND OPTICAL EFFECTS,
PART II

8

In this chapter, you'll create a plasma explosion and a shockwave ring. The first is an ever-expanding blob of hot gas (not unlike some fading radio talk-show hosts), and the second is an effect popularized in some recent science-fiction films.

Now that you've seen how to create cool disintegration effects, you'll take a breather from complex Material Editor settings and move on to some simpler pyrotechnics. Let's get blasting, shall we?

Your Everyday Plasma Bomb

This first effect is fairly simple. By using a combination of an animated Sphere, Lens Effects Glow, animated Noise maps, and the Noise modifier, you can create a nifty fireball that dissipates into a cloud of gas.

For this optical effect, you'll create a simple sphere and transform it into an outer-space fireball. To do so, follow these steps:

1. Load MAX, or save your current work and reset the program.

2. Go to Rendering|Environment. Click on the Environment Map button under Background, to open the Material/Map Browser. From the Material/Map Browser, select Bitmap, open the Material Editor, and drag the Environment Map button to an empty material slot. Make it an Instance, not a Copy.

3. Go to the new Environment bitmap slot in the Material Editor. Under Coordinates, change Environment: Mapping from Spherical to Screen, then click on the Bitmap Name button (in the Bitmap Parameters rollout).

4. Select STARS640.JPG from the \MAPS directory of the companion CD-ROM. (This was one of the most widely used images from the original *3D Studio MAX f/x* book's outer-space tutorials. It's simply a scattering of grayscale pixels that I airbrushed in Autodesk Animator Pro.) After you load the image, close the Material Editor and the Environment windows.

5. In the Top viewport, create a sphere in the center of the screen. Set Radius to 1.0, and set Segments to 10. (You'll animate these parameters during the course of the scene.)

6. In the Left viewport, create a Targeted Camera and place it at approximate XYZ coordinates X 0, Y -450, and Z 160. (You may need to zoom out in the viewport to place the camera first.) Drag the Camera01 target to the center of your screen.

7. Next, right-click on the Play Animation icon to bring up the Time Configuration menu. Set the End Time parameter under Animation to 60 frames instead of 100, and then click on OK.

8. Select the Sphere01 object (you can either select it from the viewports using the tool tips or press the H key to bring up the

Select By Name menu). Click on the Animate button, drag the Time Slider to frame 15, and from the Modify panel, change the Sphere Radius setting to 100. Then go to frame 60, set Radius to 200, and set Segments to 200 as well.

You've now set keys for the "growth" of the sphere. If you play back or preview this animation, you'll see the sphere growing rapidly from a tiny, low-resolution dot to a large, complex ball that fills your screen.

However, you'll notice that the sphere seems to grow to its full size around frame 52 and then begins to recede again on frames 54 through 60. You can fix this in Track View by changing the tangent type on the last Radius key.

9. Open the Track View window, expand the listings for Objects/Sphere01/Object (Sphere), and click on the Function Curves button in the Track View toolbar. If you highlight Radius, you see its function curve appear, as shown in Figure 8.1.

10. Click on the Radius animation curve or the green controller triangle to show the keys, select the key on frame 15, then right-click on the key. The Properties menu appears.

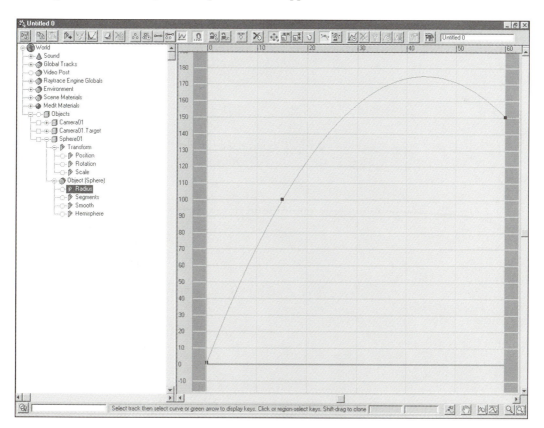

Figure 8.1 The Radius keys and function curve for the Sphere01 animation.

11. Open the Out flyout and change the Bezier Tangent setting from Smooth to Custom. Click on the arrow to the right of the Out Custom flyout to pass this tangent type to the In flyout on the frame 60 key. Close the Key Properties dialog box. Finally, adjust the Bezier spline handles of both keys until you get a smooth slope, as shown in Figure 8.2.

12. Close the Track View window and make sure you drag the Time Slider back to frame 0. For now, keep Animate on.

Smoke Gets In Your Eyes

Just when you thought you've seen enough of the Noise map...well, don't worry. You're going to use a new procedural map instead. To create the Plasma material effect, first do the following:

1. Open the Material Editor, click in any material slot, and change Type to a new Blend material. (When the "Replace Material" alert appears, discard the old material and click on OK.) Change this new material's name to Plasma Bomb and apply it to Sphere01.

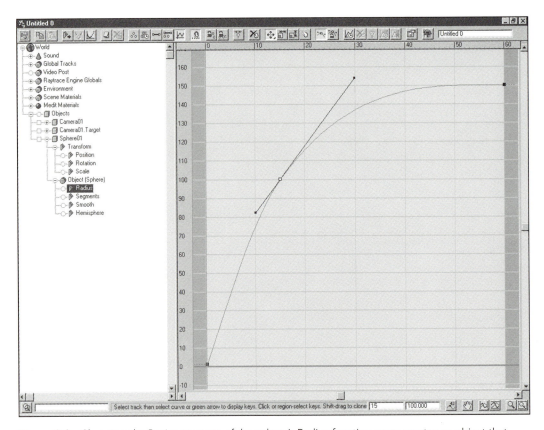

Figure 8.2   Changing the Bezier tangents of the sphere's Radius function curve creates an object that grows smoothly.

2. Open the Material 1 slot and name this material Outer Ring. Change both Ambient and Diffuse colors to RGB 0, 0, 0, or pure black. Set the Shininess and Shininess Strength to 0, set Self-Illumination to 100, then check 2-Sided.

3. Open the Extended Parameters rollout. Set Opacity Falloff to In, change Amount to 100, and change Type to Additive. This will help emphasize a bright halo around the edges of the sphere.

4. Open the Diffuse slot in the Maps rollout, and select Smoke from the Material/Map Browser. This is a new procedural texture that somewhat resembles MAX's Turbulence Noise type, although it's more "gaseous" and less "ropy." Under Smoke Parameters, change Size to 20. Change Color #1 to a bright yellow, or RGB 255, 255, 0, and change Color #2 to dark red, or RGB 128, 0, 0.

5. Next, click on the Go To Parent icon to return to the Outer Ring rollout, and drag this Diffuse Smoke map down to the Opacity map slot. Make it an Instance, not a Copy—you'll want any changes you make in the Diffuse map to update automatically for the Opacity map.

6. Click on the Go To Parent icon again, then click on the Mask button. From the Material/Map Browser, pick Falloff, keep the default settings, then click on the Go To Parent icon again. Now, drag the Outer Ring material down to the Material 2 slot. Make this a Copy, not an Instance, because you're going to set different parameters for this material. Open this new material and change its name to Inner Core.

7. Here is where the changes come in. Under Extended Parameters, change the Falloff amount to 0, then open the Diffuse map slot. Change Color #1 to pure red, or RGB 255, 0, 0, and Color #2 to yellow (RGB 255, 255, 0).

8. At this point, it's time to set some animation parameters for this material. Drag the Time Slider to frame 60, then change the Inner Core's Z Offset to 60 (this creates a billowing fiery effect as the sphere expands). Click on the Go To Parent icon to return to the Inner Core rollout.

9. The effect you want to produce now is of a gas cloud that dissipates from the middle outward, leaving a glowing outer ring. So, drag the Time Slider back to frame 30 and change the Diffuse amount from 100 to 99. (This is simply the starting key for the fade-out.) Go to frame 50 and turn Diffuse down to 0. The inner core fades to black.

10. If you want, you can open Track View and adjust the function curves and tangent of these keys as you did in the preceding section when you set keys for the growth of the sphere. In addition, you can set "bracketed keys" by setting a Diffuse value one unit below the current level, advancing one frame, and changing the value back up one unit.

11. Click on the Go To Parent icon and open the Outer Ring rollout. Go to frame 45 and change the Diffuse amount to 99. Then, go to frame 60 and change Diffuse to 0. The outer edges of the material will "lag behind" as the inner core fades out.

12. Next, go to frame 30 and render a test image of your Camera01 viewport as shown in Figure 8.3.

As your rendering and Figure 8.3 indicate, you now have a glowing sphere with a "hot" outside edge and a gaseous red core.

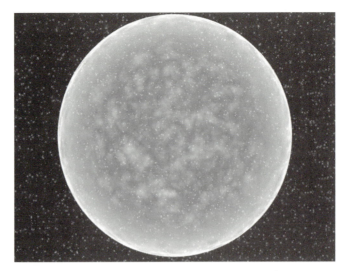

Figure 8.3 The plasma sphere with the glowing Outer Ring and Inner Core materials.

From Noise To Plasma

To create the final effect of this expanding ball of gas dissipating into the ether, you'll add a Noise modifier and animate its settings:

1. Select Sphere01 and choose Noise from the Modify panel. In the Noise Parameters rollout, make sure Scale is set to 100 on frame 0. Do *not* check the Animate Noise box—you'll set keys with specific values on certain frames and not just have the Noise modifier animating randomly. Make sure you're at frame 0, and check the Fractal box.

2. With the Animate button still on, go to frame 30 and change Scale to 99 (you'll just set an "anchor" key here). Change Strength from 0.0 to 5.0 on X, Y, and Z. Go to frame 60, change Scale to 75, and change Strength to 50.0 on the X, Y, and Z axes.

3. Turn off the Animate button and drag the Time Slider back and forth to scratch through the animation. You'll see the sphere expand suddenly from a small point; then, as the Noise modifier takes over, you'll see the surface become greatly distorted as you near the end of the sequence.

4. If you want, select Render|Preview and render a quick preview of the sphere geometry expanding and then distorting. (If you don't want to wait, select File|View File and play the PREVIEW.AVI file from the \CHAP_08 directory of the companion CD-ROM.)

5. Now you can render frames of this sequence to check the effect. Figures 8.4 through 8.6 show frames 30, 45, and 55; these frames illustrate how the animated Noise modifier, and the Outer Ring

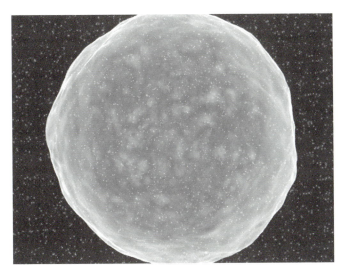

Figure 8.4   Frame 30 of the plasma sequence. The sphere reaches maximum size. It also begins to show slight surface distortion as the Noise modifier increases in strength.

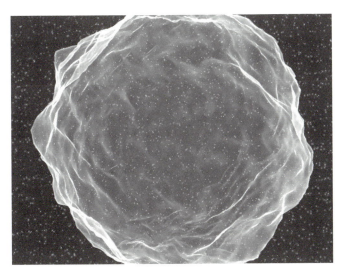

Figure 8.5   Frame 45 of the plasma explosion. The inner core has almost faded out, and the Noise modifier has distorted the sphere's surface considerably.

and Inner Core materials, create the illusion of an expanding cloud of plasma.

6. At this point, you can render your own test animation at whatever resolution you want. (To enhance your plasma sequence, you should set an effects channel on the Plasma Blend material and then apply the Lens Effects Glow filter in Video Post. This will soften the geometry and augment the "glowing cloud" effect.)

Again, if you don't want to wait for your own rendering, select File|View File and choose the PLASMA.AVI animation from the \CHAP_08 directory on the companion CD-ROM.

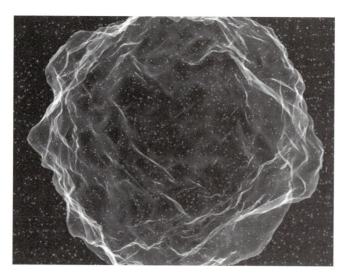

Figure 8.6 Frame 55 of the plasma explosion. The Inner Core material is gone, the Noise modifier is reaching maximum distortion, and the Outer Ring material is disappearing.

This animated plasma explosion has a basic Lens Effects Glow filter applied to it. Size has been set to 2.5 and Intensity to 50.0. (These are the same settings used in the previous chapter to create the Cellular map "lightning" crawling over the sphere.)

7. When you're finished viewing the animation, close your Preview window.

This plasma explosion effect is useful for outer-space settings, either by itself or combined with MAX's particle systems or digitized explosion elements. (You can find the latter on the VCE Pyromania or Artbeat ReelExplosions CD-ROM. For more information on these products, see Appendix B.)

Another way to use this plasma effect is to render it against a black background, save it as an AVI file or a series of still images, and use the rendering as an animated texture map for things other than explosions. (For instance, you could use it to simulate an impact against a force field, as shown in the film *Independence Day*.)

You can save this scene to your local 3DSMAX\SCENES directory; a version of this scene is saved in the \CHAP_08 directory as PLASMA.MAX. The Plasma Bomb material is also saved in the MAXFX2.MAT Material Library, located in the \MATLIBS directory of the companion CD-ROM.

Ring Of Fire

Now that you've seen how to create an expanding plasma cloud, here's another interesting optical effect that uses bitmap imagery, geometry,

Note: *If you're going to combine this plasma geometry effect with a Combustion apparatus, you should render the effects separately and then composite them together in Video Post or a third-party program such as Adobe AfterEffects; simply placing an object inside a volumetric combustion effect reveals the geometry's contours, even if the object's materials make the standard object invisible.*

and Video Post filters to achieve its results. In this example, you'll create a shockwave—an expanding, toroidal ring of fire.

You've probably seen this popular science-fiction effect in various *Star Trek* films, in *Stargate*, and in the Special Edition re-releases of *Star Wars* and *Return of the Jedi*. Basically, the effect involves an object exploding with cosmic force and then a flattened shockwave ring emerging from the initial blast point. Although scientifically questionable, the effect looks nifty, and (even though it's becoming overused) I would be remiss in my geeky effects duties were I *not* to tell you how to duplicate it. So, here's a quick and dirty way to produce this effect:

1. Load MAX, or save your current work and reset the program. Turn on 3D Snap Toggle, activate your Front viewport, and enlarge it to full screen.

2. As you did with the plasma bomb earlier in this chapter, load the STARS640.JPG image into Environment: Background as an Environment: Screen image. (See Steps 3 and 4 under "Your Everyday Plasma Bomb" again if you're unsure of how to do this.)

3. Next, go to the Create Panel and select Shapes|Splines|Circle. In the center of the Front viewport, create a circle with a radius of 100 by dragging outward from the center of the screen to the right. (The first vertex should be the one on the far right, or the three o'clock position.)

4. Go to the Modify panel and apply an Edit Spline modifier to the circle. Select Subobject: Vertex, then right-click on the vertex on the far left, or the nine o'clock position. The Properties menu appears. Go down to Vertex Type and change it from Bezier to Corner. The circle now looks like a fat teardrop lying on its side.

5. Select the top vertex of the circle (noon position) and move it on the Y axis -80 units (down). Move the bottom (six o'clock position) axis on the Y axis 80 units (up). Then, select both axes and move them on the X axis 40 units (to the right).

6. Finally, right-click on the first vertex on the far right and change it from Bezier to Smooth. The circle should now resemble a sleek teardrop, or an "airfoil" shape, like the cross section of an aircraft wing. The exact shape is shown in Figure 8.7.

Extruding And Bending

Now you're ready to create the ring itself:

1. Click on the Min/Max Toggle icon (or press the W key) to return to the four viewports, then go to the Modify panel and apply an Extrude modifier to the circle. Set Extrude Amount to -5000, and set Segments to 100 (the extrusion should be fairly high resolution because you'll be bending it back on itself).

2. Under Capping, set both Cap Start and Cap End to Off so you don't have to delete these faces later. Then, click in the Generate Mapping Coordinates checkbox to activate it.

3. Go to the Modify panel and apply a Bend modifier to this very long airfoil shape. Set Bend Axis to Z and Angle to -360 degrees. This bends the extruded circle into a completed ring shape. (You now have an object that looks somewhat like an Aerobie, the long-distance flying ring.)

4. Next, in the Top viewport, move the ring to the right on the X axis about 800 units—it should be centered in your scene. (The pivot is still centered on the original circle spline, but don't worry; you'll change its placement later.)

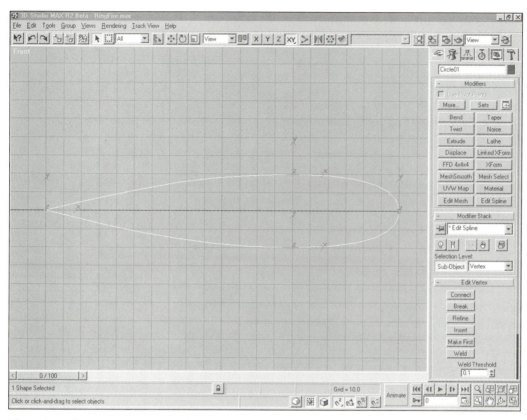

Figure 8.7 The proper cross section for the shockwave effect.

5. Press the A key to activate Angle Snap Toggle, go to Create Panel, and select Cameras|Target. In the Top viewport, zoom out somewhat, place the camera at approximate XYZ coordinates X 0, Y -1300, Z 0, and place the Target in the center of the Ring object. Activate the Left viewport, and drag the Camera01 body up on the Y axis approximately 500 units.

6. Right-click on the camera in the Front viewport, select Rotate, and rotate (or roll) the camera approximately 40 degrees. Finally, select the Camera01 Target, and in the Top viewport, move it to XYZ coordinates X -300, Y -500, Z 0. (These settings are approximate; you should have a good view of the ring's leading edge.) Your screen should look something like Figure 8.8.

7. Click on the Circle01 object and rename it Shockwave Ring.

Mirror Tile

Now, it's time to create the material for the shockwave effect:

1. Open the Material Editor, select a Standard material, and name it Ring of Fire 2. Select the Shockwave Ring object, then click on the Assign Material To Selection icon to assign it to the Shockwave Ring object. Change Diffuse and Ambient to solid black, or RGB 0, 0, 0. Change both Shininess and Shininess Strength to 0, and change Self-Illumination to 100.

2. Open the Extended Parameters rollout and change Falloff Type to Additive.

3. Go to the Maps rollout and open Diffuse. Select Bitmap from the Material/Map Browser and then select RFIR2000.IFL from the \MAPS directory of the companion

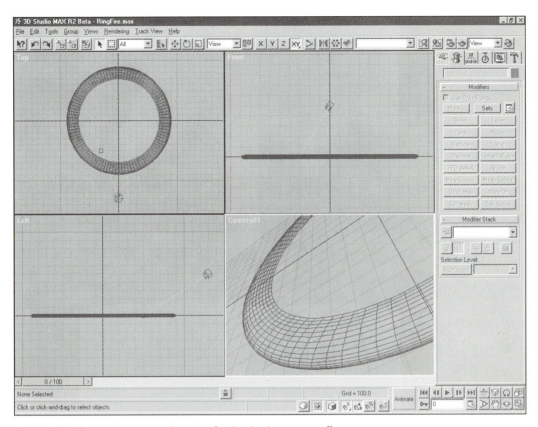

Figure 8.8   The proper camera alignment for the shockwave ring effect.

CD-ROM. Click on the View Image button to view the first frame of this 90-frame sequence; the image is also shown in Figure 8.9.

I created this 90-frame sequence from original digitized fire imagery (used by permission) from Visual Concepts Engineering's Pyromania 1 CD-ROM. This CD contains several different fire, smoke, and explosion elements and is a must for many desktop CGI effects artists. For more information on how to locate this and other useful CD-ROMs, see Appendix B.

However, the original imagery consisted of orange-red flames; to change them into the multicolored, electric imagery of the final versions, I used the batch processing features of Adobe Photoshop 4.0. By running each image through a combination of filters, such as Glowing Edges and Wind, I then created the psychedelic

effect. The resultant looping image sequence is well suited for the fantasy shockwave ring effect. (For more information on image manipulation in Photoshop, see Chapter 17.)

4. Close the VFB window to load the Image File List sequence into the Material Editor, then go to the top of the Diffuse rollout. Click in the Mirror checkboxes under Coordinates for both U and V Tiling, but leave Tiling itself at 1.0. Under Angle, change W to 90.0. Change Blur offset to 0.005; this will help minimize the aliasing of the stretched bitmaps along the periphery of the ring.

5. Click on the Go To Parent icon, and drag the Diffuse map down to Opacity. Make this an Instance instead of a Copy.

6. Next, activate the Camera01 viewport and render a test image, as shown in Figure 8.10.

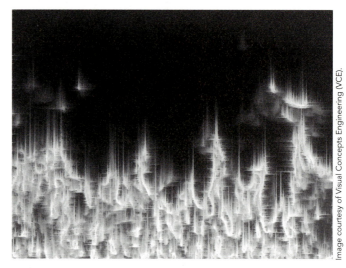

Image courtesy of Visual Concepts Engineering (VCE).

Figure 8.9   The first frame of the RFIR2000-RFIR2089.JPG sequence.

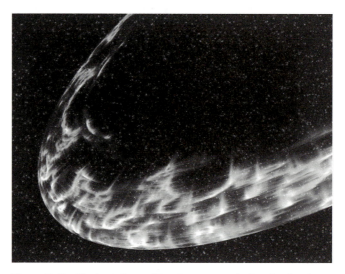

Figure 8.10   The basic Ring of Fire 2 texture applied to the Shockwave Ring object.

You'll now see how the Tiling settings in the Diffuse bitmap rollout produce the final effect. The RFIR images "wrap around" the outer edges of the ring. The bottoms of the mirrored bitmaps meet along the "equator" of the ring and are stretched along the top and bottom. The tops of the bitmaps point in toward the center of the object, creating the effect of an expanding ring of fire. (The effect is the same whether you're looking at the "top" or "bottom" of the ring.)

You'll notice that the Ring of Fire 2 texture makes the Shockwave Ring seem somewhat two-dimensional; it also doesn't seem as bright as it should be.

7. Return to the Material Editor and check 2-Sided on the Ring of Fire 2 texture, then render another test image.

The texture now appears thicker and brighter as you see it on the back faces of the object.

Playing With Fire

Now that you've seen the basic effect, it's time to set up a simple shockwave explosion. To begin, you need to make this geometry glow to enhance the fiery bitmaps. Follow these steps:

1. Return to the Material Editor, open Material Effects Channel, and assign #1 to the Ring of Fire 2 material.

2. Select Rendering|Video Post, select Add Scene Input event, select Camera01, and click on OK. Then, click on the Add Image Filter Event icon, select Lens Effects Glow, and click on the Lens Effects Glow Setup button. You'll see the Lens Effects Glow setup menu appear.

3. Click on the Preview button to display the Lens Effects Glow defaults, which are shown in the image window at the top of the menu. You'll make some basic changes to them, so make sure the Properties tab is active, select Material ID under Source, and set it to 1.

4. Click on the Preferences tab. Under Effect, change Size to 2.5, and under Color, change Intensity to 25.0. As you do, you'll see the glow effect in the Preview window change to match the new settings.

5. Click on OK to return to the Video Post menu, then click on the Execute Sequence icon. Select Single (frame 0), select 640×480 resolution, and then click on Render. After a while (how long depends on the speed of your PC, of course), the rendering appears on your screen; it should look like Figure 8.11.

The Lens Effects Glow filter provides extra *oomph* (a quantum physics unit that measures visual neatoness) to your shockwave ring.

"With This Ring, I Thee...Blam!"

Finally, you'll set up a basic explosion effect with the ring. All you really need to do is have the ring start off tiny in the frame, expand quickly, and blast by the camera. To set up the basic explosion effect, follow these steps:

1. Select the Shockwave Ring object and click on the Hierarchy tab of the Command Panel. Click on Affect Pivot Only under Adjust Pivot: Move/Rotate/Scale. Select Center To Object under Alignment. The pivot snaps to the center of the shockwave ring. Click on the Affect Pivot Only button again to deactivate it.

2. Turn on the Animate button, right-click on the Ring object, and when the Properties menu appears, select Scale. On frame 0, scale down the ring from 1 to 5 percent of its current size. Then, go to frame 100 and scale the ring up until its near edge is very close to the camera, or approximately 2,500 percent of the frame 0 size. (If you want, you can enlarge it even more so that it goes past the camera.) Then, turn off the Animate button.

3. To see more of the leading edge of the ring as it expands, go to the Left viewport and drag the Camera01 Target down on the Y axis approximately 300 units. (Again, unless you want a camera movement added as the ring expands, make sure the Animate button is turned off.)

If you play back the animation in your viewports, you'll see the shockwave ring exploding outward as it scales up.

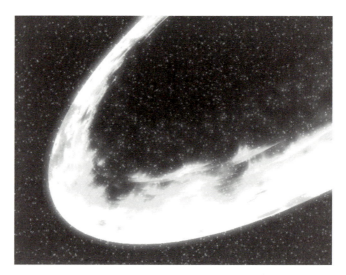

Figure 8.11   The shockwave ring with a Video Post Lens Effects Glow filter.

Now you can render your own animation of this sequence, but again, you can check out a prerendered preview of this effect that I've already done for you.

4. Select File|View File, then load and play the RINGFIRE.AVI animation from the \CHAP_08 directory.

Here, you'll see the final expanding shockwave effect. The animated RFIR bitmap loop creates the illusion of colorful fire burning from the leading edge. The Video Post glow filter punches up the effect and gives it energy.

Now, barring a camera move off of the ring effect, you may still see the far edge of the ring off in the distance, even if the ring grows substantially. For your own effects shots, you may want the shockwave effect to simply fade out by a particular frame. As with the plasma bomb effect described earlier in this chapter, you can simply set animation keys for the Diffuse map amount of the Ring of Fire material and drop Diffuse down to 0 when needed.

5. When you're finished playing with this scene, you can save it to your local \3DSMAX\SCENES directory. Again, these scenes (called RINGFIRE.MAX and RINGFIR2.MAX) and their materials are saved in the \CHAP_08 and \MATLIBS directories of the companion CD-ROM.

Other Ideas

As you've already seen, you can punch up this basic shockwave ring effect with more complex materials, modified geometry, different Video

Post filters, or combinations of these. Here are some variations you can try:

- Instead of using a Standard material, change it to a Double-Sided material and keep your original Shockwave Ring material as a submaterial. Drag-copy this first material to the second material slot (make it a Copy, not an Instance), then change the U Tiling of the second material's Diffuse and Opacity maps to, say, 3 or 5. Use odd numbers of layered, tiling materials to help conceal the fact that they're repeating. (You can also use this technique to break up texture maps on giant surfaces that are mostly planar, such as aerial views of plowed fields, the surface of the *Star Wars Deathstar* in close-up, and so on.)

- Experiment with animated Noise, Smoke, or Cellular procedural textures in the Diffuse and Opacity map slots, and use the RING bitmaps as masks for these textures.

- Use Falloff or other maps to mix between different materials.

- Use Gradient mask with animated bitmaps or procedural textures loaded.

- As with the plasma bomb effect earlier in this chapter, apply a Noise modifier to the Shockwave Ring object, then animate both the Noise settings and the material settings. When this technique is done properly, you can produce the effect of an expanding, fiery ring of energy that dissipates into a softer gaseous form as it comes close to the camera.

Moving On

In this chapter, you've taken an "explosively brief" diversion into animated materials and optical effects. In the next two chapters, contributors James Green and Michael Spaw show you some brand-new attributes of MAX's Material Editor: dynamics and ray-traced materials.

With dynamics, you can apply physical properties, such as friction, collision, elasticity, and the like, to your MAX Release 2.5 geometry. Don't want to set keyframes for a pool table simulation? Don't worry—with dynamics, MAX will do all the work and animate the objects for you.

Then, you'll see how to work with a first in *any* version of 3D Studio: native raytracing. It's not just for chrome balls and checkerboard floors anymore.

MATERIALS AND
DYNAMICS

9

BY

JAMES GREEN

In earlier chapters of this book, you explored how MAX's materials let you create unusual surface effects, such as realistic metals and retro-CG and X-ray looks. In this chapter, you'll see how to use MAX's new Dynamics utility in conjunction with Material Dynamics settings to impart physically correct movement to simple objects in your scenes.

Although you may know that 3D Studio MAX R2.5 includes Dynamics among its new features, you may be wondering exactly what the new Dynamics utility does.

Let's start with a definition. "Dynamics" could be called "the branch of mechanics in physics that deals with the motion of bodies and the action of forces in producing or changing their motion." Whoa—what a mouthful! Okay, it's time to look at this more carefully. "Mechanics" is the study of the motion of objects; for example, a ball flying through the air or across a room.

Examine the second part of the previous definition—"the action of forces in producing or changing [object] motion." Hmm.... Gravity is a force. What if there's gravity in the space the ball is traveling through? Then it's possible that the ball, instead of *flying* through space, is now *falling* through space as gravity pulls it down. What about when the ball hits the floor? When the ball collides with the floor, the floor exerts a force (a fixed resistance) on the ball and the ball rebounds, that is, it bounces off the floor. Consequently, dynamics can include the motions of balls bouncing, gears turning, planes flying or breaking up on impact, planets orbiting, and too many others to mention.

You may ask yourself, What does Dynamics do for me? Can't I just keyframe the motions of flying or falling objects in my scenes? Yes, you can, but when you need to handle the motions of multiple objects interacting—that is, colliding—with other objects and you want physically realistic movements, Dynamics can save you time by calculating the motion paths, acceleration, and deceleration for you.

In this chapter, you'll be presented with some basic steps for setting up objects and motions in your scenes for the Dynamics utility to solve. Note that the algorithms involved with Dynamics are very complex, and the calculations to solve the scene take time, much like complex rendering. Let's face it—with Dynamics, you're depending on MAX to simulate real-world physics. Much like raytracing, solving for a dynamics simulation is resource-intensive. You will start with small scenes and small numbers to try to keep solve times from taking too long. You should be aware that small changes for the values of objects and forces can result in large and possibly unpredictable results.

In the first tutorial, you'll work through a simple example that covers the features in the Dynamics rollout and the use of material properties in the Material Editor's Dynamics Properties rollout. The second example will demonstrate more advanced topics, using linked objects

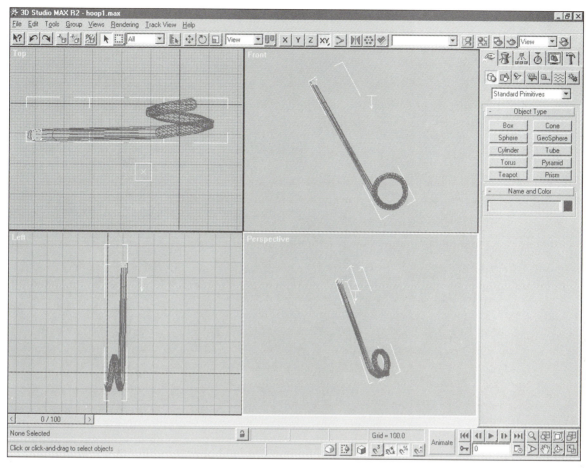

Figure 9.1   The initial state of the hoop Dynamics simulation.

and substitute (or stand-in) objects. Finally, in the last example, you'll employ two Dynamics space warps to create a couple of simple effects. So, take a deep breath and jump in.

Dynamics Basics, Part I

It's time to set up the first Dynamics example. Keep in mind that MAX's Dynamics utility works by generating keyframes from a simulation in which you specify the objects, collisions, and effects (forces). You must first set up the initial state of the scene, give an object (or two) a little push, and then let Dynamics calculate, or solve, the rest, as you'll see here:

1. Load MAX, or save your current work and reset the program.

2. Load HOOP1.MAX from the \CHAP_09 directory of this book's companion CD-ROM. Your screen should look like Figure 9.1.

> **Note:** The examples in this chapter were solved using fast PCs (either dual Pentium Pro 200MHz or single Pentium II 266MHz CPUs). Please be patient while solving some of the example files if you're running MAX on a slower machine.

LOFTY AIMS

For best lofting results, use a contiguous spline primitive as your path. Splines that are constructed from multiple attached splines may produce incorrect results.

The HOOP1.MAX scene is composed of a hoop (or a loop-the-loop track), a sphere, and a Gravity space warp. I constructed the hoop simply by lofting the track shape along a helix spline.

The hoop will act as a track for the sphere to follow. The sphere will go down the ramp, zip through the loop, and then fly off. The sphere has an initial velocity (speed) and will be affected by gravity.

3. Click on the Play button and you'll see that the sphere has an initial motion—a small push down the track over the first three frames.

The sphere has an initial transform on it to give it enough speed to make the loop with the current Gravity setting that you'll use. Both objects are no longer parametric; that is, their modifier stacks have been collapsed and they're now Editable Meshes with uniform (all outward-facing) normals. Finally, Gravity strength is set to 1.5.

4. Click on the Dynamics button in the Utilities tab to open the Dynamics rollout. (If the Dynamics button isn't part of your current Utilities setup, click on the More button and then select Dynamics.) Click on the New button, which is under the Simulation Name field. You should see "Dynamics00" appear in the field. You're now ready to move to the next phase of building the Dynamics simulation.

5. Click on the Edit Object List button in the Dynamics rollout. (This button is actually the Which Objects Do You Want To Be Part Of Your Dynamics Calculations? button, but that would have been a really big button for the user interface, so....) The Edit Object List dialog box appears, as shown in Figure 9.2.

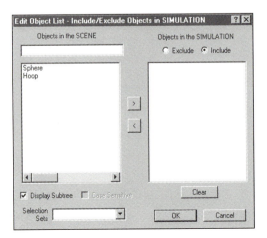

Figure 9.2   The Edit Object List dialog box of the Dynamics rollout.

You'll notice two name fields in Edit Object List dialog box: Objects In The *Scene* and Objects In The *Simulation*. If you move the first set of objects to the Objects In The Simulation field, they will be included in the Dynamics calculations for generating keyframes.

6. In the Dynamics dialog box, highlight the hoop and sphere in the left list window, click on the right arrow (the *move* button) to move the objects to the right list window, then click on the OK button.

7. Click on the Edit Object button (below the Edit Object List button in the Dynamics rollout). Your screen should look like Figure 9.3.

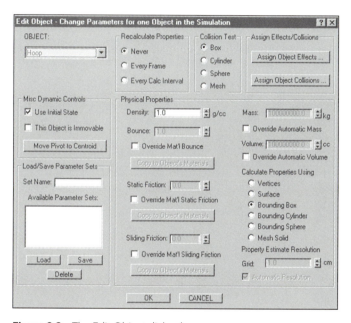

Figure 9.3 The Edit Object dialog box.

The Edit Object dialog box is where you'll tell MAX what properties your objects have and how you would like all of the different objects to react. These properties will have a direct effect on the number of keyframes generated and how long it takes to generate the keyframes.

8. Highlight Hoop in the Object field.

The hoop is what I call a base object. A *base* object is an object that is unaffected by gravity or collisions; it is immovable, and all (or most) of the other objects interact with it. (A perfect example of a base object is the ground, which is pretty darn immovable unless you're in an earthquake zone.)

9. Click on the This Object Is Immovable checkbox in the Misc. Dynamics Controls. An immovable object is immovable for the entire simulation; once its properties are calculated, you don't need to recalculate them again during the simulation, so the Recalculate Properties area of the dialog box is grayed out.

Collision Test

Now, the Collision Test area warrants some description. Dynamics can test for collisions between objects, but first you must tell MAX how accurately you want it to calculate those collisions. MAX must test for collisions between every face on one object and every face on the other, so the fewer faces you use to calculate potential collisions, the faster the calculations will be—but they'll not necessarily be more *accurate*. The Box, Cylinder, and Sphere options use a bounding primitive shape that *roughly* matches your object's size rather than its exact shape. An object with a teardrop shape, for example, will not have a tapered bounding primitive object. The Bounding Box option trades off collision accuracy for faster calculation speed. If you use the Collision Test cylinder for a cone, you won't get a very accurate representation of a collision at the apex of the cone, but the results for a collision at the base of the cone may suffice. It will also calculate much faster than if you choose the Mesh option, which uses the actual geometry's faces to calculate the collision surface.

When you choose a collision bounding, it's important to make sure your bounding object begins a simulation that is already intersecting with any object with which you've set it to collide. For example, let's say you have a wineglass on a table. You have a bounding box collision for the table and a bounding cylinder for your wineglass. The wineglass is directly on the table; in this initial state for the scene, the collision primitive for the wineglass may protrude through the collision primitive for the table. When this happens, you may get unpredictable and undesirable results for your Dynamics solution. Always check your Collision Bounding primitives and the initial positions of the objects they represent before you click on the Solve button. Now, you'll set up the collision parameters for this scene:

1. Select the Mesh checkbox in the Collision Test area of the Edit Object dialog box, which is the only choice for the hoop. As mentioned before, the Mesh option in the Collision Test area uses the actual surface of the object as the collision shape. This option takes longer to solve, but gives the most accurate results.

2. Next, you'll assign collisions to the hoop. For collisions to work, you must include objects that will collide and objects to collide against. Click on the Assign Object Collisions button in the Assign Effects/Collision area, as shown in Figure 9.4.

3. In the Assign Object Collisions dialog box, click on Sphere to highlight it. Next, click on the move arrow to move the hoop to the Collisions For This Object field.

If you look at the hoop in any of the viewports, you'll see that it's not selected. Be aware that selecting objects in a viewport doesn't mean that they'll also be selected in the Dynamics utility (or vice versa). If you have a scene with 12 bouncing balls and you select Ball06 in one of the viewports (either by clicking on it or by using the Select By Name menu), Ball06 still won't be displayed or selected in the Dynamics utility.

You won't be assigning any effects to the hoop because you don't want it to move. When you get to the sphere, you'll assign gravity to it so it will have a continuing motive force in the simulation.

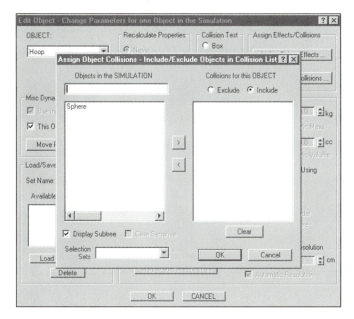

Figure 9.4 The Assign Effects/Collision area.

Physical Properties

The last area to cover in the Edit Object dialog box is the Physical Properties area. The properties of the objects are friction, bounce, mass, surface, and volume. For this first example, you'll focus on bounce. In the following examples you'll incorporate the remaining properties.

You can define the physical properties in two ways: by the object itself or by the Dynamics properties stored in the material you've assigned to the object. You'll start with object properties first (you'll deal with materials a little later on in this chapter):

1. Check the Override Mat'l. Bounce checkbox; for this scene, the sphere shouldn't bounce off the track when it collides with the hoop. Enter a value of 0.01 in the Bounce field (so the sphere won't bounce much).

What you've just done is set the bounce coefficient of the hoop to a very low value, which would be comparable to the bounce coefficient value of a bag of sand or a lead ball. A value of 1.0 would be similar to the value of a child's rubber Superball. In physics terms, if you have two identical balls that collide head-on and they both have a bounce coefficient of 1.0, they would both bounce back equally in opposite directions. Their entire energy or momentum is transferred to the other, which is called an *elastic* collision.

In addition, if one ball is twice as massive as the other ball and they collide, the smaller ball will move in the opposite direction with twice the speed, and the larger ball will continue in the same direction with half its original speed. If both balls had a coefficient value of 0.2 and identical mass, not all of their energy or momentum would be transferred when they collide. This is called an *inelastic* collision. (Car or train crashes are, unfortunately, perfect examples of inelastic collisions.) If you had this same collision but both balls were perfectly elastic, after colliding with the large ball, the small ball would reverse direction, and travel with twice the speed. The large ball wouldn't change direction but would lose some speed.

That's it for the hoop. Now, you'll focus on the sphere.

2. The sphere is travelling down a narrow channel and we want it to react as accurately as possible, so select the Sphere in the Object list box in the Edit Object dialog box and set Collision Test to Mesh.

3. Click on Assign Objects Effects in the Assign Effects/Collision area. You'll want the Sphere to be affected by the Gravity space warp. The gravity is planar; it's a uniform force moving in one direction.

4. Highlight Gravity01 in the left list window and click on the move arrow to move it to the Effects On This Object list window. Your screen should look like Figure 9.5.

5. Click on OK, then click on the Assign Object Collisions button in the Assign Effects/Collision area. Highlight Hoop and click on the

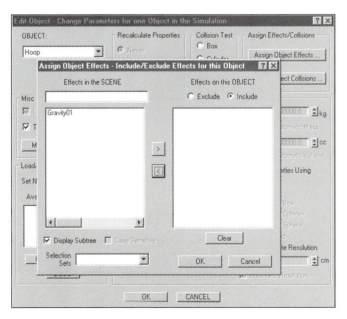

Figure 9.5 Adding gravity to the mix.

move arrow to move it to the Collision For Object field. If you don't assign the collision to both the hoop and the sphere, the sphere will "fall through" the hoop. Remember that you need to tell MAX how you want collision to be tested, and that MAX tests between each face of the object with each face of an assigned object.

6. Check Override Mat'l. Bounce in the Physical Properties area. Enter a value of 0.01 in the Bounce field.

7. Check Override Automatic Mass and enter in a value of 1250.0. This doubles the mass calculated from the size of the sphere alone and should get the sphere really cranking!

8. Click on the OK button at the bottom of the Edit Object dialog box. This covers the setup for the objects in the scene.

Calculation Intervals: Sub-frame Sampling

Now that you're back in the Dynamics rollout, you're almost ready to generate a Dynamics solution. You've already assigned effects and collisions, but you're not yet ready to solve, so pass over the Solve area. The next step is to set a start time for the Dynamics utility to take over. The Timing & Simulation area is where you'll tell the Dynamics utility on which frames to generate keyframes, how many calculations to make per frame, and how many frames per keyframe.

Note that Dynamics does not affect keyframes that are set before or after the specified range in the Timing dialog. Dynamics *will* overwrite keyframes that you've set previously if they're in the specified range. The initial keyframe generated by the Dynamics utility can be affected when you check the Use Initial State box in the Edit Object dialog box. In this hoop scene, the sphere has an initial speed, and you want the Dynamics utility to take this

into account. To set the timing and simulation values, follow these steps:

1. Enter 2 in the Start Time dialog box in the Dynamics rollout. This will begin the simulation calculations on frame 2.

Now, you're ready to set up the Calculation Intervals Per Frame value, but you may be wondering, Why set this value higher than 1? Simple—when MAX calculates several objects (including space warps) that are interacting, especially if they're moving quickly, you may need to set a sub-frame sampling rate to ensure better Dynamics solutions.

You also may want to set this value above 1 if you notice a failed collision after solving a simulation. A failed collision is when two objects pass through one another rather than acting as if they had collided. Imagine a scene in which two spheres are traveling toward each other in 3D space at a rate of more than one 3D environment unit per frame of animation. As you envision the animation, imagine that the spheres start moving toward each other. They eventually get close to touching in one frame, and in the next frame, they pass through each other. But Dynamics didn't calculate a collision event because they hadn't yet touched in one frame, but in the next frame, they were overlapping and had already passed the point at which the Dynamics utility could register a collision. By increasing the number of calculations per frame, you increase the chances that Dynamics can solve fast-moving animations and collisions.

Note that this added calculation comes with a price: the more calculations per frame, the longer MAX takes to generate a key per frame. If you find that objects in your scene aren't colliding properly, increase the number of calculations.

2. In the Calculations Interval Per Frame field, enter a value of 3.

SIXTEENTH-CENTURY PHYSICS

Do you remember when Galileo dropped the two stones of different masses off the Leaning Tower of Pisa? (I don't either, but I think my Dad was there.) In the 16th century, Galileo discovered that a stone with twice the mass of another stone fell at the same rate as the second except for the small part that air resistance played. If you were in a near-vacuum, such as on the surface of the moon, and you released a feather and a bowling ball simultaneously, they would hit the lunar surface at the same time.

Air Resistance

At the bottom of the Dynamics rollout is the Air Resistance field. Air resistance is the percentage of air density. A good way to visualize this is to consider how many molecules are in a given volume. A value of 0 would be comparable to the air density of a vacuum (or a complete lack of air resistance), whereas an air density of 100 percent is comparable to the air density at sea level (or 14.7 pounds per square inch, to be precise). You can increase the air density to model heavy gases and even to approximate water. (I say approximate, because Dynamics currently doesn't calculate wakes, drag, or turbulence. These factors can create the back-and-forth motion you see if you drop an object into clear water. A falling leaf possesses this type of movement in air because of the leaf's large-size-to-low-mass ratio.)

If you have an air density value of 0, your objects will not be affected by air resistance. Air resistance acts on each leading face of an object in motion. For most of my simulations, I enter a value of at least 1.0 for air density.

1. Consequently, enter a value of 1.0 in the Air Density field. This will give us a scene with 1 percent of air molecules; not a vacuum, but not enough to impart noticeable air resistance.

2. Before you click on the Solve button, you may want to save this scene to your local MAX \SCENES directory. (Call it HOOP1B.MAX, if you want or select File|Hold, and Fetch this scene later, if necessary.)

3. If you have a fast machine (a Pentium Pro or PII), or if you don't mind waiting, you can check the Update Display With Solve checkbox. This will display your scene in the viewport as it solves. You can watch the bar display at the bottom of the screen to see the solving progress. Then, click on the Solve button, and, if you don't have a Pentium pro or PII, go grab something to drink—you'll have some time to kill.

4. When the Dynamics simulation is solved, click on the Play icon to watch the simulation. You should see the ball sliding down the ramp and picking up a little spin as it goes through the loop and shoots off into space.

This is not a bad little simulation, but the ball should really *roll* down the ramp, rather than slide down it. You can make that happen in the next example.

Dynamics Basics, Part II: Dynamics Properties

Now, how do you get the sphere to roll? In the real world, a ball rolls along the ground because of friction (to be more accurate, sliding friction).

In most cases, once an object starts sliding, it takes less force (push) to keep it sliding. The force that acts against the push once an object is moving is a *sliding friction* force. Sliding friction is the contact friction between a moving object and the object with which it's in contact. Another example of sliding friction is when you rub your hands together vigorously; the heat produced is a by-product of this friction. In MAX R2.5, when an object begins to slide, the Dynamics utility uses the Sliding Friction parameter instead of the Static Friction parameter to solve its calculations.

1. Open the Material Editor and click on Slot #2. This is a Multi/Sub-object material named Sphere Colors. It's composed of three materials, two of which are assigned to the sphere. You'll assign one texture for the base color and one for the stripe.

2. Click on SubMaterial #2. Rename the material Sphere Friction.

3. Open the Dynamics Properties rollout in this material, as shown in Figure 9.6. As you can see, it has some now-familiar options.

4. Enter 0.01 in the Bounce Co-efficient field. Enter 0.02 in the Sliding Friction field.

You may wonder now why there's no value set for Static Friction. Remember that when you set the Timing Solve Range value in the Dynamics Utilities rollout in the Material Editor, the ball was already in motion in the scene. When an object is in motion at the start of the simulation, Dynamics uses the Sliding Friction value for its calculations.

5. Click on the Go To Parent icon and then repeat Step 4 for SubMaterial #3. Name this material Sphere Stripe.

A CAUSE FOR FRICTION

Friction is the result of contact between two objects whose surfaces are not smooth. (Actually, almost no surface is perfectly smooth; when you get down to the microscopic level, a piece of smooth paper looks like the surface of the moon.)

There are two types of friction: static friction and sliding friction. Suppose you have a heavy wooden crate and you push on it to try to get it to slide across a concrete floor. Depending on how much force you apply, the crate may not budge. Now that you've applied a force on the crate—the push—you can say that the crate has a *static friction* force. Static friction force is defined as the force between two objects by virtue of contact that opposes sliding. If your floor was made out of something very smooth, such as Teflon, you would have a very low static friction. (An example of a near frictionless surface is an activated air hockey table; the playing pucks actually float on a cushion of air, with minimal contact with the plastic playing surface.) In MAX R2.5's Dynamics, Teflon or an air hockey table surface would effectively have a Static Friction value of 0. If you were to push your crate on a Teflon floor, it would probably begin to slide.

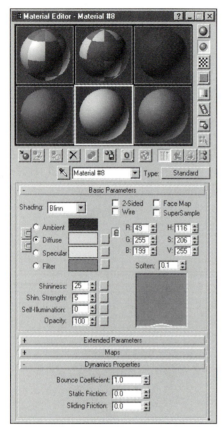

Figure 9.6 The Dynamics Properties rollout of the Sphere Friction material.

6. Next, assign this Multi/Sub-object material to the Sphere object.

You've added a material with friction to the surface of your sphere. Now, you need to go back to the Dynamics utility and reset the checkboxes in the Edit Object dialog box to reflect these changes.

7. Close the Material Editor and open the Dynamics Utility rollout. Click on the Edit Object button and select Sphere in the Edit Object dialog box. Uncheck Override Mat'l Bounce in the Physical Properties area, then click on the OK button.

You're almost ready to solve the Dynamics simulation. The sphere's initial speed is still the same, but when it contacts the hoop faces, the added sliding friction will slow down the sphere and it

won't make it over the loop. You need to compensate for it.

8. Edit Gravity01 and enter a Strength value of 1.3. Save this scene to your \SCENES directory as HOOP2B.MAX.

9. Click on the Solve button, and when the animation's finished, click on the Play icon.

You should now see the ball roll down the ramp and do an almost-complete loop. This illustrates how friction will affect your object's speed. By increasing the initial speed of the object or by setting gravity to 1.4 or more, the sphere will make the complete loop.

10. If you don't want to wait for the solution, load HOOP1FNL.MAX from the \CHAP_09 directory to view the completed loop animation.

You've now completed the basic steps for creating a Dynamics simulation. It's important to remember the following points:

• Initial object position is important.

• Collapse object stacks before doing Dynamics calculations.

• Use basic splines to loft objects in a scene.

• Save your scene before starting your solve.

Again, perhaps the most important thing to remember is that you may need to increase the number of calculation intervals per frame for your simulation to solve correctly. Here are some other things to try in this scene:

• Vary the gravity value.

• Change the air density value.

• Give the ball more sliding friction.

More Bounding Objects And Collisions

As you've seen, the Dynamics rollout is fairly straightforward; the most critical thing is to think carefully about how to set up your initial scene. The example you've just completed is fairly simple, so it's time to move to something a little more complex.

Earlier in this chapter, you learned how bounding objects can decrease solve times, but only at the expense of collision accuracy. However, it's time to look at bounding shapes from a different perspective. As you have already seen, the bounding shapes in Dynamics are based on how the object was created initially. If you've worked through the MAX Release 2.5 Dynamics online demo, you know that complex objects and simple (nonspherical) objects that have been rotated from their initial creation position do not have bounding shapes that lend themselves to the collision bounding options in the Dynamics feature.

But what if you're not worried about the accuracy of the motions or collisions? Let's say you want to create a simulation that looks (mostly) real, but you want to save time. You can calculate a Dynamics solve on a simplified mesh and then *link its motion* to more complex geometry for the final effect. Here's an example:

1. If you haven't restarted MAX or reset it from the last example, reset the program now. Load COLUMNS.MAX from the \CHAP_09 directory of the companion CD-ROM. Your screen should resemble Figure 9.7.

In this scene are three columns that rest on a box; the box represents the ground. Around the three columns are three bounding objects. These bounding objects are less complex than the columns themselves, except at their base and top. For this simulation, the ground will shake back and forth, like earth moving during a quake, and the columns will shake and then tumble.

2. Select Column01, click on the Display tab, and hide the unselected objects.

3. Click on the Arc Rotate button and rotate the scene in a wireframe viewport so that you can see the bottom of a column in a three-quarter view.

In the previous example, you saw that successful collisions depend on the type of collision and the number of calculation intervals per frame. However, there are a couple of additional ways you can tweak this scene's collision potential—you can increase the number of polygons and also alter the initial position of the objects.

Examine the first option. You'll notice that the column has many cap faces—48 quads or 96 triangles—more than would appear necessary at first. If you have a simple object and you can increase the number of faces (without going overboard for the final rendering), you may be able to save time when you calculate the collisions by relying on an increased number of collision faces rather than increasing the number of calculation intervals per frame. The more faces the object has, the more normals the Dynamics utility has to check for collisions. As I mentioned earlier, when you assign collisions in MAX, the program checks a face of the object with all the other faces of the objects it has been assigned to collide with. It does some of the collision calculations based on the normals of an object.

4. In the Display tab, unhide all the objects.

In the first hoop Dynamics example, you saw that the initial position was important for establishing speed. In this columns example, the initial movement of the base sets the velocity and momentum for toppling the columns. If you look closely, you'll notice that the column bases are slightly above the "ground"; this ensures that the columns and base will collide correctly and not pass through each other. In this case, it's better to get a little distance between the columns and the base than to have the columns

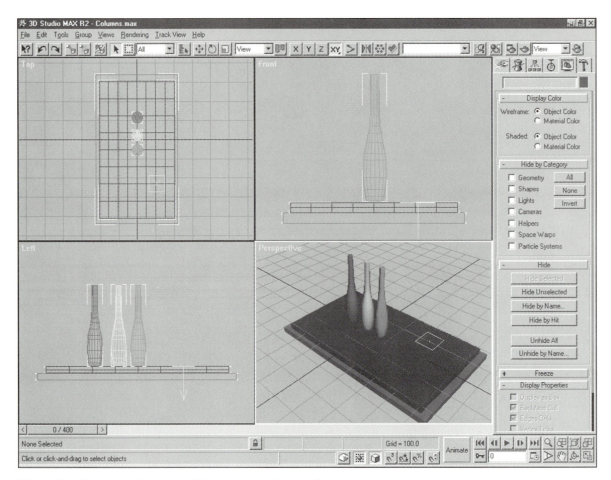

Figure 9.7   This basic columns scene illustrates an earthquake effect.

collide at the edge or vertex. *If this happens, your results may be unpredictable.*

5. Select all three columns, then hide them. (To make sure you've selected only the Column01 through 03 objects, press H to bring up the Select By Name menu.) From the Display panel, hide the selected objects. You should now have just the three bounding shapes, Mo-base (short for motion capture base), and Floor objects displayed.

6. Open the Dynamics rollout and create a new Dynamics Simulation named Dynamics00.

7. Click on the Edit Object list. Highlight Bounding01, Bounding02, Bounding03, Mo-base, and Floor objects. Click on the move

arrow to move the objects to the Objects In Simulation list, then click on the OK button.

8. Click on the Edit Object button. Highlight Floor in the Edit Object dialog box and check This Object Is Immovable. Select Box in the Collision Test area. Check Override Mat'l Bounce and enter 0.05 in the number field.

9. Click on the Assign Object Collisions button. In the Assign Object Collisions dialog box highlight Mo-base and click on the move arrow to assign the Floor a collision with the Mo-base. Click on OK.

What you've done is give the Mo-base a ground object. The Floor object allows you to see the Mo-base move, yet the Mo-base will not produce unpredictable results from the collisions of the bounding objects and gravity.

10. Now, it's time to set up the Mo-base. Highlight Mo-base in the Edit Object dialog box. Check This Object is Immovable. Select Mesh in the Collision Test area. Check Override Mat'l Bounce and enter 0.05 in the number field.

11. The Mo-base will need sliding friction to get the columns to wobble and fall over. For Sliding Friction, in the Physical Properties Area, check Override Mat'l Sliding Friction box and enter 0.75 in the number field.

12. Click on the Assign Object Collisions button. In the Assign Object Collisions dialog box, highlight Bounding01, Bounding02, and Bounding03, click on the move arrow, and then click on OK. Now you have the Mo-base ready to go.

13. Select Bounding01 in the OBJECT list. Select Mesh in the Collision Test area. Click on the Assign Object Collision button. In the Assign Object Collisions dialog box, highlight Mo-base, Bounding02, and Bounding03, click on the move arrow, and then click on OK.

14. Repeat Step 13 for Bounding02 and Bounding03.

15. Click on OK to close the Edit Object dialog box. You should now be back in the Dynamics rollout. Go down to the Timing And Simulation rollout. Enter a Start Time value of 7. The End Range value should be set to 400. (If you have a slower PC, you can enter an End Time value of 150. That should give you the gist of the simulation.)

16. Enter a value of 7 in the Calc Intervals Per Frame textbox. Enter an Air Resistance value of 80. Save the file to your \SCENES directory as COLUMNSB.MAX.

17. Now you're ready to solve, but note that this is an extremely complex scene, and it may take a great deal of time to calculate its solution. If you don't want to wait, load the COLUMNSB.MAX file from the \CHAP_09 directory and view the results.

18. When the Dynamics simulation is done (or you've loaded the finished simulation), click on the Play button to watch the animation. You should see the bounding objects wobble, fall down, and roll off the Mo-base object or tumble off into space.

Linking The Objects' Motion Data

Now that you've created the keyframes for the bounding objects, it's time to impart their motion to the columns by linking the two types of objects:

1. In the Display tab, unhide all the objects in the scene.

2. Select the Bounding01 object and click on the Select And Link icon on the toolbar.

3. Press the H key to bring up the Select Parent dialog box, highlight Column01, and press the Link button. You have now linked all of Bounding01's transforms and rotations to Column01.

4. Repeat the last two steps, linking Bounding02 and Bounding03 to Column02 and Column03, respectively.

5. Click on the Select icon (to get out of Linking mode), then press the H key to bring up the Select By Name dialog box. Select the Bounding01, 02, and 03 objects, go to the Display tab, and hide them.

6. Click on the Play icon. The columns now have the same motion imparted to them as the original bounding box objects.

Yes, this is cheating in a way. But that's what filmmaking and 3D graphics are all about—creating the illusion of something real. In this case, you used the less-complex Bounding objects to generate motion data for the more complex Column objects.

You've seen again that the objects' initial positions have a large impact on the results of the scene. In addition, always consider the balance between creating simulations with simple meshes and bounding objects and/or using complex meshes to achieve your final results.

A Little Metal Man And Some Really Thick Atmosphere

In this last Dynamics example, you'll take a quick look at how some odd Dynamics values can create some unusual effects. First, however, you'll have to change the way you look at real-world physical properties.

When we think of air, we think of it as a gas. That's true, but in some cases it performs much like a liquid. (No, I'm not crazy—I'll prove it to you.)

We use water to lift things. Early elevators were lifted by long pistons that were pushed up out of their cylinders by water pumped in underneath the base of the piston. Now we use an oil, or hydraulic, fluid. Large earth-moving equipment uses thick-walled cylinders to contain hydraulic fluid under heavy pressure to lift its blades or shovels in order to move mountains of dirt. Industrial robots use pneumatic air cylinders and actuators to perform tasks ranging from the very crude to the most precise. My point here is that water, hydraulic fluid, and air can all behave similarly.

So what does this mean for the Dynamics utility? The Air Density setting for the air at sea level is about 100, yet the slider goes much higher than that. Consequently, you can simulate heavy gases and thick atmospheres. (Note that, at present, MAX R2 and R2.5 do not have the ability to model liquids and create accurate liquid Dynamics with drag, turbulence, and wakes.)

However, you can use the high Air Density values along with Wind and Gravity space warps to model soft collisions for some fun effects. (For instance, you can set negative values for gravity so it repels rather than attracts—sort of an alternate wind effect.) This next example will demonstrate a way of doing "soft" collisions with linked objects, Gravity and Wind.

AVOID MIRRORED OBJECTS FOR DYNAMICS

If you use mirrored objects to duplicate, say, a figure's arms and legs, the mirrored objects will not behave properly in your Dynamics simulation. You can avoid having these objects react in an unexpected manner by exporting your model as a .3DS or DXF file and then reimporting it. You must then reassign its linkages, space warps, and so on. You can also select the mirrored objects and reset their transforms in the Hierarchy panel, or by using the Reset Xform Utility.

1. Reset MAX and load CLDYGUY.MAX from the \CHAP_09 directory of the companion CD-ROM. Your screen should look like Figure 9.8.

2. Press the Play icon to see the animation assigned to the wind. (This scene is a low-polygon model of a robot man. In this example, he's floating above multiple moving Wind space warps.)

3. Press the H key to bring up the Select By Name dialog box, then click in the Display Subtree checkbox. This will show you how the objects are linked together.

4. Select all the objects except for the Wind space warps and click on OK.

5. Next, click on the Hierarchy tab, the Pivot button, and then the Affect Pivot Only button in the Adjust Pivot rollout. (You'll see that all the pivots are roughly where they should be for an articulated robot man.)

6. Select the Chest object and click on the Link Info button at the top of the Hierarchy rollout.

All the objects for this model have the same settings. I've locked all the moves as well as Y axis rotations. I've locked these axes to avoid having the man's limbs twisting in the wind, as it were. (Without IK object dampening, this would be a very difficult effect to limit.)

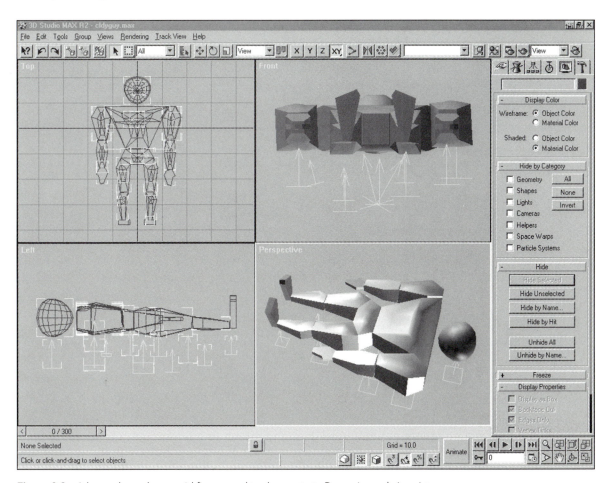

Figure 9.8 A low-polygon humanoid figure used to demonstrate Dynamics and air resistance.

7. Click on the Utilities tab and open the Dynamics Utility rollout. As you can see, all the options are active.

8. Click on the Edit Object button. In the Edit Object dialog box, select the Pelvis and click on Assign Object Effects. You'll see that the only effect assigned to the Pelvis is Wind Pelvis. Each object has its own Wind space warp assigned to it. The hands and feet have the Wind space warp assigned to their respective parent objects. Click on OK to exit the Assign Object Effects dialog box.

9. Notice that in the Calculate Properties Using area, the Pelvis object (and all other objects) are set to Surface. Surface is the setting used for calculating volume. This example uses air density, so the volume of the robot will give him his buoyancy. Surface is also the setting to use for flying objects. Click on OK to exit the Edit Object dialog box.

10. Back in the Dynamics rollout, go to the Air Resistance area and enter 10,000 in the Density field. Setting this value so high allows you to have less-than-precise wind and mass parameter values. It also means that the robot won't fly apart and that he'll move a little slower than he would at sea-level air density.

11. In the Solve area, set Start Time to 2 and Calc Intervals Per Frame to 3.

12. Before you continue, save the file to your local \SCENES directory as CLDYGUYB.MAX, click on the Solve button, and away you go! (This 300-frame animation actually solves fairly quickly.)

13. When the animation is finished, click on the Play icon.

Your animation should look like a robot floating on his back; you'll see his limbs move slowly up and down as a reaction to the Wind space warps. This is okay, but you can give this guy a little extra push.

14. Open CLDYGUY2.MAX from the \CHAP_09 directory of the companion CD-ROM.

You'll see the same little robot you saw in the previous scene, but a Spherical gravity warp has been added. I've also increased some of the Wind Strength settings; Wind Lower Left Leg, Wind Lower Left Arm, and Wind Head are all set to 10 to give them more force to compensate for the new gravity. (The Wind space warp transforms haven't changed.)

15. Select Gravity02, click on the Modify Tab, and click on the Play icon.

As you can see, the Gravity strength settings vary from 2.0 to -4.0. That's right—you can have negative gravity, which can push or repel a mesh.

16. Take a look at this Gravity's function curve. Open the Track View dialog box and expand all the tracks for the Gravity02 space warp. Open the Object (Gravity) track; you'll see tracks for Strength and Decay. If you open Strength, you'll also note a track for an Ease Curve.

17. Highlight Strength, then click on the Function Curves icon in the Track View dialog box. You should now see an interesting function curve for Gravity02's strength, as shown in Figure 9.9.

The default setting for Gravity is a Bezier curve, but for this example, I used Custom Tangents.

18. Right-click on any key to bring up the Properties menu so you can see all of the settings I used. (If you're not familiar with these tangent types, check out the 3D Studio MAX R2 or R2.5 User Guide.)

The value is set to 2.0 at frame 0 and decreases to 0 at frame 100. At frame 120, there's a sharp decrease

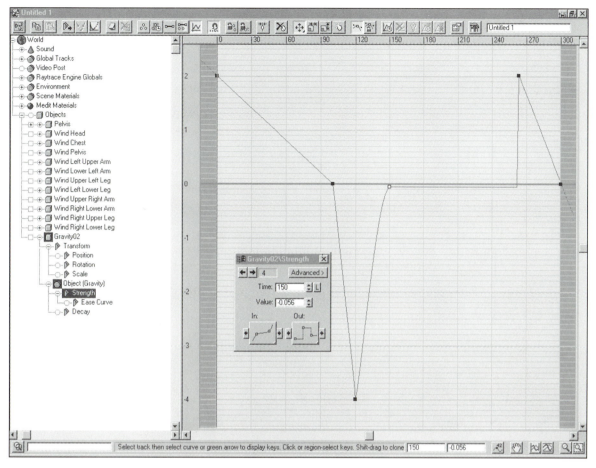

Figure 9.9   The function curve for Gravity strength.

to –4.0—the gravity, which is set to repel, pushes the robot against the Wind space warps. At frame 150, the repelling force diminishes as quickly as it came—back to near 0.

If I had left the Gravity02's tangents as the smooth default Bezier curves, the robot might fly apart. (If you want, you can change the tangent types on these keys back to Bezier, resolve the simulation, and check the effect. Don't do it right away, though—you have an additional simulation to do.)

19. Close the Track View dialog box, return to the Dynamics rollout, and click on Solve. After a few minutes, when the simulation is finished, play the animation.

You'll now see that the robot is being pushed down (as if he's in an acceleration couch in a spaceship, say), and then you'll see him recoiling. This animation illustrates the sharp increase and decrease in repelling force you saw in the Track View example earlier in the chapter.

20. As a further experiment, return to the Track View dialog box and change the values of the keys via the Properties dialog box; you can also click on the Move Keys icon and physically move the keys to change the results.

You've learned some basic techniques and features of MAX R2.5's Dynamics utility. The main points you need to remember from all the examples in this chapter are:

PHYSICS RESOURCES

If you want to increase your knowledge of dynamics and physics, you may want to check out the following books:

Hewitt, Paul G. *Conceptual Physics*. Massachusetts: Little, Brown and Co., 1985. ISBN: 0-316-35974-2. This is a great book to start with if you want to learn the concepts of physics. The emphasis is on the concepts without the burden of complex math. The math involved does not go above basic algebra. There are several different editions, and any edition will do. I highly recommend it if you are going to use the Dynamics utility in your animations.

Halliday, David and Robert Resnick. *Physics, Part 1*. New York: John Wiley and Sons, Inc., 1977. ISBN: 0-471-71716-9. This book covers dynamics and mechanics. I recommend it for those of you who wish to deepen your knowledge of physics. The math involved in this book gets into some calculus.

- Set up your scene's objects carefully and make them as simple as possible (collapse them into Editable mesh objects).

- Choose the correct bounding object(s) for your collisions.

- Adjust the number of calculations per frame.

- Save your work *before* you click on Solve! (You may want to go back to your original parameters quickly without having to go to Track View, and then deleting a huge number of new Dynamics keyframes.)

Moving On

In this chapter, you learned about MAX Release 2.5's Dynamics utility and how it interacts with MAX's Material Editor. Of course, this was by no means an exhaustive look at Dynamics; it was only a quick run-through of some techniques that aren't covered in the MAX Release 2.5 manuals.

In the next chapter, you'll explore illumination of a different sort. You'll see how you can use MAX's new Raytrace Material and Map types to create striking material effects—from glass and shiny metals to fluorescence and even rubber.

BENDING LIGHT: RAYTRACING 101

10

BY

MICHAEL SPAW

Although raytracing can produce excellent results, there are various issues you should consider when you use it in your MAX work. In this chapter, you'll find some hints on how to use MAX's new raytracing features in your 3D scenes. You'll also learn about some specific settings to create particular effects.

Note: *Because raytracing is computationally intensive, the renderings in this chapter's tutorials may require that you exercise a little patience for the final results—especially if you have a slower computer. Example renderings are included in the \CHAP_10\FIGURES directory of this book's companion CD-ROM.*

Raytracing has long been considered the pinnacle of 3D rendering technology. Even though scanline renderers, such as Pixar's Photorealistic Renderman, are capable of completely believable results, true raytracing can produce extraordinary renderings and create "hyper-realistic" reflections and refractions on shiny, translucent, or transparent surfaces.

Although 3D Studio/DOS (versions 1 through 4) and 3D Studio MAX R1 have relied on native scanline rendering, 3D Studio MAX Release 2.5 has incorporated selective ray-traced rendering. Developed by special-effects house Blur Studio, of Venice, California, the raytracer works on either a material or map basis. This selective raytracing enables you to apply raytracing rendering to objects that specifically need it and use more conventional scanline rendering for the rest of your 3D scene.

Raytracing: A Little History

Raytracing as a rendering method originated in the 3D graphic research labs in the early 1980s. It has worked its way into commercial 3D software—first on high-end workstation platforms, then on to less-expensive desktop computers.

Raytracing works by calculating, or "tracing," the path that your light would take through your 3D scene. In the real world, a light source—both natural, like the sun, or artificial—emits light, which then propagates throughout an environment, either outdoors or indoors. The light strikes surfaces, where it's reflected or absorbed until it finally reaches your eye. (That is, if you're standing around to see it—sort of a variation of the "tree falling in the forest" question, I suppose.)

Raytracing generally works in the opposite direction—that is, a 3D program traces light by starting out at a particular pixel and working its way through the scene until it reaches the light source. Raytracing works in this apparently backward manner because it would take an unbelievably large number of rays cast from the light to eventually strike the image plane that makes up the final image. By working from the image plane to the light, the program can guarantee that each ray that is calculated will count toward the final image. As the rays travel through the scene, they gather information about the color, reflectivity, refractivity, and intensity of the surfaces they strike. The program then combines this information to form an image of where the light has been. It can take quite a while to calculate this path, especially if the scene is complex. For this reason, ray-traced renderings are almost always slower than standard scanline renderings of the same scene. However, the resultant ray-traced image can contain accurate reflections and refractions that cannot be easily achieved any other way.

Introducing MAX Raytracing

Most of us have been waiting so long for a built-in raytracer in 3D Studio/DOS or MAX that, now that we have one, we're willing to throw caution to the wind and use raytracing for every object in our scenes. However, before we all go crazy with this new tool, it's important to take an objective look at what it can really do for us.

With raytracing, two things—reflections and refractions—can be reproduced with excellent results. When you are re-creating the look of polished chrome or a wineglass from a standard material, almost no amount of tweaking will beat the look of raytracing.

The reflections generated by MAX's Raytrace map and Raytrace material are more accurate than those created by using the Reflect/Refract map. Raytracing also allows you to generate reflections in surfaces where neither Flat Mirror nor Reflect/Refract maps will work. It is also possible to use raytracing to create multiple reflections within an object's surface (something that you can't do using Reflect/Refract maps). All of these abilities come at a price. It is typically much slower to render objects with raytracing than it is when you use other techniques. Even so, depending on the complexity of the scene and the relative size of the objects in the view, raytracing in MAX Release 2.5 can be less of a speed hit than you would think.

Reflections

When you use raytracing to capture the reflective qualities of a surface, it's often more important to consider what the surface reflects than the surface

In the Beginning...

At first, 3D computer graphics artists thought raytracing was the perfect solution for creating realistic imagery. This was mainly because of its ability to reproduce accurate reflections and refractions in materials like glass and metals. However, the computational cost limited the use of raytracing in most production animation environments; thus, it was reserved for stills and short animation experiments. Oddly enough, another problem with raytracing is often the ultrarealistic look it provides. Although it can produce physically correct reflections and refractions for ideal surfaces, the result is sometimes "too perfect," leading to a cold, sterile look. What's often missing are the imperfect reflections and blurring caused by irregularities in the surfaces of most objects. Very few real-world surfaces are perfectly reflective, like a mirror. You should take these considerations into account when you do your 3D renderings.

itself. This is especially true when you are creating polished metal materials. Chrome is a perfect example of a surface defined by what it reflects.

To take a look at a ray-traced chrome material, select File|View File in MAX, and click on TEAPOT1.TIF in the \CHAP_10 directory of this book's companion CD-ROM. This image is also shown in Figure 10.1.

Figure 10.1 The look of this metal teapot is determined almost completely by its surroundings.

The material on this teapot is called RT Polished Chrome; it's included in the MAXFX2.MAT Material Library. In a moment, you'll load this teapot scene and create your own ray-traced chrome material.

Refractions

The second real strength of raytracing is its ability to replicate the look of transparent materials. When light passes through a transparent surface, the light is typically bent or distorted. This distortion is known as *refraction*, and the amount of refraction is known as the *index of refraction* (IOR). The IOR results from the relative speed of light as it passes through a transparent material relative to the medium the viewer is in. Often, the more dense the object, the higher the IOR will be.

At 1.0, the approximate IOR of air, the object behind a transparent object does not distort. At 1.5, the object behind distorts greatly, like a glass marble. At an IOR slightly less than 1.0, the object reflects along its edges, like an air bubble seen from underwater.

Table 10.1 includes indexes of refraction for several common transparent materials. You can use these settings to simulate a particular material correctly, or you can use them as a starting point for materials of your own.

Table 10.1   Index of refraction.

Material	IOR
Air (at STP)	1.0003
Water	1.33
Ethyl alcohol	1.36
Glass	1.50
Lucite or Plexiglas	1.51
Crown glass	1.52
Sodium chloride (salt)	1.53
Quartz	1.544
Flint glass	1.58
Diamond	2.42

An example of how various refraction indexes change the look of transparent materials is shown in the following scene:

1. In 3D Studio MAX Release 2.5, reset Max and load IOR.MAX from the \CHAP_10 directory of the companion CD-ROM. You'll see a simple scene consisting of five spheres sitting on a striped floor.

2. Activate the Camera01 viewport and render the scene; your rendering should look like Figure 10.2.

3. To see the materials for the five spheres and how they differ, open the Material Editor and examine the IOR settings for each of the ray-traced materials. (Note that these materials are all saved in the MAXFX2.MAT Material Library on this book's companion CD-ROM.)

4. Hide all but one of the spheres, change the refractive index on one of the materials, and apply it to the sphere. Then, create your own test renderings and check the results.

The Raytrace Map And Raytrace Material

As mentioned at the beginning of this chapter, MAX Release 2.5's raytracing is selective—rather than raytrace the entire scene, you only

Figure 10.2 Here are several spheres, all with differing indexes of refraction. From left to right, the materials are underwater (IOR: 0.7), hot air (IOR: 0.98), water (IOR: 1.33), glass (IOR: 1.5), and diamond (IOR: 2.42).

need to apply a ray-traced map or material to the objects in your scene that require physically correct reflections and refractions.

MAX Release 2.5's raytracing features also enable you to select the objects in the scene that will and will not be "seen" (either locally or globally) by the raytracer. This selectivity is a substantial time-saver when you're rendering complex scenes. Finally, both the Raytrace map and Raytrace material give you a great deal of control over the depth to which the surface will be traced (i.e., the number of reflections) and the amount of anti-aliasing that will be used.

You may be wondering, why does MAX Release 2.5 have both a Raytrace map and a Raytrace material type? Simple—if you have both, you'll have a great deal of flexibility when you're tweaking your final renderings.

The Raytrace map provides an easy way to integrate either ray-traced reflections or refractions into a material you've already created or a preexisting one you're modifying. This is the easiest way to get ray-traced effects on your objects—you simply load the Raytrace map as you would any other map type.

If you have a metal or glass material in your Material Library that you'd like to use in your scene, just add the Raytrace map to the Reflections and/or Refractions map slot in the material. (For special effects, you can place the Raytrace map in material slots other than Reflection or Refraction, which I'll discuss later in this chapter.) The biggest plus to using the Raytrace map is that it usually renders more quickly than the Raytrace material.

The Raytrace material is a new material type, and it enables you to create accurate reflections and refractions for objects in your scenes. Unlike the Raytrace map, the Raytrace material gives you the ability to create translucency, fluorescence, and other special effects in your scene.

The Tabletop

Now that you've learned the basics of MAX Release 2.5's Raytrace material and map types, you'll load a simple scene and experiment with the material settings. After you work through this tutorial, you may want to play with the materials in the scene to become more familiar with the new raytracer's possibilities. You'll start out by using both the Raytrace map and material in a simple MAX scene:

1. Select File|Load File (or press Ctrl+O), and load TABLETOP.MAX from the \CHAP_10 directory of this book's companion CD-ROM. You'll see a small tabletop set up inside a room.

For those of you who started out with 3D Studio/DOS, this scene should look vaguely familiar. It's an homage to Jack Powell's original 3D Studio/DOS modeling tutorial, in which you created a tabletop, wine goblet, and covered serving tray. Here, I've replaced the serving tray with the ubiquitous rendering teapot. This scene provides a good environment in which to try out various settings with both the Raytrace map and Raytrace material.

2. Activate the Camera01 viewport and render the scene; your rendering should look like Figure 10.3.

Now, you'll make some improvements to the materials in the scene. To start out, you'll create a chrome material for the teapot. Previously, if you wanted to create materials that re-created the look of chrome, you would use either Automatic Reflection mapping or a standard Reflection map. Although this type of "cheat" is fine for many scenes and objects, the resultant reflections are not physically correct and, in some cases, simply look wrong. For example, automatic reflection maps can work well for curved surfaces, but often fall apart when there's a combination of curves and flat areas. Moreover, both of these mapping types fail to capture reflections within reflections. The Raytrace map can solve these limitations.

> **Note:** The Raytrace map and Raytrace material share the same raytracer rendering code and Global Parameters settings. It's important to keep this in mind when you're modifying any of the global parameters because all of the materials in the scene will be affected. If you need to change the parameters for ray-traced anti-aliasing, raytrace depth, and blurring, you'll most likely want to change them at the Local Parameters level.

Figure 10.3 Here you see the tabletop with all standard materials in place. Note that, at this point, raytracing hasn't been applied to any of the materials.

3. Open the Material Editor and click on the Polished Chrome material in Material Slot #1. Open the Maps rollout and scroll down to the Reflection Map slot. Currently there is a Reflect/Refract map in place. To make this material more realistic, change it to a Raytrace map.

4. Click on the Reflection Map button, select New, and choose Raytrace from the Material/Map Browser. When the Replace Map dialog appears, click on OK to discard the old map. Click on the Go To Parent icon to return to the main Polished Chrome Standard material rollout.

5. Next, activate the Camera01 viewport and rerender the scene to see the change in the teapot's reflection. Your rendering should look like Figure 10.4.

One of the first things you'll notice is that the reflection is more realistic—you can see the reflection of the knob on the teapot lid in the rest of the lid, for example. The base of the teapot also reflects the table correctly, unlike the earlier example with the Reflect/Refract map. Now that the teapot is done, it's time to move on to the goblet.

6. In the Material Editor, click on the Polished Gold material in the second material slot. Open the Maps rollout and go to the Reflection Map slot.

Figure 10.4   With the use of the Raytrace map, the teapot correctly reflects its surroundings.

Like the material for the teapot, there's a Reflect/Refract map in the Reflection Map slot. To make this material more realistic, you'll change it to use a Raytrace map.

7. Click on the Reflection Map button and choose Raytrace from the Material/Map Browser. When the Replace Map dialog appears, click on OK.

8. Look a little closer at the settings for the Raytrace map. There are the Trace Mode options in the Raytracer Parameters, in the Material Editor rollup. These radio buttons tell the raytracer whether the rays should reflect or refract the scene. As long as you use the Raytrace map in either the Reflection or Refraction Map slots, the Raytrace map should know how it is being applied. (There is one exception—when you use a strong Bump map, you should not use the Auto Detect option; instead, select either reflection or refraction.)

9. Click on the Global Parameters button to display the Global Raytracer Settings dialog box.

The Global Raytracer Settings dialog box gives you a great deal of control over how the raytracer will render the ray-traced objects in the scene. It controls the reflection recursion level, Global anti-aliasing, and renderer acceleration. By familiarizing yourself with the various controls, you can sometimes decrease the amount of time the renderer will take to raytrace materials within the scene. For example, you can do a few things now to speed up your final renderings.

10. Under Ray Depth Control, you'll see the Maximum Depth is set to 9. The Recursion depth tells the renderer how many levels deep the reflections should extend. If two or more reflective surfaces reflect one another, the reflections will continue to bounce back and forth in the surfaces. This is the "hall of mirrors" effect. By default, Maximum Depth is set to 9, but you often don't need this high of a recursion level. To speed up the rendering, set this value to 3.

11. Next, take a look at the Adaptive Antialiasing section. This controls how the raytracer applies anti-aliasing to the materials. Click on the checkbox next to Adaptive and change Max.Rays to 10. This will allow at most only 10 rays per pixel to be calculated for anti-aliasing. Then, click on the Close button and click on the Go To Parent icon to return to the main Polished Gold Standard material rollout.

12. Activate the Camera01 viewport and rerender the scene to see the change in the goblet's reflection and the teapot; your rendering should look like Figure 10.5.

Figure 10.5 The goblet now reflects its surroundings correctly, as well as the reflections in the teapot.

Like the teapot, the goblet is now reflecting its environment accurately. Some of the visible changes include the reflections captured inside the goblet and the reflection of the goblet itself in its base.

The glass ball sitting on the tabletop could also benefit from some raytracing. You could use the Raytrace map again for both the reflection and refraction, but here, you'll use the Raytrace material instead. To use the Raytrace material for the Glass Ball, you'll need to create a new material in the Material Editor.

13. The fourth material slot in the Material Editor currently contains the Glass Ball material as it is applied in the scene. To create the new Glass Ball material, click in Material Slot #5. Next, click on the Type: button to bring up the Material/Map Browser. Choose Raytrace from the Material/Map Browser, then click on OK. Finally, in the Name field, change the name of this material to RT New Glass.

14. At this point, the new Raytrace material looks much like the Standard material. Look at the Basic Parameters rollup. The first thing you'll do is change the material's Specular attributes. In the Specular Highlight section, change Shininess to 80 and Shininess Strength to 175. (Notice that the Raytrace material allows you to set this value above 100.) You'll see the material changes occur on the sample sphere in the RT New Glass slot.

15. Click on the color swatch box next to Transparency: Value to bring up the Color Selector. Set the Value to 255, or pure white. Notice how the material sample sphere is now transparent. The Raytrace material uses the value to control the material's opacity. Black makes the material opaque; white is fully transparent.

16. Next, you'll set the Diffuse color. Click on the color swatch next to Diffuse: Value and change the colors to RGB settings 0, 0, 255, or pure blue. You'll see that the sample sphere is still transparent. Reflection and transparency effects are layered on top of the Diffuse result. When Reflect or Transparency are pure white, the Diffuse color isn't visible.

17. To create the effect of colored glass, you'll need to do one more thing. Click on the Diffuse color slot and drag the saturated blue color to the Transparency slot. When the Copy Or Swap Colors dialog appears, select Copy. Now, in the material sample slot, you will see that the sample sphere looks like tinted glass.

Figure 10.6 The glass ball now correctly refracts and reflects its surroundings. (In your rendering, you'll also notice that it casts a colored shadow.)

18. The ball should also reflect its environment, so click on the color swatch next to Reflect: Value. Set the value to 30, then close the Color Selector.

19. Finally, you'll need to set the IOR for the material so that it will refract the scene as real glass does. Set the Index Of Refraction value to 1.5.

20. Select the glass ball in the scene and click on the Assign To Material Selection button (or drag this material to the glass ball).

21. Activate the Camera01 viewport and rerender the scene; your rendering should look like Figure 10.6.

As a final touch, you could change the Table material to use the Raytrace map to add subtle reflections (keep the level of reflection low).

Creating Raytraced Metals

One of the primary reasons you may want to use raytracing in MAX Release 2.5 is to produce accurate reflections in metal and other reflective materials. However, as I mentioned earlier, ray-traced reflections are often "perfect," and very few real-world surfaces, with the exception of mirrors and polished metal, are perfectly flat and reflective.

Most reflective materials have some degree of roughness to them. Small surface imperfections or grime on the surface of an object will blur out the reflection. Oily fingerprints on glass or the brushed aluminum of an auto wheel are good examples of this effect. By blurring the reflection slightly in a ray-traced material, you can add a great deal of realism to the surface.

In the following example file, I've created three ray-traced materials, each with different amounts of blur to its reflections. These differences in blurring create vastly different-looking surfaces. Now, you'll take a look at the materials for the three spheres and see how their settings differ:

1. In MAX Release 2.5, load SPHERES.MAX from the \CHAP_10 directory of the companion CD-ROM. You'll see three spheres inside a box environment.

2. Activate the Camera01 viewport and render the scene; your rendering should look like Figure 10.7.

Figure 10.7   Here are three metal spheres with differing amounts of blur in their reflectivity. The first sphere could represent polished steel. The second is less polished, and the third looks as if it's been sandblasted.

3. Open the Material Editor and click on the RT Polished Steel material in Slot #1. Notice that the material is not 100 percent reflective. You can see this by clicking on the Reflect color slot. It currently contains a Value setting of 180. Unless they're mirror-smooth, most metals will retain some of their diffuse color.

4. Notice that Shininess Strength is set to 130. MAX Release 2.5's Raytrace material allows you to set this value above 100, which creates very strong specular highlights. Finally, look at the Soften

parameter. This lets you soften and spread out the specular highlight, creating the look of a more matte surface.

5. Click on the second material slot, look at the RT Steel material and compare its settings with that of Material #1. Finally, click on Slot #3 and compare the RT Sandblast Steel material to the previous two. The main changes between the three materials are in the appearance of their specular highlights. As the surface becomes more matte and less reflective, the highlights become broader and softer.

6. Next, take a look at what really makes the reflections appear differently between the three materials. Click once again on the RT Polished Steel material and open the Raytracer Controls rollup. In the middle of the rollup is a checkbox that enables you to override the global settings, which allows you to modify each Raytrace material or map to meet specific anti-aliasing or Blur/Defocus needs. The Blur/Defocus parameters enable you to change the reflection blurring of the three materials. For the RT Polished Steel material, I've used the default settings.

7. Click on the RT Steel material and examine the Blur/Defocus settings. You'll see that Blur Offset is increased to 5.0. This new setting softens the reflection and gives the appearance of a less-polished surface.

8. Click on the RT Sandblast Steel material. Blur/Defocus is set to 10.0, which softens the reflections further. Note that you can also use the Blur/Defocus parameter to eliminate aliasing in reflections or refractions. If you see aliasing in these areas in your renderings, increase the Blur/Defocus value in small increments until you get the effect you want.

9. Note that the Blur Aspect parameter has also been changed for the RT Sandblast Steel material. When the reflection is blurred by a large amount, you may need to change the Blur Aspect parameter to change the shape of the blurring. As MAX Release 2.5's online documentation notes, "If you see aliasing that occurs mostly along horizontal lines, try increasing Blur Aspect to 1.5. This changes the shape of the blurred effect. The reverse is also true. If aliasing occurs mostly along vertical lines, try decreasing Blur Aspect to 0.5."

10. Finally, look at the parameters in the Adaptive Control area of the rollup (I've changed them for the last two materials). When Adaptive has been checked, it allows you to set the initial and maximum number of rays that will be sampled for each pixel. The greater the number of rays cast, the better each pixel will be anti-aliased against its neighbors. Generally, the default settings are adequate, but in the case of very blurry reflections, the number of rays may need to be increased.

11. Look at the Initial Rays and Max Rays settings for all three materials and compare the settings. (Although blurring the reflection can add realism to some materials, it's important to note that it can also add considerably to your rendering time.)

The Lantern Scene: Translucency

One material effect that's been difficult to render properly in MAX (until now) is true translucency. Translucent materials permit light to pass through but diffuse it so that an object on the other side is not clearly visible. Frosted glass, rice paper, and candle wax all show this effect. Another result of

Figure 10.8   This image shows how a semitransparent ray-traced material with a light inside the object looks when rendered without the use of translucency. Notice that the glass does not appear to be lit from within.

this effect is that shadows cast on a translucent surface from the back will be visible from the front.

To see an example of translucency in action, you'll take a look at frosted glass in a lamp:

1. Load LAMP.MAX from the \CHAP_10 directory of the companion CD-ROM. You'll see a cylindrical lamp sitting on a flat surface.

2. Activate the Camera01 viewport and render the scene. Your rendering should look like Figure 10.8. (Note that in this file, I've turned off anti-aliasing to speed up the render time.)

3. Now, take a look at how the material for the lamp is set up. Open the Material Editor and click on the RT Frosted Glass material in Slot #1. In the Basic Parameters rollup, you'll see that the material is set up to replicate a semi-transparent, matte-finished surface. The Diffuse color is off-white to help convey the warmth of the light from the lamp. The Transparency: value is set to 210 so that the glass is only partially transparent. I've set the IOR value to less than that of glass (perhaps it's plastic). Finally, the Shininess and Shininess Strength values provide a soft specular highlight.

4. Open the Extended Parameters rollup. At the top of the rollup is the section for Special effects. In the center of the effects section are the Translucency controls. The controls consist of a color swatch box and a map slot button.

5. Click on the Color box next to Translucency. When the Color Selector appears, change the RGB values to 243, 243, 219. As you modify the color, you'll notice that the material sample window displays the changes.

Figure 10.9 Now the frosted glass looks as if it's diffusing the light from within the lamp.

6. Activate the Camera01 viewport and rerender the scene. Your rendering should look like Figure 10.9.

As your rendering shows, the translucency effect can add a lot to the realism of semitransparent materials.

When you re-create these types of (Standard) materials with the new Raytrace material, make sure you set up the rest of the parameters for the material to reproduce the desired look before you play with the translucency. This is important because adding translucency may have the tendency to hide some of the subtlety of the material's Specular component.

To further explore the effects of translucency, set up a translucent glass block lit from behind. Place a second object between the light and the block to cast a shadow onto the block to see the effect's shadow-catching ability. You can also play with the color of the translucency or use a map to mask

the effect to replicate the look of sandblasted or acid-etched art glass.

Other Cool Effects

By now you've seen the advantages of using raytracing for creating reflections and refraction. As if basic raytracing wasn't enough, there are other options in the Raytrace material that can help you create specific effects. In many cases, these techniques don't require the use of either the reflection or refraction capabilities of the material, which decreases the time it takes to render them.

Rubber

You can create a subtle but cool surface effect with the Raytrace material's Soften parameter, which lets you soften the specular highlights that are visible on the material.

In Standard materials, the Soften feature helps soften specular highlights when they're seen at glancing angles on the surface of your objects. However, unlike the Standard Soften feature, which has values that range from 0.00 to 1.00, you can set Soften in the Raytrace material to values larger than 1.00. If you create a Raytrace material with a very large soft highlight, it can give the material a semimatte appearance, much like that of a rubber ball. To see an example of this effect, follow these steps:

1. Load RUBBER.MAX from the \CHAP_10 directory of the companion CD-ROM. When the scene appears, activate the Camera01 viewport and render it. The resulting image should look like Figure 10.10.

Figure 10.10   The ball has a ray-traced material; with the Soften setting set above 1, the ball takes on a rubbery appearance.

2. Take a look at the Material settings for the ball's material. Open the Material Editor and click on the Rubber Ball material in the first material slot. Unlike the previous examples of the Raytrace material, the Rubber Ball material uses neither the Reflection nor the Refraction properties typically associated with ray-traced renderings.

3. Next, look at the Soften parameter in the Specular Highlight section of the Basic Parameters rollup. Currently, Soften is set to 2.5, which gives the ball its soft, matte appearance.

4. To see how Soften can change the appearance of the Specular highlight, change the setting to 2.0, 1.5, and then 1.0, and render each setting.

Fluorescence

Fluorescence is an effect often associated with 1960's and 1970's psychedelic posters and roller-skating rinks. Technically, fluorescence is the emission of radiation, especially visible light, from a material when it is exposed to external radiation. More importantly for us, this new MAX Raytrace material effect can simulate the look of commercial fluorescent paints and black light. It can be used to imitate phosphorescent pigments of certain animals, like deep-sea fish.

To accomplish this effect, the Raytrace material uses the lights within your MAX scene, regardless of their color, to illuminate the material as if it were lit by purely white light. The material appears to glow by itself. The effect is especially apparent when the lights in the environment are colored very differently than the color of the fluorescent material. The effect also uses a Bias to increase or decrease the influence of the lights.

As the MAX Online Help feature notes, "At 0.5, the Bias makes Fluorescence behave just like diffuse coloring. Bias values higher than 0.5 increase the fluorescent effect, making the object brighter than other objects in the scene. Bias values lower than 0.5 make the object dimmer than other objects in the scene." To see an example of Fluorescence in action, follow these steps:

1. Load FLUORESC.MAX from the \CHAP_10 directory of the companion CD-ROM. The scene contains a watch body within a gray room environment. Activate the Camera01 viewport and render the scene. The resulting image should look like Figure 10.11.

2. Next, look at the Material settings for the watch hands. Open the Material Editor and click on the Fluorescent Green material in Slot #1. Open the Basic Parameters rollup and take a look at the settings. Currently, the material has a soft specular highlight and no added Luminosity value.

3. To make the material appear to fluoresce, you'll need to modify the Fluorescence value. Open the Extended Parameters rollout. The Fluorescence color swatch box is under Special Effects. By simply setting the Fluorescence value to the same value as the Diffuse color, you can give the watch hands an appropriately colored glow.

4. Click on the Diffuse color swatch and drag it to the Fluorescence color swatch; you'll see the sample material slot change to reflect the new effect.

5. To make the effect brighter than the environment, set the Fluorescence Bias value to 1.0. If you want, close the Material Editor.

Figure 10.11   The watch hands on this model could benefit from the Fluorescence effect in the Raytrace material. (I've hidden the watch's crystal, which has a ray-traced glass material, to speed up rendering times.)

6. Finally, drag the Time Slider to frame 100; you'll notice that the lighting dims. (I animated the light value settings in this file.) As with most Fluorescent materials, you can see the effect better when the surrounding environment is darkened.

7. Activate the Camera01 viewport and rerender the scene; your rendering should look like Figure 10.12.

Figure 10.12   The watch hands appear to glow (bright green, in your rendering) regardless of the blue color present in the room light.

RAYTRACING TIPS AND TRICKS

Here are some suggestions for getting more out of the new raytracer:

- Turn off anti-aliasing in the Global Options dialog when you're first designing ray-traced materials. This will save you a great deal of time when you're waiting for the final result and you're still tweaking the materials' appearance.

- As you look around your real-world environment a little closer, you'll notice that many surfaces are slightly reflective. You can increase the realism of a surface by adding a small bit of reflectivity to it. However, make sure the reflectivity is generally less than 5 percent for most nonmetals. Higher values look interesting, but they aren't realistic.

- To help speed up rendering times with the raytracer, make sure you've welded the cores of Lathed objects. You should also check to make sure your objects' faces have unified normals and that the objects aren't degenerate, that is, have missing faces, overlapping vertices, and so on.

- If you don't need to keep the modifier stack for your ray-traced objects, collapse them into Editable Meshes before rendering your scene.

In addition to these suggestions, here are some additional tips from animator Greg Tsadilas, who produced excellent MAX work at Blur Studio. (As mentioned earlier, Blur developed the raytracing code that ships with MAX Release 2.5 and has used it in film and TV productions.)

- If Object #1 is inside transparent Object #2 (which uses the Raytrace material), Object #1 will have its Material ID passed through to Video Post filters. So now, you can have an object glow inside another object.

- As mentioned earlier, Shininess Strength is not clamped in the Raytrace material. This means you can crank it up to 100, 200, 500, 1000...whatever! This lets you create very "hot" specular hightlights, and it works great for creating metallic materials.

- Under Globals, you'll find that the default setting for Maximum Depth is 9. That's overkill for most basic scenes. Unless you want a "hall of mirrors" effect in reflective objects that are also reflecting each other, a setting of 2 or 3 is usually sufficient, and much faster.

- Many people seldom use the Manual Acceleration settings under Globals. Depending on your scene, you can decrease your render time by using Single or Dual pipeline. I usually start by using Single in complex scenes; if necessary, I'll try switching to Dual. One of them usually decreases render time significantly.

- Here's a fun trick to try. Let's say you want your Raytrace Material object to reflect the background (or more correctly, a plane with an image that's acting as your background mapped to it), but you don't want the plane with the image to appear in the render. For the solution, follow these steps:

  1. Create a duplicate plane that's in front of the one with the image mapped to it. (Actually, it just needs to be between the camera and the image-mapped plane.)

  2. Assign this plane a Shadow/Matte material.

  3. Exclude this Shadow/Matte plane from the Global Exclude list in the Raytrace material.

The final effect is that your objects will reflect the image that's mapped onto the plane, but the plane itself will not be rendered because it's hidden by the Shadow/Matte plane. Naturally, this works if you want to reflect any object but still exclude it from the final rendered image.

Information courtesy of Michael Spaw, Phillip Miller (Kinetix), and Greg Tsadilas.

Figure 10.13   Each of the three spheres is filled with differing densities of self-illuminated fog.

Fog

You can also use the Raytrace material to simulate the look of fog within an object. This effect is much like having a volume light inside the surface; as the MAX Online Help states, Fog "is a thickness-based effect. It fills the object with a fog that is both opaque and self illuminated." To see an example of this effect, follow these steps:

1. Load FOG.MAX from the \CHAP_10 directory of the companion CD-ROM. When the scene appears, render the Camera01 view. The resulting image should look like Figure 10.13.

2. Now, you'll take a look at how the materials for the three spheres differ. Open the Material Editor and click on the Full Fog material in the first material slot. Open the Extended Parameters rollup; in the Advanced Transparency section you'll see that the Fog box is checked. This enables the fog to be rendered in transparent materials.

The Start and End controls modify how the fog appears within a material based on the object's overall size. Start sets the position within the object where the fog begins to appear. End sets the location within the object where the fog reaches its full Amount value. The Amount value sets the fog's overall density. In addition to controlling the color of the fog, you can use a map to modify its appearance.

3. Take a look at the next two materials and compare their Fog settings. The Medium Fog material has a higher End value, giving the fog a less-dense appearance. The Light Fog material has an even higher End value, further decreasing its density at the sphere's edge. It also has the Fog Amount value decreased to 0.8, lessening the overall density possible.

Moving On

Now that you've learned some of the basics of raytracing, I hope you'll be able to use this new and exciting MAX feature in interesting ways. (Just don't go overboard with chrome spheres sitting on checkerboard floors—and for heaven's sake, keep those scenes off your MAX demo reel!)

This chapter concludes this book's look at MAX Release 2.5's new material capabilities. In the next section, you'll explore modeling (both polygonal and NURBS), object modifiers, and space warps.

PART II

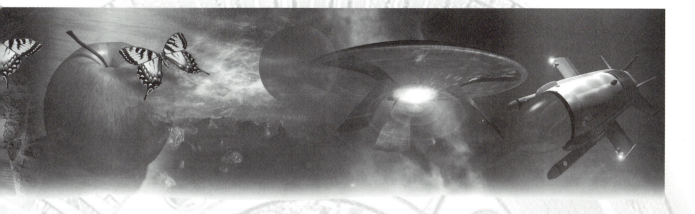

MODELING
TECHNIQUES

MODELING AND MODIFIERS

11

In this section, you'll begin to learn about modeling effects: both traditional polygonal modeling and MAX Release 2.5's powerful new NURBS implementation. In addition, you'll see how to use some of Release 2.5's wide array of object modifiers to modify your geometry.

In the last section, you saw how to use MAX's powerful Material Editor to create a wide variety of surface textures—from glossy metal and ray-traced glass to water and physical properties.

In this chapter, you'll see how to use Release 2.5's new renderable splines and a Noise modifier to create a simple, fun lightning effect. You'll then take a quick look at MeshSmooth and how it can change a blocky "paw" into a realistic human hand. You'll see how you can use Release 2.5's new Connect Compound Object option to attach the blocky hand seamlessly to an arm and turn them into realistic appendages.

Then, in Chapter 12, you'll concentrate on MAX's new Compound Scatter Object feature. With it, you'll create an entire scene of a desolate, deep-space planetary surface. Then, you'll see how you can use a QuadPatch, FFD deformation, Noise, and MAX's Top/Bottom material to create a snow-capped mountain range.

Thunder And Lightning

In the original 1933 Universal film *Frankenstein*, propbuilder Kenneth Strickfaden constructed a wide array of weird electrical machinery to bring life to Frankenstein's monster. Many of the devices used Tesla coils and bare wire terminals to show crackling electrical arcs coursing through the air. (The machinery used in the film survived for decades; it appeared in numerous other Universal productions and even made an appearance in Mel Brooks's 1973 film *Young Frankenstein*.)

For this chapter's first (simple) effect, you're going to duplicate the bare electric arcs seen in *Frankenstein* to create a "Jacob's ladder"—an electrical arc that travels repeatedly up the terminals of a piece of "Frankensteinian" lab equipment. You'll use Release 2.5's new renderable splines, a Noise modifier, and a little bit of Track View tweaking. To begin, follow these steps:

1. Load MAX, or save your current work and reset the program.

2. Load FRANKSTN.MAX from the \CHAP_11 directory of your companion CD-ROM. Your screen should look like Figure 11.1.

This simple scene consists of a table with a piece of Kenneth-Strickfaden-inspired equipment on it—a pseudo-1930s-style electrical generator with bare terminals on top. A rocky wall (a QuadPatch with Noise applied) serves as a backdrop; note that for this scene and the figures, the wall is being displayed in Box mode. Several spotlights

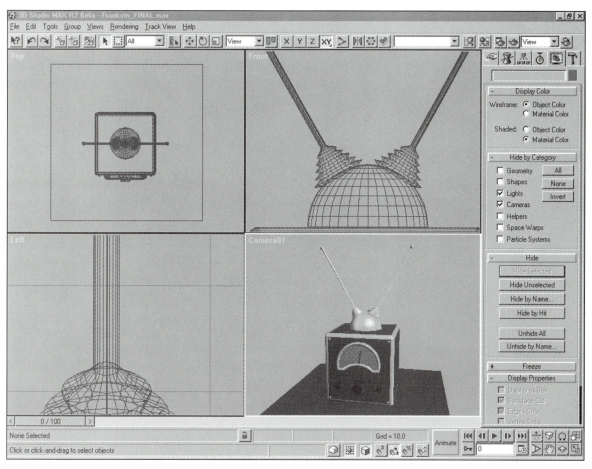

Figure 11.1 The test model and scene for the "Jacob's Ladder" effect.

provide moody, theatrical illumination; a garish green spot provides primary lighting, and blue fill spots highlight the geometry edges.

You're going to create an animated spline that travels constantly from the bottom of the terminals to the top, disappears, and then repeats. You'll then add a Glow effect to the spline to give it extra energy.

   3. Activate the Front viewport and zoom in on the top of the terminal box until you can see just above the capacitors at the base of the terminal wires, as shown in Figure 11.2. (If you want, enlarge the viewport to full screen by pressing the W key, or the Min/Max Toggle icon.)

   4. Select Create|Shapes|Splines from the Command Panel and select Line. In the center of the Front viewport, click in the middle of the left wire terminal (just above the capacitor) to place the first vertex of the line.

   5. Next, draw a horizontal line from the middle of the left terminal to the right terminal, left-clicking repeatedly (about 20 to 30 times) to place vertices along the length of the spline, as shown in Figure 11.3.

The spline should have a large vertex count so that the Noise modifier (which you'll apply in a moment) can distort the spline into a jagged electrical arc. If you want, you can draw a rough, jagged lightning shape as you create the spline, but it's

THE AUTHOR TELLS A WEIRD SHORT STORY

Now, here's a bit of weird, useless (but interesting) trivia: It's appropriate that I present a "Frankenstein-style" effect...

...because I'm related personally to the Frankenstein family.

Seriously.

My wife, Joan Gale Frank, had grandparents who were immigrants: Her mother's grandparents came from a small village in Ukraine; her father's father came from London (and his family was originally from Austria and Poland).

When Archibald, Joan's grandfather on her dad's side, left London and came to the United States in 1910 (23 years before the premiere of the Universal film), an official at New York's Ellis Island Immigration Station suggested that he shorten his name to Frank...

...from Frankenstein.

My wife keeps her maiden name—Frank—but jokes occasionally about changing it back to her family's real name...

...which I guess would make me The Husband of Frankenstein.

not really necessary. The Noise modifier will impart an undulating movement to the vertices of the spline, but if you want exaggerated "cartoony" lightning, then make the spline as "scratchy" as you want.

6. Change the name of Line01 to Lightning, click on Renderable under General Parameters|Rendering, and change Thickness to 0.5. This is another of Release 2.5's new features—with a simple button click, you can turn 2D splines into renderable objects of varying thickness and activate mapping coordinates for them.

7. In the Modify panel, apply an Edit Spline modifier. Sub-object: Vertex is selected as the default, so draw a selection box around all the vertices of the Lightning spline and then right-click over the selected vertices to bring up the Properties menu. Change the vertex type from Bezier to Smooth. This will help make the entire lightning spline undulate smoothly as it travels up the wire terminals.

Snap, Crackle, Pop

Now it's time to make the spline into a lightning bolt:

1. Use the Zoom and Pan features to center only the terminals in the Front viewport, then turn off the Edit Spline Sub-Object: Vertex selection level.

2. In the Modify panel, apply an XForm modifier to the entire spline. You'll use the XForm modifier to both move and scale the spline along its Y axis. (If you simply try to use Non-uniform Scale on just the spline, without the XForm modifier applied, you'll get a nasty warning that the Non-uniform scaling will be applied after all the transforms in the stack, which is a no-no. Don't do it.)

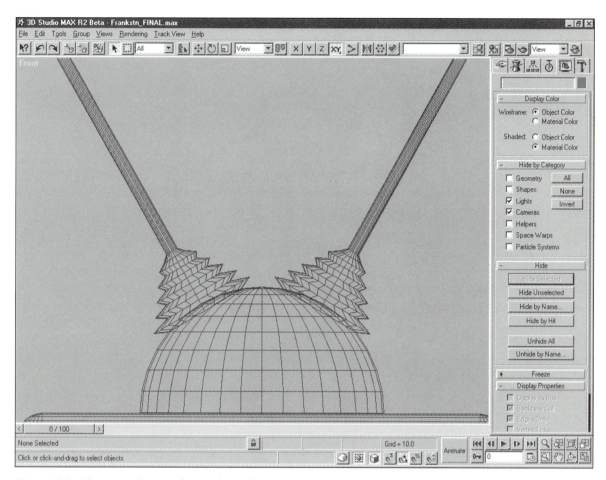

Figure 11.2   The starting location for the electrical arcs.

3. Turn on the Animate button, go to frame 20, and move the Lightning spline on the Y axis until it's just below the knobs at the ends of the terminals. (You may want to click on the Restrict To Y Axis icon to keep the spline centered between the two terminals.)

4. Click and hold on the Scale icon to open the Scale flyout and choose the Select And Non-uniform Scale icon. Select Restrict Axis To X, then scale the spline along the X axis until its end vertices are centered again in the wire terminals, just below the "knobs," as shown in Figure 11.4.

5. Drag the Time slider back to 0; you should see the Lightning spline move down and scale itself back to its starting point just above the capacitors.

6. Turn off the Animate button, then use Region Zoom to zoom in close to the spline and base of the terminals again (as you did

Note: *To center the spline properly between the terminals, you may have to alternate between moving and scaling the spline on the X axis.*

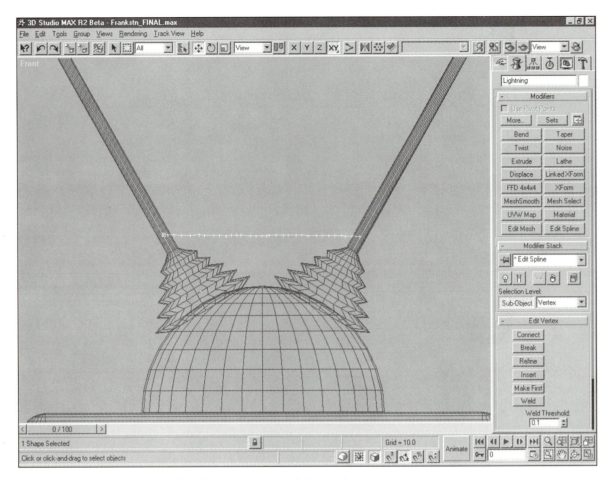

Figure 11.3 A complex spline with multiple vertices arrayed along its length.

earlier). From the Modify panel, apply another Edit Spline modifier. As you do, you should see all the vertices along the spline selected.

7. Click in the Front viewport outside the spline to deselect all the vertices, then draw a selection box around every vertex except for the first and last, as shown in Figure 11.5.

8. Select Noise from the Modify panel to apply it to the selected vertices. Under Parameters, change Scale to 10, click in the Fractal checkbox, then turn Strength on the X, Y, and Z axes to 10.0 on each. Finally, click in the Animate Noise checkbox. As you can see on your screen, the Noise Modifier distorts the selected vertices of the Lightning spline but leaves the end vertices untouched.

9. If you zoom back somewhat so you can see the entire length of the terminals and then drag the Time slider to frame 100, you'll see the Lightning spline travel up the terminals to the top. It then stops at frame 20, and the Noise modifier continues to make the stationary spline dance around throughout the animation.

10. Finally, you'll need to make sure the Lightning spline doesn't cast shadows on the back wall, so right-click on the selected spline to bring up the Properties menu, turn off Shadow Casting, and click on OK.

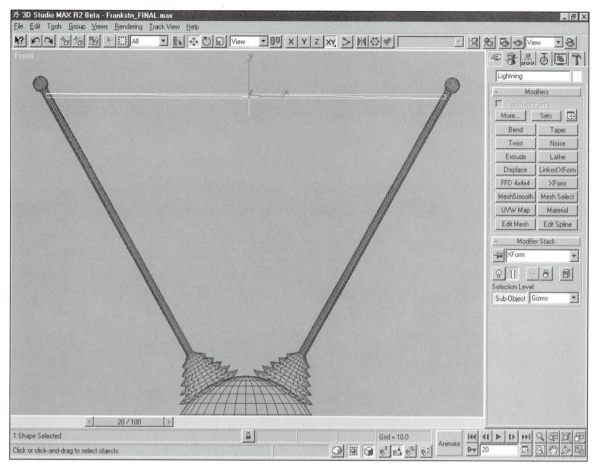

Figure 11.4 The topmost position for the Lightning spline cycle.

Making Lightning Strike Twice

To make the spline travel repeatedly up the terminals every 20 frames, you need to cycle it in Track View:

1. With the Lightning spline selected, open Track View. Click on the Filters icon, click in Animated Tracks under Show Only, and click on OK.

2. When you return to the Track View menu, you'll see the Arrow indicator (inside the front dial) and the Lightning objects. (As you dragged the Time Slider back and forth, you may have seen the Arrow twitching back and forth, as if measuring fluctuating voltage. I simply set up random Rotation keys to produce the indicator's movement.)

3. Under Lightning, open Modified Object, then open all the tracks for Noise and Xform. Hold down the Control key, and under Xform/Gizmo, click on Position and Scale to select them.

4. Click on the Parameter Curve Out-Of-Range Types icon, and from this menu, click on the Out curves button under Cycle, as shown in Figure 11.6 (the figure shows the correct button just above the mouse cursor).

5. Close Track View and then click on the Play Animation button. In the Front viewport, you'll see the indicator needle flashing back and forth and the Lightning spline cycling repeatedly up the terminals.

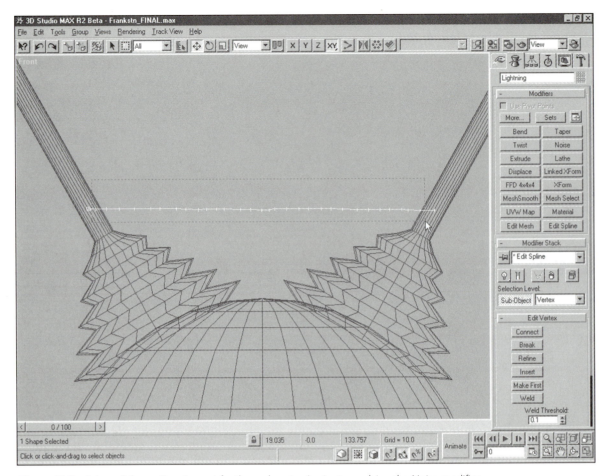

Figure 11.5 Select all the vertices (except for the end vertices) prior to applying the Noise modifier.

6. Turn off Play Animation and press the W key to return to the four viewports.

7. Bring up the Material Editor and assign a self-illuminated material to the Lightning spline—white, blue, yellow, or whatever color you want. Next, assign Material Effects Channel 1 to the Lightning spline, then close the Material Editor.

8. Open Video Post; you'll see that Camera01 is active in the queue. Click on the Add Image Filter Event icon, select Lens Effects Glow from the list, and click on the Lens Effects Glow Setup button. The Lens Effects Glow setup menu appears.

9. Click on the Preview button to display the Lens Effects Glow defaults, which are shown in the image window at the top of the menu. Click on the Properties tab, select Material ID under Source, and set it to 1. Click on the Preferences tab. Under Effect,

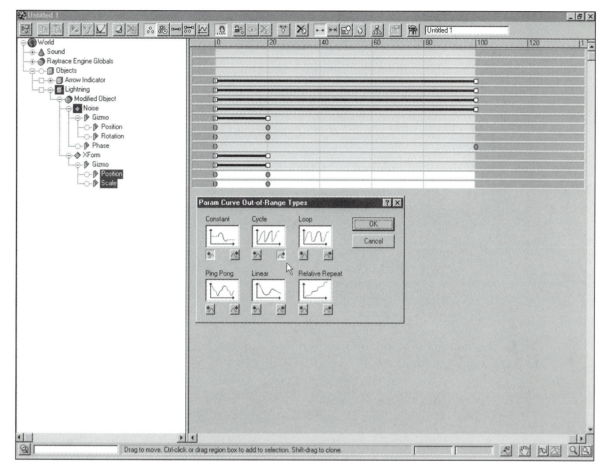

Figure 11.6 The Parameter Curve Out-Of-Range Types menu enables you to produce repeating values in your animations without copying multiple sets of keys.

change Size to 2.5; keep Intensity at 100.0. You'll see the Glow effect in the Preview window change to match the new settings.

10. Click on OK to return to the Video Post menu. Click on the Execute Sequence icon, select Single, change the frame number to 20, and render a 640×480 image of the scene. After a moment, the scene appears, then the Lens Effects Glow filter is calculated, and your rendering should look like Figure 11.7.

11. Close the Camera01 VFB window.

12. You can now render your own test animation of this sequence, or you can select File|View File and preview FRANKSTN.AVI in the \CHAP_11 directory of the companion CD-ROM.

As the animation shows, a glowing electrical arc travels up the terminals, snaps off, and then repeats.

Figure 11.7 The Lens Effects Glow filter imparts otherworldly energy to the lightning bolt.

There are other uses for this technique: By attaching dummy objects to the end vertices of a Lightning spline and then employing Linked Xform, you can animate lightning strikes from and to any point (you could use this to simulate futuristic energy weapons, for example). By adding renderable splines to the barrel of a laser cannon, you could simulate the projection of powerful energy bolts from the muzzle.

Finally, by animating the Noise gizmo itself (perhaps rotating it) and/or the Noise strength values, you can make the lightning effect as subtle or as outrageously frenetic as you want.

A Quick Look At MeshSmooth

Now that you've seen how to create a simple lightning effect, you'll examine some basics in MAX's Edit Mesh and MeshSmooth modifiers, and Face Extrude. With these MAX features, you can build complex industrial shapes, or even organic shapes, without having to use NURBS. (Of course, for certain types of complex modeling, NURBS are exactly what you need, as you'll see later on.)

For this chapter, you'll need to be fairly familiar with MAX's EditMesh modifier and how to build meshes by selecting and extruding faces. So, instead of completing a step-by-step tutorial on simple model building, you'll load some low-resolution, "blocky" models from the companion CD-ROM. You'll then apply MeshSmooth to them, tweak the settings, and check the results.

Give Yourself A Hand

MAX's MeshSmooth modifier rounds off blocky, hard-edged geometry into smoother forms. By applying different levels of smoothing to your object and adjusting the edge parameters, you can either create a flowing Henry Moore type of sculpture or simply add smoothed bevels to sharp corners.

For the first simple example, you'll see how MeshSmooth enables you to start from a parametric box and create a cartoon character hand. By applying MeshSmooth to it several times, you can smooth the blocky geometry into a rounded, organic form. To create the cartoon hand, follow these steps:

1. Save your current work and reset MAX. Load HAND.MAX from the \CHAP_11 directory of the companion CD-ROM. Your screen should look like Figure 11.8.

As your screen and Figure 11.8 indicate, this simple hand model looks as if it were assembled from a child's blocks. That's actually not too far off the mark; the hand began life as a parametric box primitive.

2. Select the hand model and go to the Modifier panel. Under Modifier Stack, you'll see Edit Mesh applied. Click on the Remove Modifier From Stack icon; you'll see the boxy hand revert to its original parametric box.

3. Click on the Undo icon; the box reverts to the hand object.

To create this hand, I first created a box primitive and applied an Edit Mesh modifier to it. I then selected specific faces and extruded them to create

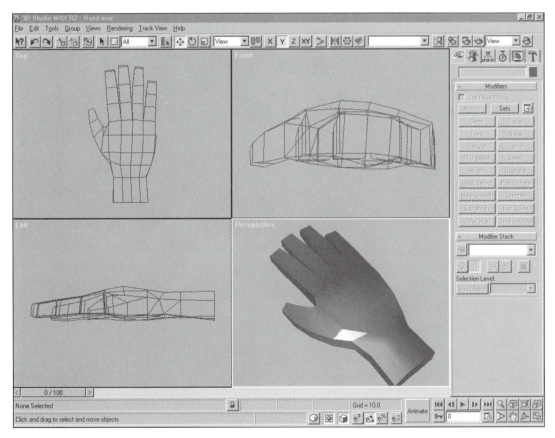

Figure 11.8 The initial hand model prior to applying MeshSmooth.

the fingers and thumb. With each extrude, the original box looked as if it were budding squared "boxes" off the initial shape. I alternated between selecting faces and selecting vertices; I then moved and welded the latter as necessary to produce the tapered fingers and the fleshy "web" of the thumb.

4. Click on Unhide All on the Display panel, then click on the Zoom Extents All icon. You'll see a succession of geometry to the left of the hand model, as shown in Figure 11.9.

5. Enlarge the Top viewport to full screen and take a look at the progression of geometry (from left to right) that leads up to the final hand model.

The progression of geometry is as follows:

- Box01 on the far left is the original parametric box primitive, as you saw when you removed the hand's Edit Mesh modifier in Step 2. If you select Box01 and examine it in the Modify panel, you'll

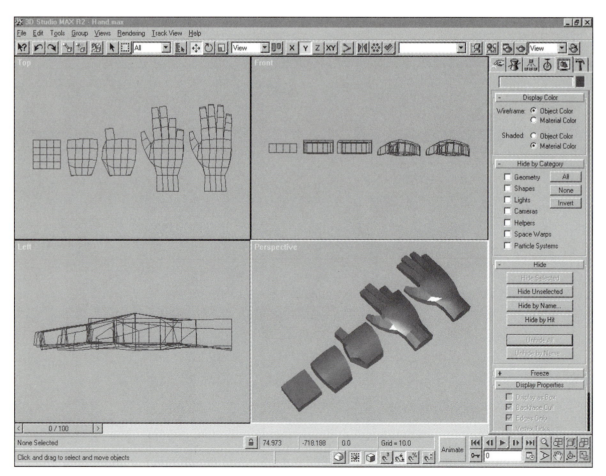

Figure 11.9 The basic progression of Edit Mesh (faces and vertices) used to build the rough hand geometry from the original box primitive.

see that it has a length and width of 100 units and a height of 30 units. The Length and Width Segments settings are both set to 4 to provide adequate cross sections for the initial hand shape. Height is set to 1; the MeshSmooth modifier will round off the hand sufficiently to obviate the need for additional "thickness" cross sections.

- Box02 shows the beginnings of "sculpting" as I applied an Edit Mesh modifier and began to move its vertices into a basic hand/palm shape.

- Box03 shows the effects of selecting faces as sub-objects and extruding them to form the base of the thumb and the index finger. You also see how certain vertices for the thumb base have been welded together to further refine the shape.

- Box04 shows additional face extrusions for the thumb and all the fingers, as well as a new "wrist" piece on the back of the hand. I used additional vertex scaling and rotating to taper the fingers and also to take some of the flatness out of the hand (most noticeable in the Front viewport).

- The final hand model shows fairly accurate hand proportions, and its rough sculpting work is done.

A MeshSmooth Manicure

Now you're ready to apply the MeshSmooth modifier:

1. Press the W key (or click on the Min/Max Toggle icon) to switch back to the four viewports, click on the hand model to select it, and click on Hide Unselected on the Display panel. Then, click on the Zoom Extents All button to center the hand model in your viewports. (If you want, use the Zoom feature to zoom in somewhat in the Perspective view so the hand is larger in the screen. You can also change your various viewports to wireframe or shaded mode to better gauge the MeshSmooth effect.)

2. Go to the Modify panel and apply a MeshSmooth modifier to the hand. You'll see the hand's blocky contours smoothed off, as shown in Figure 11.10.

The MeshSmooth modifier, with an iterative setting of 1, has already made this simple geometry into a more realistic hand (at least, for a stylized CG character).

If you take a look in the Modify panel, you'll see that the MeshSmooth modifier has several new settings distinguishing it from its MAX Release 1 version. Check the Quad Output box and note the results in

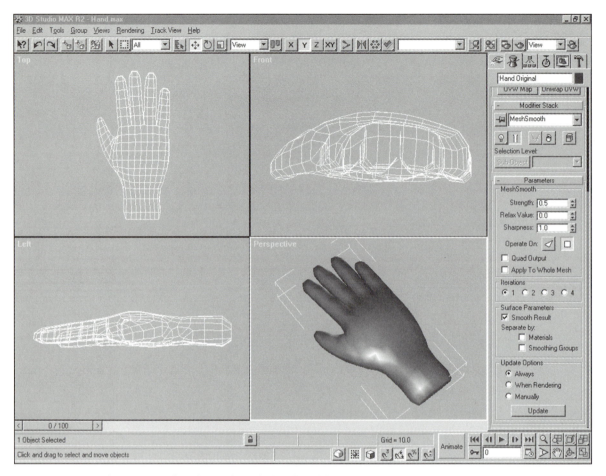

Figure 11.10 The first iteration of MeshSmooth on the hand model.

your view-ports. Quad Output produces only four-sided (visible-edged) facets on your MeshSmoothed object. The desired result here is for the hand surface to be rounded further without adding another iteration.

However, if you're like me, you can't help yourself—you've just got to smooth this hand model even more.

3. Change Iterations from 1 to 2, and if you have Shaded mode active in any of your viewports, check the Smooth Result box under Surface Parameters. You'll see the hand become even smoother and more rounded, as shown in Figure 11.11.

At this point, you should see a more realistic human hand, built originally from a box primitive and a little bit of face and vertex editing.

4. If you go to the Perspective viewport and use the Arc Rotate feature to orbit the hand model, you'll see how MeshSmooth has rounded off the stretched vertices of the palm into a more anatomically correct shape.

The hand is now ready for further editing, or perhaps to be joined onto a human figure's arms using either Boolean or (better yet) Release 2.5's new Connect compound object.

Now that I mention it, I think you'll do that right now.

The Hand Bone's Connected To The Arm Bone...

Connect—a compound object that's useful for both modeling and animation—is yet another new feature of 3D Studio MAX Release 2.5.

Essentially, Connect enables you to create a transition between two disparate pieces of geometry. You can use it to join between two mechanical pieces, such as a square bolt head merging into a round threaded rod, or between two organic models, such as the previously mentioned hand and arm. By placing two objects close to one another, deleting selected "facing faces" on each object, and then turning them into Connect compound objects, you can create a smooth transition between the two. You can "dial in" the number of segments for the seam (or fillet), adjust the tension (pulling it inward or bulging it outward), and even animate these attributes.

Another useful aspect of Connect is that you don't have to make sure the missing faces on each object have the same number of vertices surrounding the holes. The Connect compound object does a "best fit" between the two. With Connect, you can also create quick-and-dirty transitions between multiple "slices" of geometry, which is similar to MAX's Lofting functions.

To use Connect, do the following:

1. Save HAND.MAX to your local \SCENES directory, if you want, and then load HAND_ARM.MAX from the \CHAP_11 directory of the companion CD-ROM. Your screen should look like Figure 11.12.

MESHSMOOTH AND SUB-OBJECTS

An important thing to remember is that MeshSmooth also works on a sub-object level in the Modifier Stack: you can have an entirely MeshSmoothed object, apply an Edit Mesh modifier, select certain faces, and then apply a second MeshSmooth modifier to affect the previously selected faces in the stack. This is useful for smoothing the joints of certain extruded faces and creating fillets. (For example, you may be satisfied with a certain level of "roundness" or smooth contours over the body of an aircraft fuselage. However, problem areas—such as the intersection of a wing into the body of the craft—may need additional smoothing. Applying multiple levels of Edit Mesh/Face modifiers and MeshSmooth may do the trick.)

Also, be aware that one excellent way of editing your models is to manipulate vertices in the bottom of the stack and apply a MeshSmooth modifier above. This way, you can move sets of vertices and/or faces (in Edit Mesh mode) on lower-resolution geometry and then go back up to the MeshSmooth level and gauge the results.

Finally, one additional feature of Release 2.5's MeshSmooth is the Apply To Whole Mesh setting. When it is checked, this feature adds MeshSmoothing to the entire object to which it's applied and ignores sub-object selections passed up the stack. However, other modifiers will continue to pass their parameters up the stack based on previous sub-object selections.

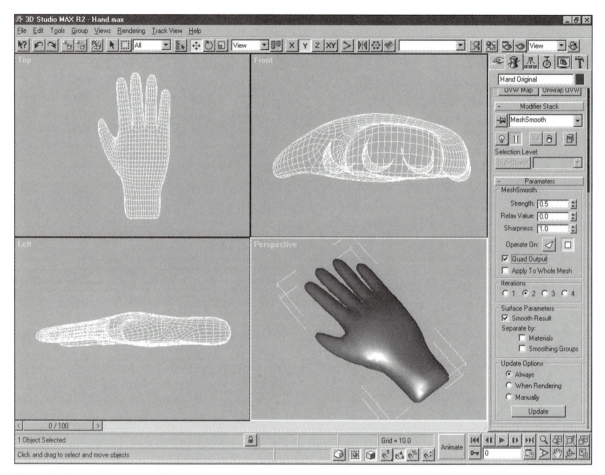

Figure 11.11 Two iterations of MeshSmooth on the hand model (with Quad Output active).

HAND_ARM.MAX contains a variation of the hand model you were working with a moment ago. I've pulled the wrist vertices out somewhat to align them better with the contours of the rough arm model just below it. However, there's a large gap between the two pieces of geometry, and the lower arm terminates well above the hand.

To fix this, you could select the end faces of either the hand or arm, extrude them several times, delete the end faces, attach the objects, and then adjust and weld their vertices by hand. That's precise, but tedious; the Connect object makes this process much easier.

2. Before you create the Connect compound object, you'll need to delete the respective "wrist" faces of both the hand and the arm models. Select the hand model, go to the Modify panel, and turn on Sub-object: Face. Make sure you've got Window Selection active (check the Crossing/Window Selection radio icon on your menu bar at the bottom of the screen). Then, in any of

CONNECT LIMITATIONS

Although you can use Connect to create an active blend between two pieces of geometry and then animate their operands or the blend itself, you shouldn't rotate and animate the operands. If you do, the Connect blend recalculates the connection on every frame, spoiling the effect.

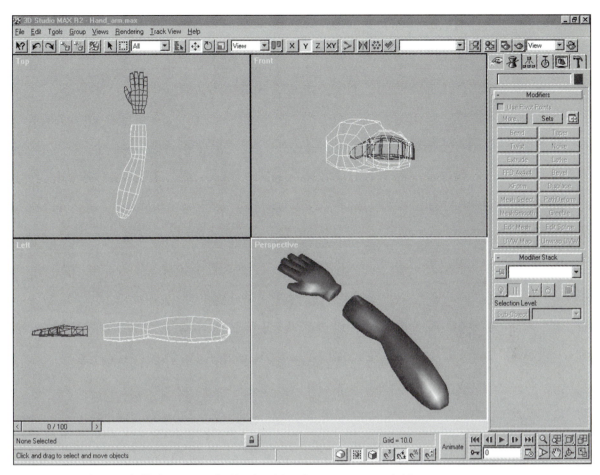

Figure 11.12   The sample file for creating the Hand and Arm Connect compound object.

your orthographic viewports, select the end faces of the hand's wrist. Press the Delete key to delete them (and delete isolated vertices as well).

3. Deselect Sub-object mode, select the Arm object, and repeat the process in Step 2—delete the end faces of the wrist and turn off Sub-object mode for the arm. If you now go to the Perspective window and use ArcRotate to orbit the geometry, you should see "holes" where each hand and arm wrist face each other.

4. Select Geometry|Compound Objects in the Create panel and select Connect. With the arm still selected, click on Pick Operand from the Connect rollout, then click on the Hand object. You'll see new polygonal faces appear to bridge the gap between the two models. To smooth their appearance in the Shaded Perspective viewport, check Bridge and Ends under Smoothing; the seam appears much less noticeable.

5. In the Connect rollout under Interpolation, change Segments to 5. You'll see the seam become more complex as more faces are created to smooth the transition between hand and arm.

6. Next, click on the Tension slider, drag it up and down (say, -2.0 to 2.0), and note the effect. You'll see how the wrist faces either collapse inward or balloon out. You can use

Tension to create the appearance of a new seam in otherwise solid geometry or to create a (skintight) glove or sleeve effect for either the hand or the arm. (Note that the Tension parameter, like most features in MAX, is animatable, of course.) When you're finished playing with these settings, change Segments back to 0 and Tension back to 0.5.

7. Go to the Modify panel and apply a MeshSmooth modifier to this new Compound object. Check Quad Output and change Iterations to 2. You'll see the entire blocky arm geometry become much more smooth and organic and the seam between the hand and arm become invisible, as shown in Figure 11.13.

8. You can save this file to your local \SCENES directory, if you want. Note that the file you've just created is in the \CHAP_11 directory as ARMFINAL.MAX.

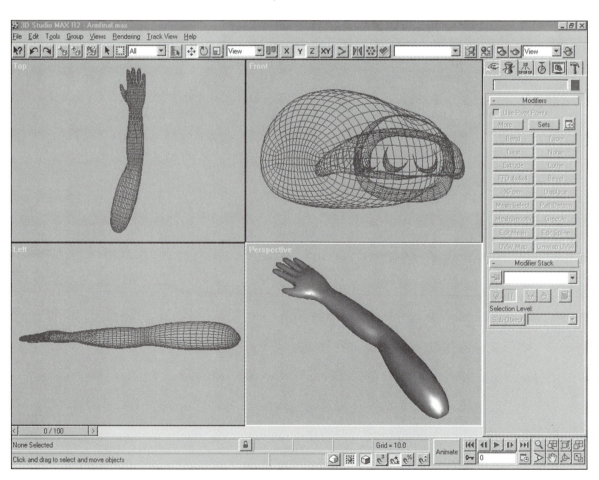

Figure 11.13 The MeshSmooth modifier, applied on top of the Connect compound objects, turns the blocky hand and arm geometry into a smooth appendage.

Moving On

In this chapter, you saw how to create some simple modeling and animation effects using MAX Release 2.5's modifiers and compound objects. In the next chapter, you'll continue exploring modeling techniques as you create two landscapes—a forlorn alien world with scattered rocks and distant nebula and an earthly mountain range with volumetric clouds.

You'll see how to use MAX Release 2.5's new Scatter compound object to produce forced-perspective terrain that includes various sizes of rocks as visual cues. You'll use a Top/Bottom material to place snow on your mountain peaks. Then, by adding Volumetric Fog, you can create either a barren, alien, planetoid atmosphere or cloud-wreathed mountains.

MODELING LANDSCAPES:
ALIEN WORLDS AND
EARTHLY MOUNTAINS

12

In this chapter, you'll use a Quad Patch, Noise modifiers, and Release 2.5's new Scatter routine to create your own forlorn planetoid surface. Then you'll use a Quad Patch, a Noise modifier, and volumetric fog to create a more terrestrial mountain range. You'll also see how you can use MAX's Top/Bottom material to turn these distant hills into snowcapped peaks.

Note: *The following tutorial is very resource intensive. You will be dealing with complex object modifiers and creating a great deal of geometry, so if you have a slow PC and video card, please be patient—some of the steps might take a few moments. You may want to create fewer scattered objects or build your own lower-resolution rock objects.*

If you're like me, you probably enjoyed seeing the new NASA photos from the surface of Mars when the *Pathfinder* probe and its nifty little Sojourner vehicle landed during the summer of '97. Millions of people were thrilled to be able to view the brand-new photos of the rock-strewn Martian surface. In addition, being able to get immediate updates—and see the images—on the Internet allowed everyone on this planet with a computer and a modem to participate in this interplanetary adventure.

With this recent adventure as inspiration, you'll create your own forlorn planetoid surface and dress up the scene with some prebuilt rocks, a couple of spheres (to represent planets), a nebula starfield background, Environmental Fog, and some complex layered materials. You'll end up with a lonely, dusty landscape that looks as if it's light years from here.

Building An Alien Landscape With Scatter

Here are the basic steps to get started with your landscape scene:

1. Save your current MAX scene and reset the program.

2. Activate the Top viewport, press the S key to turn on 3D Snap toggle, select Geometry|Patch Grids from the Create panel, and choose Quad Patch.

3. Create a Quad Patch that is approximately 2000×2000 units and centered in the Top viewport (and world); or you can zoom out and draw it in the viewport instead of entering the specific values. (You may want to change the Top viewport to full-screen to make this easier; press the W key or use the Min/Max Toggle icon.) Change both Length and Width Segments settings to 10—you'll need a very large, relatively high-density surface for this landscape—and then check Generate Mapping Coordinates. Name this object Landscape.

4. Go to the Modify panel and apply a Noise modifier to the Landscape. Under Noise Parameters, change Scale to 1.0, check Fractal, and change Strength to X 25, Y 25, and Z 25. Click on the W key (or the Min/Max icon) to return to the four viewports, if necessary. You should now see a gently rolling landscape.

5. Go to the Create panel, select Cameras|Target, and create a camera just below the bottom edge of the Landscape patch in the Top viewport. (The approximate XYZ coordinates are X 0, Y -1100, Z 0.) Drag the Camera01 target about three-quarters of the way up to the topmost edge of the patch (in Camera01 view, this would be the distant horizon).

6. In the Left viewport, drag the Camera01 body up on the Y axis approximately 100 units, then turn 3D Snap toggle off. Change the Perspective viewport to Camera01 (press the C key).

Let There Be Light

Now it's time to create a harsh, unidirectional light to simulate a distant sun:

1. Go to the Create panel and select Lights| Standard|Target Direct. In the Top viewport, place the light origin at approximate XYZ coordinates X 2000, Y 0, Z 0. Drag the Directional light target down to the left to XYZ coordinates X -1500, Y -500, Z 0.

2. In the Left viewport, select the Directional light body and drag it up on the Y axis ap-

proximately 700 units. (You'll want a fairly low light in the sky to produce stark shadows.)

3. With the Directional light selected, go to the Modify panel and change the light attributes as follows: change the light color to RGB 255, 255, 128, or pale yellow; under Directional Parameters, crank up the Hotspot value to around 1500—this ensures that the light will cover the entire landscape; under Shadow Parameters, check Cast Shadows and change Map Size to 512—you'll want the map quality to be higher than the default. (For high resolution renderings, you might want to adjust it to a much greater value than this.) Your screen should look something like Figure 12.1.

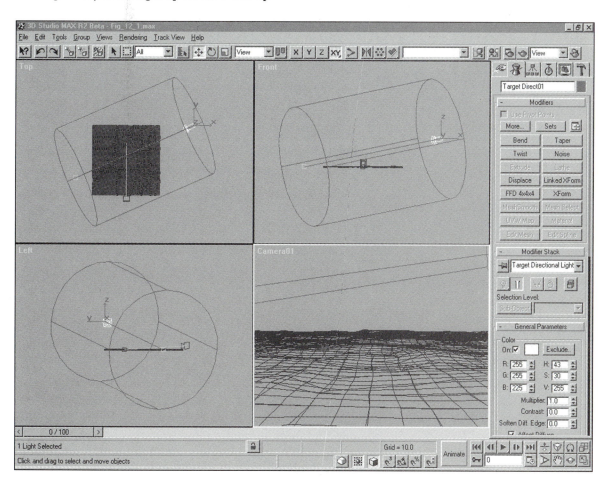

Figure 12.1 The basic setup for the planetary landscape scene.

Note: In 3D Studio MAX f/x: Creating Hollywood-Style Special Effects, the predecessor to this book, I presented an entire chapter on how to use simple geometry and successions of modifiers to create complex rocky objects. For more information, see Chapter 19 of that book, "Space Rubble: Creating Asteroids," pages 299 to 318.

Rolling Stones

Now, it's time to merge in some rocks that will give a greater illusion of depth to this scene:

1. Select File|Merge File and choose ROCKS.MAX from the \CHAP_12 directory of the companion CD-ROM. When the Merge window appears, select All and click on OK. In a moment, you'll see four irregularly shaped boulders sitting in the middle of the viewports. The largest boulder is Rock01; the smallest is Rock04.

I created these rocks fairly easily. They began as low-resolution Geospheres to which I then applied Noise modifiers. Through a combination of Noise, Edit Mesh, Tessellation, and Optimize modifiers, I created the four boulders you see here. The boulders already have mapping coordinates and materials applied, which you'll see in a moment.

You'll now use the Scatter compound object to distribute these rocks across the surface of your landscape.

2. Activate the Top viewport and press the W key to enlarge it to full screen. Click on the Landscape patch to select it, then go to the Modify panel. Click on the Edit Stack icon, then click on Convert To: Editable Mesh. You'll use this Editable Mesh Landscape as your Distribution object.

3. With the Landscape object selected, select Sub-object: Face and make sure Window Selection is active. (Click on the Crossing/Window Selection icon on the bottom of your MAX desktop to toggle between these two features.) Draw a selection box around the bottom half of the Landscape faces, as shown in Figure 12.2.

Forced Perspective

Next, you'll use successive layers of ever-diminishing boulders to create a *forced-perspective* scene; this will make the landscape horizon appear to be much farther away from the camera than it really is. Forced perspective is a very old special-effects technique, used extensively with miniature sets.

One of the most extensive uses of miniature sets occurred in Gerry Anderson's "puppet" TV series *Thunderbirds* and *Captain Scarlet* and his live-action series *UFO* and *Space: 1999*. British effects masters Derek Meddings (*Goldeneye*) and Brian Johnson (*Alien*, *The Empire Strikes Back*) used large-scale models to create fantasy landscapes of great complexity and depth. Their forced-perspective techniques made the "tabletop" miniatures appear to be miles across and miles deep.

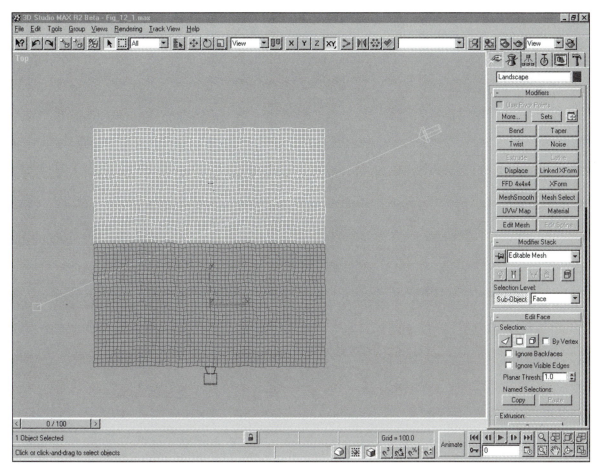

Figure 12.2   These selected faces will be the area over which the largest rocks will be scattered.

Although computer graphics, digital composites, and matte paintings are largely supplanting miniature sets, you can still apply the lessons of these old techniques to your cutting-edge CG work. To create your forced-perspective scene, follow these steps:

1. Press the H key to bring up the Select By Name menu and select Rock01 from the list.

2. Go to the Create panel and select Geometry|Compound Objects|Scatter. The Scatter rollout will appear.

The Scatter feature enables you to clone and distribute selected objects throughout your scene. You can use either a set of scale, transform, and rotate values to distribute the objects, or you can select a Distribution object, which will serve as a Scatter template.

Under Pick Distribution Object, the default setting is Instance. This creates an instanced duplicate of the selected Distribution object, which in this case will be the Landscape mesh. However, you should check Move instead—this will move the selected object into the Distribution object.

3. Check Move, click on Pick Distribution Object, and click on the Landscape mesh. You'll see both the Rock01 and the (former) Landscape mesh become selected; Rock01 also moves to a new position on the Landscape mesh. The Landscape object and Rock01 have become a new Compound Object.

4. Scroll down to the Source Object Parameters section in the Scatter menu. Enter 10 under Duplicates and check Use Selected Faces Only under Distribution Object Parameters. This scatters the Rock01 objects across the selected faces of the original Landscape object. Check Random Faces under Distribute Using. This "breaks up" the distribution of the Rock01 objects so they're not evenly spaced.

5. To change their appearance even more, you'll introduce random rotations into the duplicated Rock01 objects. Scroll down to the Transforms section of the Scatter rollout and enter X -175, Y 249, Z -308 in the Rotation transforms. (You can actually enter whatever numerical settings you want; just make sure they're at least double-digit values.)

6. To enter "further randomness" into these rocks, go down to the Local Translation section and enter random values there as well (say, X 17, Y -25, Z 39). This will move the rocks slightly up or down relative to the Landscape object.

As you can see, using the Scatter Compound Object feature saves you the trouble of duplicating, placing, and rotating each of these objects by hand. You can also distribute objects precisely along the surfaces of other objects—perfect for creating large amounts of tiny details, such as buildings for distant cityscapes, kit-bashed model parts (otherwise known as "greebles," "wiggets," or "nernies") for spacecraft hulls, or natural phenomena such as trees and plants. (In Chapter 18, you'll also see a way you can create procedural details on your objects by using Tom Hudson's Greeble 1.0 modifier, included on this book's companion CD-ROM.)

Rock On

Now, it's time to increment the distribution area for the second-largest series of boulders. First, though, you'll detach and reuse the original Landscape element to keep your overall face count down. To do this, follow these steps:

1. Go to the Modify panel and apply an Edit Mesh modifier to the Rock01/Landscape object. Select Sub-object: Face, click on the Element icon under Selection, then click on the original Landscape mesh itself to select it. (Don't select one of the Scattered rocks by mistake.) You should see the Landscape mesh become selected.

2. Under Miscellaneous in the Edit Mesh rollout, click on Detach, again name the new object Landscape (it will default to Landscape01), and click on Yes to delete isolated vertices.

3. Next, turn off Sub-object selection mode for Rock01 and select the resurrected Landscape mesh (you can choose it from the Select By Name menu, if you want). Click on Sub-object: Face and make sure your selection set is Polygon, not Element. (Otherwise, you'll select the entire landscape.) This time, select the bottom, say, two-thirds of the Landscape faces, as shown in Figure 12.3.

4. Use the Select By Name menu to choose Rock02, then go to the Create panel and select Scatter again. Check Move under Pick Distribution Object, click on the Pick Distribution Object button, and select the Landscape mesh again. The Rock02 object is moved to Landscape.

5. Go to Source Object Parameters and change Duplicates to 35. You'll see the Rock02 objects scattered about the Landscape surface. Check Use Selected Faces Only, check Random Faces, and open the Transforms rollout.

6. As you did with the Rock01 object, enter widely varying XYZ Rotation values for Rock02 and more-subtle XYZ values for Local Translation. (Don't enter the same values as Rock01; make them different.)

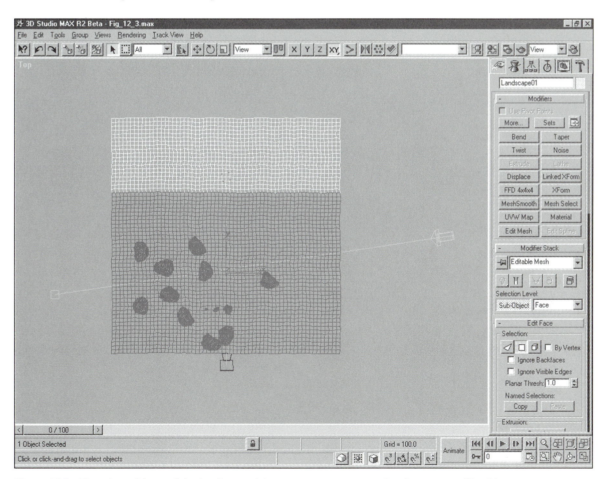

Figure 12.3   The selected faces of the Landscape object, preparatory to scattering the next set of boulders.

7. Go to the Modify panel again, apply another Edit Mesh modifier to the selected object, and select Sub-object: Faces. Click on the Element icon, select the original Landscape mesh, and detach it again as Landscape.

8. Select the Landscape mesh again, select Sub-object: Face, change the Selection level back to Polygon, and select, say, the bottom five-sixths of the mesh, as shown in Figure 12.4.

9. Choose Rock03 from the Select By Name menu and select Scatter again from the Create panel. Check Move under Pick Distribution Object, click on the Pick Distribution Object button, and select the Landscape mesh again.

10. Under Source Object Parameters, change Duplicates to 75. Check Use Selected Faces Only, check Random Faces, then open the Transforms rollout. Again, enter widely varying XYZ Rotation values for Rock03 and more-subtle XYZ values for Local Translation.

11. Go to the Modify panel again, apply another Edit Mesh modifier, and select Sub-object: Faces. Click on the Element icon, choose the original Landscape mesh, and detach it again as Landscape.

Now that you're on the final pass, you don't need to select specific faces; you can just use the entire detached Landscape object.

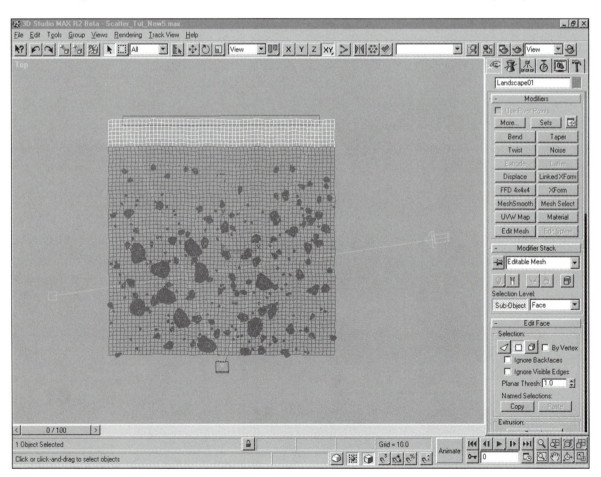

Figure 12.4   The selected faces for the Rock03 distribution.

12. Select Rock04, select Scatter, and check Move under Pick Distribution Object. Click on the Pick Distribution Object button and select the Landscape mesh again. The Rock04 object is moved to Landscape.

13. At this point, you can enter whatever duplication number you're comfortable with; if you have a fast PC (such as a Pentium Pro or Pentium II), you might enter a value as high as 200. (Your scene should now have more than 100,000 faces; if this bogs down your system too much, reduce the number of duplicates.) Then, go to Transforms and enter widely varying XYZ Rotation values and more-subtle XYZ values for Local Translation.

14. Finally, apply another Edit Mesh modifier to the Rock04 compound object, select the Landscape element, detach it again, and rename it as Landscape.

Terraforming And Finishing Touches

You should now have a complex landscape covered with rocks. The diminishing scale of the rocks as they approach the horizon enhances the effect of distance, as shown in Figure 12.5.

Now, it's time to add the finishing touches. With some layered materials, a little Environmental fog (tinted with a bitmap), a Background image, and a moon in the sky, you can finish off this landscape nicely:

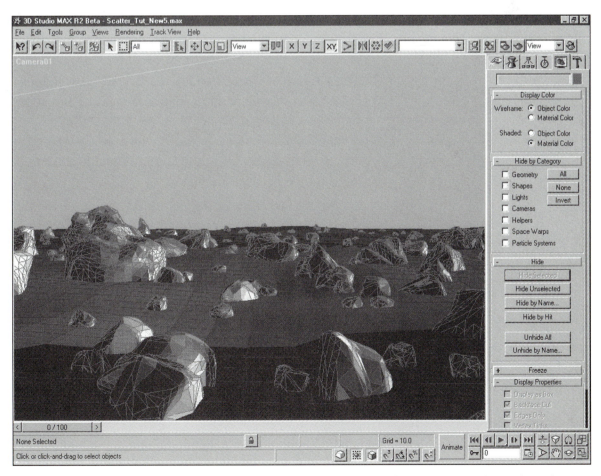

Figure 12.5 The Scattered rocks (large to small) accentuate the apparent depth of the scene and the horizon line. (The Camera01 scene is displayed in Smooth + Highlights/Edge Faces mode.)

A WARNING ABOUT PROXY MESHES

Be careful when you are collapsing a Modifier stack of Scatter objects. If you are displaying the Scatter objects as Proxies (to speed your screen redraw), you will collapse the original objects into low-res Proxy meshes. Note that if this happens, you can undo the action in 3D Studio MAX Release 2.5.

1. First, you'll need to set the Camera ranges for the Fog dropoff. Click on the Camera01 body to select it and go to the Environment Ranges section of the Modify panel. Check Show and change Far Range to around 2100 units. In the Top viewport, you'll see the Camera Far Ranges change to encompass the far end (horizon line) of the Landscape.

2. Open the Material Editor first, then select Rendering|Environment. Click on the Environment Map Name button under Background and select Bitmap, click on OK in the Material/Map browser. When the Map (Bitmap) appears, drag the map name button over to an empty Material Editor slot and copy it as an Instance. Under Coordinates, change mapping from Environ: Spherical to Screen.

3. Click on the empty Bitmap Name button, select STARNEB4.JPG from the \MAPS directory of the companion CD-ROM, and click on View. The STARNEB4.JPG image is a heavily modified image of a starfield combined with a public-domain NASA nebula image. This 800×640 resolution bitmap will serve as your deep-space background. Click on OK to load the image.

4. Go back to the Environment window. Under Atmosphere, click on Add and select Fog from the Atmospheric Effects list. Click on the Environment Color Map Name button under Fog Parameters and select Bitmap from the Material/Map Browser. Drag this Map (Bitmap) file over to a Material Editor slot, select Instance, and click on the Bitmap name field.

5. Select MARSCLDS.JPG from the \MAPS directory of the companion CD-ROM and click on View. This bitmap (shown in Figure 12.6) is another heavily modified 800×640 image. I took a stock cloud background image, added deep orange coloration and Gaussian blur, and then extended its lower half. Click on OK to load the image; then, in the Material Editor, change the Environmental Mapping coordinates to Screen.

6. Under Fog Parameters: Standard in the Environment window, check the Exponential box and change Far Percentage to 35 percent. Then, close the Environment window.

7. Next, press the H key to bring up the Select By Name menu, select the objects Landscape and Rocks01-04, and click on OK.

Figure 12.6 The MARSCLDS.JPG bitmap will tint the Environment Fog used in the planetoid landscape.

8. Go to an open slot in the Material Editor, click on the Get Material icon, and when the Material/Map Browser appears, select Browse From: Material Library. Click on File: Open and load MAXFX2.MAT from the \MATLIBS directory of the companion CD-ROM. When the library loads, scroll down to the Planet Landscape 2 texture and double-click on it to load this material into the open Material Editor slot.

9. The Planet Landscape material is a Standard material that uses Specular bitmaps, several Mix maps in the Diffuse and Ambient slots, and Release 2.5's new Cellular procedural texture as Shininess and Bump maps. (The latter provides excellent craters and rocky surface relief.)

If you want, open the various map slots and shader trees and view the bitmaps and procedural map settings that make up this material. The rocky textures feature a variety of colors; the different tiling settings and the use of Noise as a Mix map help keep the overall material from repeating.

10. Click on the Put Material To Selection icon to apply this material to the selected Landscape and Rock objects.

Planet-Building Made Easy

Next, you'll dress up this scene by building a nearby planet (or a moon) to put in the sky. You'll then apply textures to all the elements in the scene and render it. Follow these steps:

1. Press the W key to enlarge the Top viewport to full screen and click on the Zoom Extents icon to center the Landscape and Directional light in your viewport. Press the S key to activate 3D Snap.

2. Select Geometry|Standard Primitives from the Create panel and then select Sphere. In the Top viewport, place your mouse cursor at approximate XYZ coordinates X 370, Y 1270, Z 0. Drag outward to create a sphere with a radius of *approximately* 250 units. Change

Segments to 60, then check Generate Mapping Coordinates. (You can then rename this object Planet, if you want.)

3. Press the W key again (or the Min/Max Toggle icon), and in any of the four viewports, drag the Planet sphere up on the Z axis until it's above the horizon line, as shown in Figure 12.7.

4. Open the Material Editor, click in an unused material slot, then click on the Get Material icon. Load the material MARS PLANET 2 from the MAXFX2.MAT material library. You'll see a tan-colored texture loaded in the Diffuse and Bump map slots.

5. If you want, open either of these slots and view the MARS_NEW2.JPG bitmap.

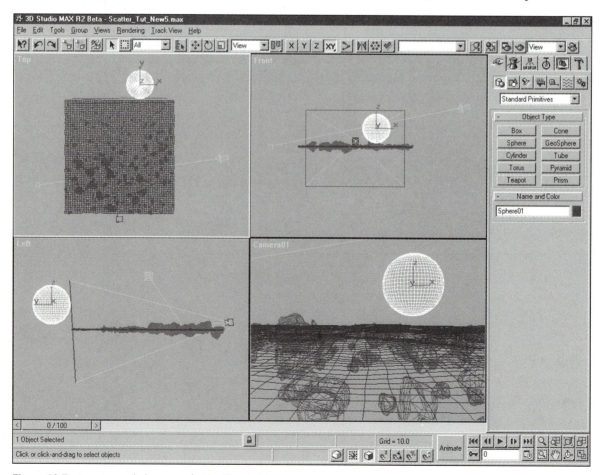

Figure 12.7 A suggested placement for the Planet object.

I created this 1024×512 bitmap from a series of very high-resolution, public-domain NASA images of Mars. I took sections of three images of Mars, cut features from each of them, and then built a Mars-type planet. This 2:1 bitmap is designed specifically for spherical mapping. (Note that there are other planet bitmaps in the \MAPS directory of the companion CD-ROM.)

6. Click on the Go To Parent icon, select the Planet sphere, and apply this material to the Planet object.

7. Next, click on the Directional light and increase its Hotspot values in the Modify panel to include the new Planet (about 2000 should do it).

8. Finally, activate the Camera01 viewport and render a test image of at least 640×480. Depending on the speed of your computer, it may take a few minutes to render this complex scene, which is shown in Figure 12.8.

Figure 12.8   The final version of the desolate planetoid landscape.

As this rendering indicates, you now have a dusty, desolate planetary landscape. The forced-perspective rocks scattered on the gently rolling surface provide a great feeling of depth, as does the Environmental Fog. In addition, the MARSCLDS.JPG image used to tint the fog adds streaks of color to the scene. Finally, the stark lighting helps to emphasize the lonely nature of this deep-space vista.

9. Close the Camera01 VFB window.

10. You can save this file to your local 3DSMAX \SCENES directory for later study. (Note that it is included in the \CHAP_12 directory of the companion CD-ROM as PLANETOD.MAX.)

If you have a fast computer and video card, you can try to create an even more complex version of this scene with additional rocks, more planets and moons in the sky, or different background or geometry textures.

Things To Try

There are many more uses for Scatter besides simply strewing rocks around a distant alien landspace, of course. With Scatter, you can create effects that are much more terrestrial in nature. Here are some suggestions:

- Place trees, bushes, and other vegetation in a forest setting.

- Scatter details around an interior set. For example, you can use Scatter to create similar objects strewn about a room after a hurricane or a ransacking by burglars.

- Apply hair or fur to an object. For instance, you could begin by selecting the faces representing the hairline of a human head model. Then, by creating very thin, triangular shapes—or even renderable splines—and scattering them, you could produce a quick-and-dirty hair effect on the head.

- Place repetitive details on an industrial surface (such as the wall or ceiling of a factory), distant buildings in a cityscape, or even "greebles" on the outside of a *Star-Wars*-style spaceship.

- Here's an interesting trick created by Martin Foster, an excellent 3D Studio MAX artist: Apply tiny, scattered objects on the outside of a larger piece of geometry, such as a sphere or a flattened torus. Then, if you animate the larger Distribution object's size (making it grow rapidly), you can produce an explosion or shockwave effect.

Creating An Earthly Mountain Range

Now that you've seen how to create an alien environment, it's time to bring the tutorials back to earth.

In the second part of this chapter, you'll turn a Quad Patch into a rocky mountain complete with snowcapped peaks. To build the geometry, you'll use a combination of modifiers: Noise, free-form deformation (FFD), and Tessellation. You'll then create a Top/Bottom material for the snow material and add clouds and atmospheric haze via Environmental Fog. To begin, follow these steps:

1. Save your current work and reset MAX.

2. Activate 3D Snap (press the S key) and select Create|Geometry|Patch Grids. Create a Quad Patch object that is centered in the Top viewport and has both a length and width of 200 units. Change both Length and Width Segments settings to 10 and check Generate Mapping Coordinates. Finally, change the name of this object to Mountain.

3. In the Modify panel, apply an Edit Mesh modifier to the Mountain Quad Patch, deselect Sub-object: Vertices, and apply an FFD 4×4×4 modifier. You'll use this to "bow" the flat patch into a rounded hill shape.

4. Click on Sub-object: Control Points and select the four control points in the middle of the FFD "cage." Press the spacebar to lock the selection, then move the FFD control points up on the Y axis approximately 200 units, as shown in Figure 12.9. You now have the beginnings of a hilltop.

5. Turn off 3D Snap (press the S key again), turn off Sub-object: Control Points on the FFD cage, and apply a Noise modifier to the Mountain object. Change Scale to 50.0, check the Fractal box, and change Strength to X 10, Y 10, and Z 75. The Noise modifier then distorts the

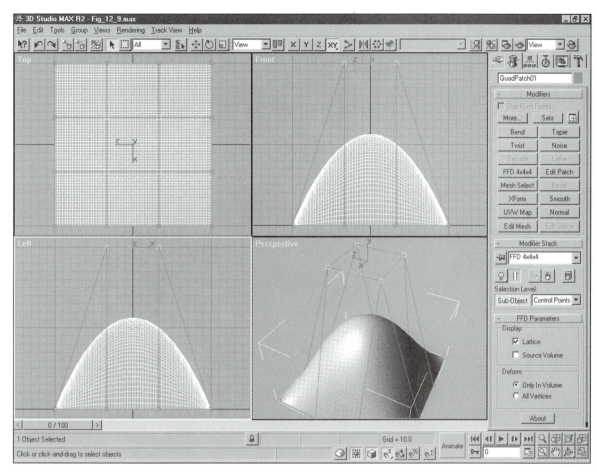

Figure 12.9 Pulling up the middle set of FFD control points turns the flat Quad Patch into a rounded-off hill.

rounded hill shape into a rocky mountain peak, as shown in Figure 12.10.

Although the new Mountain object now looks like its namesake, it may still not have enough detail for your liking. This is still a parametric MAX object (assuming you haven't collapsed the stack), so you can increase the Mountain's complexity by increasing the original Quad Patch's Length and Width Segments settings.

6. Go to the Modifier panel and click on the down arrow to open the Modifier Stack rollout. You should see Noise, FFD 4×4×4, Edit Mesh, and then Quad Patch. Go to the Quad Patch level of the rollout and change both the Length and Width Segments settings

from 10 to 25. You'll see the Mountain become even craggier. (This isn't surprising; the Mountain object has gone from 7,200 faces to 45,000, as File|Summary Info indicates.)

Making Snowcapped Peaks

Now, it's time to create the material for the mountain range. You'll use a Top/Bottom material to place (Noise) snowcaps on the higher elevations and a Blended bitmap for the mountain texture:

1. Open the Material Editor, click on the Type button for Material #1, and when the Material/Map Browser appears, change Material #1 from Standard to Top/Bottom (click on OK to discard the old material).

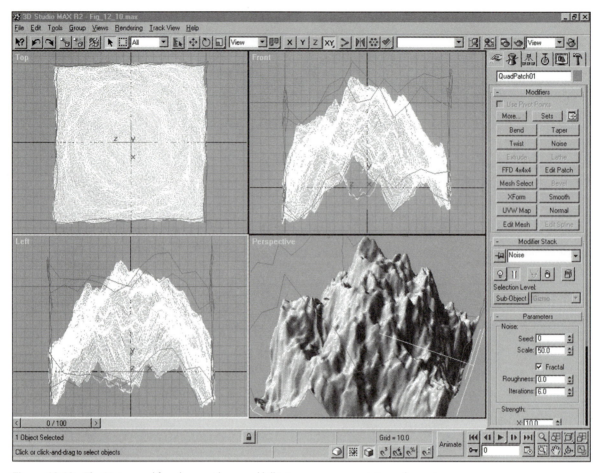

Figure 12.10 The Noise modifier changes the round hill into a craggy mountain peak.

2. Click on the Top Material button to go to this material level. Change Ambient to pure white, or RGB settings 225, 225, 255, then change Diffuse and Specular RGB 255, 255, 255. Change Shininess Strength to 75 and Shininess to 100.

3. Click on the Bump map button in the Maps rollout. Click on the Type button, select Bitmap from the Material/Map Browser, and click on the Bitmap button.

4. Click on MOUNTAIN.JPG in the \MAPS directory of the companion CD-ROM to view it. This 640×640 resolution bitmap is a combination of various rocky textures (scanned from real photographic elements) that were layered in Photoshop. Click on OK to load it,

change both U and V Tiling to 2.0, then click on the Go To Parent icon. Change this material name to Snow.

5. Click on the Go To Parent icon again and select the Bottom material. Change Ambient to RGB 16, 16, 0 and change Diffuse to RGB 96, 96, 0. The default Blinn material's Shininess value is low, so leave it as it is.

6. Open the Diffuse map slot in the Maps rollout and click on the Type button; when the Material/Map Browser appears, click on Get From Material Editor and click on OK. From the Material Editor Browser window, click on the map slot and load the MOUNTAIN.JPG bitmap. Make it an Instance and click on OK.

7. Click on the Go To Parent icon, drag the Diffuse MOUNTAIN.JPG bitmap down to the Bump map slot, and make it an Instance. Then change this Bottom material name to Mountain and click on the Go To Parent icon again.

8. You should now be back in the Basic Parameters section of the Top/Bottom material. Change Blend to 2 and Position to 90. You'll see the white snowcap shift to the very top of your sample sphere (or box) in the Material Editor. (It looks somewhat like a polar ice cap on a dark planet.) Keep Coordinates set to World, not Local.

9. Finally, change this Top/Bottom material to Snowcapped Peaks, then assign it to the selected Mountain object. Don't close the Material Editor—you'll need it open for the next step.

Partly Cloudy; Chance Of Volumetric Fog Tonight

Now, it's time to set up your Environmental fog—both atmospheric haze and volumetric clouds. But before you go to the Environment editor, you'll need to set up an Atmospheric Apparatus Gizmo to place a layer of clouds around the mountain range:

1. Go to the Create panel, click on Helpers, change from Standard to Atmospheric Apparatus, and select BoxGizmo. In the Top viewport, draw a BoxGizmo that encompasses your Mountain object (with Length and Width settings of around 200 units). Make Height approximately 35 units.

2. In the Left viewport, drag the BoxGizmo up on the Y axis about 65 units, as shown in Figure 12.11.

3. Click on Rendering|Environment. Click on the Environment Map Name button and select Bitmap from the Material/Map

Browser. Drag this bitmap over to Material Editor slot #2 and make it an Instance.

4. Go to Material #2, click on the Bitmap Name button, and click on and view CLOUDNEW.JPG in the \MAPS directory of the companion CD-ROM. This 800×600 bitmap image of clouds will serve as your background. Click on OK to load the image, and make sure the coordinates are set to Environ: Screen (not Spherical).

5. In the Environment menu under Atmosphere: Effects, click on Add and select Fog. Under Fog Parameters, check the Exponential box under Standard, leave the Near percentage at 0.0, and change the Far percentage to 50.

6. Click on the Add button again and then select Volume Fog. Click on the Pick Gizmo button under Gizmos and click on BoxGizmo01 in your scene. Change Soften Gizmo Edges to 1.0.

7. Check Exponential under Volume, change Density to 60.0, and change Noise Type to Fractal. Under Noise Threshold, change High to 0.3, Low to 0.2, and Size to 20.

8. Close the Environment menu and the Material Editor.

A Cyberspace Ansel Adams

Okay, now it's time to place your cameras and lighting in the scene and render this scene:

1. In the Top viewport, select Cameras from the Create panel, place a Target Camera at approximate XYZ coordinates X 0, Y -135, Z 0, and drag its target into the center of the Mountain object.

2. In the Left viewport, drag the Camera01 body up on the Y axis about 110 units, then drag the Target up on the Y axis about 95 units. Change the Perspective viewport to the Camera01 key (activate this viewport and press the

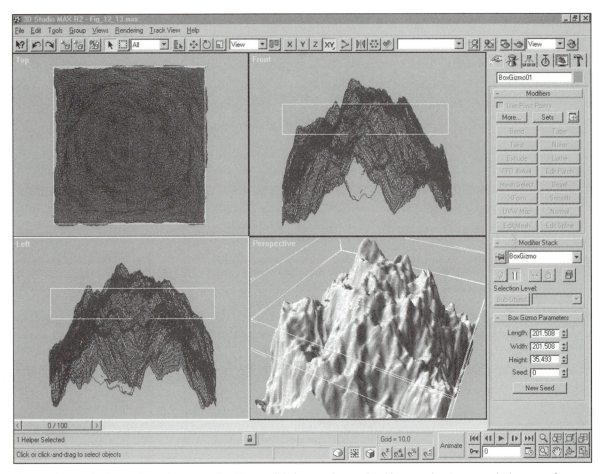

Figure 12.11   The Atmospheric Apparatus BoxGizmo will help you place a cloud layer so that it surrounds the tops of the mountains.

C key). If you find that your camera view doesn't resemble Figure 12.13, adjust your camera and target placement as desired. You want to have the top half of the Box Gizmo visible so you can see a cloud layer.

3. Select Camera01, then go to the Modify panel. Under Environment Ranges, check Show, keep Near Range set to 0, and change Far Range to about 225—enough to encompass most of the Mountain object.

4. Go back to the Create Panel, select Lights, and place a Target Directional light in the Top viewport at approximate XYZ coordinates X -170, Y -125, Z 0. Drag the Target into the center of the Mountain object.

5. Go to the Left viewport and drag the Directional light up on the Y axis about 200 units so that's it's shining down on the Mountain at an approximate 45-degree angle.

6. Go to the Modify panel and change the Light color to RGB 255, 255, 225, or a whitish-yellow. Under Directional Parameters, change Hotspot to around 155—or large enough to encompass the entire Mountain object. Finally, click on the Cast Shadows parameter and change Shadow Map Size to 512. Your desktop should look something like Figure 12.12.

7. Render at least a 640×480 version of this scene. After a few minutes, your scene should appear, as shown in Figure 12.13.

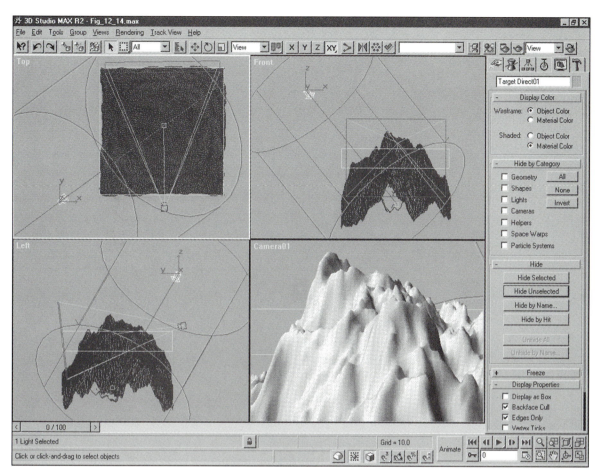

Figure 12.12 The proper placement for your Camera and Directional light.

Figure 12.13 The final rendering of your mountain scene.

As Figure 12.13 and your rendering indicate, you've created the effect of a distant mountain range with fleecy, low-lying clouds near the snowy summits; atmospheric fog adds additional depth to the scene. The Top/Bottom material caps the high areas of the mountains with snow, and the MOUNTAIN.JPG bitmap provides dark coloration for the rest of the terrain.

If you want, you can go into the Material Editor and change the Blending and Position values of the Snow material versus the Mountain material; a lower Position figure will make the snow heavier and give more of an arctic appearance to the mountains.

You can alter the Mountain's appearance by adding more modifiers. To create a more pronounced peak, try adding a Taper modifier to the overall object. You can, of course, also alter the Noise settings, add a Displacement modifier to further perturb the surface, or collapse the modifier stack entirely if you're satisfied with this topology.

8. Close the Camera01 VFB window. Note that the scene you have just created is in the \CHAP_12 directory on the companion CD-ROM as MOUNTAIN.MAX.

Moving On

Now that you've created these two complex pieces of rugged terrain, both alien and earthly, it's time to take a look at "smooth" modeling—Release 2.5's new NURBS implementation.

In the next two chapters, you'll learn how to use MAX's NURBS (Non-Uniform Rational B-Splines) to create organic models. With NURBS, you can create anything from a seamless human face to fantasy creatures and animals. Stay tuned!

An Introduction To
NURBS Modeling, Part I

13

BY

KEN ALLEN ROBERTSON

In this chapter and the next, contributor Ken Allen Robertson will introduce you to the wonders of organic modeling with NURBS.

Probably nothing has defined the division between high-end and low-end 3D graphics packages more than the inclusion of NURBS capabilities. NURBS is a strange acronym, and when added to the list of features in a particular 3D program, it has magical qualities. The feature it represents, when included in a 3D software package, can drain a bank account at unheard-of speeds; it can make a user feel and act superior to those without it in the manuals of their software packages, and its inclusion (or mere mention thereof) can sell 3D software at a premium. (Hence, the last reason provides the rationale for the first.)

Now, finally, the veil of mystery has lifted, the magic has been revealed as a real and tangible tool without the evil side effects, and bank accounts of 3D artists everywhere are breathing a sigh of relief. True NURBS capabilities have come to MAX.

What Are NURBS, Anyway?

NURBS stands for *Non-Uniform Rational B-Spline*, a definition that isn't much more helpful than the acronym. So, let's break it down to make it more comprehensible:

- *Non-Uniform* means that different areas along NURBS objects (curves or surfaces) can have different properties (weights) and are not completely equal.

- *Rational* means that a NURBS object can be defined with mathematical formulae.

- *B-Spline* is any line in three-dimensional space that has the ability to curve in more than one direction.

So, a NURBS object is one or more curved lines in three-dimensional space with varying properties (weights) that can be rationally defined with mathematics.

Simple. Sort of.

The important thing to remember about NURBS objects is that, at some point, NURBS curves are critical to the realization of the object. In fact, the most useful definition of a NURBS object is "a bunch of curves thrown into three-dimensional space and connected in order to make a surface."

So, what's all the hullabaloo about? Because NURBS surfaces are always defined by curves (whether you actually see any of them or not), they are extremely organic and smooth. (In fact, it's almost impossible to create a hard edge within a NURBS surface.)

In addition, NURBS surfaces will adjust themselves in order to maintain their defining curves. This means that when you animate NURBS sub-objects (curves or points, mainly), the surface will always maintain those organic curves, and a hard edge will never be created within a single surface, even if the NURBS object has to adjust its entire surface topology. Therefore, animation of a NURBS surface will produce results that more closely resemble organic skin rather than animation of polygonal or patch-based objects.

Core Concepts

Although each NURBS system has its own peculiarities, the NURBS paradigms in MAX Release 2 and 2.5 are quite simple and organized and fall into broad concepts that apply across the sub-objects that make up a NURBS surface.

NURBS Sub-objects: Points, Curves, And Surfaces

All NURBS surfaces consist of three sub-objects: points (or control vertices), curves (which are determined by their points or control vertices), and surfaces (which are controlled by either curves or their own points or control vertices).

Points are, well, just that—points. They lie precisely on the surface or on the curve they affect, almost exactly like a standard vertex. However, unlike a standard spline vertex, they cannot use Bezier, corner, or Bezier corner manipulation. They behave very much like a smooth spline vertex.

Control vertices (or CVs) are points that control the amount and placement of curvature in a surface or curve but do not lie on the surface or curve they control. Instead, they form a lattice that is similar to the control points in a standard MAX free-form deformation (FFD) modifier. Unlike an FFD, CVs have a weight, an amount of influence over the curve or surface. The higher the weight, the more a

surface or curve is drawn toward a CV's position; the lower the weight, the smaller the influence a CV has over the curve or surface. But weights are relative. This means that if all of the CVs of a particular surface were set to a high value, there would be no change because the influence over the surface is even. Only when certain CVs have a higher or lower relative weight than their neighboring CVs can you see a difference. This is also the closest way to approximate a hard edge in a single NURBS surface or curve.

Control vertices and points are the basis for everything in NURBS. They are, however, mutually exclusive. A surface or curve is made up of one or the other, never both—thus the distinction, in the initial object creation, between a point curve or surface and a CV curve or surface.

Dependent Vs. Independent

In addition to the differences between point and CV objects, points, surfaces, and curves may also be either dependent or independent.

In MAX R2 and 2.5, you can manipulate (sculpt or animate) an independent point, curve, or surface by its own points or CVs, or you can manipulate the curve or surface itself. MAX draws independent objects in white while you're editing the NURBS object (except points, which are drawn in green). You can't make an independent curve or surface directly into a dependent surface. However, the exercises later in this chapter will provide a method for getting around this limitation.

A dependent curve or surface has no active CVs or points of its own. Instead, you can control it by a combination of curves and/or surfaces, even if you're animating them. Note that you can make a dependent curve or surface independent. When you're editing MAX Release 2.5 dependent NURBS objects, they're drawn bright green.

Fortunately, you'll always know whether the object you're creating is dependent or independent before you create it. Without listing every possible object and whether it is dependent or independent, here are some easy ways to know what type of object you are creating:

- If the object you are creating needs other objects (curves, surfaces, or points) to be in place before you can build your new object, it will be dependent.

- Simply look at the creation box when you are creating the object; independent and dependent objects are separated in the main panel of the NURBS modifier rollout.

In general, while the second method for identifying dependency is largely foolproof, I prefer to keep the principles of the first method thoroughly embedded in my mind so I always know what to expect and never have to guess or take the time to look at the rollout panel.

The benefit of a dependent object is that it will always attempt to maintain a smooth curve or surface across the independent objects that determine how it's formed, allowing for extremely organic animation. The downside of a dependent object is that it cannot be manipulated or sculpted by itself. For example, if you create a u-loft surface (a dependent NURBS surface created from two or more NURBS curves), you can only use the u-loft curves or their CVs (instead of the surface CVs found in an independent surface) to sculpt the surface and still maintain its dependent state.

As a general rule, dependent surfaces are better suited to animation and macro-modeling (creating the large details), while independent surfaces are better for micro-modeling, or creating fine details in the surface of the model.

Fortunately, MAX R2 and 2.5 has provided some very useful tools to allow you to go back and forth from dependent to independent surfaces, allowing the user to utilize the best of both paradigms at the optimal time in the creation procedure.

Surface Rules

NURBS objects are created from one or more NURBS curves and/or surfaces. You can make curves renderable with a definable thickness, but surfaces are the core sub-object of a solid (that is, a "surfaced") NURBS model.

Now that you know the basic construction paradigms of all NURBS sub-objects, you'll take a closer look at what you can and cannot do, as defined by the "three NURBS surface commandments."

Thou Shalt Not Have Holes In Thy Surface

All NURBS surfaces must be a single solid piece, similar to patches. To make a hole in a NURBS object, you must create two or more NURBS surfaces and join them in such a way as to create a hole. However, they will remain separate surfaces.

Some NURBS modelers have included a particular feature called trimming (or trims) that allows you to slice part of a NURBS surface, leaving a clean edge with which to blend other objects, or extract a curve for modeling other surfaces. Although this feature was not implemented in MAX Release 2, Kinetix has incorporated NURBS trimming features in MAX R2.5.

Thou Shall Have Only One Texture Per Surface

Just like patches, each patch can have only one texture and cannot be subdivided to hold more than one map per surface. To have more maps over the area of a single given surface, the surface sub-object must be broken into more surfaces.

Thy Polygons Shall Be Built Only At The Time Of The Rendering

When you see your NURBS surface in the main MAX interface, what you are seeing is an iso-surface (in a shaded display) or iso-parms (in a wireframe display). It's only a representation of the object, albeit a good one. NURBS surface polygons (necessary for proper lighting and map placement) are created only when the object is rendered. Therefore, NURBS objects can take a little more time to render than a polygonal model because the geometry has to be calculated and built for each frame before it can be drawn. But remember, the benefit is that it is almost impossible to get a hard-edged line within a NURBS surface, even during animation. So that extra rendering time comes with a big bonus.

If an iso-surface needs more geometry to make it smoother at rendering time, you can adjust the rendered complexity of the surface in the Surface Approximation rollout of the NURBS Surface Modifier panel. I won't present a complex and lengthy technical explanation of this process here; consult your MAX Release 2.5 User's Guide or the Online Help feature for the exact parameters.

Basic NURBS Modeling Methodology

A good general rule of thumb for all 3D modeling (not just NURBS) is "start simple, then add detail." However, this rule is vital to NURBS modeling in particular.

Most of your NURBS model creation will take place in the NURBS Surface Modifier panel, so it will be beneficial to start with some sort of simple or primitive surface (spherical, conical, cylindrical, or flat), or curve to serve as the master component. Then, you can add detail by sculpting and refining the surface and extracting other NURBS components from this. This "master component" could be

a simple point or CV surface, a standard primitive object that you then convert to a NURBS surface, or a single curve that will be used later to create a surface. In general, the simpler the starter object, the easier it will be to add detail later; there will be less clutter to deal with, allowing you to focus detail only where it is desired.

Here are some things to keep in mind when you are creating this master component:

- Will this component need to be attached or blended to another surface edge?
- If so, where?
- Will this surface be animated, and if so, how?
- Does it need to be dependent or independent?

The good news is that almost all of these items can be changed, with varying levels of success, at almost any stage in the modeling process. But if you have reasonably solid answers to the preceding questions before you begin, you can focus your time on modeling and not fixing the model.

And now, on with the show.

Creating An Alien Head

Now that you've learned a smattering of technical basics that you'll need to successfully create NURBS models, let's dive into some practical applications.

In the following exercises, you'll create a NURBS model of an alien creature's head and learn the benefits and detriments of using differing NURBS methodologies to build it. The goal here is to make you familiar with the concepts of starting with basic NURBS objects and then sculpting them into complex models.

Stage 1: Creating The Master Surface Object

You'll build an alien head starting from a single NURBS curve. The first step is to create the Master Surface Object:

1. In MAX, click on the Shapes tab in the Create panel. Choose NURBS Curves from the drop-down list and click on the CV button.

2. In the Front viewport, create a CV curve that resembles one-half of a side profile of a humanoid head, similar to Figure 13.1.

3. With the curve still selected, go to the Modify panel. Click on the Edit Stack button, and when the Convert To options list pops up, change the curve to a NURBS Surface.

4. Open the Create Surfaces section of the NURBS Surface rollout panel, click on the Lathe button, then click on the NURBS curve to make a lathe NURBS surface. If the surface looks like an inverted wine glass (as in Figure 13.2), go to the very bottom of the rollout (which has expanded to include the parameters for Lathe Surface creation), click on the Max button, and set the Degrees spinner to 360.

5. If the surface appears as anything other than what is shown in Figure 13.2 or 13.3, make sure the Y Axis button (under Direction in the Lathe Surface rollout) is selected. The surface should look like a squashed lightbulb, as in Figure 13.3. This will serve as your master object.

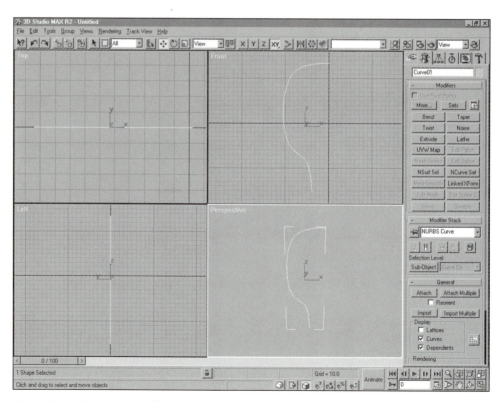

Figure 13.1 The starting profile of a humanoid head.

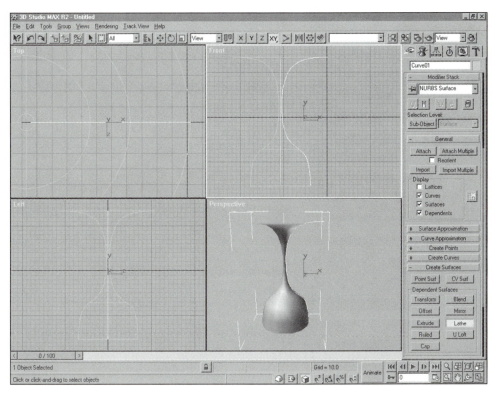

Figure 13.2   An example of a NURBS curve lathed with the axis improperly set.

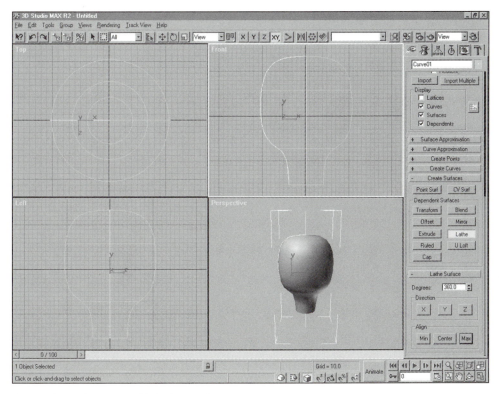

Figure 13.3   The corrected lathed NURBS curve.

Don't be concerned if the surface has a seam along one side—this is a detail that you can fix easily when you start adding the final details to the model in Stage 3.

Stage 2: Adding Gross (Not Grotesque— Yet!) Detail

Now you're ready for Stage 2—adding details. Follow these steps:

1. Click on the Sub-object button and select Surface from the Sub-object list. Then, click on the Lathe surface to select it.

2. Click on the Make Independent button in the Surface common panel. This will free your surface from being bound by the single profile curve. Just to clean up after yourself, select Curve in the Sub-object list and select and delete the original curve.

3. Next, select Surface from the Sub-object list. Select the surface again, and then click on the Make Loft button. When the Loft dialog box appears, click on the From V Iso Curves button and set the number of curves to 15. You should then have 15 vertical curves that define your surface, as shown in Figure 13.4.

4. Select Curve CV in the Sub-object list. All of the CVs for the V Iso curves should appear in bright green on the screen. In the Left viewport, select a few of the CVs on the right side of the display where the spherical part of the surface (the head) curves into the cylindrical area (the neck), as in Figure 13.5. You may need to use "Fence Selection Region" to select the correct CVs.

5. Lock the selected CVs (click on the lock in the status bar or press the spacebar) and pull them to the right and down until you have a good muzzle or chin shape, similar to Figure 13.6. Next, make a selection set called chin by typing the name into the selection set box on the top toolbar, just in case you lose the CVs before completing the next step. (Release 2 lets you create selection sets from sub-objects.)

6. In the Top viewport, deselect the middle CVs, leaving only one selected row on either side of the chin selection set, as in Figure 13.7. Make sure your Axis coordinates are set to Screen and the active axis is "restrict to Y", then move them back toward the top of the screen (middle of the model) until you see the chin rounding out and looking less like an animal's muzzle.

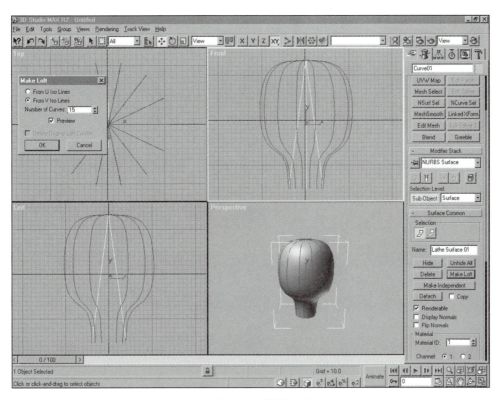

Figure 13.4   Fifteen vertical curves now define your NURBS surface.

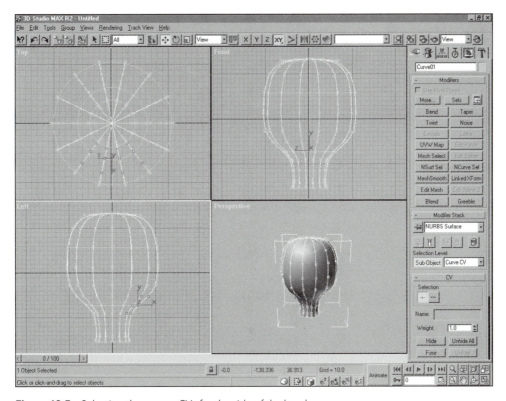

Figure 13.5   Selecting the proper CVs for the side of the head.

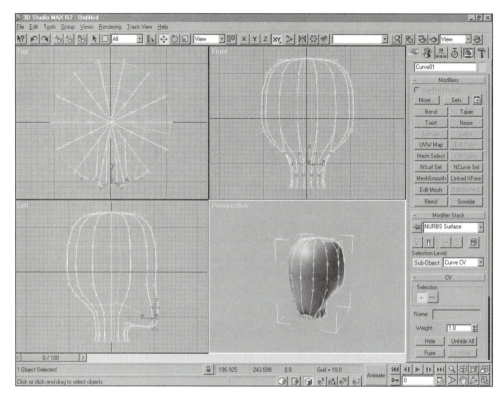

Figure 13.6 Moving the chin CVs.

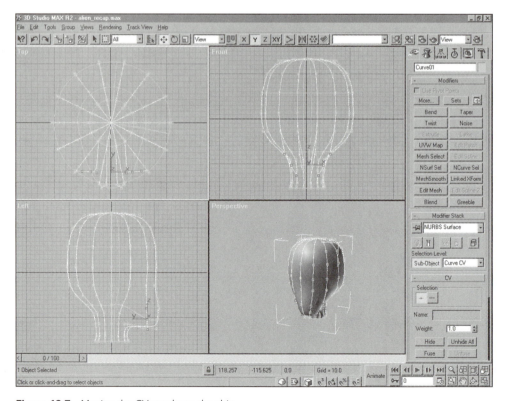

Figure 13.7 Moving the CVs to shape the chin.

Now, it's time to build the mouth:

7. Reload the chin CV selection set so that you can more easily see the exact area in which you'll be working. Under the top menu list, select Edit|Select Invert to select all but the chin CVs. Hide the selected CVs by clicking on the Hide button in the CV Sub-object panel.

8. Next, identify the two columns of CVs that make up the frontmost part of the mouth bulge. Click on the Refine button in the CV Sub-object panel and insert a new CV on each of the frontmost CV columns just above the top chin CV, as seen in Figure 13.8. If they are placed in the correct columns, the rest of the CVs in each column will automatically unhide themselves. The new CVs will serve as the upper lip.

9. In the Left viewport, select the two CVs at the front of the muzzle (the CVs below the ones just created). Drag them back into the head, just above the center of the neck. This should put a nice orifice in the alien face, as shown in Figure 13.9.

10. Before going on to the next step, feel free to sculpt the CVs around the mouth to add as much (or as little) detail as you

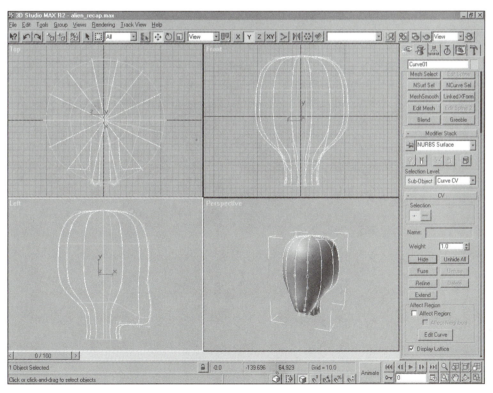

Figure 13.8 After adding the CVs that will serve as the upper lip of the alien, all of the CVs in the refined columns appear.

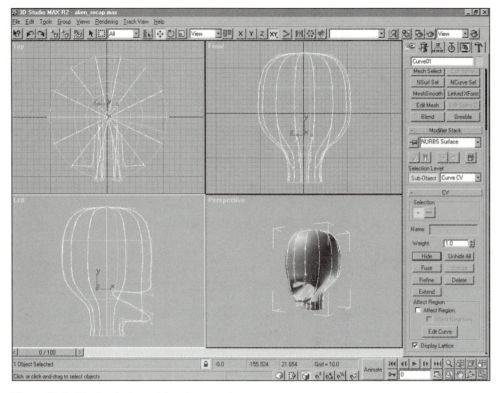

Figure 13.9 The beginnings of the alien mouth.

wish. In my examples, I'll add a little sharpness and weight to the jawline through the same process of selective refining and sculpting. I'll also pull in the corners of the mouth for a more gaunt appearance and pull the upper lip down a bit until I have what you see in Figure 13.10. Feel free to customize the alien any way you wish—no two aliens ever look alike.

Once you have the mouth sculpted to your liking, it's time to adjust the cranium (after all, alien races need extra space to hold those large, spacefaring brains). To do so, follow these steps:

11. Click on Unhide All in the CV rollout to unhide the hidden CVs, then select all of the CVs on the cranial area of the head, as seen in Figure 13.11.

12. In the Top viewport, scale the selected CVs on the (View) Y axis until you get a nice bulge. Then, go into the Left viewport and scale the CVs on the View Y axis again to stretch the cranium upward, resulting in something similar to Figure 13.12.

13. Next, move the vertices up so that the base of the cranial bulge lies near the center of the entire head model, resulting in what you see in Figure 13.13.

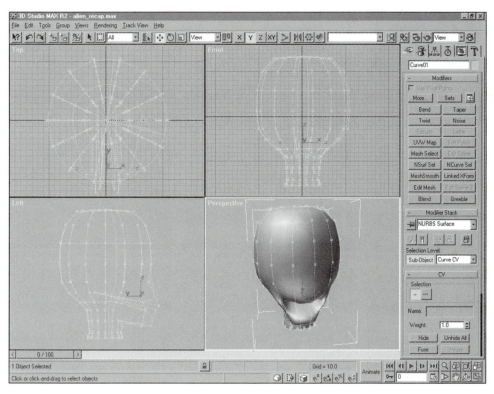

Figure 13.10 The basic alien head.

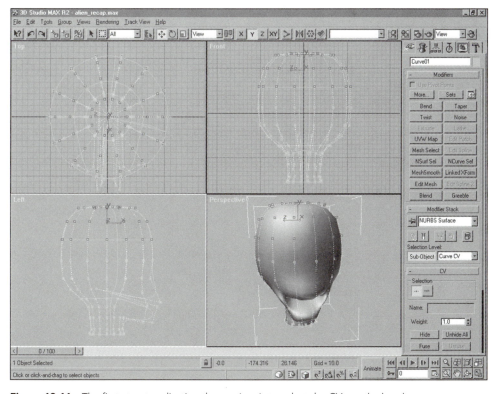

Figure 13.11 The first step to adjusting the cranium is to select the CVs on the head.

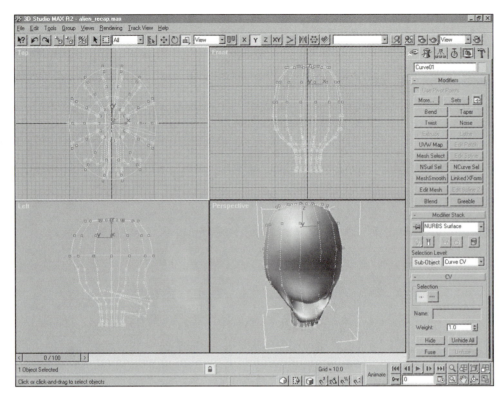

Figure 13.12 Scaling the CVs results in the alien getting a swelled head.

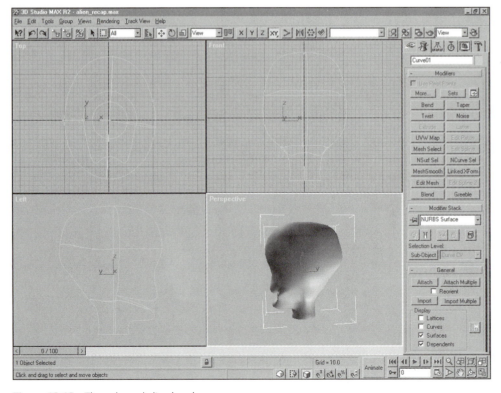

Figure 13.13 The enlarged alien head.

You're now finished with the gross detail of the head. (If you want, save this file to your MAX \SCENES directory as ALIENHED.MAX.) In the next sections, you'll add more details to the face, including features such as the eyes and nose. To do this more easily, you need to "chunk down" the surfaces, breaking them into manageable parts that allow you to focus in on individual details without disturbing those areas already finished or not yet touched. In addition, for time and accuracy, you'll cut the head in half and work only on one side. But through the miracle of NURBS modeling, you'll be able to see your results on a dependent symmetrical copy of the head surfaces.

Stage 3: Breaking The Model Into Detail-Focused Surfaces

Now, you're ready to create the finer details of the alien head:

1. Select Surface from the Sub-object list, select the head surface, and click on the Make Independent button. The head surface is no longer defined by the curves created from the v-loft. Just for cleanliness, select Curves from the Sub-object list, select all of the loft curves, and delete them.

2. Go back into the Surface Sub-object panel. Select the surface and go to the bottom of the rollout panel. Click on the Break Rows button, then go into the Top viewport. Move the cursor until you have a blue line that bisects the face, as shown in Figure 13.14.

3. Left-click on the head. The surface will now be divided into two parts: one that is a quarter of the total (the left side of the face) and the other a three-quarter section. Click on the surface just to the left of the bisecting line you created and delete it. You should be left with three-quarters of the head surface.

4. Repeat the Break Rows procedure, but this time, move the bisecting line so it cuts across the middle of the back of the head. Again, select the surface section to the left of the bisecting line and delete it. You should then be left with nearly an exact half of your original head model, as shown in Figure 13.15.

Now, you'll begin separating out the individual detail areas, such as the eyes and nose, using the same surface breaking procedures but with a bit more finesse. The important thing to keep in mind here is how all these parts will be rejoined to create the final detailed head. Always focus on clean edges that will easily blend back into the appropriate areas. To begin separating out the individual detail areas, follow these steps:

The Break Rows And Break Columns Functions

The Break Rows and Break Cols (columns) functions divide the selected surface at the point indicated between the origin of the surface and the termination of the surface. In this case, because you started with a lathe surface, the Break function breaks the surface into what resembles a one-quarter and a three-quarter model. Because the original curve was at the left side of the head, a bisecting line down the middle of the face represents approximately one-quarter of the lathe distance from the original defining curve. Always keep these basic rules in mind and the Break Rows and Break Cols functions become powerful and predictable tools.

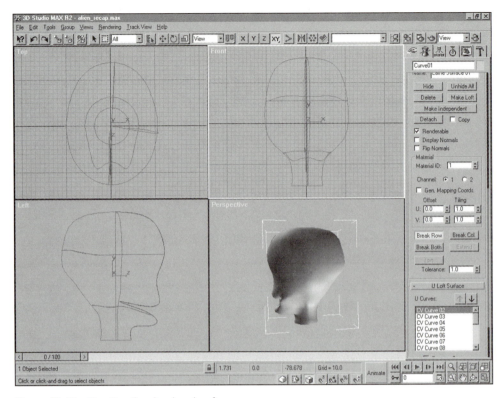

Figure 13.14 Bisecting the alien head surface.

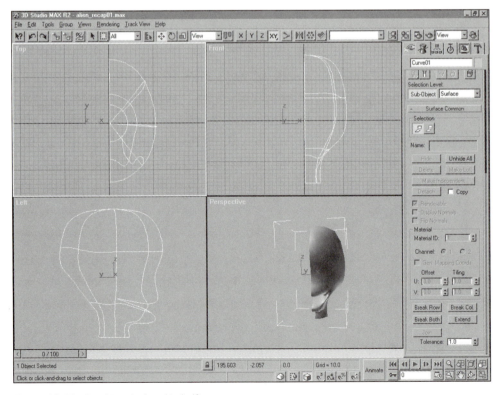

Figure 13.15 Breaking the head in half.

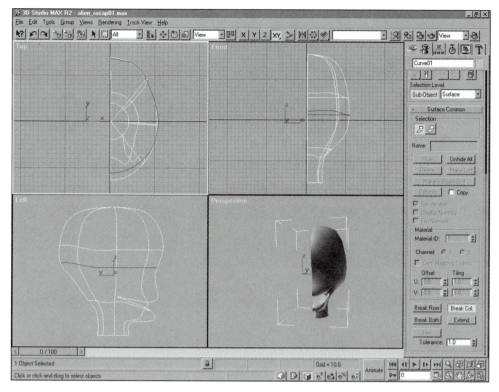

Figure 13.16 Drawing the bisecting line for the eye placement.

5. Click on the Break Cols button and go to the Left viewport. Draw the bisecting line at approximately the center of where you want the eye line to be (as shown in Figure 13.16). The head surface should now be in top and bottom halves. Move the top half up just a bit so you can easily see the separation between it and the bottom half.

6. In preparation for building the nose (which you will add before you add the eyes), you'll cut a few surfaces out of the front of the face to sculpt. Click on the Break Both button and move it across the lower half of the model so it creates two bisecting lines; the lines will separate a small corner of the face corresponding to the lower tip of the nose, as shown in Figure 13.17. Left-click to complete the operation. Repeat the operation on the upper half of the face to create a surface for the upper half of the nose.

7. In the Front viewport, select all of the surfaces on the right side and move them on the X axis a tiny distance, just enough to create a visible space between the surfaces. Select the upper nose surface and the lower nose surface and scale them down a bit on the Y axis to create a small space isolating these surfaces as well. You should end up with something that looks like Figure 13.18.

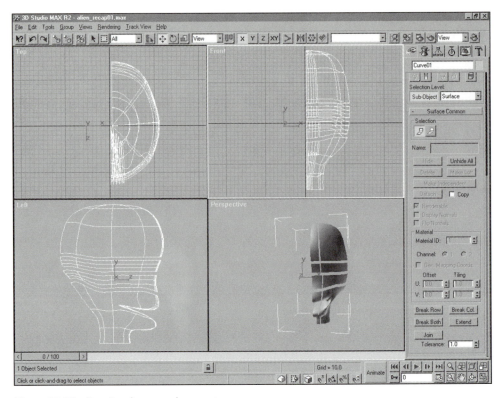

Figure 13.17 Creating the nose placement.

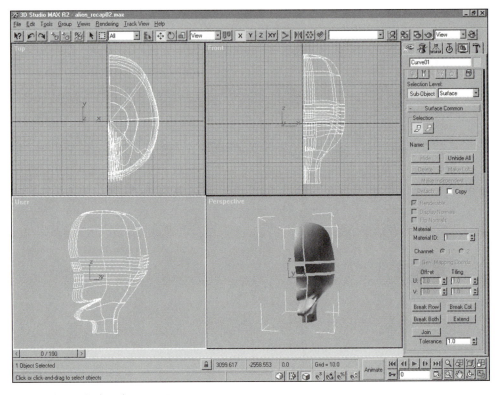

Figure 13.18 Scaling the nose pieces.

Stage 4: Detailing The Nose

Now, you're ready to add detail to this alien's proboscis:

1. Turn off the Sub-object button and go into the main NURBS Surface Modifier panel. Expand the Create Surfaces rollout and click on the Blend button. Begin blending all of the horizontal edges of the new surfaces by clicking on one edge and dragging to another (don't worry about the vertical edges for now). You should end up with a series of dependent green blend surfaces and some vertical spaces, as shown in Figure 13.19.

2. Go back into the Surface Sub-object mode and select all of the surfaces except the nose surfaces and the blend surfaces coming from them. Hide the selected surfaces.

3. Turn off Sub-object mode again and go back into the main NURBS Surface Modifier panel. Expand the Create Surfaces rollout again, but this time click on the Mirror button. Go into the Front viewport, select each surface (independent and dependent) one at a time, and create a mirror surface of each across the X axis (check the X radio button in the Mirror Surface parameters panel). Adjust the Offset amount in the Mirror Surface

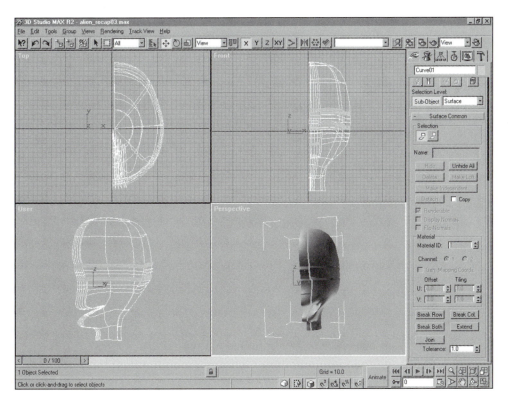

Figure 13.19   Blending the horizontal edges of the surfaces.

parameters panel until the new dependent mirror surfaces are close to the original surfaces, as seen in Figure 13.20.

4. Turn on the Sub-object button and select Surface CVs from the list. Select all of the displayed CVs for the independent nose surfaces and create a selection set called Nose CV in the Named Selection box.

5. Next go into the Surfaces Sub-object panel and click on the Unhide All button. All of the surfaces will reappear, making it easier to see what the nose will look like in conjunction with the entire face. Repeat Step 3 with all of the newly unhidden surfaces.

6. Go back into the Surface CV Sub-object mode and select the Nose CV set from the Named Selection list. Invert the selection and hide all of the other CVs so that only the nose CVs remain visible. You may also wish to uncheck the Display Lattice box at the bottom of the Surface CV dialog box to make it easier to see the CVs.

7. Now, you can begin sculpting the nose (finally!). Start sculpting by using the inner nose CVs to pull out the bridge of the nose. Then continue sculpting, adding whatever details you wish by pushing and pulling CVs and refining and deleting CVs as

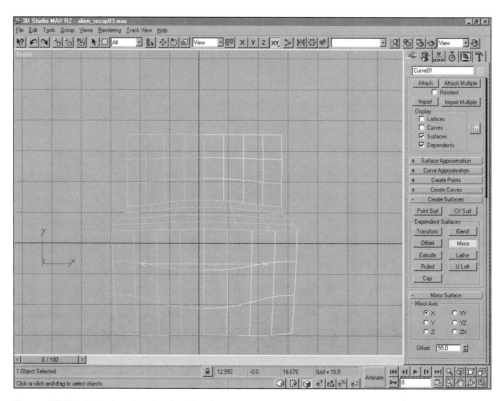

Figure 13.20 Mirroring the alien head surfaces.

needed. Again, this is a good place to add as little or as much
detail as you desire.

In the example model, I have given the alien a rather humanoid-
looking nose by adding a bit of tapered width to the bridge and some
nostrils to flare when his/her/its plans for galactic domination start
to go awry, resulting in what you see in Figure 13.21.

Now you can start detailing the eyes.

Stage 5: Detailing The Eyes

Your alien has a nose; now it needs some optical equipment:

1. Begin by deselecting the NURBS head altogether and going
   into the creation panel. Click on the Geometry tab, create a
   GeoSphere the size of an appropriate eyeball, and move the
   sphere into the eye position on the head, as seen in Figure 13.22.

2. Next, reselect the NURBS head, go back to the Modify panel, and
   with the Sub-object button turned off, click on the Import button.
   Click on the new GeoSphere to import it into the NURBS head model.
   If the operation is successful, the eye-sphere will no longer be drawn
   in polygonal mode but will be represented by NURBS iso-parms.

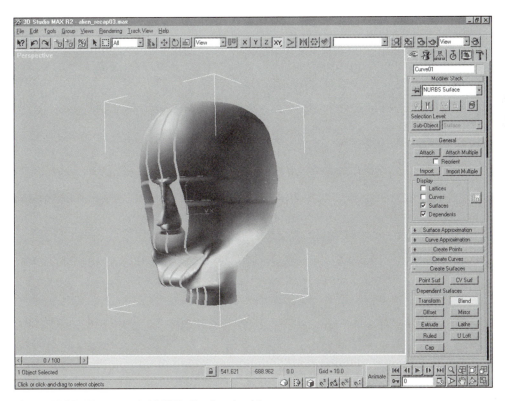

Figure 13.21   The example NURBS alien (head only).

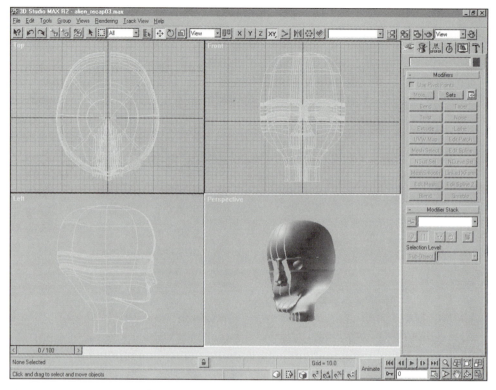

Figure 13.22 Creating eyes for the alien.

3. Click on the Sub-object button again, select Imports from the drop-down list, and select the eyeball. It should turn red and be displayed in its original polygonal form. Scale and rotate the eyeball until it resembles Figure 13.23.

4. Select Surface CVs from the Sub-object drop-down list and click on the Unhide All button in the Surface CV panel. All of the independent surface CVs should reappear (most of them were hidden when you were constructing and detailing the nose).

5. Select all of the CVs around the eyeball import, as shown in Figure 13.24. Invert the selection and hide these CVs.

6. In the Front viewport, select the CVs at the top of the blend surface above the eyeball and the CVs at the bottom of the blend surface below the eyeball. Select only the CVs that are centered around and aligned with the eyeball itself, as shown in Figure 13.25. Add in the corresponding CVs one row above the top selection and one row below the bottom selection (again, only those CVs aligning with the eyeball import object).

7. Lock the selection and (still in the Front viewport) perform a non-uniform scale along the screen Y axis, pushing these CVs out

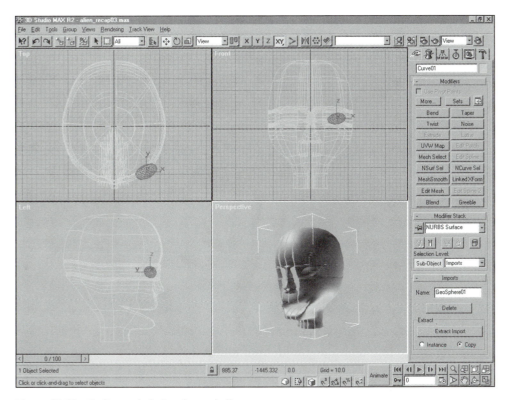

Figure 13.23   Scaling and placing the eyeball.

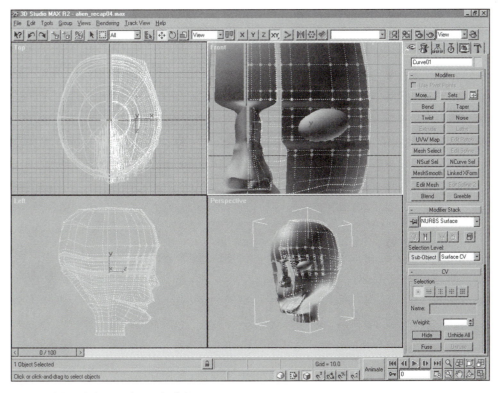

Figure 13.24   Selecting the eyeball CVs.

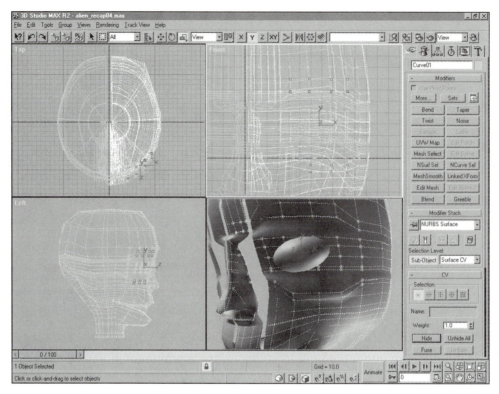

Figure 13.25   Selecting the CVs around the eyeball itself.

from the eyeball; the result will be similar to what you see in Figure 13.25.

8. Select the CVs that align with the eyeball along the bottom edge of the top blend surface. Lock the selection and then go to the Top viewport. Move the selected CVs out from the head and over the top of the eyeball. (You may need to refine the rows or columns to add more CVs to create a smooth eyelid.)

9. Go back into the Front viewport and pull these CVs down just over the top edge of the eyeball. Place them in a named selection set called Top Eyelid and deselect them. Then, start moving them one at a time to cover the top of the eye more closely, until you have a result that looks similar to Figure 13.26.

10. Go to the CVs along the far left edge of the eye surface (near the nose) in the Front viewport. Click on the Fuse button in the Surface CV Sub-object panel. Find the CV that's closest to the inside lower edge of the eye, then locate the corresponding CV along the left edge of the eye surface. Click and hold on the CV just above the CV you just located and drag to the CV on the corner edge of the eye. Go to the next CV up and repeat the process.

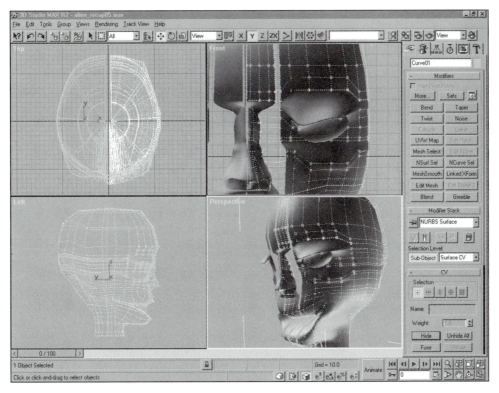

Figure 13.26   Creating and aligning the eyelids.

Continue doing this until you fuse the CV on the bottom of the top blend surface.

11. Repeat this process with any other CV columns between the left edge of the eye surface and the CV column nearest the eye. Do not fuse the CV column nearest the eyeball import object. In the end, you should have an eyelid resembling what you see in Figure 13.27.

12. Repeat the fusing procedure with the CV column on the other side of the eye (one column should be sufficient to get the proper results here).

13. Repeat the previous two steps using the top CVs on the bottom blend surface. Your final result should be similar to Figure 13.28.

14. Next, go back to the CVs that you adjusted earlier in Step 6. Start with the top row of CVs along the top blend surface and pull them down just above the eyeball. In the Top viewport, move these CVs just a little toward the inside of the head, creating a good clean line over the top of the eyeball itself. Do the same with the bottom row of CVs along the bottom blend surface. Your end result should look something like Figure 13.29.

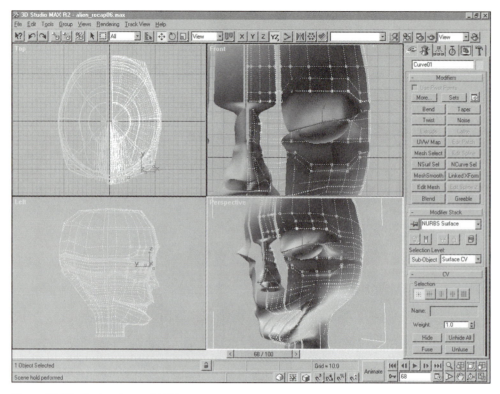

Figure 13.27 Fusing the eyelid CVs.

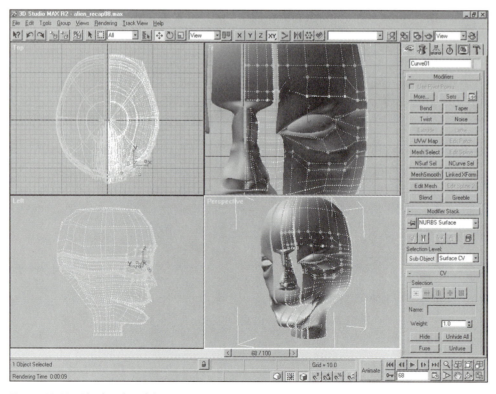

Figure 13.28 The fused eyelid CVs.

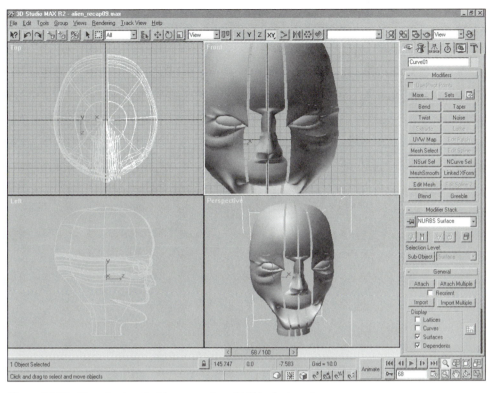

Figure 13.29   The alien head with eyes and eyelid CV adjustments.

15. If you have problems with the eyelids showing through the eye-
    ball surface, select the CVs at the back of the eye socket, scale
    them apart (and the X and Y axes), and pull them further inside
    the head. If you still have problems, check to make sure the
    normals on the eyeball surface are pointing outward from the
    center of the eye.

Detailing Your Alien Eyes

In Chapter 4, contributor Michael Spaw showed you how to use a
ray-traced material, two spheres, and a digitized photo of a sheep's
eye to create an extremely realistic eyeball, complete with spherical
corneal distortion. In the \CHAP_13 and \MAPS directories of this
book's companion CD-ROM, you'll find several files called
ALIENEYE*.JPG. Feel free to use these bitmaps to dress up your
alien's extraterrestrial orbs!

Finishing Touches

All that remains to complete the model is to create blend surfaces
across the remaining gaps in the head. If the blend surfaces leave
harsh lines, simply move the defining surfaces (the surfaces from

Note: *The alien head example file
I've created for this chapter's
figures is included in the
\CHAP_13 directory of this book's
companion CD-ROM as
ALIENHED.MAX.*

which the blend surface was created) in small increments until the line is gone. Occasionally, you may have to go so far as to adjust the CVs along the edges of the defining surfaces to smooth out the blend seam. Adjustments performed in this manner need a delicate touch, but the results are visible and rewarding.

Voila! You now have a being from another planet to put to whatever fiendish purposes you can devise.

Moving On

Now that you have had an in-depth look at NURBS tools and methodology, you'll take NURBS to the next level, where they really shine.

In the next chapter, you'll construct a similar (but seamless) NURBS model. By starting with a simple cone, then stretching it, flattening it, and adding detail, you can build a hooded cobra, complete with venom-laden fangs.

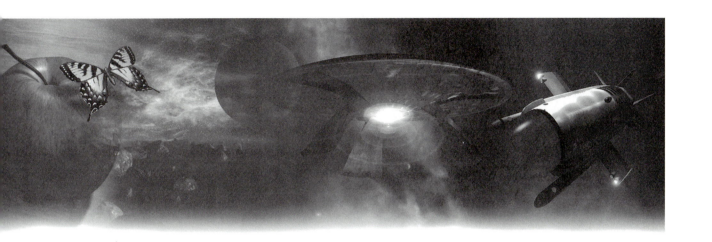

AN INTRODUCTION TO
NURBS MODELING, PART II

14

BY

KEN ALLEN ROBERTSON

In this chapter, you'll build a cobra. You'll start with a lowly polygonal cone and then add more detail and more parts to the creature. You'll also explore new methods of using the power of MAX NURBS.

In the last chapter, you were given a useful (and more easily understandable) definition of a NURBS surface and what benefits it has over traditional polygonal models or patch surfaces. You learned that NURBS surfaces are always determined by curves, and that therefore, it's difficult (almost impossible, actually) to create a hard-edged line in a NURBS surface. In this chapter, you'll create an entire creature—a cobra—rather than just part of one, like the alien head you created in the last chapter.

Creating A NURBS Cobra From A Geometric Primitive

The first stage of building the NURBS cobra is to build the body. You'll then progress to eyes and fangs. To begin, reset Max and follow these steps:

1. Click on the Geometry button in the Create panel. In the Front viewport, create a cone with a Radius 1 (base radius) setting of 50 units, a Height setting of 300 units, and a Radius 2 (top radius) setting of 0. Don't worry about the number of height or cap segments; they won't be a factor when you convert the object to a NURBS surface.

2. With the cone still selected, click on the Edit Stack icon in the Modify panel. Select NURBS Surface from the Convert To options list, turn on the Sub-object button, and select Surface from the drop-down list.

3. In a Perspective (or User) viewport, rotate the NURBS cone so you can easily see both the bottom cap and the sides of the cone. Click on the bottom of the cone to select just the surface that makes up the end cap of the cone and then delete it. You should now have a bottomless NURBS cone, as shown in Figure 14.1.

4. Select the remaining cone surface and click on the Close Cols button at the bottom of the Surface Sub-object rollout. This will make the surface continual, without a starting and ending edge.

5. With the cone surface still selected, click on the Make Loft button in the Surface Sub-object panel. Click on the U Iso-curves radio button in the Make Loft pop-up window and set the number of curves to 10.

6. Select Curve from the Sub-object drop-down list. Select all of the curves in the Left viewport and scale them along the X axis (View orientation) until the surface is a long, broom-handle-like object (about 2,000 percent).

3D Studio MAX R2.5 F/X and Design Color Studio

On the following pages, you'll see color examples of the effects tutorials presented in this book. In addition, you'll see the work of several noted 3D Studio MAX artists for film, TV, multimedia, games, and print.

From Chapter 3, "Lux Aeterna," by Michael Spaw. A standard three-light studio setup showing a key light, fill, and kicker. This type of real-world lighting arrangement also works well for demonstrating computer graphics lighting techniques.

A finished rendering of the lighting example. This image combines all the light types, reproducing a full studio lighting setup.

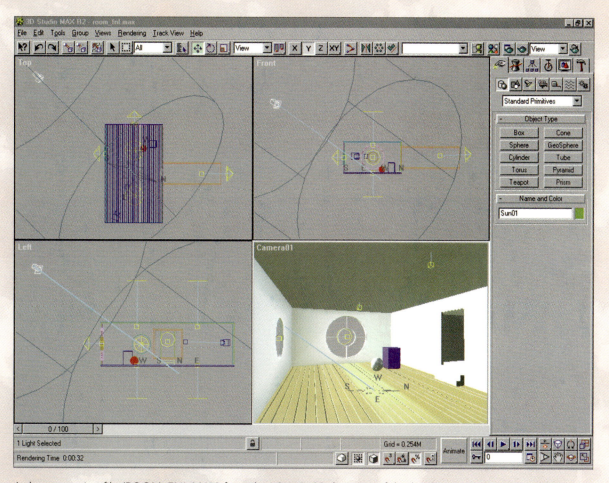

A demonstration file (ROOM_FNL.MAX) from the \CHAP_03 directory of this book's companion CD-ROM; this file demonstrates advanced lighting techniques for room interiors.

An example of a realistically-illuminated room, from Chapter 3. With careful placement of lights, you can create interiors that display a richness in color values and tonality that rival images produced with a radiosity renderer.

An example of a radiosity rendering of a room interior, done with the 3D Studio MAX rendering plug-in RadioRay.

Image courtesy of Kinetix.

Real-world textures, such as digitized images of rocks, bricks, metals, earth, tree bark, and animal skins can improve the quality of your final 3D renderings greatly. By using Adobe Photoshop, the author has taken this digitized photo of a rock face and has made it seamlessly tileable on the top and bottom edges, and on both sides. This map is included in the \CHAP_04 and \MAPS directories of this book's companion CD-ROM.

A digitized photo of an industrial electrical junction box. By loading textures such as this into an image editing or painting program, you can cut and paste interesting sections of the image together to form new maps. This map is included in the \CHAP_04 and \MAPS directories of this book's companion CD-ROM.

Another way to create realistic-appearing materials is through the use of third-party MAX plug-ins, such as DirtyREYES from REM Infografica (www.infografica.com). DirtyREYES creates procedural highlighting, smudges, and dirt along the edges of your 3D geometry, as shown here. The top flintlock pistol has DirtyREYES applied; the bottom simply has a default gray material. (A demo version of this plug-in is included in the \INFOGRAF\PLUGINS directory of this book's CD-ROM.)

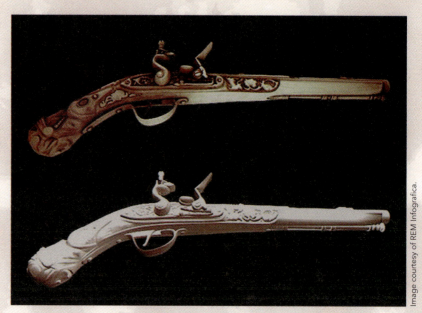

Image courtesy of REM Infografica.

Although it's a simple technique, the use of beveled and chamfered edges on your 3D geometry can enhance the appearance of your renderings. In this simple example, note how slight bevels on the right box's edges catch specular highlights, resulting in a less flat appearance.

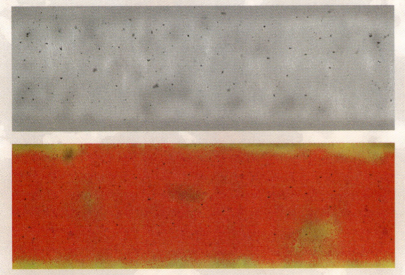

If you're a skillful 2D artist with a good eye, you may be able to paint Diffuse and Bump maps for your 3D objects that are indistinguishable from their real-world versions. In this figure, the top grayscale bump map and the colorful Diffuse map below it serve as the outer skin texture for an apple. These maps are included in the \CHAP_04 and \MAPS directories of this book's companion CD-ROM.

The finished apple rendering. (File APPLE.MAX in the \CHAP_04 directory.)

These digitized images of glass taxidermy eyes can help you create very realistic-appearing 3D fauna. These maps are included in the \CHAP_04 and \MAPS directories of this book's companion CD-ROM.

An example of a digitized sheep's eye (seen horizontally in this rendering) combined with a raytraced corneal dome provides a startling 3D effect. (File EYE.MAX in the \CHAP_04 directory.)

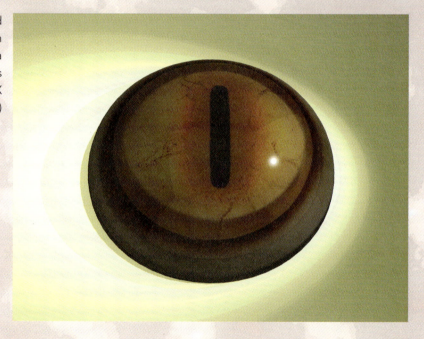

Martin Foster 1997

Careful attention to lighting and subtle details (such as this bat's fur) can greatly enhance your 3D creatures, as seen in this beautiful rendering done by MAX artist Martin Foster.

Image courtesy of Digimation.

Although not strictly plausible as a real-world animal, this creature is made whimsical by an application of procedural hair, courtesy of Digimation's Shag:Fur plug-in.

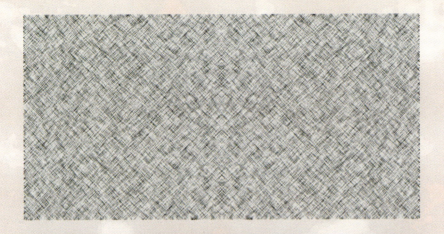

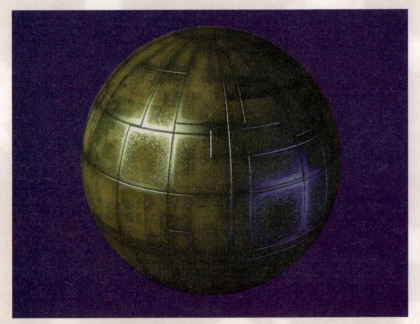

The combination of Diffuse, Shininess, Shininess Strength, Specular, and Bump maps, combined with Phong and Metal-shaded materials in a Blend material, creates the appearance of a scratched, scuffed metal surface. (Files METAL_1.MAX and METAL_2.MAX in the \CHAP_05 directory; example maps are included in the \MAPS directory.)

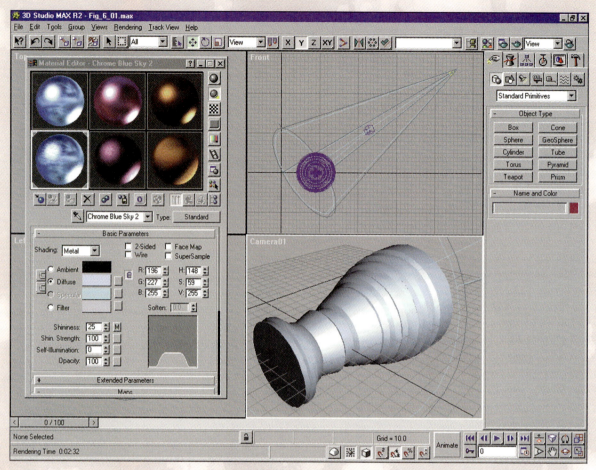

The METAL_3.MAX scene file from \CHAP_06 demonstrates the use of various Shininess, Bump, Reflection and Falloff maps to create convincing metallic textures.

The final rendering of the METAL_3.MAX scene file shows the Blue Sky 2 material, which uses 3D Studio MAX Release 2's new Falloff map type to reduce the amount of reflection on the edges of your 3D objects.

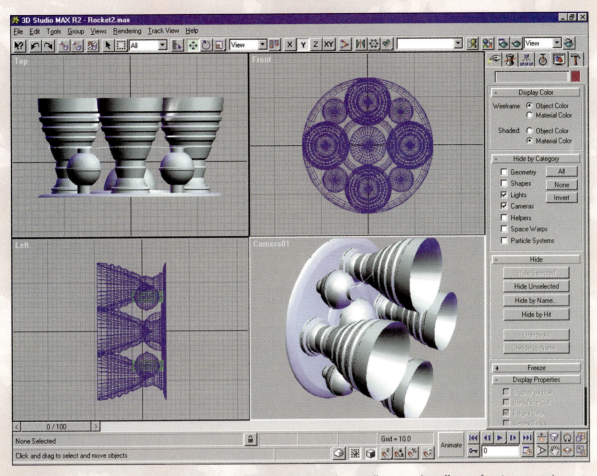

Another "rocket thruster" example uses complex geometry to better illustrate the effects of various metal materials. (File ROCKET2.MAX in the \CHAP_06 directory.)

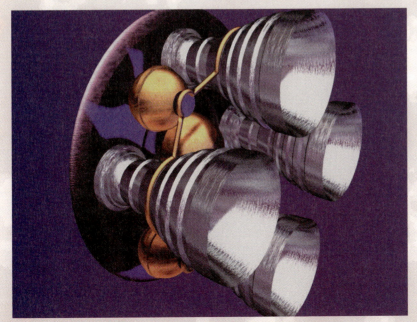

In this rendering, different metal textures (included in this book's MAXFX2.MAT Material Library) are applied to the thrusters, piping and mixing tank geometry.

Another example of the Falloff map used in a Mix map, this time creating an "X-ray" effect on the rocket thruster geometry.

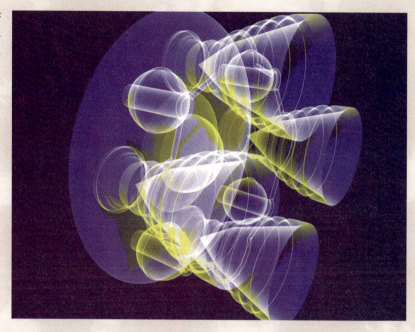

By using the Falloff map to blend between two Reflection maps, you can create an abalone-shell "mother of pearl" texture, as shown here.

A combination of the Cellular texture and MAX's Lens Effects Glow Video Post filter creates the illusion of lightning arcing across this spherical surface. (File DISINTG1.MAX in the \CHAP_07 directory.)

By combining the glowing Cellular lightning with an animated Opacity map and mask, you can create the effect of lightning "eating away" the sphere. (File DISINTG2.MAX in the \CHAP_07 directory.)

A combination of a sphere, an animated Noise modifier, and the Smoke and Falloff maps creates this effect of an expanding cloud of plasma. (File PLASMA.MAX in the \CHAP_08 directory.)

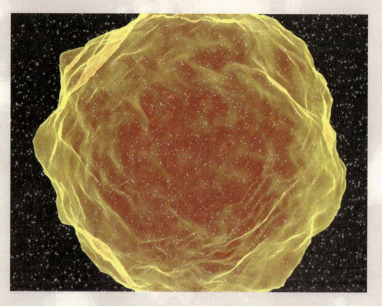

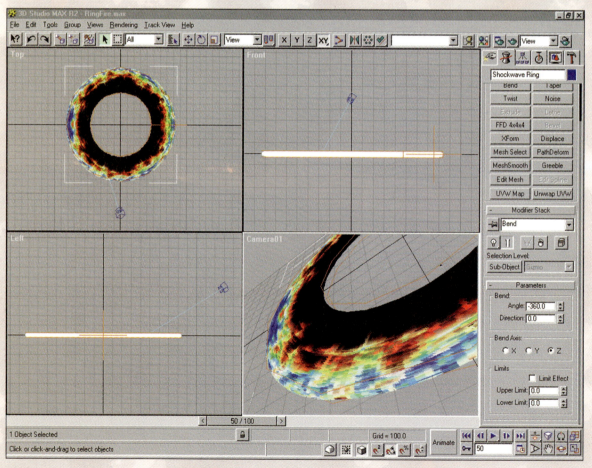

By creating an airfoil shape, extruding it, bending it into a ring, then animating its size, you can create the effect of a science-fictional explosive "shockwave" ring, as seen in the *Star Trek* and *Star Wars* films. (File RINGFIRE.MAX in the \CHAP_08 directory.)

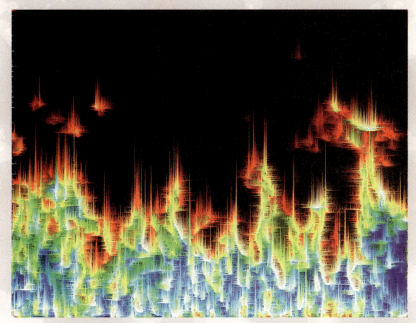

A still frame of the animated texture applied to the shock-wave ring geometry. The author created this texture by using Photoshop to manipulate digitized fire imagery from the VCE Pyromania CD-ROM. (This texture sequence is included in the \PYROMANI and \MAPS directories of the companion CD-ROM. Textures used by permission of Peter Kuran and VCE, Inc.; for more information, go to www.vce.com.)

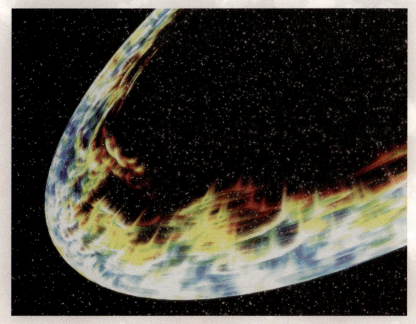

The finished shockwave rendering.

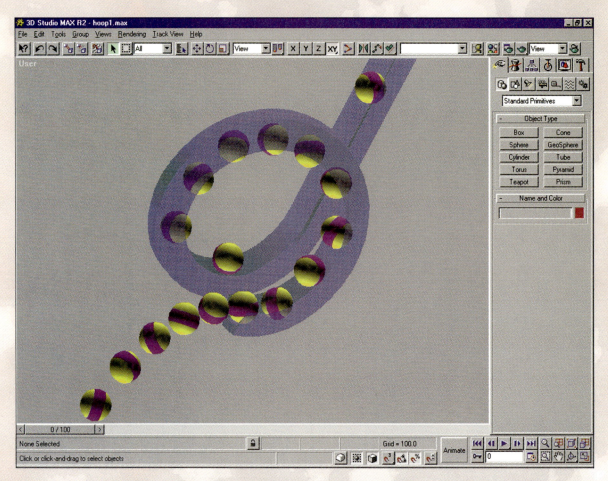

From Chapter 9; this example of snapshot geometry shows how MAX's Dynamics utility imparts friction to a ball rolling down a looping track. The ball slides and rotates properly as it moves down the track. (File HOOP1B.MAX in the \CHAP_09 directory.).

3D Studio MAX Release 2's new Raytrace material type enables you to set the Index of Refraction (IOR) for your specific material needs. This image from Chapter 10 shows five spheres, each with a different IOR that corresponds to real-world refraction properties. From left to right, top: underwater (IOR: 0.7) and hot air (IOR: 0.98); bottom: water (IOR: 1.33), glass (IOR: 1.5), and diamond (IOR: 2.42).

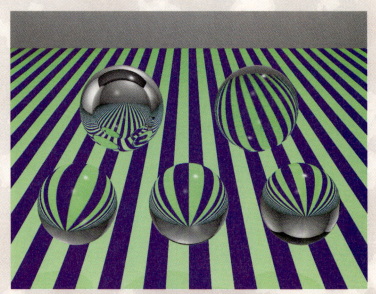

This example of three metal spheres illustrates how you can use the Blur settings in MAX's Raytrace Material to create different metal types—polished steel, plain steel, and sandblasted steel.

A tabletop setting illustrates MAX's Raytrace Material and Map types. Note how the teapot lid reflects its own handle, and the blue-tinted shadow cast by the blue glass sphere. (File TABLETOP.MAX in the \CHAP_10 directory.)

A chromed watch demonstrates both the refractive properties of MAX's Raytrace material (on the crystal) and the Fluorescence feature on the glowing green hands. (File WATCH.MAX in the \CHAP_10 directory.)

Although many 3D artists use raytracing to create accurate reflections and refractions in shiny objects, MAX's Raytrace material allows you to adjust Shininess Strength above 100, resulting in large, soft specular highlights, as shown on this rubber ball example. (File RUBBER.MAX in the \CHAP_10 directory.)

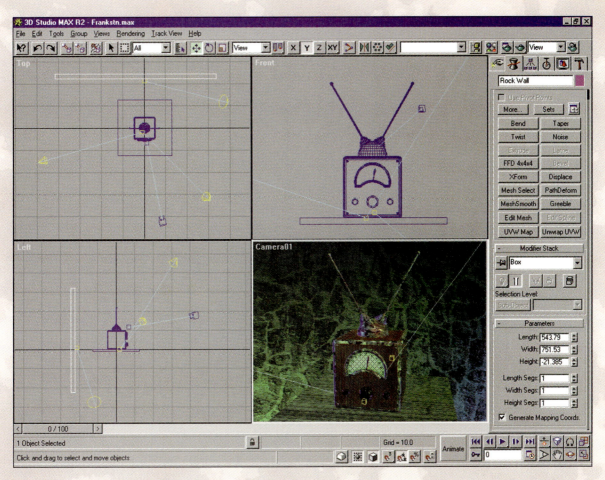

From Chapter 11, a piece of "Dr. Frankenstein" (or other mad scientist) lab equipment (file FRANKSTN.MAX in the \CHAP_11 directory). By applying a Noise modifier to an animated, renderable spline, you can create an electrical arc that travels repeatedly between the two metal contacts.

The finished rendering of the "mad scientist" electrical device. A Lens Effect Glow filter applied in Video Post creates the glowing effect on the renderable spline.

A blocky human hand model, created by extruding faces from a simple box, then pulling and welding certain vertices. By applying a MeshSmooth modifier to the model, you can turn this blocky geometry into a more organic appendage.

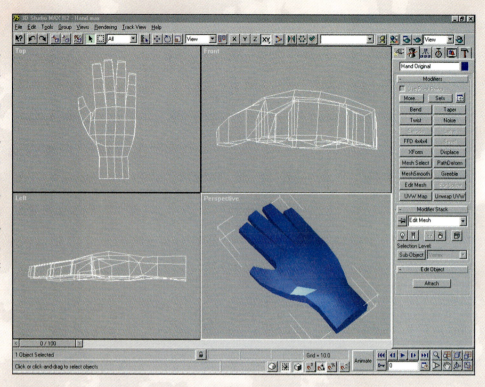

The original blocky human hand model with the MeshSmooth modifier applied, two levels of Iteration, and the Quad Output is checked.

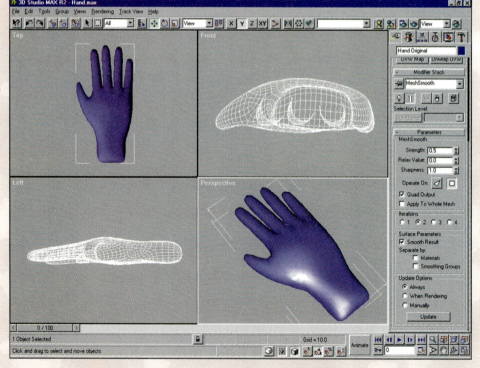

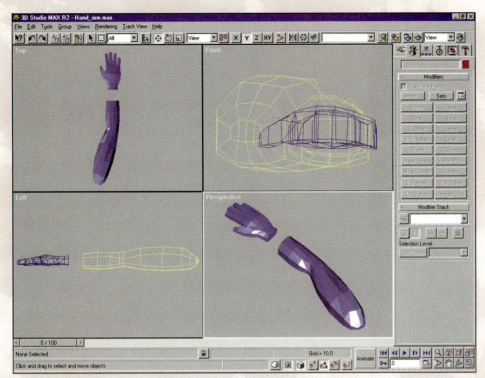

Simple geometry of a human hand and arm, before application of the Connect and MeshSmooth modifiers. (File HAND_ARM.MAX in the \CHAP_11 directory.)

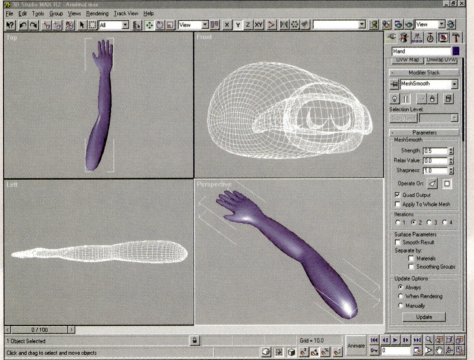

The same human arm geometry with the Connect and MeshSmooth modifiers applied. Notice how the original rough geometry has now achieved a much more realistic appearance; you can also collapse it into a single smooth mesh object. (File ARMFINAL.MAX in the \CHAP_11 directory.)

From Chapter 12, a Quad Patch "landscape" object with "rock" geometry strewn across it using the Scatter Compound Object.

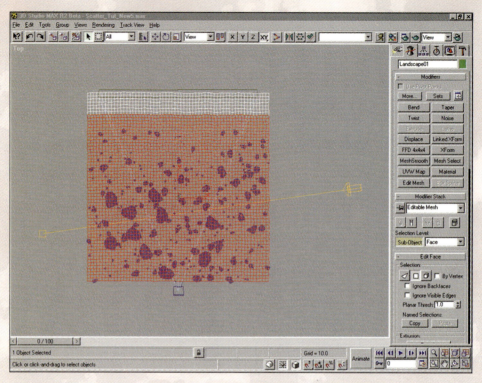

A shaded, camera's-eye view of the finished landscape geometry, with lighting applied.

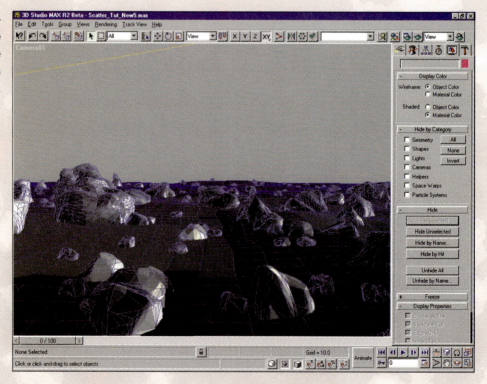

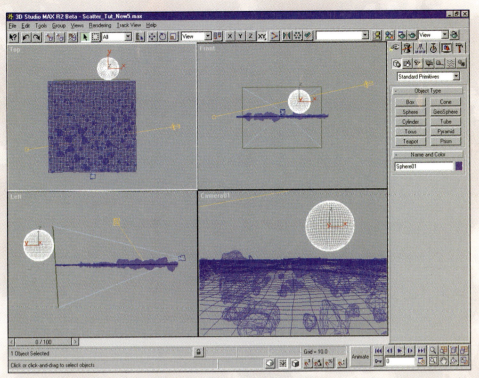

A parametric sphere above the horizon provides a distant planetoid for the scene. (File PLANETOD.MAX in the \CHAP_12 directory.)

The finished alien landscape rendering depicting a distant, dusty planetoid surface. Atmospheric fog, complex landscape materials, custom environment maps, and stark directional lighting create the final effect. (Note that all materials and maps for this scene are included on this book's companion CD-ROM.)

The beginnings of a distant mountain range. A QuadPatch object with an FFD modifier applied (its middle vertices pulled up) provides the initial "hill" shape.

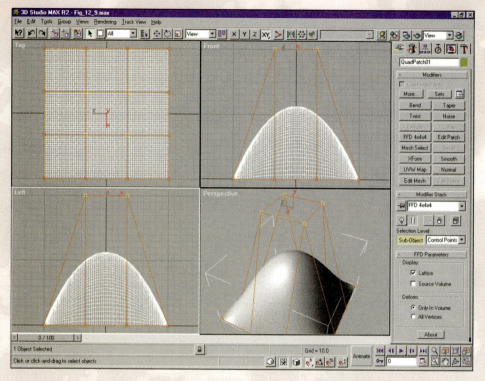

The QuadPatch mountain with Noise applied, and a Directional light illuminating its surface.

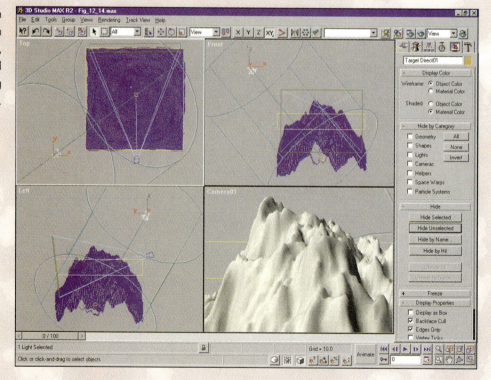

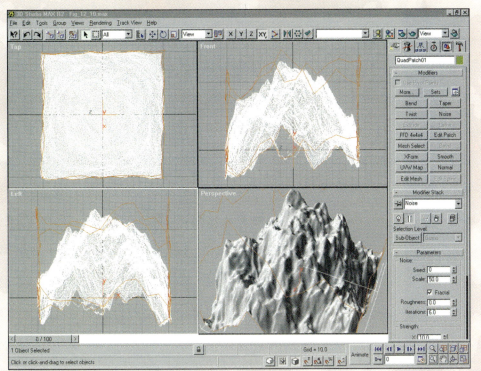

The QuadPatch mountain with additional Noise and Tessellation of its faces to create a more craggy surface.

The final mountain range rendering. A Top/Bottom material creates the illusion of a rocky surface with snow-capped peaks. Atmospheric haze is created with Linear and Volumetric fog; a digitized cloud photo used as an Environment background completes the effect. (File MOUNTAIN.MAX in the \CHAP_12 directory.)

From Chapter 13; an extraterrestrial head takes shape from these basic NURBS splines. (File ALIENHED.MAX in the \CHAP_13 directory.)

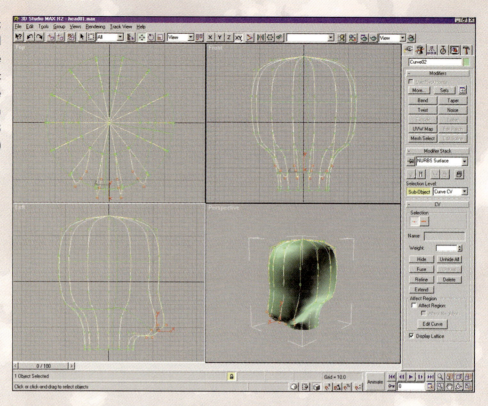

By adjusting the NURBS CVs (control vertices), you can sculpt soft features into organic shapes.

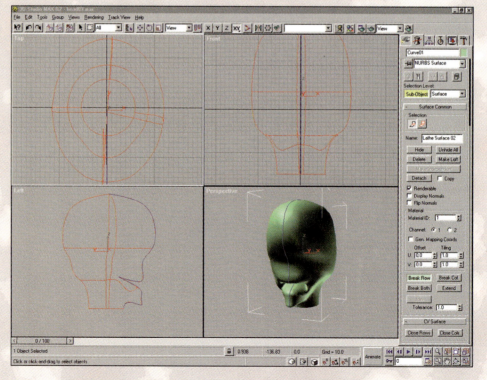

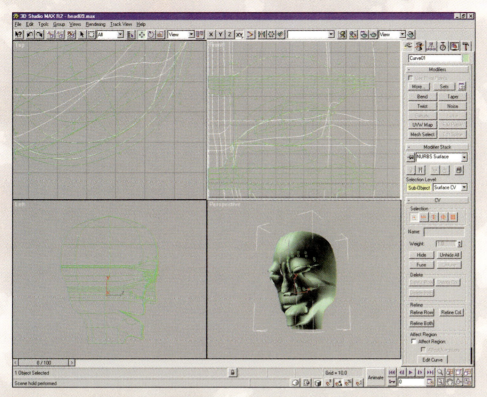

Further CV adjustments and the addition of new NURBS surfaces creates eyes, their sockets, and eyelids.

A rendering of the finished NURBS alien head, with the Cellular map applied, and Environmental fog added for atmospheric haze.

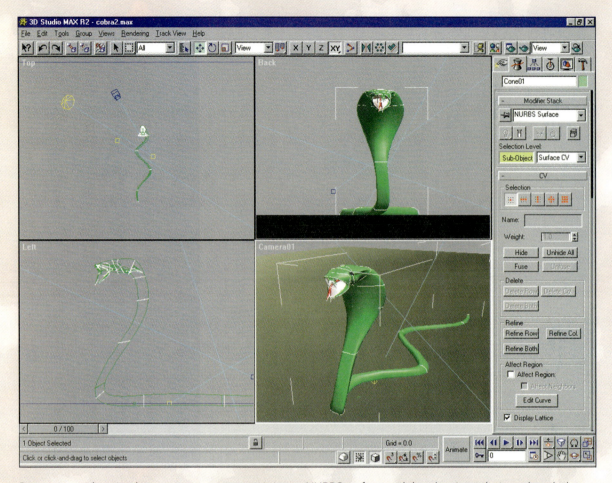

By starting with a simple cone, you can convert it into a NURBS surface and then begin sculpting a hooded cobra. (File COBRA.MAX in the \CHAP_14 directory.)

The NURBS cobra model with a simple Cellular Diffuse and Bump map texture.

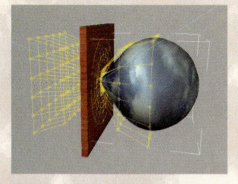
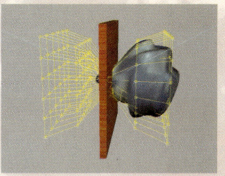

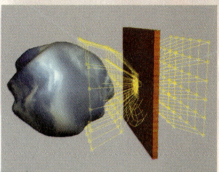

From Chapter 15. You can use an FFD (free-form deformation) lattice Space Warp to squeeze an object through a small opening, as these images illustrate. (File SQUEEZE.MAX in the \CHAP_15 directory.)

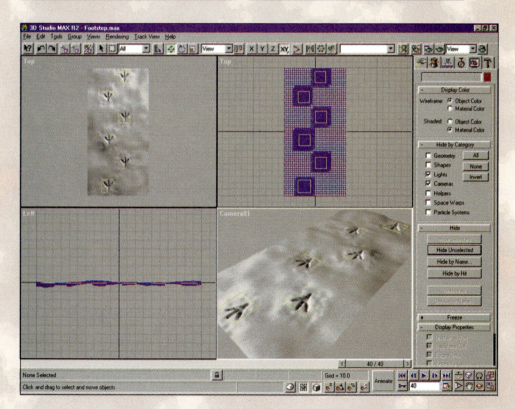

A series of animated Displacement Space Warps creates the illusion of invisible footprints (in this case, bird tracks) appearing across a snowy landscape. (File FOOTSTEP.MAX in the \CHAP_15 directory.)

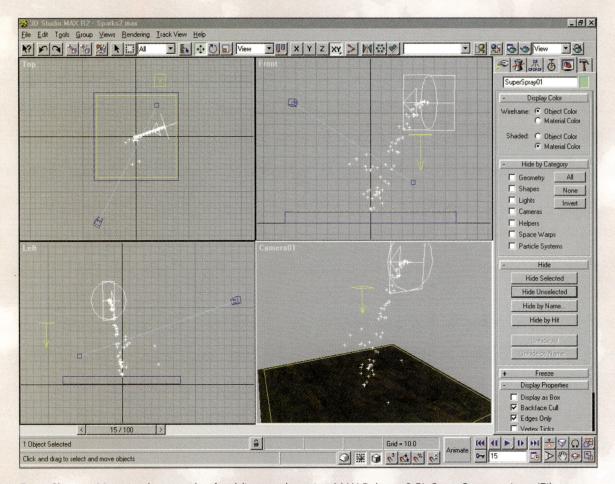

From Chapter 16; a simple example of welding sparks, using MAX Release 2.5's SuperSpray emitter. (File SPARKS2.MAX in the \CHAP_16 directory.)

A finished rendering of the welding sparks using Image Motion Blur, and with the Lens Effects Highlight filter applied in Video Post.

An example of a MetaParticles setup, with a stream of particles dropping down along a helical spline and spinning around into a wooden bowl.

Frame 30 of the MetaParticles rendering. (File MERCURY2.MAX in the \CHAP_16 directory.)

From Chapter 17, a still frame from a "blobby particle" MAX animation sequence.

The "blobby particle" image with the Photoshop Stylize/Wind filter applied. By using the Action batch file features in Photoshop 4.0 or above, you can create stylized image processing effects to MAX-rendered image sequences.

Image courtesy of Artbeats Software (www.artbeats.com).

A still frame from a digitized explosion sequence before Photoshop manipulation. The entire image sequence is included in the \ARTBEATS directory of this book's CD-ROM.

The same still image after a Photoshop Radial Blur/Zoom filter has been applied, then the original frame composited atop the blurred version in MAX's Video Post. The Photoshop .ATN files used to create this sequence are included in the \CHAP_17 directory.

A real-world example of "greebles"—styrene plastic detailing and model kit parts create this science-fiction-style object.

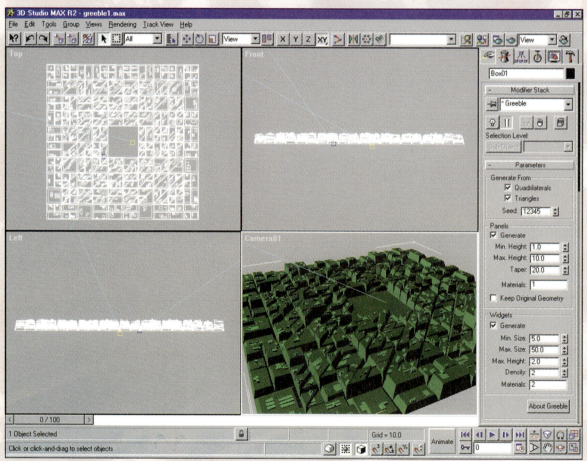

From Chapter 18, an example of Tom Hudson's "Greeble" object modifier applied to various faces of a QuadPatch object. With Greeble, MAX users can create and apply complex details quickly to the surfaces of their objects. The Greeble 1.0 plug-in, developed exclusively for this book, is in the \CHAP_18 directory.

A rendering of the Greeble-modified QuadPatch object, with custom textures applied. These textures are included in the MAXFX2.MAT Material Library.

Three Standard Primitive objects—a sphere, cylinder, and pyramid—with the Greeble modifier applied.

An example of Harry Denholm's Ishani:Bulge modifier plug-in applied to a cylinder. This plug-in, along with almost two dozen others, is included in the \CHAP_18 and \PLUGINS directories of this book's companion CD-ROM. Ishani plug-ins courtesy of Harry Denholm.

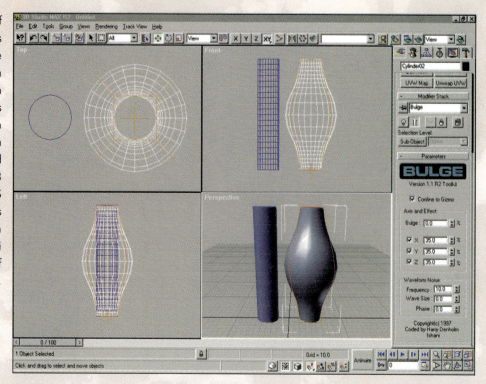

Harry Denholm's Ishani:Decay modifier (included on this book's CD-ROM) applied to a Box primitive.

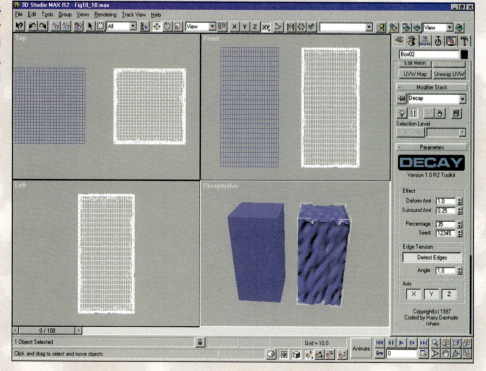

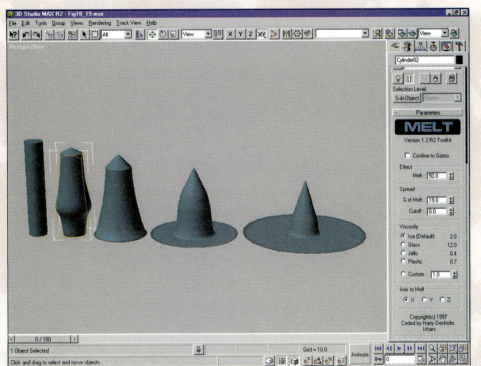

An example of Harry Denholm's Ishani:Melt modifier applied to a succession of cylinders. The plug-in is included on this book's CD-ROM.

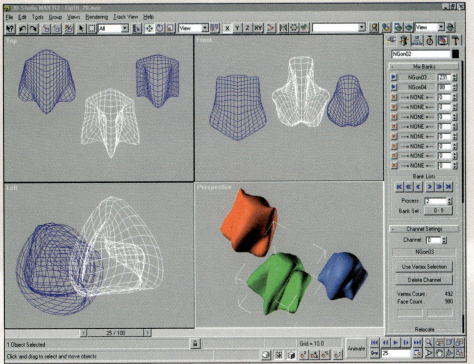

With the Ishani:Mix modifier, you can blend between 10 different channels of weighted morph targets, and animate the settings. This feature is especially useful for blending between different 3D character face targets, enabling you to create lip-synched dialogue and animated expressions. The plug-in is included on this book's CD-ROM.

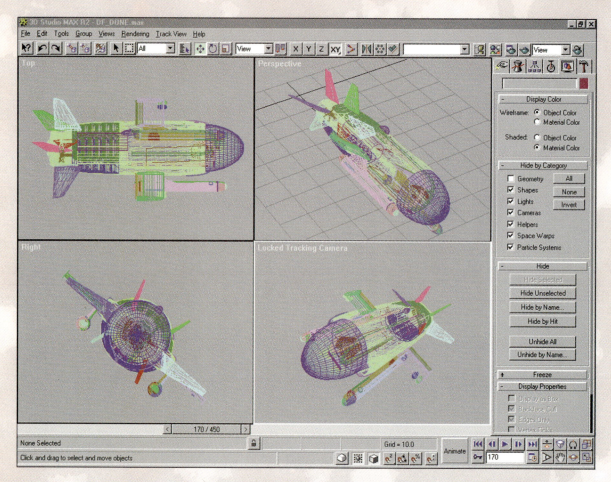

From Chapter 19, contributor Scot Tumlin shows you how to use MAX's Expressions feature to control the diving planes of the Deep Flight I mini-submarine. (Deep Flight I model built by Scot Tumlin and Jon A. Bell.) The model and all its maps are included in the \CHAP_18 and \MAPS directories on this book's CD-ROM.

A rendering of the Deep Flight I minisub. Deep Flight I designed by Graham Hawkes, of Hawkes Ocean Technologies, Pt. Richmond, CA. (For more information, go to www.deepflight.com.)

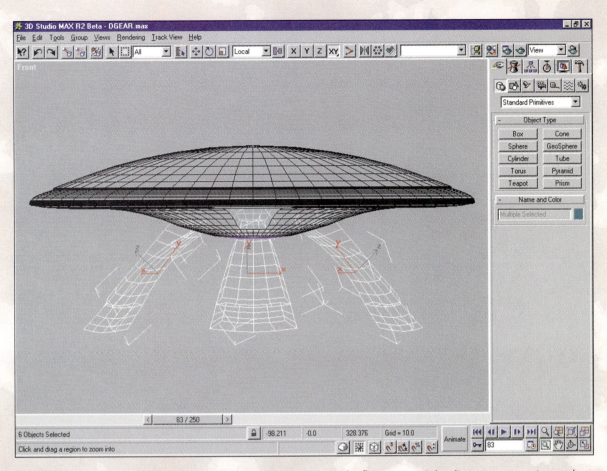

In Chapter 21, contributor Scot Tumlin shows you how to control a flying saucer's landing gear extension and retraction through the new MAXScript feature.

A rendering of the flying saucer model included in the \CHAP_21 directory of this book's CD-ROM.

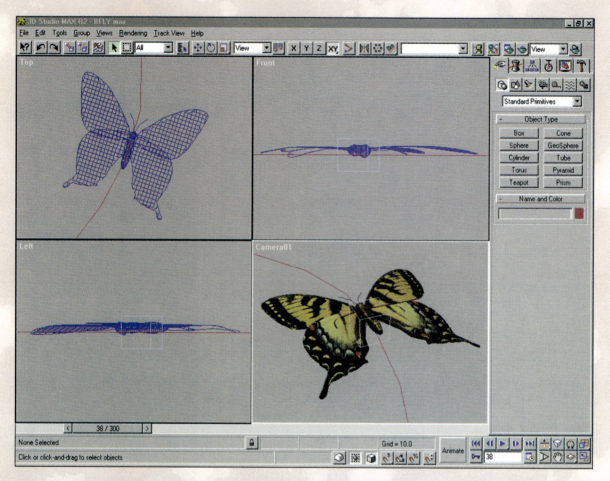

In Chapter 22, Scot Tumlin shows how to use MAXScript to control the flapping of a butterfly's wings, and to reproduce the butterfly's swooping motions along a path.

A final rendering of the butterfly model.
Model and maps included in the
\CHAP_22 directory of the CD-ROM.

"Shaman's Heaven," by Jon A. Bell. Originally developed as an animated piece for Kinetix's 1996 National Association of Broadcaster's (NAB) reel introducing MAX Release 1. Inspiration for this transcendental imagery came from the visionary art of painter Alex Gray, Douglas Trumbull's visual effects sequence for the climax of the movie "Brainstorm," and the psychedelic writings of Terence McKenna.

(c)1997 Ron Lussier

"Mars: 2036" by Ron Lussier. An extremely complex MAX scene with a 40-entry texture for the ground cover, this image was created with extensive use of Displacement and Scatter for the ground surface.

"Cartoon Alien" by John W. Stetzer III. Although 3D Studio MAX has several "cartoon" rendering plug-ins available, Stetzer created the "toon" look of this whimsical character study by using several shareware MAX material plug-ins, including Blur Studios' (www.blur.com) Sidefader and Shadow/Light for the surface, and Solidify for the outline.

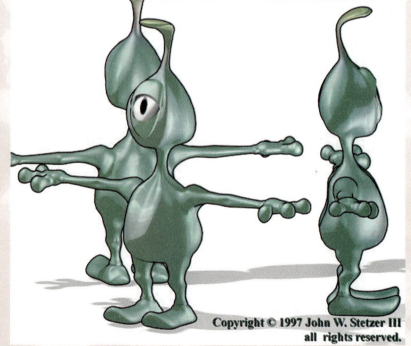

"Clown Alien," by Victor Pietrzynski. An imaginative mixture of deep shadow and splashes of color, along with excellent organic modeling, mark this striking image.

"Reptilian Alien and Angel" by
Victor Pietrzynski. Beautiful
organic modeling is enhanced
with great scaly textures in this
fantasy image.

"Lesser Oracle" by Phelan F. Sykes. From the New World Computing/3DO release "Might and Magic VI." This image uses complex instanced geometry for the straw and rocks on the ground; the human figure was clothed using Peter Watje's Surface Tools plug-in from Digimation. For the proper volumetric lighting effect, Sykes modeled each board in the toolshed and turned the lights' Shadow Filtering on high.

"Cathedral" by Phelan F. Sykes. From the New World Computing/3DO release "Might and Magic VI." Complex textures (created in Photoshop) and a statue created with Peter Watje's Surface Tools plug-in (for MAX R1) enhance this evocative interior. Due to the absence of shadow-casting Omni lights in MAX R1, Sykes used a huge number of shadow-casting spotlights—more than 190 in all!

"Canyon Run" by John W. Stetzer III. Two "bumblebug" fighters attack a larger starship. Modeling done in Rhino; rendering in 3D Studio MAX.

"Plant Life" by Mike Malloy. An alien intelligence develops in a floral womb.

"Earth: 3042 B.C." by Ron Lussier. Another exploration of complex, multi-layered materials, with high-resolution, Displaced geometry and a raytraced lake surface.

"Ancient Evil" by Neil Blevins. A brilliantly twisted MAX modeling and rendering job, from the heavy-metal-loving MAX-master Blevins.

"The Enforcer" by Mike Murguia, New Pencil. Modeling done in Rhino; rendering in 3D Studio MAX, for the "Blattaria" video project.

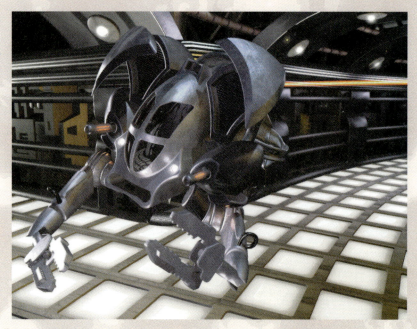

"Reptilian Monster" by Mike Murguia, New Pencil. Excellent modeling and use of textures for both the creature and the stone blocks are the highlights of this scene. Modeling done in Rhino; rendering in 3D Studio MAX.

"Deep Flight II-A and II-B" by Jon A. Bell; models and textures by Eric Hobson and Jon A. Bell. This is a rendering of the proposed Deep Flight II mini-submarines. In the foreground is the double-hull configuration of the modular Deep Flight II design, linked to a work package equipped with manipulator arms and vertical positioning thrusters. In the background is a single-hulled version of Deep Flight II. Both submarines are designed by Graham Hawkes, of Hawkes Ocean Technologies, Pt. Richmond, CA. (For more information, go to www.deepflight.com.)

Image courtesy Matte World Digital, Novato, California.

Image courtesy Matte World Digital, Novato, California.

Two before-and-after special effects shots created in MAX by Matte World Digital for the 1998 film *Great Expectations*. In these shots, Matte World was entrusted with "extending" the live-action portion of the sets with 3D models. In the top shot, you see the MAX wireframe extension of the set; in the bottom shot, the finished effects composite. Animated pigeons (also done in MAX) fly up from the floor and through the opening in the ceiling, and help tie the live-action and CGI elements together.

Image courtesy Matte World Digital, Novato, California.

Image courtesy Matte World Digital, Novato, California.

Two more Matte World Digital special effects shots for the 1998 20th-Century Fox film *The Newton Boys*. In these two before-and-after images, Matte World Digital enhanced a back lot setting with digital matte paintings to depict Chicago in the 1920s. In the first image, the black mask at the top center of frame prevents the key light from flaring the camera lens. The matte paintings in the second image were based on reference models built in 3D Studio MAX (foreground). The matte painting also includes Chicago's famous landmarks, the Tribune and Wrigley buildings. Matte World Digital also used MAX to create interactive lighting on the buildings produced by the MAX-built "El Train" seen in the distance.

"Elephants at the watering hole" by REM Infografica (www.infografica.com). Possibly the most realistic MAX "creature" rendering this author has ever seen. Modeling done with REM Infografica's MetaREYES plug-in.

Jose Maria De Espona 1997. REM 3D MODELS BANK

"Poison Arrow Frog" by Mike Malloy. A colorful South American frog sits on a tropical leaf; the frog's bright colors alert would-be predators to the frog's toxic nature.

(C) 1996 Mike Malloy

"Scaled Dragon," by Mike Malloy. The "snakeskin" textures on the dragon's head and neck help accentuate the nature of this beast.

"Alien Abduction" by Mike Malloy. Volumetric backlighting and stark shadows add mystery to this depiction of an archetypal "gray" alien being.

"Impact" by Neil Blevins. A traditional outer-space science-fiction image, with Neil's characteristic attention to detail.

Neil Blevins '97

"Robot Factory" by Neil Blevins. Another dark image from the H.R. Giger of the MAX world.

Neil Blevins '97

©1997, Johnny Ow–johnny@ywd.com; http://www.ywd.com/jow

"Raytraced Porsche" by Johnny Ow. This shiny new vehicle in its futuristic enclosure was rendered in 3D Studio MAX Release 2 using MAX's raytraced maps and materials.

"Vortex" by Daniel Manahan. A striking rendering that shows how 3D graphics can be used to produce beautiful "art" pieces for a variety of media.

"Particle Rain" from Animation Science (www.anisci.com). This image demonstrates the motion-blurred particles of the MAX Outburst plug-in, from the company that developed the particle systems for Softimage Extreme.

"Schooling Fish," from Animation Science. Another demonstration of the Outburst particle system, used to generate and control the flocking behavior of instanced geometry— in this case, a school of tropical fish.

"Hairy Billiard Ball" by Digimation (www.digimation.com). An example of Digimation's Shag: Fur plug-in, applied to an unorthodox subject. A demo version of this plug-in appears in the \DIGIMATN directory of this book's companion CD-ROM.

"Cartoon Bee" by Boyd Lake. A friendly "toon-style" bee, who would be right at home in the "Toy Story" universe, waves at you from the suburbs of Anytown, U.S.A.

"Gnaw" by Mike Malloy. An evil-looking, bloodsucking beastie snarls at you and its host in this startling image. Depth-of-field provides helps sell the "macro photography-feel" of this shot.

(c) 1996 Mike Malloy

"Tornado" by Boyd Lake. A dark funnel cloud, courtesy of MAX's particle systems, tears up a suburban neighborhood.

"Hatred 2" by Neil Blevins. Sometimes, you just have to wonder how computer graphics artists work out their deep, innermost feelings in the 3D realm....

"Saurian Crystalmancer" by John W. Stetzer III. This fantasy creature features the Cellular procedural texture quite extensively, as well as MAX Release 2's second UVW channel to hide texture seams where parts of the head join, and in areas where the UVW mapping gets overly stretched.

"Pseudo-Flubber" by Greg Tsadilas. In these images from an animation sequence, former Blur Studios animator Tsadilas created his own MAX simulations of the titular effects seen in the 1997 Disney Studios film *Flubber*. Tsadilas created these gelatinous figures by using Digimation's Clay Studio Pro metaball plug-in, with MAX Release 2's RayTrace materials. The interior bubbles are Geospheres linked to the closest metaball or clay spline. Tsadilas linked the metaballs to a dummy hierarchy that represents the body structure. As the dummies are moved and rotated, the "bubbles" move and rotate with them, giving the illusion of secondary motion.

As the dummies are scaled to expand or contract the metaballs, the "bubbles" follow suit, completing the illusion that they are suspended within the "liquid."

"Strike!" by Ron Lussier. In homage to the cover of *The Renderman Companion* book, Ron created this in MAX. The bowling ball and pins use MAX Release 2's Dynamics utility for their motion. Real-world textures combined with object and image motion blur complete the illusion of frozen motion.

The "mascot" of this book is "MAX-02." This robot model, inspired by Japanese *anime* designs, is included in the \CHAP_03 and \SCENES directories of this book's companion CD-ROM. Model and textures by Jon A. Bell.

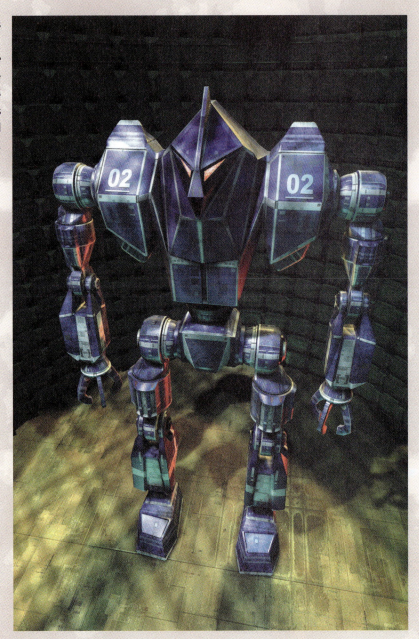

7. While you're still in the Left viewport, select the second curve in from the open end of the cone surface—this will become the head of the cobra. Lock the selection and go to the Front viewport. Scale this curve on the View X and Y axes until it's about the same size as the largest visible curve, which will be the front curve. It doesn't have to be precisely the same size, and in fact, a little over or under will make the final cobra model look more natural. Repeat this process with all but the last two curves (those farthest away from the open end). The result of this process is shown in Figure 14.2.

8. Select the second to the last curve and, in the Front viewport, scale it up along the View X and Y axes until the surface forms a gentle slope from the last curve you adjusted in Step 7. Repeat the process with the last curve (the only curve as yet untouched). The final result should look something like Figure 14.3.

9. Select Curve CV from the Sub-object drop-down list and go to the Front viewport. Select all of the CVs on the bottom of the larger loft curves (those toward the front of the snake) and pull them up toward the center of the body, making the body cross section into a more organic, oblong shape with a semi-flat bottom (forming the belly of the cobra). Repeat the procedure with the smaller loft curves at the back of the body.

10. To finish the process, move the smaller loft curves downward so the bottoms lie roughly in line with the bottoms of the larger loft curves, creating the illusion that the body lies flat along a ground plane. The result should look something like Figure 14.4.

Sculpting The Head And The Hood

Now that you have the basic shape of the body, it's time to add the details that make the cobra look like a cobra. There are two major features missing thus far: the hooded cobra head and, of course, a mouth complete with venom-dripping fangs.

You'll remedy the first situation next:

1. Turn off the Sub-object selection and go to the main NURBS Modifier panel. Check the box next to Curves in the Display subpanel. Select the Left viewport ; this will be critical in the next few steps.

2. Open the Create Curves rollout and click on the U Iso Curve button. Zoom in on the front portion of the body (near the open

> **Note:** As I've stated in this chapter and the previous one, it's very difficult to create a hard edge within a NURBS surface. However, when you convert Standard primitives (you can't convert Extended primitives to NURBS surfaces) from the MAX geometry Create panel, the new NURBS object seems to defy this "hard edge" rule, leaving hard corners and edges in the exact spots they existed on the polygonal primitive. In actuality, what the NURBS surface conversion process does is create a new surface that is isolated by every hard parametric edge it finds. A continually rounded surface (such as a sphere or torus) is converted as a single surface. But all end caps on cylinders, cones, pyramids, and tubes become separate surfaces, as does every side of a box or a prism. (Just for kicks, create a Primitive teapot and then convert it to a NURBS surface. Those wacky Kinetix development folks loaded some interesting parameters in there for your enjoyment and enlightenment.)

Close Cols Function

As I noted in the last chapter, a NURBS surface always has a starting place and an ending place (generally curves). The Close Cols function tells the surface to make a continual loop, and act as if the start and end are the same, creating the illusion of a continuous smooth surface.

end of the surface) in the Left viewport so you can clearly and easily see the three Iso curves nearest the front end of the surface.

3. While you're still in the Left viewport (and with the U Iso Curve button still active), move the cursor about one-third of the distance from the Iso curve at the open end of the surface and the next curve. A large blue representation of where the new curve will be created appears on the surface, so it should be easy to identify your position. Click to create a new U Iso curve. The new curve will be displayed as bright green, signifying that it is a dependent curve (something you'll change in the next step).

4. Repeat the procedure; you'll create another curve about two-thirds of the distance between the curve at the open end and the next curve. Then, create two more curves between the second and third loft curves of the body surface; use the same procedure and the same relative spacing, as shown in Figure 14.5.

5. Click on the Sub-object button and select Curve from the drop-down list. Select all of the curves you just created (they should still be drawn in green) and click on the Make Independent button. The curves turn white after they've been deselected.

6. While still in Sub-object mode, select Surface from the Sub-object list. Click on the body surface and go to the U Loft rollout at the very bottom of the panel. In the U curve list, select the third CV curve from the top. The curve should turn blue in the viewports. Click on the Insert button just below the U curve list and select the newly independent Iso curve just to the left of the blue CV curve in the Left viewport. The new Iso curve should now appear in the U curve list just above the CV curve previously selected, as shown in Figure 14.6.

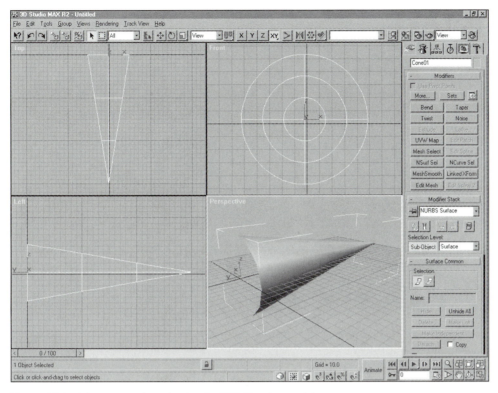

Figure 14.1 A basic cone shape begins the NURBS cobra model.

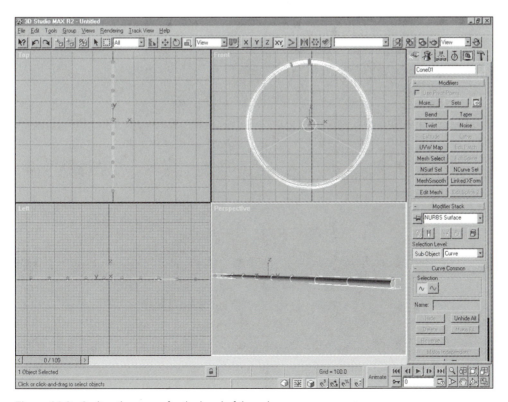

Figure 14.2 Scaling the curves for the head of the cobra.

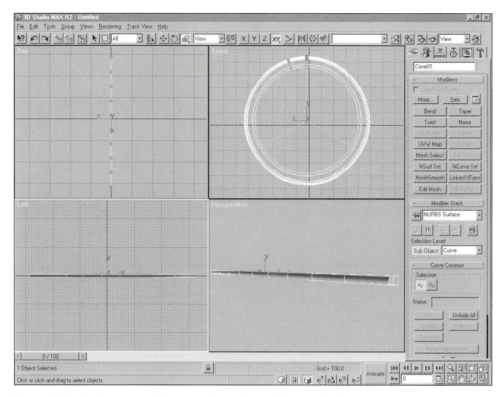

Figure 14.3 Scaling the remaining curves helps the snake body take shape.

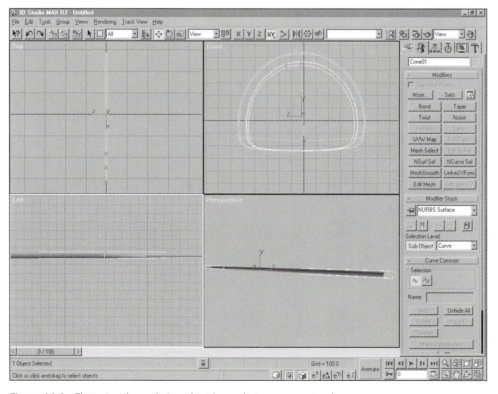

Figure 14.4 Flattening the snake's underside results in a more natural appearance.

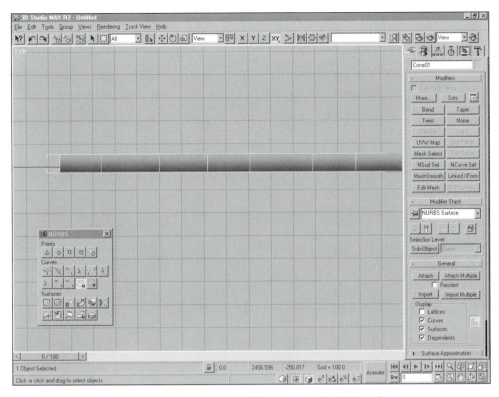

Figure 14.5   The four inserted U Iso curves that will be used to sculpt the hood.

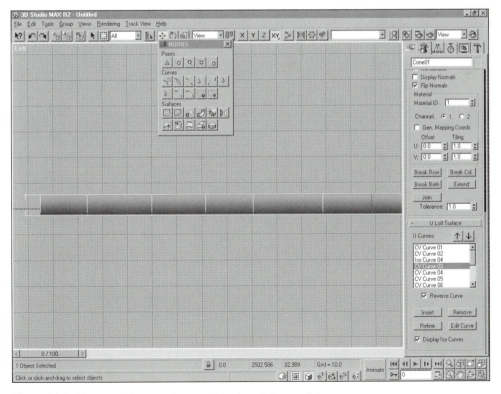

Figure 14.6   The new U Iso curve inserted into the u-loft curve list.

7. Select the next added Iso curve from the list and repeat the insert procedure. Then, repeat the insert procedure with the next two CV and Iso curves. Your U-Loft surface should have four new defining U curves, as shown in Figure 14.7.

8. Select Curve CVs from the Sub-object drop-down list. Select the CVs in the middle of the fifth, sixth, and seventh U iso-curves in the Left viewport. Lock this selection, and in the Top viewport, scale them out on the X axis until you get a nice hooded shape, as shown in Figure 14.8.

9. Still in the top viewport, scale out the outer CVs of the middle hood curve just a bit extra (to about 139%) to create a slight diamond shape. In the Left viewport, pull all of the outer hood CVs up on the View Y axis until they are just below the top body CVs. Place the outer hood CVs in a named selection set called Hood.

Modifying The Head

Now, it's time to begin sculpting the head:

1. In the left viewport, select all of the CVs on the far left side of the cobra's body (at the open end of the surface) and move them farther to the left until the space between these curve CVs and those immediately to the right has roughly quadrupled (roughly -150 units on the View X axis. Then, go to the CVs in the middle of this curve in the left. Select them and pull them back to the right toward the body, creating an open mouth as shown in Figure 14.9.

2. In the Top viewport, select the CVs at the very top of the cobra (what has now become the nose). They should be rather squared off because they are still aligned to the original flat end you started with. Start sculpting the nose by selecting the two centermost CVs on both the top and bottom of the mouth-end iso-curve (a total of four CVs) and pulling them ever so slightly upward. Then, select the next four CVs (outward from the centermost CVs you just adjusted) and move them upward to a position just below the centermost CVs. Continue the procedure until you have created a blunt but nicely organic snake nose, as shown in Figure 14.10.

3. Next, change to Curve Sub-object mode and select the two head curves (the mouth curve and the curve between the mouth and the first hood curve). Scale them out along the View X axis in the Top viewport until you get a more obvious blocky head bulge, as seen in Figure 14.11.

Note: *Cobra's hoods only expand when they rear up; it's the expansion and flattening of the snake's ribs that produces the effect. The rest of the time, when they're just slithering around, they look like any other nonhooded snake (but with cobra coloration, of course). However, by having a semblance of the hood in place (a feature that's easily undoable), you can see how the head and hood will look when you pose your cobra so it looks as if it's getting ready to strike.*

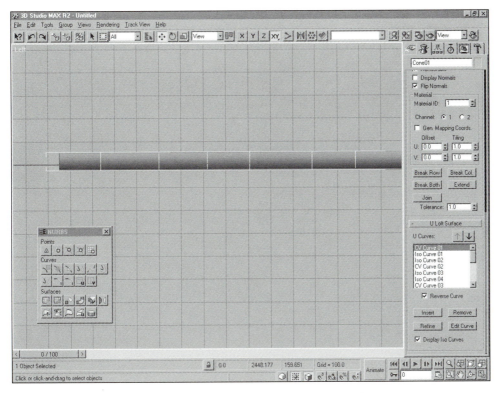

Figure 14.7   The four new U Iso curves now included in the u-loft cone surface.

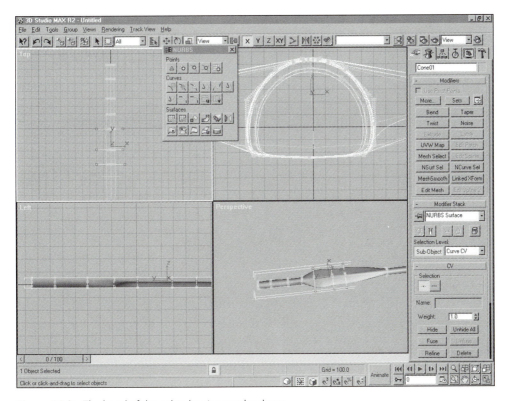

Figure 14.8   The hood of the cobra begins to take shape.

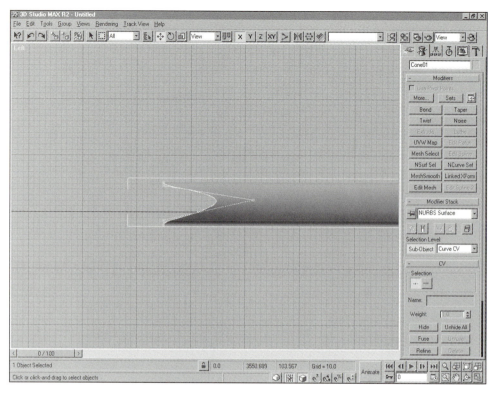

Figure 14.9 The first formation of the mouth.

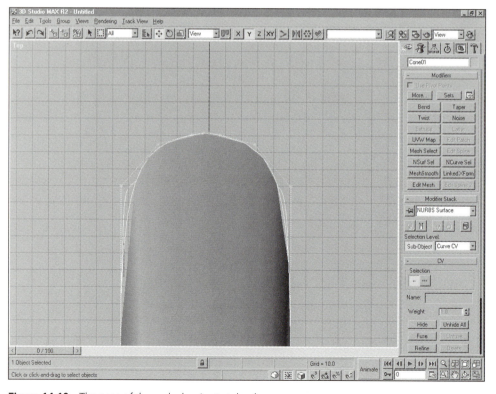

Figure 14.10 The nose of the snake begins to take shape.

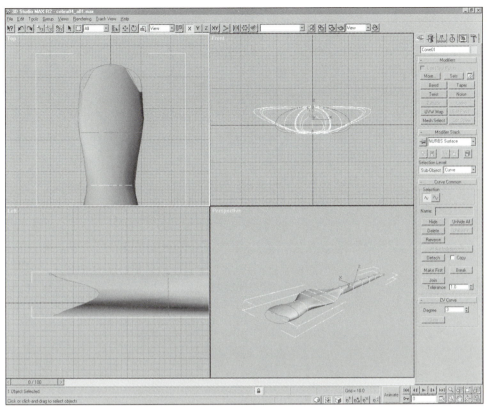

Figure 14.11   The blocky, yet organic, shape of the cobra's snout.

4. Go back to the Curve CV Sub-object panel. In the Left viewport, select the CVs on the main head curve from the middle up, leaving only the CVs at the bottom of the main head curve unselected. Lock the selection and move the selected CVs up along the View Y axis until the bottom CVs of the selection line up with the top CVs of the mouth, creating a cranium (albeit a small one) for the cobra.

Creating The Interior Of The Mouth

Now, it's time to create the business end of the snake—its mouth. To create the inside of the mouth, follow these steps:

1. Select the mouth curve in Curve Sub-object mode. In the Left viewport, hold down the Shift key and move the selected mouth curve back into the body (toward the right) a small amount (about 20 percent of the distance to the head cranium curve) to create a clone of this curve.

2. With this curve still selected, go to the Front viewport and perform a Non-uniform Scale on it (along the View X and Y axes)

Note: Cobras have surprisingly blocky heads, so feel free to make the head less snakelike and more bulky. Note that most animals, except, say, insects with spiky carapaces or other arthropods, don't have "corners"; virtually any other animal you can think of is "rounded off." Keep tweaking those gentle rounded edges until they look good and organic. Fortunately, with NURBS, this is one thing that's easier done than said.

so it's just slightly smaller than the original mouth curve. Perform the Shift-clone/Scale operation two more times, moving the next clone about 10 percent farther toward the cranium curve and scaling it up (close to the size of the original mouth curve). Next, move the last clone curve back near the position where the hood meets the head and scale it down quite a bit (to about 30 percent of its original size). The three new curves are shown in Figure 14.12.

3. Select all of the mouth curves (the original and all of the new clones), invert the selection so it selects all of the other curves, and then hide the non-mouth curves. (Use the Hide button in the Curve Common Rollout in the Modify Rollout.)

4. Turn off the Sub-object button and go to the main NURBS Modifier panel. Expand the Create Surfaces rollout and click on the Cap Surface button. Select the last clone curve (the smallest one) to create a cap surface that will serve as the back of the cobra's throat. (If it doesn't appear to be visible when you peer into the cobra's mouth, pause here to go to the Surface Sub-object panel and check the Flip Normals box.) Click on the U-loft surface button.

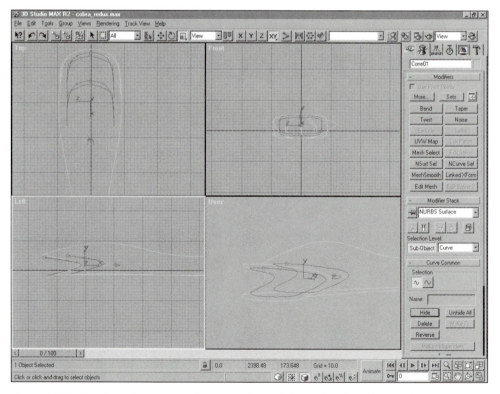

Figure 14.12 The three cloned curves that create the basis for the interior of the mouth.

5. Start the u-loft surface by clicking (and holding) on the back-of-the throat curve, dragging and clicking on the middle mouth curve (the second clone curve), and then dragging and finishing the surface with the first clone curve. (Again, if you need to flip the normals, do it before proceeding—it'll be easier than attempting a correction later.)

6. To finish the inside of the mouth, click on the Blend surface button, click and hold on the frontmost edge of the inner mouth surface, and drag to the original mouth curve (yep, you guessed it—flip any undesired normals). The interior of the mouth should now be complete. (To get a better view of the inside of the mouth, change the Left viewpoint to shaded and use the Arc Rotate button. Remember to flip the normals use Sub-Object Surface.)

Creating The Tongue

Your cobra needs a tongue so it can smell properly. (Snakes smell with their tongues by "tasting" particles in the air—that's why they flick their tongues in and out. And you thought that this book was going to teach you only about 3D stuff, didn't you?) To create the cobra's tongue, follow these steps:

1. Select the mouth's interior surface, the back of the throat, if you will, in the Surface Sub-object panel. Invert the selection and hide the selected surfaces (the body and lip surfaces).

2. Turn off the Sub-object button and expand the Create Points rollout in the main NURBS Modifier panel (or launch the NURBS Creation floater). Click on the "surface point" button in the Create Points rollout (or the Creation floater) and create eight points on the lower part of the mouth's interior surface in a roughly centered ellipsoid shape, as shown in Figure 14.13. Make sure there's one point that lies roughly in the center of the ellipsoid shape at each extremity (top, bottom, left, and right).

3. Open the Create Curves rollout on the main NURBS Modifier panel and click on the Fit Curve button (or click on the Fit Curve button in the NURBS Creation floater). Left-click and hold on point and drag it to the next point (clockwise from the selected point). Click and release on this point, then proceed clockwise to the next point. Continue until you've created a complete curve from all of the points created in Step 2. Make sure to close the curve by dragging from the last point selected to the first point selected, then right-click to stop drawing the curve.

Note: You may ask yourself, why go through this long multisurface process when I could simply extend the current body surface loft to include the new curves that make up the interior of the mouth? Glad you asked! Remember, NURBS surfaces are always defined by curves, whether they are visible or not. If you extended the body loft surface, it would interpret a curve between the outer mouth curve and the inner mouth curves, resulting in a rather bulgy sucker-type mouth like that of a leech. In addition, you wouldn't be able to define a semihard edge between the gums (do snakes have lips?) and the palates in the mouth. Also, creating the other surfaces (the interior u-loft and the cap surface) gives you the ability to add different materials from the exterior body to the inside of the mouth. Remember, one surface, one material.

Note: *In the previous procedure, all of the curves changed shape except the original fit curve defined by the surface points. That's because the fit curve is a dependent sub-object defined by the surface points and the surface points are dependent on the surface they were placed upon. This means that, no matter what you do to the mouth's interior surface (the dependent surface points), the dependent fit curve they define, and therefore the dependent origin of the tongue surface, will be bound to the mouth's interior surface. Since you created the other curves as clones (through the standard Shift-Transform clone operation), they were created as independent objects and are unaffected by the mouth's interior surface.*

Multiple dependencies allow for some very intriguing animation possibilities, which is a tremendous benefit of using MAX NURBS. Try moving the mouth's interior surface a little (not so much that it can't be easily realigned to its original position; you still have to finish this model!) and check out how it affects the tongue.

4. Turn on the Sub-object button and go to the Curves Sub-object panel. In the Top viewport, select the curve you just created, hold down the Shift key, and move this curve along the View Y axis about a third of the way between the original curve's position and the opening of the mouth (towards the top of the viewport); this will create a clone. Clone this curve two more times, positioning the next (second) clone about halfway between the last curve you created and the opening of the mouth. Position the third clone just below the opening of the mouth, as seen in Figure 14.14.

5. Turn off the Sub-object button and expand the Create Surfaces rollout in the main NURBS panel. Click on the U-loft button (or the U-loft button in the NURBS creation floater, if it's still active), and create a u-loft surface starting with the fit curve you created in Step 3 and including each of the clone curves you created in Step 4. (Make sure the surface normals aren't inverted. If they are, go to the Surface Sub-object panel, select the newly created tongue surface, and check the Flip Normals check box.)

6. Turn on the sub-object button and select the Points Sub-object panel. In the Front viewport, select the top-center and bottom-center points in all of the curves you just created. Scale them along the View Y axis until they resemble a rounded dog-bone shape, as shown in Figure 14.15.

7. To finish the tongue, let's put the fork into it. Click on the Fuse button in the Points Sub-object menu. In the Top viewport, fuse the top-center and bottom-center points of the topmost curve (the one nearest the mouth opening). Fuse the three points on the right side of the tongue into a single point. Then, repeat this procedure with the three points on the left side of the tongue, leaving a flat curve (no opening) consisting of three points—one on the left, one in the middle, and one on the right.

8. Select the left and right points and move them a little toward the top of the screen. Widen them from their original position until you have a nice forked-tongue surface, similar to Figure 14.16.

Creating The Fangs

Before you continue with your 3D modeling, pause for this brief biological note.

In the real world, cobras have short fixed fangs instead of the long curved fangs we associate with North American venomous snakes such

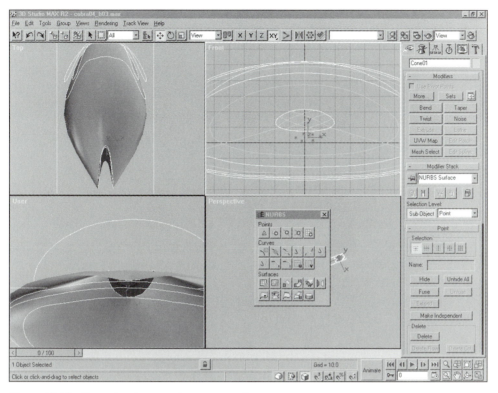

Figure 14.13   The points that start the tongue surface.

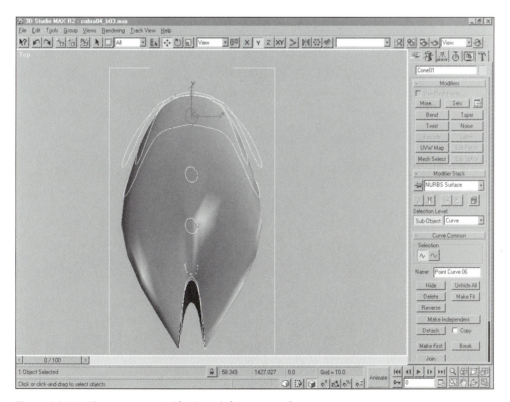

Figure 14.14   The curves created for the u-loft tongue surface.

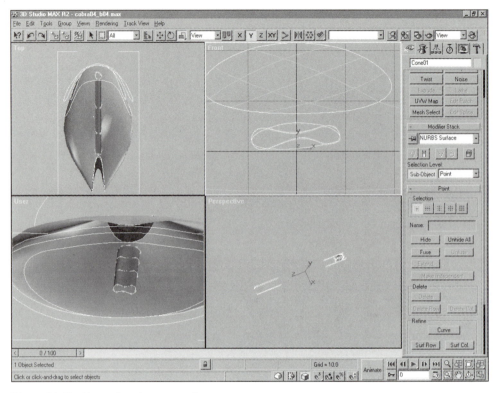

Figure 14.15 The sculpted tongue surface.

as rattlers. Because a cobra's fangs are so short, they don't retract when the snake's mouth is closed; there is no danger of the snake biting itself.

However, because the cobra's short fangs are difficult to see even when the snake's mouth is open, you may want to do a bit of virtual genetic engineering and provide your snake with the more visually nasty extending/retracting fangs. (Hey, if Industrial Light and Magic can resurrect entire extinct species, we can create a little compensation for nature's aesthetic flaws, right?)

To create the cobra's fangs, follow these steps:

1. With the Sub-object button off, open the Create Points rollout in the main NURBS Surface Modifier panel (ignore this if you still have the NURBS Creation floater open). Click on the Surface Point button again and rotate and zoom in on the snake in a User viewport until you have a clean close-up view of the upper interior of the mouth's surface.

2. On the upper mouth surface, create six surface points near the mouth opening (and about halfway between the tongue and the outer edge of the mouth's interior surface) in a roughly circular shape, as seen in Figure 14.17. Check the other viewports to ensure

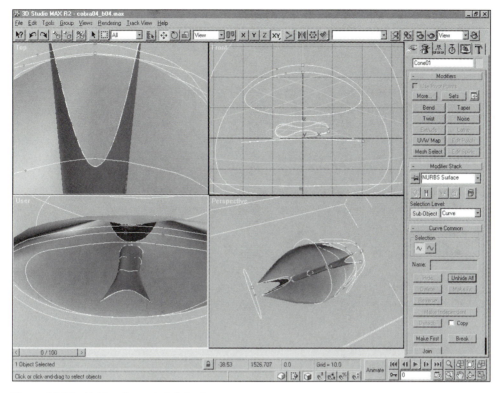

Figure 14.16 Making the snake's forked tongue.

that the points are placed and shaped correctly. The circle doesn't have to be perfect; in fact, a little imperfection looks more organic.

3. Next, open the Create Curves rollout (or go to the NURBS Creation floater) and click on the Curve Fit button. In clockwise order, click on the points you just created; this will create the fit curve. Right-click to end the curve.

4. Turn on the Sub-object button and go to the Curve Sub-object panel. Select the fit curve you created in Step 3, and in the Front viewport, clone the curve twice by holding down the Shift key and moving the curve down along the View Y axis. Place the first clone curve just above the top of the mouth's back surface and place the second one just below the bottom of the tongue surface. Turn off the Sub-object button.

5. Open the Create Surfaces rollout (or go to the NURBS Creation floater) and click on the U-Loft surface button. Create a u-Loft surface by connecting the fit curve and the two clone curves, starting at the top curve.

6. Select the bottom clone curve, lock the selection, and go to the Top viewport. Scale (Non-uniform) the bottom clone curve down

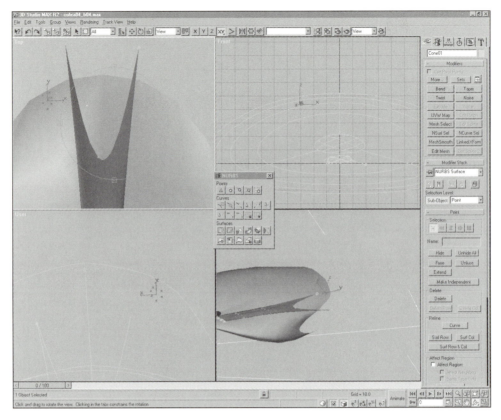

Figure 14.17 The points that start the fang surface.

along the View X and Y axes until it's no longer recognizable as a curve (it should resemble a single point).

7. Go back to the Left viewport. With the bottom clone curve still selected and locked, move the bottom clone curve back (on the View X axis) into the mouth just a bit to give this fang a nasty curve and make it look a little more lethal.

8. While you're still in the Left viewport, select the middle clone curve and move it just a bit forward (toward the mouth opening along the View X axis) to accentuate the fang's curve. The final fang surface should look like it does in Figure 14.18.

Attaching The Fangs To The Roof Of The Mouth

To complete the fang, you must now add the flap of skin that connects the back of the fang with the top of the mouth:

1. Go to the Surface Sub-object panel and select the mouth's interior surface. Hide this surface, then select the fang surface. Rotate around the scene in a User viewport until you have a

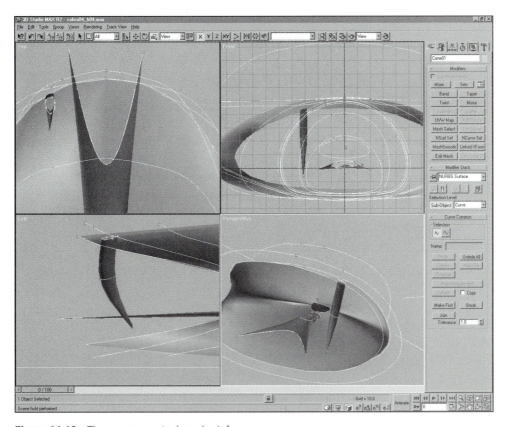

Figure 14.18 The nasty curve in the cobra's fang.

clear view of the back of the fang surface. Turn off the Sub-Object button.

2. In the main NURBS Surface Modifier panel, open the Create Points rollout (or go to the NURBS Creation floater) and click on the Surface Point button. Create a point just below the middle clone curve at the center back of the tooth. Then, about halfway between the middle clone curve and the top fit curve, create two more surface points, one on either side of the center line at the back of the fang surface. You should now have three new points along the back of the fang surface, as shown in Figure 14.19.

3. Go back to the Surface Sub-object panel, unhide all of the surfaces, then rehide the snake body and lip surfaces (leaving the tongue, mouth interior, mouth back, and fang surfaces visible).

4. Click on the Surface Point button in the Create Points rollout of the main NURBS Surface Modifier panel (or in the NURBS Creation floater). Create three more surface points, this time on the roof of the mouth surface. Make the first surface point just in back of the fork in the tongue surface (roughly aligned with the

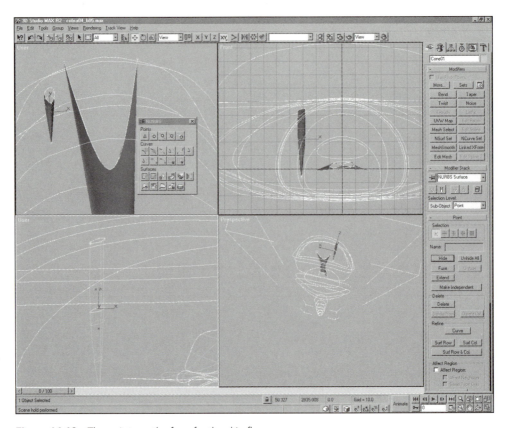

Figure 14.19 The points on the fang for the skin flap.

center line at the back of the fang surface). Then, create the other two about halfway between the first point and the back of the fang surface, placing these points just on either side of an imaginary line drawn between the first surface point created in this step, and the center line at the back of the fang surface. These points should end up looking like they do in Figure 14.20.

5. Open the Create Curves rollout and click on the Fit Curve button (or the Fit Curve button in the NURBS Creation floater). Create a fit curve consisting of the three points at the top and back of the fang (the original surface points used to create the fang fit curve) and the new surface points on the roof of the mouth surface, resulting in a vague floating-heart shape.

6. Starting with the same three points on the top of the fang surface you used in the last step, create another fit curve, but finish the curve with the new surface points created on the back of the fang surface. You should now have two new heart-shaped fit curves: one on the roof of the mouth surface and the other on the back of the fang surface, as shown in Figure 14.21.

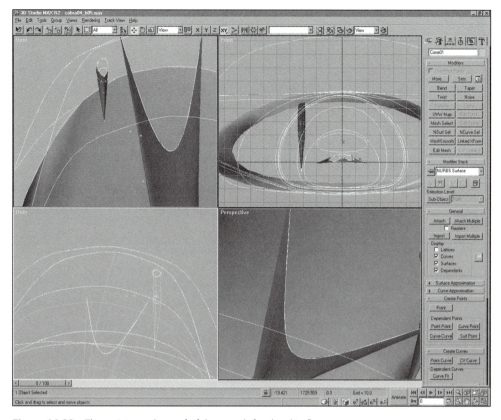

Figure 14.20 The points on the roof of the mouth for the skin flap.

7. Go to the Create Surfaces rollout in the main NURBS Modifier panel and click on the Ruled Surface button (or click on the corresponding button in the NURBS Creation floater). Create a ruled surface by clicking on one of the new "heart" fit curves and then dragging and clicking on the other fit curve. If the surface appears inverted or twisted, select the Ruled object as sub-object Surface and place a check in either (or both) of the Flip Beginning or Flip End checkboxes (at the bottom of the Create Surfaces rollout) to fix the problem.

You've created the flap of skin from the roof of the mouth to the back of the fang. However, it isn't quite "organic" enough; you can rectify this with the next few steps.

8. Expand your Left Viewport and zoom in on the flap. Click on the U Iso Curve button, in the Create Curves rollout of the main NURBS modifier panel. You will see a blue line representing the U Iso Curve you are creating. Create a U Iso curve approximately halfway between the roof of the mouth and the back of the fang surface, as shown in Figure 14.22.

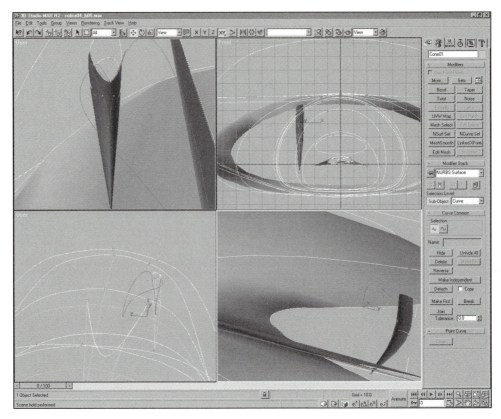

Figure 14.21 The fit curves that will determine the skin flap surface.

9. Go to the Surface Sub-object panel, select the ruled skin flap surface, and delete it (you'll replace it with something better in a moment).

10. Back in the main NURBS Surface Modifier panel, open the Create Surfaces rollout and click on the U-loft button. Create a u-loft surface by starting with the fit curve on the roof of the mouth, including the U Iso curve created in Step 8, and finishing with the fit curve on the back of the fang. If the surface appears twisted, go to the Curve Sub-object panel and try reversing the loft curves until the surface appears normal.

11. Next, go to the Curve CV Sub-object panel. You should see a set of CVs that define the middle loft curve of your new skin flap surface. Pull these up toward the area where the top of the fang meets the roof of the mouth, creating an arch in the skin flap surface, as shown in Figure 14.23.

12. Now, all you have to do to finish the mouth is create the other fang. Go back to the main NURBS Surface Modifier panel, open the Create Surfaces rollout, and click on Mirror. Select the fang in

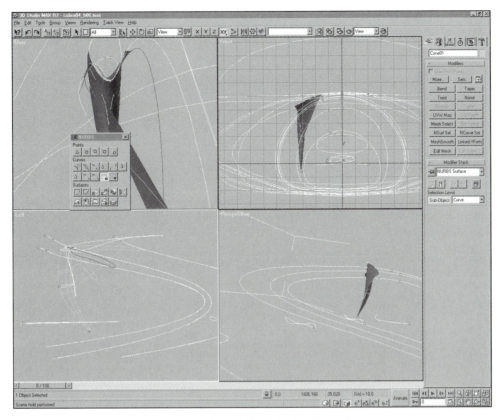

Figure 14.22 Extracting a U Iso curve in the middle of the skin flap surface.

the Front viewport to create its counterpart on the other side of the mouth. Do the same with the skin flap surface.

Creating The Eyes

When I'm creating a character or a creature, I generally like to save the eyes for last because that's what brings the model to life, as far as I'm concerned. So, this is the last set of steps for creating the cobra:

1. Unhide all of the surfaces in the Surface Sub-object panel, turn off the Sub-object button, and deselect the cobra object altogether.

2. Select Create|Geometry|Standard Primitives and create a geosphere using MAX's default settings. Position and scale it so that the back third of the geosphere is behind the first Iso curve back from the mouth, as shown in Figure 14.24.

3. Go to the Top viewport, hold down the Shift key, and Shift-clone the geosphere by dragging it (along the View X axis) to the corresponding position on the other side of the cobra's head. Re-select the cobra and go back to the main NURBS Modifier panel. Click on the Import button and then click on the first geosphere to

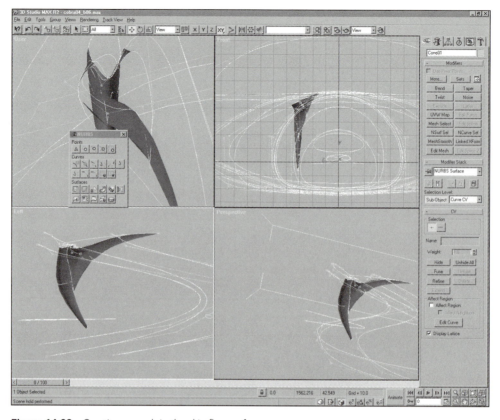

Figure 14.23   Creating an arch in the skin flap surface.

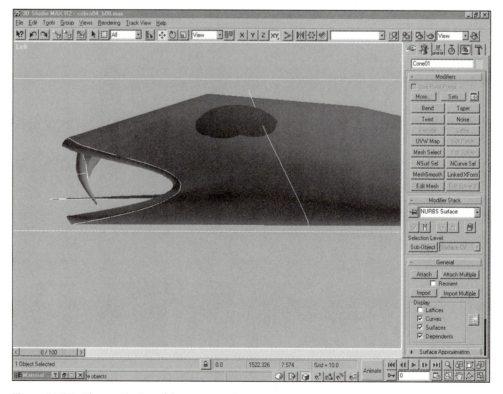

Figure 14.24   The positioning of the eye geosphere.

make it a part of the cobra object. Repeat the import procedure with the second geosphere.

4. Turn off the Sub-object button and go back to the main NURBS Modifier panel. Open the Create Curves rollout (or launch the NURBS Creation floater) and click on the U Iso Curve button. In the Left viewport, create two U Iso curves on the head of the cobra, the first near the leftmost edge of the eye and the second about half an eye-length behind the Iso curve used in Step 2 to align the eyeball, as shown in Figure 14.25.

5. Turn on the Sub-object button and select Curves from the Sub-object drop-down list. Select the two curves you just created and click on the Make Independent button.

6. Select Surface from the Sub-object drop-down list and click on the cobra's body surface. Go to the very bottom of the Surface Sub-object panel until you find the list of Iso curves that define the cobra's body surface. Click on the third curve in the list. Click on the Insert button below the list and click on the curve that's touching the eyeball (one of the curves you created in Step 5). Next, click on the second curve in the list and repeat the insert procedure with the frontmost curve (created in Step 4).

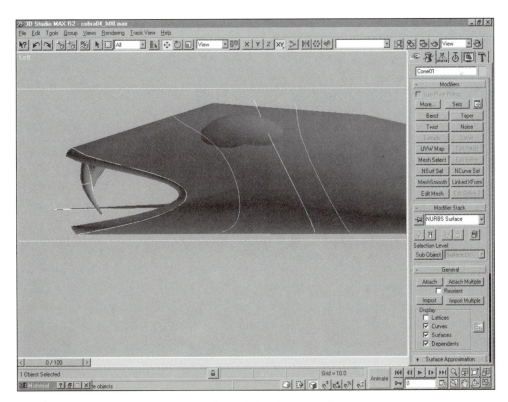

Figure 14.25   Extracting the U Iso curves for sculpting the eye socket.

7. Go to the Sub-object drop-down list and select Curve CVs. Find the Iso curve between the two curves you added in the previous step. Make sure you can see its lattice and find the CV that is aligned with the eyeball. Click on the Refine button in the Left viewport and insert a new CV just below the CV you last located. Insert another CV between the first one located in the one you just created, then insert a third new CV above the first CV you located in this step. Repeat this procedure with the same curve in the Right viewport.

Making The Final Eye Adjustments

In the next two steps, some irregular bulges may appear in the surface of the cobra from the head to the beginning of the hood. This is simply a result of the surface adjusting itself to maintain the invisible curves that define it between the visible Iso curves. Don't try to fix the bulges while you are creating them; it'll be frustrating and nearly impossible. Instead, wait until Step 3 when these surface anomalies are taken care of.

To make the final eye adjustments, follow these steps:

1. Select the CVs of the middle curve on both sides of the head that line up the middle of the eye surfaces. In the Top viewport, scale down these CV's along the View X axis so they pull into the head a bit and leave an indentation behind the eyeballs. In the Left viewport, select the two CVs on both sides of the head that are just above and just below the eyeballs. Back in the Top viewport, scale these CVs up along the View X axis so they protrude past the edge of the eyeballs a bit, as shown in Figure 14.26.

2. Select the CVs on the two new Iso curves (the ones created in the initial eye-creation stage) that line up with the eyeball. Make sure you have the corresponding CVs selected on both sides of the head. In the Top viewport, scale them up along the View X axis, which will highlight both the indentation and protrusion created in the last step. Back in the Left viewport, scale them down along the View X axis so they pull in toward the eyes.

3. Go to the Curves Sub-object panel and select the Iso curve in the middle of the eye. In the Left viewport, move this curve more toward the center of the eyeball. Go to the Top viewport and select all of the hood curves. Move them up along the View Y axis closer to the head until most of the surface smoothes out. The final result should look something like Figure 14.27.

At this point, the eyes and eye sockets are finished, but feel free to push and pull the curve CVs around until you get a customized cobra look that you are satisfied with. All that remains now is for you to pose the cobra in a cobralike stance, hood reared, ready to strike. Applying some scaly textures (either bitmaps or procedurals) to the skin and eyes will complete this cool, lethal reptile. (For realistic eyes, check out EYES.MAX in the \CHAP_04 directory of this book's companion CD-ROM, as well as the discussion of this Eyes scene in Chapter 4.)

Moving On

The addition of NURBS to MAX has opened a whole new realm of modeling and animating methods to the MAX artist. With more improvements on the way, the possibilities are staggering. NURBS are not necessarily useful for all modeling needs, but the fact that they can be combined with traditional polygon models, as well as patch models, allows a tremendous amount of flexibility. I

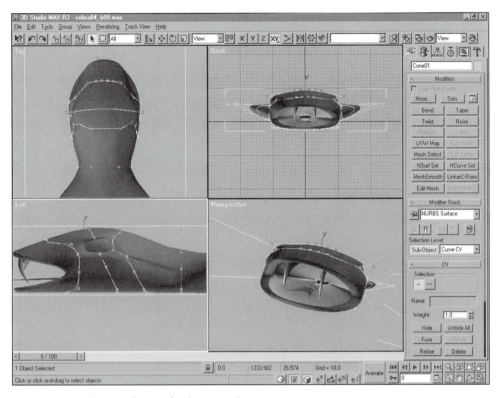

Figure 14.26   Adjusting the CVs for the eye socket.

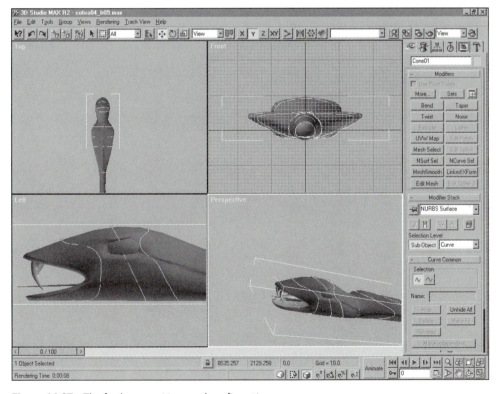

Figure 14.27   The final eye positions and configuration.

hope this chapter, like the previous one, has not only given you a good foundation in MAX Release 2.5's NURBS tools and techniques, but has also inspired you to strike out and find new techniques to explore and call your own.

Now that you've learned about modeling in MAX, it's time to move on to something more kinetic. In the next section, you'll see how to have some fun with MAX's space warps, object modifiers, and particle systems.

PART III

MOVING PARTS

MODELING AND SPACE WARPS 15

In this chapter, you'll take a brief look at some of 3D Studio MAX Release 2's Space Warps. You'll see the differences between the Space Warps in MAX Release 1 and Release 2.5, and you'll see how you can use them to create cool animated effects.

The first example you'll play with involves squeezing a sphere through a hole in a wall. This simple technique can be adapted to produce "cartoon-style" effects, such as a rubbery character oozing through a keyhole or jumping through a tiny hole in the floor. After that, you'll see how you can use Displace Space Warps to create footprints embossed into a surface such as snow.

Warp Speeds

Unlike MAX Release 1, which contained only one category of Space Warps, MAX Release 2 contains three different Space Warp types: Geometric (or Deformable), Modifier-based, and Particle/Dynamic-based:

- Geometric Space Warps, such as the new free-form deformation lattices (FFDs), Wave, Ripple, Displace, Conform, and Bomb, are used to distort MAX geometry. As you could with MAX Release 1, you can apply an FFD lattice to an object, select the lattice's control points, and deform the object's surface. (In Release 2 and above, you can animate those control points as well.)

- Modifier-based Space Warps are just what their name implies—space warp incarnations of MAX's standard object modifiers, such as Bend, Noise, Taper, Twist, Skew, and Stretch.

- Finally, Particles and Dynamics Space Warps, which make up the third and most unusual category—Space Warps, include Gravity, Pbomb (particle bomb), Wind, Deflector, Path Follow, Udeflector (universal deflector), Displace, Sdeflector (a spherical particle deflector), Push, and Motor.

Each space warp operates in a different way on various components of your MAX scene; the Displace warp can operate not only on geometry, but on particles as well. To see which categories of MAX components these warps support, look in their Creation rollout under Supports Objects Of Type.

Because you can use Space Warps as object modifiers, you can animate the Warp components separately or produce new effects by moving the Warp gizmo, the object it affects, or both. This is an extremely powerful feature—you're no longer constrained to using certain modifiers only as modeling tools. For example, you can apply an FFD lattice (as a space warp) to your geometry and deform the geometry as it moves through "world space." You'll see an example of that in the next section.

In this chapter, you'll play with two of the Space Warps—FFD and Displace. You'll take a look at Dynamics, Particles, and their associated Space Warps later in this book.

A Hole In The Wall

In the first example, you'll use some simple geometry and an FFD space warp to squeeze a large sphere through a small opening in a wall. You'll then add a Ripple warp to make the sphere "flutter" as it oozes through the opening. To begin, follow these steps:

1. In MAX, save your current work and reset the program.

2. Activate the Front viewport, press the W key to enlarge it to full screen, and press S to activate 3D Snap Toggle.

3. Select Create|Shapes|Splines from the Command panel, and select Rectangle under Object Type. Place your cursor at approximate coordinates X -100, Y 0, Z 100 and drag diagonally down and to the right until you've created a square with a length and width of 200 units. (Leave Corner Radius at 0.)

4. Select Circle and create a circle with a radius of 20 units in the center of the square (and your screen).

5. With the circle selected, click on the Modify tab and apply an Edit Spline modifier to the circle. Turn off Sub-Object: Vertex under Selection Level and click on Attach under Edit Object. Then, click on the Rectangle01 spline to attach it to Circle01.

6. Select Extrude from the Modifiers panel (if it's not already a part of your Modifiers set, click on More to bring it up). Set Amount to 10 and rename this object Wall.

You've now created a simple wall with a hole bored through the center, as shown in Figure 15.1.

Big Rubber Ball

Now, you'll create a sphere to "push" through the opening in the wall:

1. Click on the Create tab and select Geometry| Standard Primitives|Sphere. In the Front viewport, click in the center of your screen and drag outward to create a sphere with a radius of 80 units. Set Segments to 100—the sphere should have a high resolution so it looks rubbery when it oozes through the wall opening.

2. Click on the Min/Max Toggle icon (or press the W key again) to return to the four viewports and then activate the Right viewport. Using the Zoom All Icon, zoom out so that you can see the moving sphere. With Sphere01 selected, right-click to bring up the Properties window, select Transform: X, and then select Move. Drag the sphere to the right on the X axis approximately 180 units.

Now that you've placed the sphere in position, you're ready to create the FFD Space Warp.

Creating The FFD Space Warp

Unlike the standard FFD object modifiers, which create static modeling effects, the FFD Space Warps are designed to distort geometry in your scene as it animates. You can see this effect quite easily as you "push" Sphere01 through a distorted, hourglass-shaped FFD space warp. To create the FFD space warp, follow these steps:

1. Activate the Front viewport and press the W key to enlarge it to full screen.

2. Press the S key to activate 3D Snap and select Create|Space Warps|Geometric|Deformable (the default) from the Command panel. Select FFD(box) under Object Type.

3. In the Front viewport, place the Snap cursor at approximate XYZ coordinates X -80, Y 0, Z 80, then drag diagonally downward to the right to XYZ coordinates X 80, Y 0, Z -80. You'll see under FFD Parameters that this creates an FFD box with both a Length and a Width setting of 160. Make the Height setting 200.

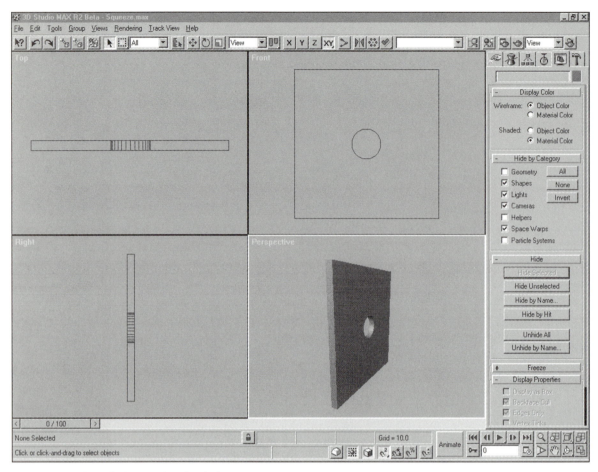

Figure 15.1 The wall object with a "knothole" opening.

4. Click on the Set Number Of Points button, set Length, Width, and Height to 6 points each, and click on OK.

5. Turn off 3D Snap, press the W key to return to the four viewports, and activate the Right viewport. Press the W key again to enlarge it to full screen, make sure the FFD box is still selected, and drag it to the right on the X axis approximately 55 units. (You can click on the Restrict To X Axis icon to make it easier to drag the box on the X axis.) The right side of the FFD box should be almost touching the high-resolution Sphere01.

6. With the FFD box still selected, turn off Re-strict To X Axis (if it's activated) and click on the Modify tab of the Command panel. Click

on Sub-Object: Control Points, and in the Right viewport, select the middle four rows of the FFD box, as shown in Figure 15.2.

What you'll do next is "pinch" the control points inward and start to create the hourglass shape.

An Hourglass Figure

To get the proper "oozing" effect, you'll squeeze the control points inward using Uniform Scaling. (If necessary, you could also simply move them in-ward individually, but for now, scaling is easier.) Follow these steps:

1. Right-click on the selected FFD box to bring up the Properties menu and choose Scaling. It will now be set to Uniform Scale. Then, in any viewport, scale the selected control

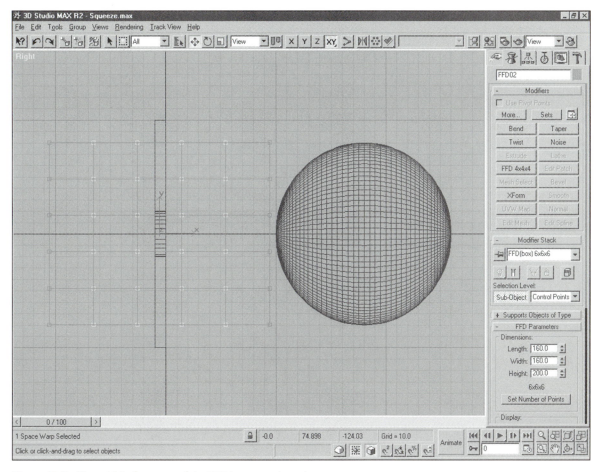

Figure 15.2 The middle four rows of the FFD box are selected.

points down approximately 75 percent on the X, Y, and Z axes, as shown in Figure 15.3.

2. Click outside the selected FFD control points to deselect them, then select the middle two rows of the FFD box control points and scale them down 25 percent, as shown in Figure 15.4.

The hourglass figure of the FFD box is now apparent. By scaling down the middle rows of the FFD box to approximately the size of the knot-hole, you can now fit the Sphere01 object through the wall.

Break On Through To The Other Side

Now, it's time to make this large sphere go through this small opening. First, you need to bind the sphere to the FFD box space warp:

1. Select the sphere and click on the Bind To Space Warp icon on the menu bar at the top of your screen.

2. In the Right viewport, move your mouse cursor over the sphere until it changes to the Bind To Space Warp cursor, then click-hold

---

FITTING IN: THE FFD SPACE WARP

Unlike the Object-modifier version of FFD (which will fit itself to a selected model or selected faces of a sub-object), your geometry must fit entirely within the outermost edges of the FFD Space Warps in order for the geometry to be deformed fully.

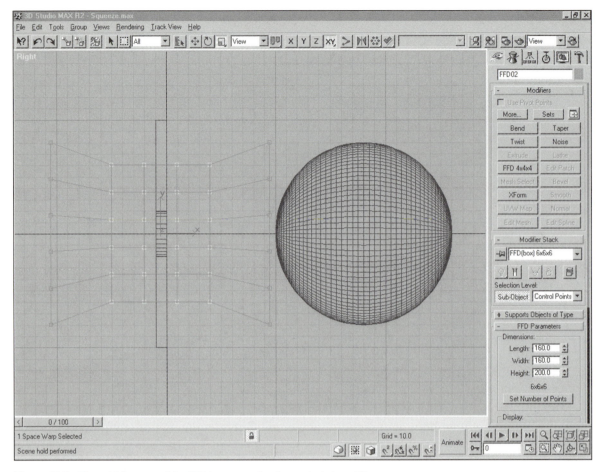

Figure 15.3 The middle rows of the FFD box control points scaled down 75 percent.

and drag the cursor from the sphere to the FFD box (you'll see a line stretching from the sphere to the FFD box). As you release the mouse button, you'll see the FFD box flash white briefly, indicating that the sphere has been bound to it.

3. Next, click on the Animate button, drag the Time Slider to frame 100, and right-click on the sphere to deactivate Bind To Space Warp mode; this also will bring up the Properties menu. Select Transform and drag the sphere to the left on the X axis approximately X -370 units.

As you drag the sphere, you'll see that it "pinched" in the middle as it approaches and then passes through the hole in the wall.

4. Turn off the Animate button, return to the four viewports, and drag the Time Slider back and forth to see the effect.

Adding A Ripple

Okay, this is a fun little effect—and it's simple. To jazz it up some more, you can add another space warp—a Ripple—to distort the surface of the sphere as it oozes through the wall:

1. Activate the Front viewport, select Space Warps|Geometric|Deformable from the Create panel, and choose Ripple.

2. In the Front viewport, place your cursor in the center of the wall and drag outward to create a Ripple space warp with a Wave

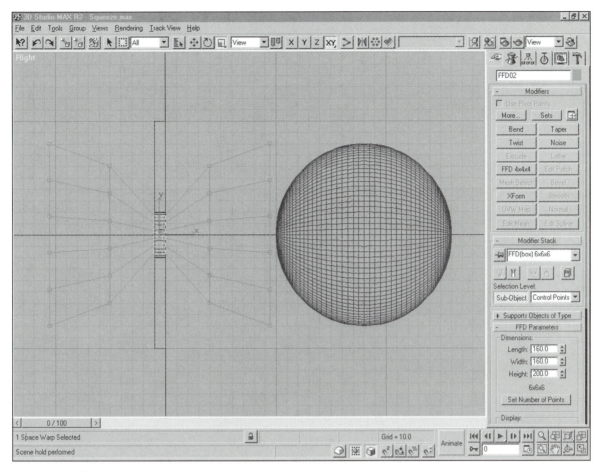

Figure 15.4   The two middle rows of the FFD box scaled down.

Length setting of 40; Amplitude 1 and 2 can be, say, 5 and 5. (These last two parameters don't matter much because you'll be changing and animating them in a moment.) Under Display, set Circles to 10, Segments to 16, and Divisions to 4.

As you did with the FFD box in Step 2 in the previous section, you have to bind the Sphere01 object to the Ripple space warp.

3. Select the sphere, then click on the Bind To Space Warp icon. Click-hold and drag the Bind cursor from the sphere over to the Ripple space warp and release. (If you have difficulty selecting the Ripple space warp instead of the FFD box, press the H button and select Ripple01 from the Select By Name menu.)

4. To deactivate the Bind To Space Warp mode, click on Select Object, then select the Ripple01 space warp again, and click on the Modify tab. Turn on the Animate button (make sure you're on frame 0), then set Ripple Amplitude 1 and Amplitude 2 both to 0.0.

> **BINDING MULTIPLE ELEMENTS**
>
> Remember that you can bind an object or particle system to many different Space Warps simultaneously—you're not restricted to just one at a time.

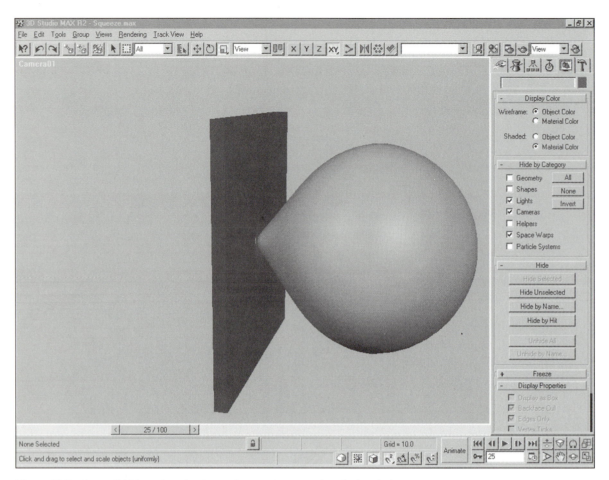

Figure 15.5 Frame 25. The sphere begins to distort as it approaches the knothole.

5. Go to frame 25 and right-click on the Time Slider button. The Create Keys menu appears; click on OK to set "anchor" keys for Position, Rotation, and Scale. (You actually need only a Rotation key here, but don't worry about it—setting the other keys won't affect the final results.)

6. Go to the Modify panel, and on frame 25, set both Amplitude 1 and Amplitude 2 for the Ripple space warp to 0.5.

7. Go to frame 50. Set Amplitude 1 and Amplitude 2 to 10.

8. Go to frame 100, set Amplitude 1 and Amplitude 2 to 0, then right-click on the Ripple space warp in the Right viewport to bring up the Properties menu. Select Rotate, then Rotate the Ripple space warp gizmo on the Z axis a full 180 degrees (Z 180). Turn off the Animate button and drag the Time Slider back and forth to see the effect.

As you drag the Time Slider back and forth, you'll see the sphere ooze through the wall with the added effect of rippling like gelatin as it squeezes through the knothole.

Figures 15.5 through 15.8 show the progression of the sphere. (Note that I've created a scene with a Targeted Camera tracking past the sphere and wall. I've also applied basic materials to the objects and created two spotlights to illuminate them. Finally, I've hidden the actual Displace and Ripple Space Warps and the viewport grid for clarity.)

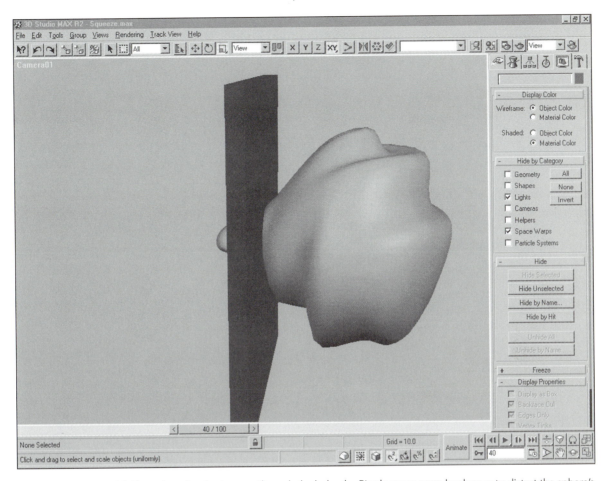

Figure 15.6 Frame 40. The sphere begins to ooze through the hole; the Ripple space warp has begun to distort the sphere's surface.

At this point, of course, you could apply materials to the objects in the scene, create lights and a camera, and then do a test animation, but again, I've done the work for you.

9. Select File|View File and click on SQUEEZE.AVI from the \CHAP_15 directory of the companion CD-ROM, to view it.

In this animation, I've added basic Diffuse color maps to the objects; spotlights and a lateral camera move so that you can see the sphere distortion effect on both sides.

10. When you've finished viewing the animation, close your Preview window. Note that the scene file used to create this animation is in the \CHAP_15 directory as SQUEEZE.MAX.

Beware The Blob

The sphere effect you've just created is somewhat reminiscent of the classic 1950s horror film *The Blob*, wherein the titular alien creature's lack of a skeleton doesn't impede it from going wherever it wants. (Alien monsters seem to have a knack for that.) A real-world equivalent, of course, might be a single-celled organism, such as an amoeba, oozing its way merrily around a petri dish.

However, another example is the common Pacific octopus, which I've seen several times while scuba diving in Hawaii. The octopus possesses the largest brain and keenest eyesight of any invertebrate (of comparable body size) and is quite adept at squeezing through the tiniest openings in search of food.

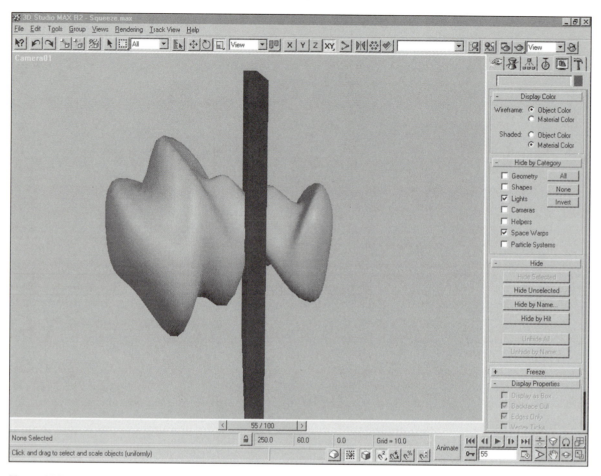

Figure 15.7 Frame 55. The sphere emerges on the other side; the Ripple space warp creates an undulating surface on the object.

Marine biologists have shown that an octopus with a 24-inch tentacle spread (and a head/body about the size of a man's clenched fist) can squeeze through an opening only a quarter of an inch in diameter. (Something to consider when you're searching for a MAX animation idea....)

Finally, the other thing this effect tells you is that whoever coined that old saying, "You can't fit a square peg in a round hole," obviously didn't have access to MAX Release 2. With MAX's Space Warps, your geometry can, uh, go boldly where it hasn't gone before.

Displacement: Space Warps Vs. Modifiers

You've created a simple Space Warps squeeze-and-ripple effect; now you'll see how to use the new Displace Space Warps to create footstep impressions, such as those left by someone (or some *thing!*) walking across a snowy field.

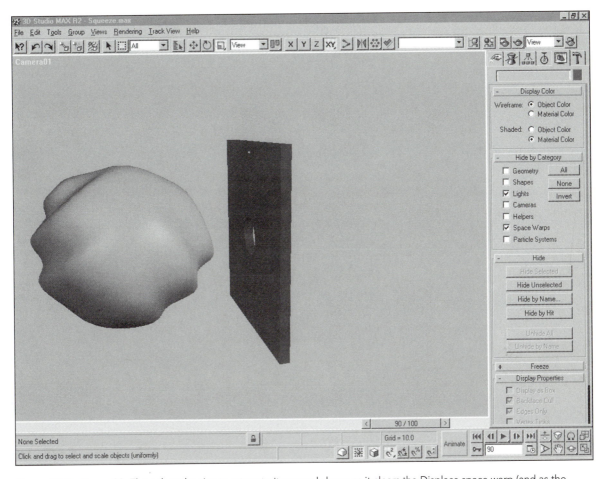

Figure 15.8   Frame 90. The sphere begins to return to its normal shape as it clears the Displace space warp (and as the animated Ripple values diminish to zero).

Both the Displace Space Warps and Displace object modifier can be used as powerful modeling tools as well. Simply load a grayscale elevation map into a Displace gizmo (applied to a high-density Quad Patch object), and you can literally make mountains out of molehills.

Now, you might be asking: Why use Displace Space Warps on an object instead of using Displace object modifiers? There are a couple of reasons.

First, you have to consider your final object complexity and the object modifier stack. Displace works best, of course, on complex geometry—the more dense the mesh, the finer the detail you'll be

able to produce with a Displacement map. However, if you're using multiple animated Displace effects on a single piece of geometry, it's best to have them affect only the areas that need to be deformed. If you have to tessellate an entire piece of geometry for one or two localized effects, your memory overhead and screen redraw times may be prohibitive.

Second, the Displace space warp is more flexible in this instance. To create this same effect using Displace object modifiers, you would have to:

- Apply an Edit Mesh or Mesh Select modifier to your Quad Patch. (As Jack Powell, MAX Documentation Manager, notes, "The Mesh Select modifier lets you pass sub-object selection up the stack to subsequent modifiers.") Some of these modifiers have been duplicated from the Edit Mesh modifier into new, discrete modifiers, such as Tessellate.

- Select the faces you want and tessellate them (or apply the new Tessellation modifier after a Mesh Select).

- Apply a Displacement modifier.

- Then, repeat the process for each displacement.

It takes (somewhat) fewer steps to create the above Displacement effect with Displace Space Warps, and it keeps the object stack more manageable. You simply:

- Apply a single Edit Mesh or Mesh Select modifier.

- Select all the (groups of) faces you want to tessellate.

- Move your Displace Space Warps over the tessellated areas, then bind the object to them.

This latter technique is what you'll do now.

Footprints In The Snow

In this example, you'll assume that the ghost of Ralph, the famous 3D Studio egret (shown in Figure 15.9), has left his DOS environs and is traipsing through a snowy MAX landscape. He's a mischievous ghost, so you'll just see his footprints.

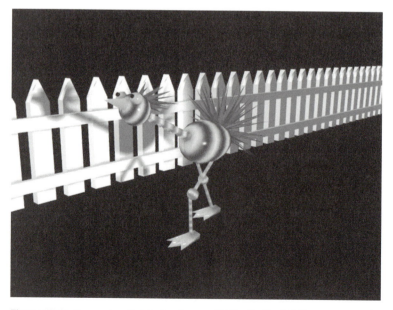

Figure 15.9 Remember Ralph, the famous 3D Studio (for DOS) egret? His polygonal soul is restless and about to leave mysterious footprints in the snow.

To create this effect, all you need is a Quad Patch, some Displace Space Warps, and a couple of bitmaps from the companion CD-ROM:

1. Load MAX, or save your current work and reset the program.

2. Press the S key to activate 3D Snap, then activate the Top viewport. Select Create|Geometry|Patch Grids|Quad Patch from the Command panel.

3. In the Top viewport, place your mouse cursor at approximate XYZ coordinates X -50, Y 100, Z 0. Drag your mouse cursor diagonally down to the right to XYZ coordinates X 50, Y -100, Z 0. This creates a Quad Patch with a length of 200 and a width of 100.

4. Set Length Segments to 10 and Width Segments to 5 and check Generate Mapping Coordinates. (You can apply a snowy texture to this Quad Patch later.)

5. Enlarge the Top viewport to full screen (press the W key or click on the Min/Max Toggle icon). Select Create|Space Warps|Geometric| Deformable from the Command panel and choose Displace.

6. In the Top viewport, place your cursor at approximate XYZ coordinates X -16, Y -85, Z 0. Then click-hold and drag outward to create a Displace space warp with a width (and length) of approximately 10 units. (You may need to scroll the Displace create panel down to see the exact size, or place the space warp and change its size in the Modify panel.)

Making Tracks

Before you make the rest of the Displace footprints, load the bitmap you're going to use to create the impression of bird tracks:

1. With the Displace space warp active, go to the Modify panel and click on the Bitmap

Name button under Image. Click on BIRDFOOT.JPG in the \CHAP_15 directory of the companion CD-ROM. This 200×200 grayscale image is shown in Figure 15.10.

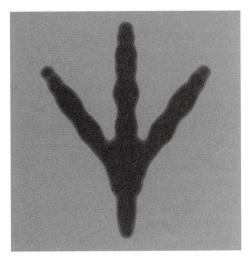

Figure 15.10 The BIRDFOOT.JPG image used in the Displace space warp.

2. Continuing in the Top viewport, create five more Displace Space Warps that are aligned evenly like footprints up the length of the Quad Patch, as shown in Figure 15.11. (Shift-clone them as Copies, not Instances. You can also make them as you made the original Displace space warp—in the Create panel— but you'll have to load the BIRDFOOT.JPG image in each one individually, of course.)

Using The Mesh Select And Tessellate Modifiers

Now that you've got the Displace footprints placed, you need to make the footprints appear properly on the Quad Patch object. Even though the Quad Patch has a relatively high face count, you should increase the resolution of the areas directly underneath the footprints so the grayscale image will distort the surface properly:

1. Select the Quad Patch and choose Mesh Select from the Modify panel. You'll see that

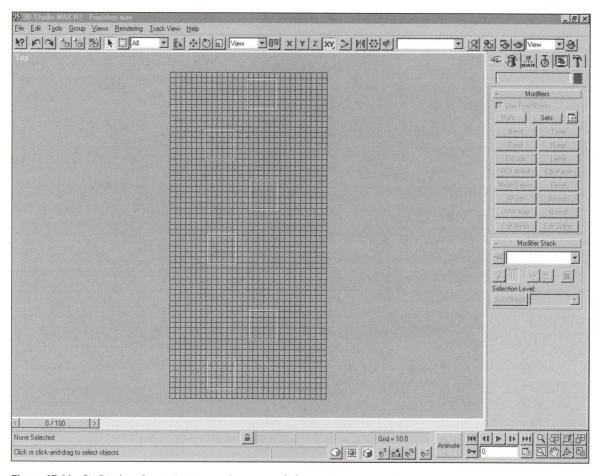

Figure 15.11 Six Displace Space Warps provide a series of "footprint" patterns in the snow.

Sub-Object: Face is already selected. The Mesh Select modifier will pass the sub-object selection (in this case, the footprint areas) up the stack to the Tessellate modifier, which you'll apply in a moment.

2. In the Top viewport, make sure you're in Select Object mode (not Move, Scale, or Rotate), then draw a square bounding box to select the faces around the first Displace space warp.

3. Hold down the Ctrl key and select the faces around each of the other Displace Space Warps, as shown in Figure 15.12.

4. Return to the Modify panel and select Tessellate (if you don't have it in your standard list of Modifiers, click on More; you'll find it under Object-Space Modifiers). When you apply the Tessellate modifier, you'll see that Iterations is set to 1 and the selected faces of the Quad Patch have become tessellated.

5. We need to have more faces to make this look more realistic. Click on 2 under Iterations; you'll see the selected faces tessellate

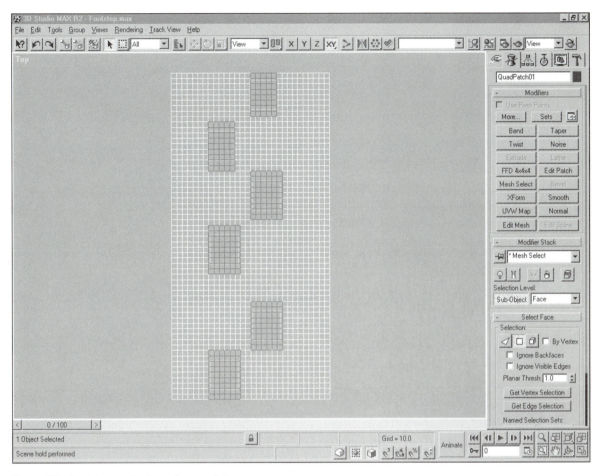

Figure 15.12   Selecting the faces for tessellation.

even more. If we were to select 3, the redraw and rendering times would be very slow.

Bound

Now it's time to bind the Quad Patch to the Displace Space Warps:

1. With the Quad Patch still selected and the tessellated faces still highlighted, click on the Bind To Space Warp icon on the menu bar at the top of your screen. The Bind To Space Warp cursor appears.

2. Press the H key to bring up the Select Space Warp menu, choose Displace01, and click on Bind (you'll see * Displace Binding appear in the Modifier Stack window for the Quad Patch).

3. Next, repeat the process to bind the Quad Patch to the remaining Displace Space Warps (02-06). Then, click on the Select Object icon again to deactivate Bind To Space Warp.

4. If you open the Modifier Stack rollout now, you'll see a list that reads:

   - Displace Binding

   - Displace Binding

   - Displace Binding

   - Displace Binding

   - Displace Binding

   - Displace Binding

   ==============

   - Tessellate

   - Mesh Select

   _____

   - QuadPatch

5. When you're finished looking at the list, make sure the last (top) Displace Binding is still selected.

A Good First Impression

Now, you need to adjust the strength of the Displace BIRDFOOT.JPG image to create the effect that it's leaving an impression on the snowy ground:

1. Press the W key to return to the four viewports, then activate the Perspective viewport.

2. By using a combination of the Pan and Zoom features, enlarge the Displace01 space warp and the Quad Patch underneath it in the Perspective window until it looks like Figure 15.13.

3. Press the W key to enlarge the Perspective viewport to full screen and right-click on the Perspective title. Change your display mode from Wireframe to Smooth+Highlights; this will enable you to see the effect of the "bird tracks" more easily.

4. Select the Displace01 space warp, then go to the Modify panel. Under Displacement,

change Strength to 5.0 and then observe the results, as shown in Figure 15.14.

Although you have a proper bird footprint in the flat Quad Patch, the grayscale bitmap background is also distorting the Quad Patch, making it look like a raised footprint tile. You can fix this by adjusting the Luminance Center of the Displace space warp.

5. In the Modify panel, click in the Luminance Center checkbox to activate it, then begin increasing the Center slider slowly. You'll see the edges of the bird-foot tile recede into the Quad Patch.

6. Continue adjusting the Luminance Center; the edges should be completely flat when the Luminance Center has a setting of approximately 0.5, as shown in Figure 15.15.

Making (More) Tracks

Now, it's time to animate the footsteps of Ralph, the Invisible Bird:

1. Right-click on the Play Animation button to bring up the Time Configuration menu. Change End Time from 100 to 40 and click on OK.

2. In the Modify panel, keep the Luminance Center value set to 0.5 and change Displacement Strength back to 0.0.

3. Turn on the Animate button, go to frame 5, and change Displacement Strength to 5.0. The bird track looks as if it's an impression in the Quad Patch. Turn off the Animate button.

   Click on the Track View icon to open Track View, maximize it to full screen, and open the Tracks for Displace01. The Track View shows the placement of the animated Strength keys from frames 0 to 5, as shown in Figure 15.16.

4. Select Displace02, and in the Modify Panel, make sure that Luminance Center is checked, and the value is set to 0.5.

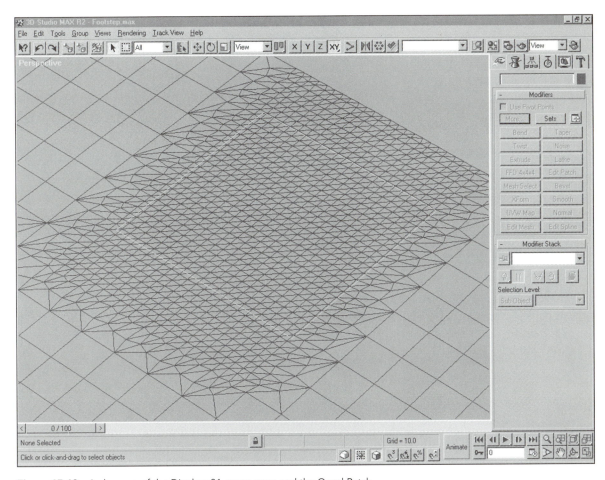

Figure 15.13   A close-up of the Displace01 space warp and the Quad Patch.

5. Open the Tracks for the remaining Displace
   Space Warps, then click on the Zoom Horizontal Extents icon.

You don't need to animate all the footsteps by
hand; you can just copy the Strength settings from
Displace01, paste them to the other Space Warps,
and then offset them.

6. Under Displace01, click on the Strength attribute under Object: Displace to select it and
   then click on the Copy Controller icon on the
   menu bar at the top of Track View.

7. Working your way down the list, hold down
   the Ctrl key and click on the Strength attribute of the remaining Displace Space
   Warps to highlight them. Next, click on the
   Paste Controller icon. Paste as a Copy and

click on OK. You'll see the same set of animation keys appear on Displace02 through
Displace06.

8. Now, you need to weed out all the extraneous
   object data, so click on the Filters icon; when
   the Filters menu appears, click on Animated
   Tracks under Show Only and then click on
   OK. When you return to Track View, you'll see
   only the keys and tracks for the Strength attributes of the Displace Space Warps.

9. To make the footsteps appear in succession,
   you need to offset each set of Displace
   Strength keys. Select the keys for Displace02
   through Displace06 (make sure the Dis-
   place01 keys aren't selected), then drag
   them to the right so the first Strength key of

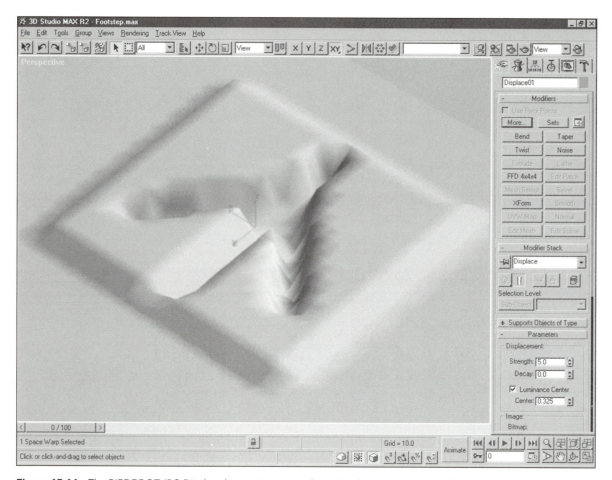

Figure 15.14 The BIRDFOOT.JPG Displace bitmap image used as a Displacement map; the Strength setting is 5.0.

02 through 06 is at frame 5 (the last frame of Displace01).

10. Deselect all the Strength keys, select the keys for Displace03 through Displace06, and drag them so the first Strength key is at frame 10 (the last Strength key of Displace02).

11. Next, drag the remaining keys over, in turn, so the first frame of each successive footstep begins on the last frame of the previous footstep, as shown in Figure 15.17.

12. Close Track View, make sure Perspective is still active, and click on the Zoom Extents All icon (or press Shift+Ctrl+Z) to zoom out in all viewports. If you want, you can zoom in somewhat in the Perspective viewport to see the effects of the footsteps more clearly.

13. With Smooth+Highlights active in the Perspective viewport, drag the Time Slider back and forth and note the results.

Ralph's ghost footprints appear across the flat ground.

At this point, you can render a shaded preview of this scene (at only 40 frames and with this simple geometry, it should render pretty quickly), or you view a prerendered scene from the \CHAP_15 directory.

14. Select File|View File, and click on BIRDFOOT.AVI in the \CHAP_15 directory of the companion CD-ROM to preview it. (Close the Preview window when you're finished—you don't want to leave it lying around where someone could stumble over it, do you?)

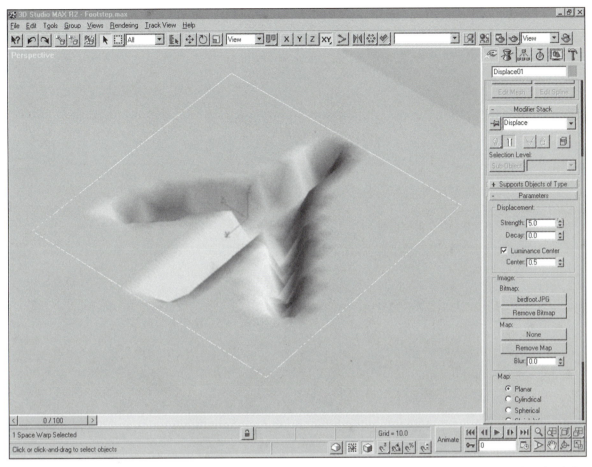

Figure 15.15 The Luminance Center of the Displacement map adjusted to "zero out" the gray values surrounding the dark bird track in the BIRDFOOT.JPG image.

MAX's Sense Of Snow

Because you applied mapping coordinates to the Quad Patch originally, there's nothing to prevent you from improving this object with a little snow texture and a Noise modifier:

1. Click on the Quad Patch to select it, then apply another Mesh Select modifier from the Modify panel. Select all the faces of the Quad Patch and choose Noise from the Modify panel.

2. Click on Fractal under Parameters and change Strength on Z to 10.0. You'll see the surface of the Quad Patch become slightly distorted.

3. Open the Material Editor and apply Material #1 to the Quad Patch. Change Ambient to RGB settings 48, 48, 64; change Diffuse to RGB 225, 225, 255. Change Shininess to 75 and Shininess Strength to 100.

4. Open the Maps rollout, click on the Diffuse button, and select Bitmap from the Material/Map Browser.

5. In the \CHAP_15 directory of the companion CD-ROM, double-click on SNOW.JPG to load it. This is a simple 400×400 pixel image I created in Adobe Photoshop. It's merely a white field with Gaussian Noise and a little Gaussian blur applied and its blue tones enhanced.

6. Under Coordinates, change V Tiling to 2.0, then click on the Go To Parent icon to return to the main Maps rollout. Drag the

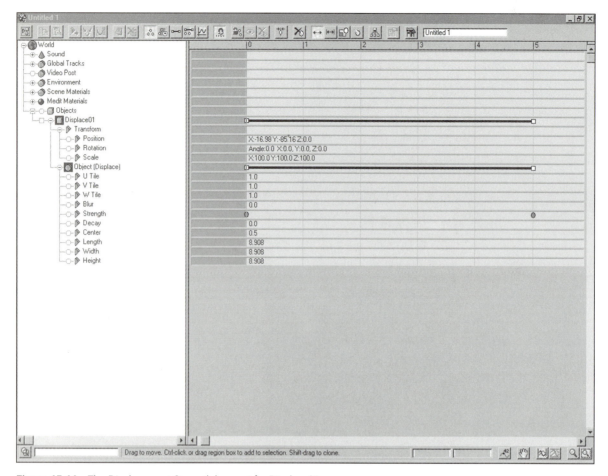

Figure 15.16 The Displacement Strength keys set for Displace01.

SNOW.JPG Diffuse map down to the Bump map slot to copy it (it doesn't matter if it's a Copy or an Instance). Then, assign this material to the Quad Patch.

7. Render a still image, with at least 640×480 resolution, of frame 40 of this shot. Now you have a snowy field with bird tracks scattered across it. (Note that you don't have to have a spotlight or Omni light set up in the scene for it to render properly. The default lighting parameters of MAX will provide overall illumination until you create a specific light.) You can set up your own lighting, atmospheric effects, and cameras and play with this scene further. (There are even human footstep bitmaps

included in the \CHAP_15 directory of the companion CD-ROM; load them and examine the effect.)

8. You can save this scene to your local hard drive if you want; it is included in the \CHAP_15 directory as FOOTSTEP.MAX.

Things To Try

Of course, you can use this effect for more than footprints of invisible birds. Other uses for Displace include:

- Tire tracks in snow

- Tank tracks across muddy ground

- A depression being blown into soft earth or sand by a helicopter's propellers

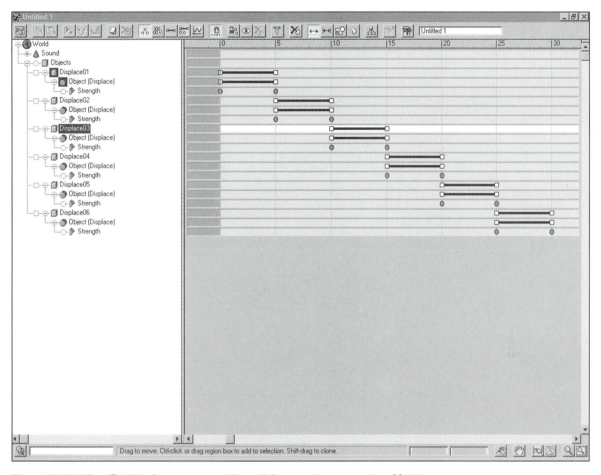

Figure 15.17   The offset Displace space warp Strength keys create a succession of footsteps.

- Pits or ruts being dug into a surface (either artificial or a landscape) by an energy beam

You can also use Displace to depict the Bugs Bunny tunneling effect (you know—the quickly moving "mole tunnels" that appeared across the ground as Bugs headed for Miami Beach). All you need is the proper bitmap image or images depicting a light-colored line moving across a dark surface. Adjust the Luminance Center and poof! You've got Bugs Bunny missing that left turn at Albuquerque.

Finally, remember that you can animate the actual Displace space warp gizmo itself, of course; by animating its position, scale, or rotation, you can produce serious distortions of your geometry.

Moving On

Now that you've played with MAX's object modifiers, you'll continue to work with "moving parts" as you take a look at Release 2's new particle systems. In the next chapter, you'll see how to create glittering sparks and swirling mercury.

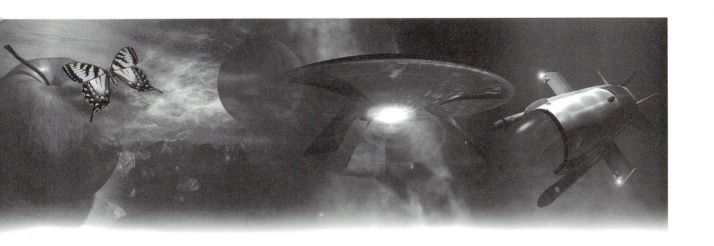

FUN WITH PARTICLES

16

BY JON BELL
AND PETER CLAY,
DIGITAL PHENOMENA

In this chapter, you'll create a couple of simple particle scenes and test the results. The effects discussed here include welding sparks (using the Video Post Lens Effects filters) and MetaParticles.

One of the most notable enhancements to 3D Studio MAX Release 2 is its advanced particle systems. Whereas 3D Studio MAX Release 1 had basic particles (Snow and Spray), Release 2 adds a great deal of new functionality to the existing particle systems. It also adds several new particle systems (such as Blizzard and Particle Array), particle types (such as MetaParticles), and space warps and other modifiers to affect the particle systems.

Much of the new particle systems in 3D Studio MAX Release 2 come from the designer/programmer team of Eric and Audrey Peterson. Eric and Audrey's previous MAX work included the All-Purpose Particles (APP), Shields Up, and MAXTrax plug-ins for Release 1; for Release 2, Kinetix and The Yost Group added the Petersons' considerable expertise to MAX's core code.

In addition to creating and testing the two particle scenes, you can load two test scenes that are included in the \CHAP_16 directory of the companion CD-ROM and then reverse-engineer them to note the effects. These test scenes consist of an interesting tornado simulation and an entire darn planet exploding. (For the latter scene, you'll need an extremely fast computer, because it contains complex geometry and a high number of particles.)

For this chapter, I'm indebted to the pioneering particle pyrotechnics of Peter Clay, resident 3D explosions expert at Digital Phenomena in Corte Madera, California. Peter has been concentrating on MAX's particle systems since Release 1 (and with APP, mentioned earlier) and generated the example files used in this chapter. With my words and his electrons, we'll soon fill your screen with jumping, falling, dancing, and sparkling particles.

Old Sparky

The first example you'll play with consists of simple "welding sparks." For this example, you'll create a collision surface upon which you'll "pour" a stream of particles. As the particles hit the surface (a flattened box), they'll spawn, or shatter, into additional fragments. Then, by applying a Lens Effects Glow to them in Video Post, you can create the effect of glowing sparks hitting a floor.

First, you'll set up the elements in your scene as follows:

1. Start MAX, or save your current work and reset the program.

2. Press the S key to activate 3D Snap, then make the Top viewport active (press the W key to enlarge it to full screen if you want). Select Create|Geometry|Standard Primitives, create a box, and center it

in the Top viewport with a width and length of 160 and a height of 10 (place your mouse cursor at XYZ coordinates X -80, Y 80, Z 0, then drag diagonally down to the right to XYZ coordinates X 80, Y -80, Z 0). Then, check Generate Mapping Coordinates.

3. Select Create|Cameras|Target Camera and place a camera at XYZ coordinates X -80, Y -160, Z 0. Drag the Camera target out to X 40, Y 60, Z 0, or the upper-right corner of the box.

4. Press the W key again, if necessary, to return to the four viewports, then activate the Left viewport. Drag the Camera target up on the Y axis 110 units, select the Camera target, and drag it up 40 units on the Y axis.

5. Activate the Top viewport again and enlarge it to full screen. Click on Create|Space Warps|Particles & Dynamics, and select Deflector. Place your mouse cursor near the upper-left corner of the box (say, X -75, Y 70, Z 0), then drag diagonally downward to the right to just inside the lower-right corner of the box (to cover its surface almost completely). The Deflector should be about 150 units in width and length. (You'll change the parameters of the various space warps after you create all of them.)

6. Next, click on Gravity in the Particles & Dynamics panel and place your cursor outside the upper-right corner of the box (the exact placement doesn't really matter). Drag out a Gravity space warp icon (Planar) about 15 to 20 units in size.

7. Press the W key again to return to the four viewports, activate the Left viewport, and move the Deflector space warp up on the Y axis about 10 units (it should be level with the top of the box). While you're at it, you can move the Gravity space warp up, too, until it's above the surface of the box.

8. Turn off 3D Snap, then select Create|Geometry|Particle Systems and click on Super Spray. In the Left viewport, place your cursor at approximate coordinates X 0, Y 20, Z 110. Drag outward to create a Super Spray icon about 25 units in size.

9. Activate the Top viewport and move the Super Spray icon to the right (X 60 units). Then, right-click on the icon to bring up the Properties menu, select Rotate, and rotate the icon counterclockwise, or Z 15 units. Right-click on the icon a second time; when the Properties menu appears, select Properties, change G-Buffer Object Channel to 1, and click on OK (you'll use this object channel for the Lens Effects Glow in Video Post). Your desktop should look something like Figure 16.1.

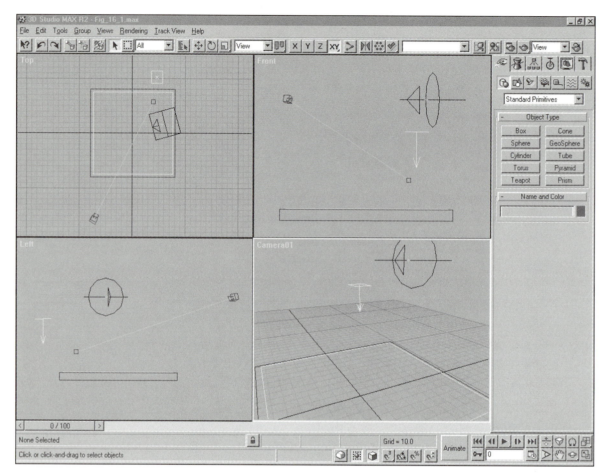

Figure 16.1   The placement for the Collision box, Deflector, and Gravity space warps. (Note that in this figure, Zoom Extents All has been selected, and the Perspective view changed to the Camera view.)

Binding The Space Warps

Now, it's time to bind the Super Spray emitter to the Deflector and Gravity space warps:

1. Select the Super Spray emitter, then click on the Bind To Space Warp icon. In the Top viewport, drag the Bind To Space Warp cursor over to the edge of the Deflector and release.

   The Deflector will flash white briefly to show that it's been selected.

2. Next, move the cursor over to the Gravity space warp and release; this space warp should flash, indicating that it's also been selected.

3. Click on the Select Object icon to deactivate Bind To Space Warp mode.

Setting The Parameters

The next step is to set the various parameters for your sparks scene. First, you'll set the particle parameters:

1. Select the Super Spray emitter, then click on the Modify tab of the Command panel. You should see the Gravity Binding in the Modify stack; click on the Down arrow and move down the stack to SuperSpray.

2. Under Basic Parameters, change the Off Axis Spread value to 10. This will make the particle stream more random and less of a narrow, linear flow. Viewport Display should be set to Ticks. If you have a fast PC, you can change the Percentage Of Particles value to 100; otherwise, keep it around 10 to 25 percent.

3. Open the Particle Generation rollout. Under Particle Quantity, check Use Total; the total number should be 100. Under Particle Motion, change Speed to 5.0. Emit Start should be 0; Emit Stop should be 15. Display Until should be set to 100, Life to 20, and Variation to 5. Under Subframe Sampling, check Creation Time and Emitter Translation.

4. Under Particle Size, Size should be kept at 1.0; Variation percentage should be 50.0. Set Grow For and Fade For both to 3.

5. Open the Particle Type rollout. Set Particle Type to Standard Particles and check Constant. Under Material Mapping and Source, check Time and set the duration to 100. Set Get Material From to Icon.

6. Open the Particle Rotation rollout; Spin Time should be set to 30. Under Spin Axis Controls, check Direction Of Travel/Mblur.

7. Skip down to the Particle Spawn rollout and open it. Under Particle Spawning Effects, check Spawn On Collision. Set Spawns to 25; Affects should be at 100. Set Variation to 10 percent and set Direction Chaos to 50.0. Set Speed Chaos to 75.0 and check the Both box (not Slow or Fast). This will impart additional wild bouncing motions to the particles. Make sure Inherit Parent Velocity is checked.

8. Under Scale Chaos, change Factor to 5 percent and check the Both box.

Rewriting The Laws Of Gravity

Now, it's time to set the parameters for your space warps. To do so, follow these steps:

1. Select the Gravity space warp, then go to the Modify panel. Set Gravity Strength to 1.0.

2. Click on the Deflector space warp; under Parameters, set Bounce to 0.4.

3. Now, you're ready to check the motions of the particles. Drag the Time slider back and forth, scratching through the animation.

As you can see, the particles emit (in midair) in a thick stream and then bounce and shatter when they hit the surface of the box (actually, the Deflector sitting atop the box). The Gravity space warp causes the particles to curve down in a gentle arc until they impact. Figure 16.2 shows frame 15 of the sequence.

> **USING CONSTANT PARTICLES**
>
> The Constant particle type is ideal for creating "pixel" particles that don't exceed a specific size, no matter how close they get to the camera. Use this setting for plankton, dust motes, and so on.

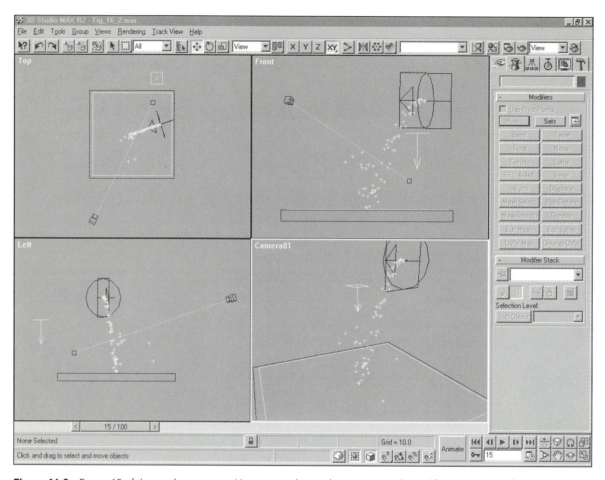

Figure 16.2   Frame 15 of the sparks sequence. You can see the sparks starting to rebound from the box surface.

Against A Dark Background

Now, you're ready to assign the materials for this scene. First, though, you need to change the background color to make the soon-to-be-glowing particles and green metallic box show up better:

1. Select Render|Environment and click on the Background color swatch. Change the background color to RGB 0, 0, 32, or a dark blue, and close the Environment menu.

2. Select the Super Spray emitter, open the Material Editor, select Slot #1, and click on the Get Material icon. When the Material/Map Browser appears, select Material Library. Load the MAXFX2.MAT library from the \MATLIBS directory of this book's companion CD-ROM. Scroll down and pick the

Spark Fadeout material. When it loads, take a look at the components that make up this Blend material:

- Material #1 (Fade-Out) is completely transparent—essentially, a "nothing" material.

- Material #2 (Glow Particles) is a glowing yellow-orange.

- The mask consists of the Particle Age map. Particle Age is a new type of map that was added to 3D Studio MAX Release 2; it enables you to fade particle colors based on the lives of the individual particles. When used as a Blend Mask between two submaterials, it creates a transition between the Glow Particles material and the Fade-Out material, causing the particles to change color and disappear.

3. After you've examined this material, apply it to the selected Super Spray emitter, then make the Material Editor Slot #2 active. Load the Metal 1 material from the MAX_FX_2.MAT library, select Box01, and apply Metal 1 to it.

At this point, you may be wondering where the lights are in this scene. For the purposes of this tutorial, you can use MAX's default scene lighting—you're more interested in seeing the particle effect than seeing specific lighting attributes. If you want, however, you can create an Omni light or spotlight to add some drama and highlights to the box.

A Healthy Glow

Before you do a test rendering of this scene, you'll need to set up a Lens Effects Glow in Video Post to give life to these sparks. To do so, follow these steps:

1. Select Rendering|Video Post; click on the Add Scene Event icon, select Camera01, and click on OK.

2. Click on the Add Image Filter Event icon, select Lens Effects Glow from the drop-down list, and click on the Setup button. When the menu appears, click on the Preview button.

As you saw in Chapters 7 and 8, the Lens Effects Glow Preview window displays a nifty little image that gives you some idea of how your final glow effect will look in the scene. For now, the glow is too bright, so you should change the Glow settings.

3. Click on the Properties tab and make sure Object ID 1 is checked. (You changed the G-buffer ID with the Properties menu earlier, remember?) Under Filter, click on Edge—this will help the particles remain visible instead of being obscured by the glow effect.

4. Click on the Preferences tab and set Size to 1.0—with Preview selected, you'll see the

Glow effect diminish considerably. Don't worry—the size will be fine for a 320×240 resolution test AVI rendering. Set the Glow Intensity to 100.

5. Click on the Gradients tab; click on the far-right slider under Radial Color to select it, then right-click to bring up the Flag #2 Properties menu. Currently, this color is blue. Click on the color swatch, change the color to RGB 255, 128, 0, or a reddish orange, and close the Color Swatch floater.

6. Click on the Inferno tab. Under Settings, change Type to Electric and check the blue box. Under Parameters, set Size to 1.0. (Although the final effect is too small to show Inferno's fractal noise patterns, you can use this setting to help force the overall glow effect to a yellow-orange cast. Later, if you want, you can increase the Glow size, animate the Inferno settings, and check the particle results.) Click on OK to close the Lens Effects Glow menu and return to Video Post.

7. At this point, you could click on the Add Image Output Event button and save an AVI test animation to your \3DSMAX2\IMAGES directory (call it SPARKS1.AVI). However, if you don't want to wait, you can preview a test animation of this scene, which I've already rendered.

   Select File|View File and double-click on SPARKS1.AVI (in the \CHAP_16 directory of the companion CD-ROM) to view it.

As the preview shows, the sparks now fall down and bounce off the green Metal 1 surface; the Glow effect adds to their fiery appearance. The sparks bounce around on (and off!) the surface before finally coming to a rest and then fading out altogether. Figure 16.3 shows frame 20 of the sparks sequence with the Glow filter applied.

MOTION BLUR: IMAGE, OBJECT, AND SCENE

Image motion blur is a post-processing rendering effect that is applied after the scanline render is finished. It blurs an object by applying a "smearing" effect based on the object's trajectory of movement. It also takes camera movement into account and usually produces better results than Scene motion blur.

Object motion blur applies blur to an object by rendering translucent subframe copies of the object and then combining them. Note that OMB is not affected by camera movement.

Scene motion blur is applied in Video Post at rendering time and affects the entire scene, both objects and camera movements. Note that Scene motion blur can usually increase your rendering times substantially, depending on your final scene.

To find more information, use 3D Studio MAX Release 2's Online Help feature and search on "motion blur."

8. Although this effect is interesting, the particles have a tendency to "strobe" due to their lack of motion blur. You can fix this by selecting the particle emitter, right-clicking on it to bring up the Properties menu, and checking either Image motion blur or Object motion blur. (You can also use the Particle MBlur map—which is applied in the Material Editor as an Opacity map—for all particle types other than Constant or Facing.) You can preview SPARKS2.AVI from the \CHAP_16 directory of the companion CD-ROM. This file shows the sparks with Image motion blur applied, as also shown in Figure 16.4.

Getting Those Sparkling Highlights

Although the Glow filter made the sparks brighter, it also made them softer. For a better "welding spark" effect, the particles should look like sharp, hot embers as they fly and bounce around.

You can create this effect by changing the Video Post Lens Effects Glow filter to Highlight. Follow these steps:

1. Open the Video Post menu, select the Lens Effects Glow filter entry, and click on the Edit Current Event icon. Select Lens Effect Highlight from the drop-down list, then click on Setup.

2. When the Setup menu appears, click on the Properties tab and set Source to Object ID 1. Under Filter, check Edge, then click on the Geometry tab. Angle should be set to 30.0, and Clamp should be set to 4. Click on the Preferences tab and change Size to 2.5 and Points to 6.

3. Finally, click on the Gradients tab. Under Radial Color, click on the far-right slider to select it, then right-click to bring up the Flag #2 Properties menu. Click on the color swatch, change the color to RGB 255, 128, 0 (or a reddish-orange), then close the Color

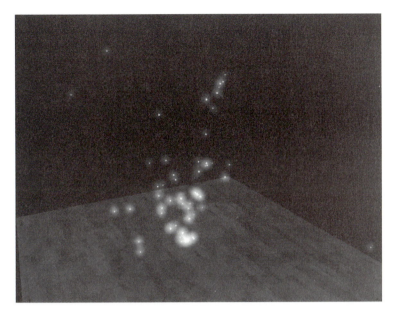

Figure 16.3 Frame 20 of the sparks sequence with the Lens Effects Glow filter applied.

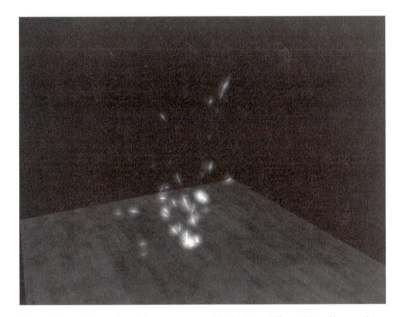

Figure 16.4 Frame 20 of the sequence with the Lens Effects Glow filter and Image motion blur (Multiplier set to 2.0) applied.

Swatch floater. Click on OK to close the Lens Effects Glow menu and return to Video Post.

4. Now, again, you can render your own test animation, or you can preview the results by selecting File|View File and loading SPARKS3.AVI from the \CHAP_16 directory of the companion CD-ROM.

As the animation shows, the particles now resemble glowing metal fragments; the Highlight filter adds a flickering glow effect that heightens the apparent energy of the particles. (Frame 20 of this sequence is shown in Figure 16.5.)

5. If you want, play with the various settings of this particle scene. Vary the Gravity and Deflector values, the number of particles, and the Lens Effects settings and check the results. Note that the files you've just created are included in the \CHAP_16 directory of the companion CD-ROM as SPARKS1.MAX and SPARKS2.MAX.

Figure 16.5   Frame 20 of the Sparks sequence with the Lens Effects Highlight filter applied.

Creating MetaParticles

One of the new features in MAX's particle systems is the metaparticle type, which consists of metaball particles that can merge and flow together. You can use metaparticles to simulate thick fluidic effects, zero-G liquids, plasma clouds, amoebas, pools of mercury, and the like.

To examine these effects, you'll load a demonstration scene and see how a spline path directs a flow of MetaParticles into a container—which in this case is a wooden bowl being filled with mercury. (Hey, it could happen!) Here's how to do it:

1. In MAX, select File|Open and load MERCURY1.MAX from the \CHAP_16 directory of this book's companion CD-ROM. Your screen should look something like Figure 16.6.

Note: This tutorial is resource intensive. You will be dealing with complex particle systems, so if you have a slower PC and video card, please be patient—scratching through the animation may take a few moments.

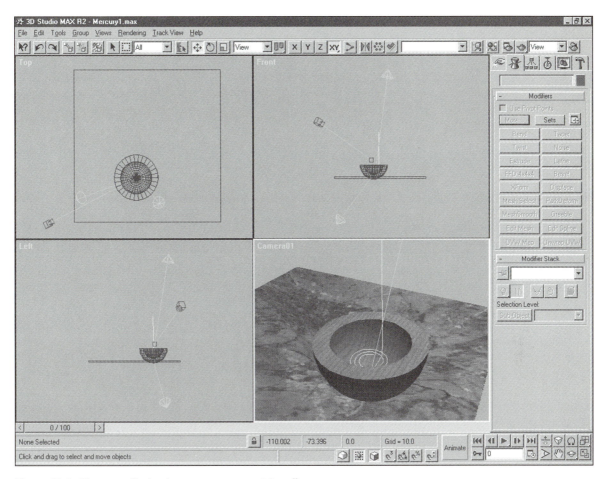

Figure 16.6   The scene file for the mercury metaparticles effect.

If you'll take a moment to examine the elements in your scene, you'll see that it consists of a flat, table-top surface with a bowl sitting on top. A helical spline extends below the emitter and runs down into the bowl. Finally, a couple of shadow-casting spot-lights provide top and fill illumination in the scene.

To produce the mercury effect for this scene, you'll need to create three things: a Blizzard particle emitter and two particle-based Space Warps (a PathFollowObject warp and a Udeflector).

2. First, you'll create the particle system and adjust its settings. Activate the Top viewport and enlarge it to full screen (press the W key). Click on the Region Zoom icon and draw a bounding box around the Bowl object

to zoom in on it, as shown in Figure 16.7 (this will make it easier to center the emitter).

3. Select Create|Geometry|Particle Systems| Blizzard, and place your mouse cursor at approximate XYZ coordinates X -5, Y 5, Z 0. Drag downward diagonally to the right to create a Blizzard emitter that is about 10 units wide and tall, as shown in the Create panel. (Note that you don't need to move the emitter up in a side viewport; the original scene elements have been adjusted so the emitter will be in the correct Z orientation above the bowl.)

4. Next, you'll enter some parameters in the Create panel. If you have a fast PC, check

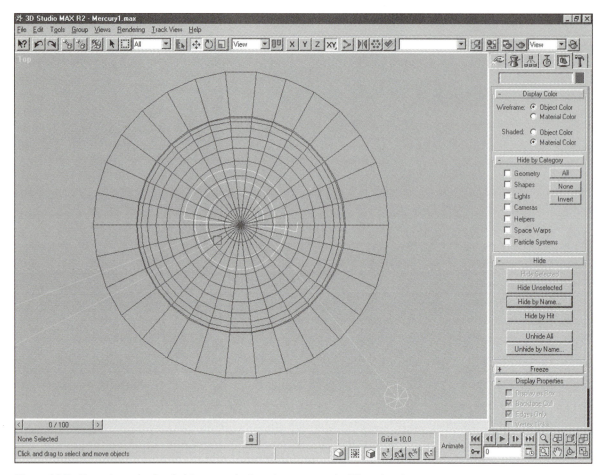

Figure 16.7 Zoom in on the Bowl object to make it easier to center the Blizzard emitter.

Mesh under Viewport Display, but change Percentage Of Particles to 10.0. This will give you sufficient feedback to gauge how the metaparticles are forming.

5. Open the Particle Generation rollout. Set Particle Motion Speed to 5.0, Variation to 25.0, Tumble to 1.0, and Tumble Rate to 3.0.

6. Under Particle Timing, set Emit Start to 0 and Emit Stop to 25. Set both Display Until and Life to 100. Check Creation Time and Emitter Translation under Subframe Sampling. Set Particle Size to 10.0 and Variation to 20.0.

7. Open the Particle Type rollout and check MetaParticles. Under Parameters, set Tension to 1.0 and Variation to 0.0. (Note that you'll

be animating some of these settings in a moment.) Select the On checkbox under Automatic Coarseness.

8. Under Material Mapping and Source, check Time; set Get Material From to Icon. (You'll apply a custom material for the particles in a little while.)

9. Open the Particle Rotation rollout. Set Phase to 360.0 and Variation to 50.0. Under Spin Axis Controls, set X Axis to 1.0 and Y and Z to 0.0. Variation should also be set to 0.0 degrees.

10. Open the Object Motion Inheritance rollout. Set Influence to 100.0, Multiplier to 1.0, and Variation to 50.0.

11. Open the Particle Spawn rollout and check None under Particle Spawning Effects.

You're now ready to animate these settings.

Animating The Particle Settings

Now that you've got this amazingly long particle modifier panel open, you'll change some of the settings on frame 100 to make the MetaParticles spew forth. You'll then create and bind the space warps to direct the particle flow. To begin, follow these steps:

1. Click on the Animate button, drag the Time slider to frame 100, then right-click your mouse button over the Modify panel to bring up the Blizzard rollout properties menu. This is a quick way to jump to a specific spot or to open or close a long rollout menu. Click on Modifiers to jump to the top of the rollout, and under Display Icon, change Width and Length to 25.

2. Open the Particle Generation rollout and set Tumble Rate to 10.0. Set Particle Size to 25.0 and Variation to 75.0 percent.

3. Open the Particle Type rollout and change Variation to 10.0 percent. Then, go down to the Particle Rotation rollout and change Phase to 360.0 degrees and Variation to 100.0 percent. Under Spin Axis Controls, change all of the X, Y, and Z Axis settings to 10.0 and change Variation to 25.0.

4. Finally, with the Blizzard emitter selected, right-click on it to bring up the Properties menu, select Rotate, and rotate (or spin) the emitter on the Z axis 720 degrees (counterclockwise). This will help the particles spin as they fall down the length of the helical spline path.

5. Turn off the Animate button and drag the Time slider back to frame 0.

Particle Space Warps: PathFollow

You're now ready to create, place, and bind the space warps to the Blizzard emitter:

1. Press the W key to return to the four viewports, then click on the Zoom Extents All icon to center the scene objects in the viewports. Select Space Warps|Particles & Dynamics from the Create panel and click on the Path Follow icon.

2. Place your mouse cursor in the Top viewport at approximate X, Y, Z coordinates X 80, Y 0, Z 0, then drag outward to create the icon. (The exact size and placement doesn't really matter. Make it about half the size of the bowl, for instance.)

3. Under Basic Parameters, click on the Pick Shape Object button, then press the H key to bring up the Select By Name menu. Select Helix Mercury Path and click on OK. Check Unlimited Range and set Particle Motion to Along Parallel Splines.

4. Set Stream Taper to 99.0 (Variation should stay at 0.0). Check Converge and set Stream Swirl also to 99.0. Finally, check Bidirectional. All of these settings combined make the particles travel down the helical path, swirl when they collide with the bowl object, and cluster together so they don't fly out of the bowl.

Particle Space Warps: UDeflector

The next step is to create your final space warp—a Universal Deflector:

1. Select Create|Space Warps|Particles & Dynamics and choose Udeflector. In the Top viewport, place your mouse cursor at approximate XYZ coordinates X 0, Y 0, Z 0, and then drag outward to create the emitter. Make it about the size of the bowl interior, or around 65 units wide.

2. Click on the Pick Object button under Basic Parameters, press the H key, and choose Wooden Bowl from the Select By Name menu. Click on OK.

3. Make the following changes under Particle Bounce: Set Bounce to 1.0 and Variation at 0.0; change Chaos to 0.4 percent and Friction and Inherit Velocity to 100.

Staying The Path

Now, you're ready to bind these two space warps, each with its selected scene objects or shapes, to the Blizzard emitter.

1. Select the Blizzard emitter, then click on the Bind To Space Warp icon. Next, either drag the Space Warp cursor over to the UDeflector gizmo and release, or pick the UDeflector from the Select By Name menu.

2. Repeat the process in Step 1, but bind the Blizzard emitter to the PathFollow gizmo. Then, click on the Select icon to toggle off Bind To Space Warp mode. Your screen should look something like Figure 16.8. Note that both the UDeflector and the PathFollow space warps have been moved for clarity; I've also zoomed in to the bowl and space warp elements in the scene.

The Mercury Is Falling

You should now be able to gauge the finished effect of the MetaParticles, objects, and space warp interactions in your scene. To do so, follow these steps:

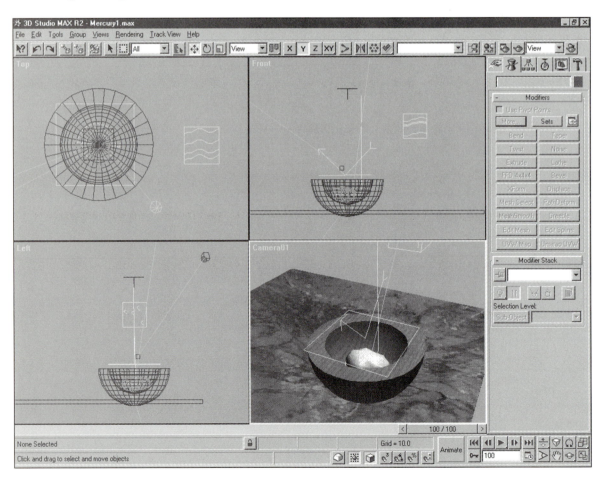

Figure 16.8 The finished Mercury MetaParticles scene (frame 100 of the final animation).

1. Drag the Time Slider slowly and take a look at the Camera viewport. As you do so, you should start seeing the MetaParticles being emitted, falling down along the helical path, and then swirling around in the wooden bowl.

2. If you want to do your own test rendering of this effect, you'll need to apply a chromelike material to the particles. Select the Blizzard emitter, then open the Material Editor. You should see a material called Mercury Particles in the second Material Editor slot. Activate it and click on the Assign Material To Selection icon to apply it to the Blizzard MetaParticles.

3. If you open the Reflection Map slot of this material, you'll notice that it uses a Mix material that includes a Cubic Environment map of the scene (featuring a faux blue sky) and a Falloff map to darken the edges. (I described using the latter map in Chapters 5 and 6.)

4. Close the Material Editor, drag the Time slider to frame 30, activate the Camera viewport, and render a test scene at (at least) 640×480 resolution. Your scene should look somewhat like Figure 16.9. (Note that the exact placement of the MetaParticles in frame 30 of your scene may vary from those in the figure.)

5. If you want, you can render your own test animation of this scene, or you can preview a finished animation instead. Select File|View File and select MERCURY1.AVI from the \CHAP_16 directory of this book's companion CD-ROM.

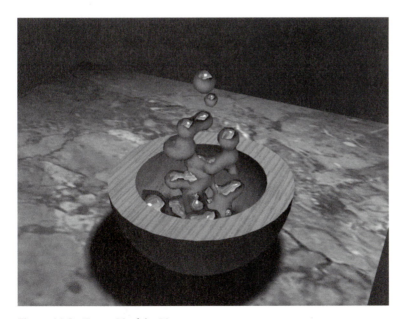

Figure 16.9 Frame 30 of the Mercury test scene.

You can now see the final effect—a scattering of mercury droplets fall into the scene, lands in the wooden bowl, swirls around, and merges together.

6. Although this effect is pretty nifty, the falling particles tend to strobe somewhat. You can fix this by selecting the Blizzard emitter, right-clicking to bring up the Properties menu, and selecting either Object or Image motion blur for the particles.

7. To see another preview of this scene with Image Motion Blur applied, select File|View File and preview the MERCURY2.AVI file from the \CHAP_16 directory of the companion CD-ROM. As you'll see, in this file, the droplets are "smeared," and the strobe effect is lessened.

Note that the scene you've just created is included in the \CHAP_16 directory as MERCURY2.MAX.

Things To Try

As you read at the beginning of this chapter, there are a couple of additional particle scenes included in the \CHAP_16 directory that you might want to play with:

- TWISTER.MAX consists of a couple of spinning helical splines with instanced particle geometry swirling around the splines to create a wispy, tornado-style effect.

- If you're feeling ambitious and have a lot of time, a very fast PC, or both, then take a look at the MARSBOOM.MAX file. This is an extremely complex scene that depicts an entire planet exploding. This scene also shows off a wide range of MAX's new particle systems, including streaming particles, Particle Array (to create actual planetary chunks), and volumetric particles to create a gaseous fireball effect. For best results, render test images or animations from the Video Post menu. You'll see a series of Lens Effects filters set up in the VP queue to enhance the final results.

Moving On

In this chapter, you learned the basics of MAX Release 2's new core particle systems. Now, it's time to move on from MAX's core code features and discuss MAX third-party support.

In the next chapter, you'll see how you can use Adobe Photoshop 4.0 to create striking texture maps for your MAX animations and how you can use its Actions feature to apply batch-image-processing to your MAX renderings. Then, in Chapter 18, you'll see some custom MAX plug-ins from Tom Hudson and Harry Denholm of Ishani Graphics.

PART IV

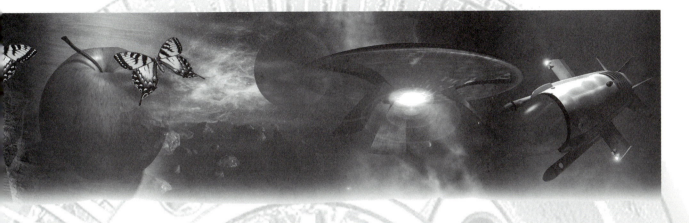

M A X
PLUG-INS AND
THIRD-PARTY
FUNCTIONALITY

FUN WITH PHOTOSHOP: TEXTURES AND FILTERS

17

In this chapter, you'll learn about different ways you can use Photoshop to augment your 3D Studio MAX work. First, you'll learn how to create original texture maps, or alter existing bitmaps, for use in MAX's Material Editor. Then you'll see how to use Photoshop's native and third-party filters combined with MAX's Video Post feature to create striking post-processing effects.

As I mentioned in Chapter 1, the majority of professional 3D artists also rely extensively on 2D painting, image manipulation, and image composition tools to augment their 3D work. It's a rare 3D artist who doesn't use a 2D paint package to create original textures or alter pre-existing ones.

The premier package for 2D painting and image manipulation is Adobe System's Photoshop. Since its introduction on the Apple Macintosh, Photoshop has become an industry standard for digital artists. Although it started out primarily as a pre-press and print production tool, Photoshop is now an indispensable tool for 2D and 3D graphics artists, game and multimedia developers, and 3D artists working on film and video productions. With its extensive feature set, its easy-to-use interface, and its expansion to Silicon Graphics and Intel-based platforms, it's regarded as the so-called "killer app"—a program that sells its attendant hardware platforms. (I've heard many people in the computer industry proclaim flatly that Photoshop is the greatest computer program ever written.)

Much of this can be traced to its original creator, John Knoll, a programmer and Industrial Light and Magic (ILM) visual effects supervisor. Photoshop actually began life as a program that John was developing at ILM to create digital matte paintings. He then used it to create environmental maps for the pseudopod (water tentacle) sequence in Jim Cameron's *The Abyss*. Since then, ILM effects artisans have used Photoshop to do frame-by-frame retouching (such as wire removal), digital environments, and countless other image manipulations.

Whether you're an ILM employee working on the next *Star Wars* trilogy or a CG hobbyist working at home, you'll find Photoshop invaluable for enhancing your 3D work. For obvious reasons, this chapter requires that you have a copy of Photoshop version 4.0 (or higher).

Textures #1: Tweaking Metals With Grime

Back in Chapters 5 and 6 , you saw various ways to use custom bitmaps to create complex layered metal materials. Here, you'll be presented with a quick series of techniques for creating a wide variety of bitmaps you can use as Shininess, Shininess Strength, Specular, and Diffuse maps.

The first example shows how to use a Bump map image to add dirt and grime to the panel lines of an industrial bitmap texture:

1. Load Photoshop (version 4.0 or higher). If it's not already active, select Window/Show Layers to bring up the floating

Layers|Channels|Paths window. This step is important—without these floating windows present, you won't be able to check the effects as easily.

Note: This chapter's tutorials require that you have a copy of Photoshop for the PC and that you're familiar with its basic features. You can use versions 2.5 to 3.0 for some of the Texture tutorials. However, for batch processing, you'll need Photoshop version 4.0 or higher.

2. Select File|Open and load MTLBMP.JPG and MTLGREN2.JPG from the \CHAP_17 directory of the companion CD-ROM.

The black "panel lines" in MTLBMP.JPG correspond to the panel lines present in the MTLGREN2.JPG Diffuse map. In Photoshop, I used Layers/Multiply at 50 percent to paste the first image on top of the MTLGREEN.JPG bitmap. The MTLBMP.JPG Bump map's dark lines were added to the Diffuse map to help enhance the illusion of recessed panel seams. These images are shown in Figures 17.1a and 17.1b.

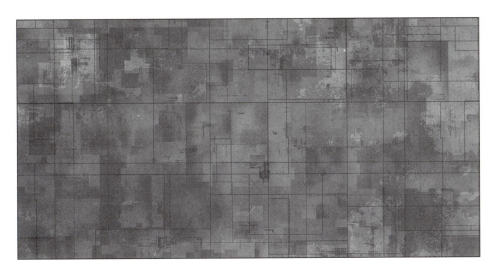

Figure 17.1a The MTLGREN2.JPG image.

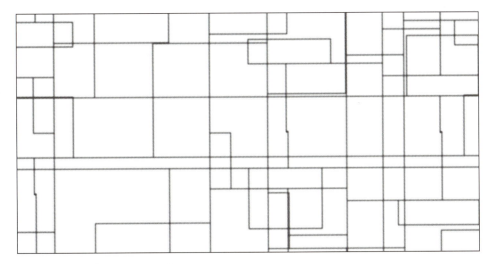

Figure 17.1b The MTLBMP.JPG image.

You can add to the MTLGREN2.JPG Diffuse map's textures by overlaying the MTLBMP.JPG again and manipulating it with various filters.

3. Click on the MTLGREN2.JPG image to make it active, select Layer|New|Layer, and click on OK to create Layer 1.

4. Make MTLBMP.JPG active, press Ctrl+A (Select All), then press Ctrl+C (Copy) to clip the image. Activate the MTLGREN2.JPG and press Ctrl+V (Paste) to paste the MTLBMP.JPG image into the new Layer 1. (Alternately, you can use Photoshop's Edit menu options to cut, copy, and paste the images.)

5. Look at the Layers window and you'll see that the white Layer 1 is selected and in Normal mode; at 100 percent, this image obscures the Background image. In the Layers window, change Normal to Multiply, Darken, or certain other modes. The dark panel lines are added to the Background but don't otherwise affect the image much. Certain other filters, such as Color Dodge, Color Burn, Difference, Lighten, and Soft Light, change the appearance of the underlying texture greatly.

6. When you're finished experimenting, change Layer 1 back to Normal.

Now that you've got MTLBMP.JPG in this layer, you can apply various filters to it and gauge the results on the underlying MTLGREN2.JPG bitmap.

7. Select Filter|Blur|Gaussian Blur, check Preview, and change Radius to 5. You'll see the black panel lines "fuzzed out" on the white background. Click on OK to accept these settings.

8. Go back to the Layers menu and change Layer 1 from Normal to Multiply (with Opacity at 100 percent). The result is that the fuzzy black lines turn into dark "smudging"

along each of the overlaid panel lines. The effect is subtle, but it makes it look as if the edges of the panel lines have accumulated dirt and grime.

9. If you want the effect to be more obvious, select Image|Adjust, choose Brightness/Contrast, and change Contrast to 50. The dark smudging around the panel lines appears more pronounced.

10. Drag the Contrast setting upward to about 75 or so (if you drag it much above 85, the effect gets overwhelming and, well, pretty ugly). You now have a new green industrial metal texture with panel lines rimmed with dark grime.

11. Save this image to your local \3DSMAX2\ MAPS directory (or \IMAGES, if you want) as a native Photoshop PSD file; call it METLTEST.PSD. The PSD file format preserves the individual layers that are present; you can change or delete them later as necessary. However, don't quit Photoshop or flatten the image in the Layers menu—you'll continue working with it in the next example.

Tweaking Metals With Panel Line Wear

Now that you've saved the METLTEST.PSD image to your local hard drive, you can continue making changes to the current image. For the next example, you'll use the bitmap in Layer 1 to add the illusion of scratches and lighter-colored, scuffed metal around the panel seams:

1. Make sure Layer 1 of the METLTEST.PSD image is active, then select Image|Adjust|Invert. You'll see that the Multiplied fuzzy black lines in Layer 1 have become lighter-colored lines against the underlying METLGRN2.JPG image. However, the current composition is too dark.

2. Change the Layer setting from Multiply to Soft Light. The image becomes slightly brighter, but it's still fairly dark.

3. Change the Layer setting to Color Dodge.

Now, you'll see much brighter highlighting around each panel line, and the overall image appears brighter. The highlighting around the dark panel lines also suggests that the green paint along the panels has become worn down to smoother, shinier metal.

4. You can make this effect appear more realistic by "scratching up" the inverted Bump map image with Noise. Go back to the Layers menu and change Color Dodge back to Normal. You're now looking at the inverted, blurred Bump map in Layer 1. Select Filter|Noise and choose Add Noise. Change Amount to 25, change Distribution from Uniform to Gaussian, and check Mono-chromatic. The result is a faint dusting of Noise pixels on the image. Click on OK to accept this filter.

5. Go back to the Layers menu and change the setting from Normal back to Color Dodge. You'll see that the Noise in the original Layer 1 image has made the paint along the panel lines appear more randomly flaked, giving a more "grainy" appearance.

6. If you want to punch up this effect further, select Image|Adjust, choose Brightness/Contrast again, and drag the Contrast higher for Layer 1—say, up to about 50. You'll see that the highlights in Layer 1 become very bright, almost "burned out."

7. Go back to the Layers menu and adjust Color Dodge Opacity back down to 65 to 75 percent. Now, the highlights are more subdued, with the brightest areas gathering in the intersections of the panel lines.

Tweaking Metals With Scratches

For the final metal texture example, you'll enhance the METLTEST.PSD image by creating another Layer, copying the existing Layer 1 to it, and then adding "scratches" to both, courtesy of Photoshop's Motion Blur filter:

1. In the Layers menu, change Color Dodge back to Normal and make Opacity 100 percent. Then, with Layer 1 active, press Ctrl+A, Ctrl+C to copy this bitmap.

2. Select Layer|New|Layer from the Photoshop menu bar and click on OK to create Layer 2. Then, press Ctrl+V to paste the copied Layer 1 into Layer 2.

> ### PHOTOSHOP .PSD FILES AND MAX
>
> Remember that 3D Studio MAX Release 2 enables you to use Photoshop PSD files as texture maps in the Material Editor.

3. With Layer 2 active, select Filter|Blur|Motion Blur. In the Motion Blur menu, check Preview, then change Angle to 45 degrees. Change Distance to 25 pixels. You'll see the whitish panel lines and noise speckles smeared diagonally up to the right.

4. In the Layer window, click on the Eye icon next to Layer 2 to toggle its visibility off. (If Layer 2 is still set to Normal and Opacity is at 100 percent, you won't see the effects you perform on the underlying layers.) Next, make Layer 1 active, select Filter|Blur|Motion Blur again, and this time, change Angle to -45 degrees. The image is smeared diagonally up to the left.

5. Click on the Layer 2 Eye icon again to toggle Visibility on, then click on Layer 2 to make it active. Change Normal to Lighten, check the Preserve Transparency checkbox, and set Opacity to 100. You'll now see the underlying Layer 1 image with a "cross-hatched" pattern where the two textures are overlaid.

6. In the Layers window, click the right arrow to bring up the Layer Options window. Click on Merge Down to blend Layers 1 and 2. (Alternatively, you can use the Layer drop-down menu, or press Ctrl+E to merge the two layers.)

7. Next, click on the Layer Type button for this new layer and change it from Normal to Color Dodge. You'll see the new layer create crosshatched scratches along the panel lines. If you zoom into the image (use Ctrl and the plus key) several times (blow it up to around 300 percent), you see the subtle "X" scratch marks, as shown in Figure 17.2.

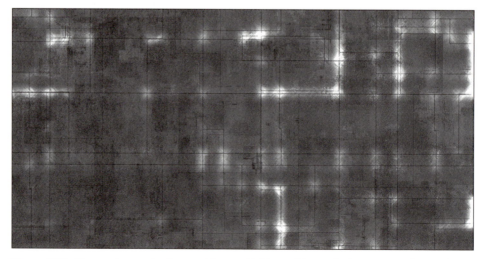

Figure 17.2 The two layers of noisy panel lines, with Motion Blur applied, create crosshatched metal scratches on the underlying texture.

I used these techniques to create the various metal textures in Chapter 5, including the "herringbone" Specular maps (MTLSPEC.JPG, and so on). As with the preceding example, I simply applied heavy monochromatic Gaussian Noise to two layers of a white background image. I then applied Motion blur to each layer (in different directions) and composited the layers together.

8. Again, at this point, you can save your current work to your local \3DSMAX2\MAPS directory. Note that the images you've just created are included in the \CHAP_17 directory of the companion CD-ROM as METLTEST.PSD and METLTES2.PSD.

Textures #2: Batch Image Processing And Filters

In Chapter 8, you saw how to create a science-fiction-style shockwave explosion effect. The effect featured an expanding, flattened toroid, mapped with a colorful, fiery bitmap sequence.

I created the bitmap sequence in Chapter 8 by applying various Photoshop 4.0 batch processes to a looping sequence of digitized fire from the Pyromania 2 CD-ROM from Visual Concept Engineering (VCE). In the following tutorials, you'll see how to duplicate these effects on some unsuspecting images. You can load a single frame into Photoshop, activate the Actions (record) feature, and practice applying combinations of filters on the test image. When you get a combination you like, you can stop recording the actions, save the ATN file to disk, and apply the action to a range of frames.

The companion CD-ROM does not contain the original Pyromania sequences. Instead, VCE has kindly given me permission to run a test frame from the Pyromania 2 "Bottom Fire" sequence and to include my altered versions of the entire sequences. You'll find them in the \PYROMANI directory on the companion CD-ROM. (Thanks go

VCE AND PYROMANIA

Visual Concepts Engineering (VCE) was founded in 1982 by Peter Kuran, a former Industrial Light and Magic (ILM) employee and an effects alumnus who worked on the original 1977 release of *Star Wars*. Since the company was founded, Kuran has specialized in optical effects for film and television and has concentrated on rotoscoping. (Rotoscoping generally means to draw certain effects, such as lightning bolts or laser beams, frame-by-frame on a live-action filmed sequence. It can also mean to trace over live-action footage, a technique used occasionally in cel-animated features.)

VCE has released three volumes in its Pyromania series; each CD features a wealth of digitized effects such as fire loops, explosions, smoke, fireworks, and the like. The effects are digitized from 35mm motion picture film and are suitable for many 3D effects scenes.

For more information, see Appendix C.

Note: *For this part of the tutorial, you must be running Photoshop 4.0 or higher.*

to Peter, Marilyn, and the gang at VCE for granting me permission to include these images here.)

One other thing to remember: The techniques you're about to explore can be applied to many different types of images, not just the ones included on the companion CD-ROM, the Pyromania CD-ROMs, or the ArtBeats CD-ROMs. Instead of using pre-rendered fire from a commercial CD, for example, you could set up a line of Combustion atmospheric apparatus in an orthographic MAX viewport and render your own CG "bottom fire" sequence.

Before getting started, modify the Pyromania test frame in Photoshop to create the "psychedelic fire" effect you saw in Chapter 8:

1. In Photoshop, select Window|Show Actions to bring up the Actions menu (if it's not already active).

2. Select File|Open, and load BFIR0000.TGA from the \PYROMANI directory of the companion CD-ROM. Your screen should look like Figure 17.3.

Figure 17.3   The first frame of the BFIR0000.TGA Pyromania 2 "Bottom Fire" sequence.

3. Click on the arrow icon in the Actions menu and select Clear Actions from the list. Click on OK to delete the actions and then click on the arrow icon again. Select New Actions from the menu, name it ColorWind, and click on Record. (The ATN file included in the \CHAP_17 directory of the companion CD-ROM is called COLRWIND.ATN.)

The first thing you'll do is eliminate the orange-red fire image and replace it with colorful "waves" of energy.

4. Select Filter|Stylize and then choose Glowing Edges. Change Edge Width to 1, Edge Brightness to 20, and Smoothness to 5 and then click on OK. You see the original flames re-

placed with "lines" of energy, like electrical arcs, as shown in Figure 17.4.

At this point, you could (but don't) go back to your Actions menu, click on Stop Recording, apply batch processing, and resave an entire directory of pre-rendered images. However, there are a few other nifty tricks you can try out here.

5. Select Image|Adjust, choose Hue/Saturation, and adjust the Saturation slider of this image up to 100. This will make the colors even brighter. Click on OK to accept these changes.

6. Next, select Image|Rotate Canvas and choose 90 degrees CCW. The bitmap rotates so the former "top" is at the nine-o'clock position. Select Filters|Stylize and then choose Wind. In the Wind menu, set Method to Wind, set

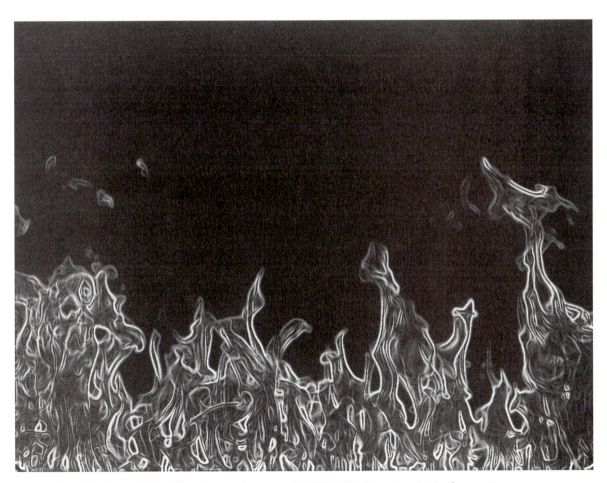

Figure 17.4 The Glowing Edges filter changes the orange BFIR0000.TGA flames into "coils of energy."

Direction to Right, and click on OK. You'll see the Wind filter create "streaks" on the electrical arcs, giving a more fiery appearance. (Note that the Wind filter operates only from the sides, hence, you'll turn the image sideways to streak the fire "upward.")

7. This effect is so nifty that you should do it again. Select Filter; Wind should be at the top of the drop-down menu (because it was your last choice). Select it again to apply a second layer of streaking to the image.

8. Next, select Image|Rotate Canvas and choose 90 degrees CW to rotate the image back to its original orientation. Your screen should look like Figure 17.5.

9. If you like these results, you can click on the arrow icon in the Actions menu, select Stop Recording, and save COLRWIND.ATN to your local hard drive.

However, don't do that yet—to create an even more interesting "streaky" effect, you can apply another two more layers of Wind—this time from the sides.

10. Select Wind from the Filter menu and apply another layer of Wind to the right-side-up image. The Wind filter creates horizontal streaks on the long, vertical Wind "spikes."

11. Select Image|Rotate Canvas, select 180 degrees, and apply the Wind filter again to this now-upside-down image. Rotate the canvas back another 180 degrees, back to its original

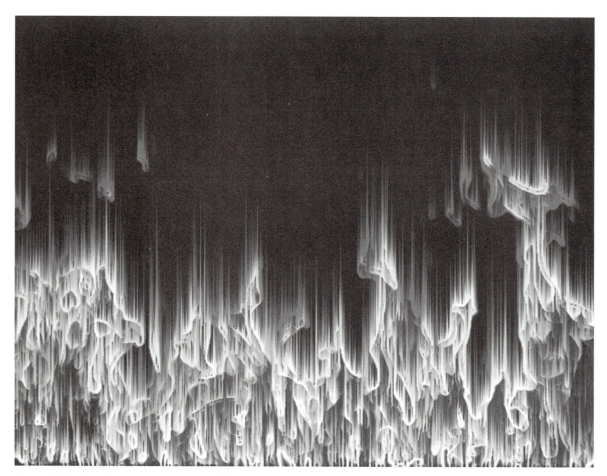

Figure 17.5 The BFIR0000.TGA image with the Glowing Edges filter and two levels of Wind applied.

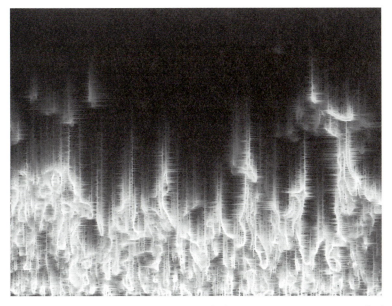

Figure 17.6 The BFIR0000.TGA image with the COLRWIN2.ATN action applied.

orientation. The resulting image looks somewhat like a shimmering Aurora Borealis, as shown in Figure 17.6.

In the \CHAP_17 directory of this book's companion CD-ROM, you'll find COLRWIND.ATN and COLRWIN2.ATN; they are Action files that are identical to the ones you've just created. (The first ATN file features every step up to the final two sideways Wind filters; the second includes these steps as well.) You'll find other ATN Action batch files, which you can load and use to experiment on other test images. There are also some original image sequences, which you'll work with right now.

Cooking Up A Batch

For the next trick, you'll run a Photoshop .ATN Action file to batch-process a looping, 50-frame sequence that I rendered in MAX.

1. Without closing Photoshop, open a Windows NT Explorer window (or Windows 95/98 Explorer, if you're running 3D Studio MAX Release 2 under these operating systems). Find and open the \CHAP_17 directory on the companion CD-ROM. You'll see various ATN files, such as:

   - Chrome.ATN

   - ColrBlur.ATN

   - ColrWind.ATN

   - ColrWin2.ATN

   - GlowEdge.ATN

These are various Photoshop Action files that you can use to process the following image sequences in the subdirectories included in \CHAP_17:

- \COLRWIND
- \GLOWEDGE
- \PARTICLE

2. Open the \PARTICLE subdirectory. You'll see a MAX file (PARTTEST.MAX), 50 JPG files (PRTCL000-PRTCL049.JPG), and PARTICLE.AVI. Double-click on this AVI to bring up your Media Player and play through the file. (Your Media Player should play this AVI file automatically. If it doesn't, consult your OS manuals and associate AVI and other movie files with your player. You can also open 3D Studio MAX and use File|View File to preview this animation.)

The PARTICLE.AVI animation is a looping, 50-frame animation sequence of amorphous colored blobs floating upward, produced with the PARTTEST.MAX file. (If you load this file and examine it, you'll see that it's simply a Blizzard particle system. A colorful Noise material and Radial gradients produce the soft balls of light.) The PRTCL.JPG files are the 320×240 images used to create this AVI. A still frame from this sequence is shown in Figure 17.7.

You'll now use Photoshop's Actions feature and one of the ATN files in the \CHAP_17 directory to process these JPG images. (As you did with

Figure 17.7   The PRTCL000.JPG image.

the RFIR0000.JPG image sequences you used to produce the shockwave effect in Chapter 8, you can then use these processed frames on your Shockwave toroid if you want.) The 320×240 resolution of the images will speed up their processing time.

3. Minimize your Windows NT Explorer window (don't close it) and return to Photoshop. Click on the arrow icon in the Actions window and save any Actions already loaded (if necessary). Then, click on Clear Actions and click on OK.

4. Select Load Actions and load the file COLRWIN2.ATN from the \CHAP_17 directory of the companion CD-ROM. You'll see that the file is composed of several layers of filters and attributes, similar to the effect you experimented with earlier. The action is:

   • Glowing Edges (filter)

   • Hue/Saturation (punch up the Saturation to 100 percent)

   • Rotate (90 degrees counterclockwise)

   • Wind

   • Wind

   • Rotate (back to original orientation)

   • Wind (applied from one side)

   • Rotate (180 degrees, or upside down)

   • Wind (applied from one side again, but now opposite the previous Wind step)

   • Rotate (back to original orientation)

5. Select Batch in the Actions window. Set Source to Folder, click on Choose, and select the \CHAP_17\PARTICLE directory. Click on Choose under Destination: Folder, select your \3DSMAX\IMAGES subdirectory, and click on OK. You'll see the PRTCL000-049.JPG images loading from the CD-ROM, being processed, and then being saved to your \IMAGES subdirectory. After a few minutes (depending on the speed of your computer

and your CD-ROM drive), you'll have processed all of the files. (Note that the processed files have the same names as the originals, which is why you chose a different destination folder. You can always rename the new files later, of course, to reflect the changes.)

6. At this point, you can go to your \IMAGES subdirectory and examine the individual files in Photoshop. The first altered image is shown in Figure 17.8.

7. You could also load 3D Studio MAX, go to Video Post, load the files as an Image Input Event, and resave them as an AVI animation. (If you select the first modified PRTCL000.JPG file, replace the numbers with an asterisk wild card (e.g., PART*.JPG) and press Enter; you'll create an IFL, or image file list, that will load the remaining files.)

8. However, as with the other examples throughout this book, I've saved you the trouble. Maximize your Windows NT Explorer again, open the \CHAP_17\COLRWIND directory, and double-click on COLRWIN2.AVI to play it.

You'll now see how the combinations of Glowing Edge and Wind filters produce a series of colorful streaks flickering upward, with sideways streaks producing a shimmering effect. You can try other combinations of Photoshop 4.0 filters, of course, on single images or image sequences.

9. To see another batch effect, go to the \CHAP_17\GLOWEDGE directory and preview GLOWEDGE.AVI. This animation uses the GLOWEDGE.ATN file on the original PART0000-49.JPG images; the resultant animation looks like glowing translucent globules dancing upward. (Electric tapioca, anyone?)

Finally, you can also try third-party Photoshop filters, such as Kai's Power Tools, or the Eye Candy filters from Alien Skin Software. (For more information on these filters, see Appendix C.)

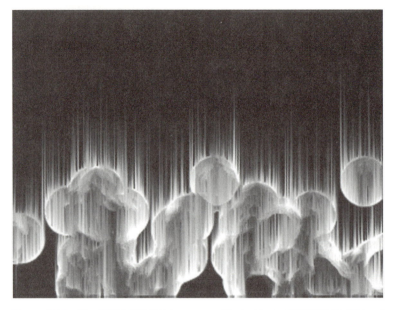

Figure 17.8 The PRTCL000.JPG image modified with the COLRWIND.ATN action.

Textures #3: Explosions With Radial Blur

For the next synthesis of Photoshop batch processing with MAX effects, you'll see how to use MAX's Video Post feature to combine two explosion elements. Video Post is a useful tool for doing quick composites of images, whether they've been rendered originally in MAX or deliberately mangled in Photoshop (as you've just seen). To begin, follow these steps:

1. Save your current work in Photoshop (if necessary) and either minimize or close the program.

2. Load 3D Studio MAX and select File|View File. Select ARTBEATS.AVI from the \ARTBEATS directory of the companion CD-ROM and view it.

This 54-frame animation is derived from an explosion element (used by permission) from the ReelExplosions I CD-ROM (published by ArtBeats Software Inc., of Myrtle Creek, Ohio). ArtBeats Software creates CD-ROMs of numerous textures for computer graphics professionals. The textures include wood, paper, marble, leather, and fabric. It also has animated textures of pyrotechnic effects such as fire and explosions, like the effect you've just seen. (Note that the full resolution bitmaps for this explosion are included in the \ARTBEATS directory of this book's companion CD-ROM.)

3. Next, select File|View File and click on and view ARTX0025.JPG and ZOOM0025.JPG from the \CHAP_17\EXPLODE directory (these images are shown in Figures 17.9 and 17.10).

Figure 17.9 The ARTX0025.JPG image.

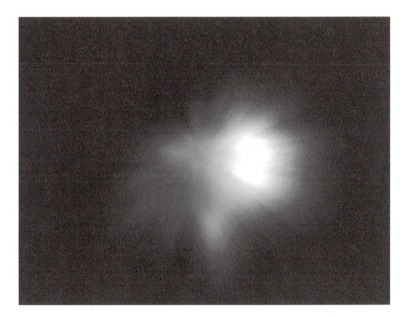

Figure 17.10 The ZOOM0025.JPG image.

The first image, ARTX0025.JPG, is straightforward enough—it shows
frame 25 of the original ArtBeats explosion sequence reduced in size to
320×240 resolution. However, the ZOOM0025.JPG image shows the
effects of batch Action filter processing in Photoshop 4.0. I applied a
Blur/Radial Blur/Zoom filter, with Amount set to 100, to the image and
then applied it again. This streaked and blurred the image outward from
the bitmap center. (The file used to create this effect, ZOOMBLUR.ATN, is
included in the \CHAP_17 directory of the companion CD-ROM.)

ARTBEATS SOFTWARE, INC.

You can contact ArtBeats Software, Inc. at PO Box 709, Myrtle Creek, OR 97457. Its phone number is (541) 863-4429, and its fax number is (541) 863-4547. You can reach domestic sales at (800) 444-9392 and international sales at (541) 863-4429. You can also check out its wares on the Web at www.artbeats.com.

Now, what happens when you combine these two effects—when you overlay the original explosion atop the "zoom-blurred" version? (A very cool effect, that's what.)

4. In MAX, select Rendering|Video Post and click on the Add Image Input Event icon. Click on Files, change to IFL Image File type, and go to the \CHAP_17\EXPLODE directory of the companion CD-ROM. Click on ZOOM0000.IFL to load it, then click on OK twice to return to Video Post. ZOOM0000.IFL loads the Radial-Blur-processed ArtBeats explosion bitmaps.

5. Click the Add Image Input Event icon again and load ARTX0000.IFL from the \CHAP_17\EXPLODE directory. This loads the original explosion bitmap sequence. You'll now see both files added to the Video Post Queue.

6. Hold down the Ctrl key and click on both ZOOM0000.IFL and the ARTX0000.IFL to select them. With both files selected (highlighted in blue), click on the Add Image Layer Event icon in Video Post. Click on the down arrow, select Simple Additive Compositor from the list, and click on OK. In the Video Post menu, you'll now see that the two Image Input Events are children of the Compositor.

7. Click outside the two selected items to deselect them, then click on the Add Image Output Event icon. Click on Files, change File Type to AVI, and save the file as COMPBOOM.AVI in your \3DSMAX\IMAGES directory. For best results, use the Cinepak Codec by Radius and set the compression quality to 100. (To change your Video Compressor settings, pick .AVI as your rendering format, then click on Setup in the Render Output File menu.) Click on OK twice to return to the main Video Post menu.

8. Click on the Execute Sequence icon. Check Range (frames 0 to 53), change Output to 320 by 240, and click on Render. You'll see the ZOOM0000-53.JPGs being loaded first and then the ARTX0000-53.JPG images composited atop the images. The sequence should compile in only a few minutes.

9. When the sequence is finished, select File|View File and click on and view the COMPBOOM.AVI sequence in your \IMAGES directory.

Neat, isn't it? The extreme Radial/Zoom blurring on the original image sequence creates a "volumetric light-streak" effect when combined with the untouched explosion element. The streaks of light help punch up the effect and enhance the effect of internal illumination. It also tends to make the explosion look as if it's happening underwater. (Of course, it could actually be occurring in the outer Magellenic Cloud, for all we know.)

You can use these compositing effects in many ways, of course. You don't have to use a real explosion element; a 3D particle explosion works nicely as well. (For an odd effect, try this using Blur/Radial Blur/Spin instead of Zoom.) By applying Gaussian blur to an image and then compositing the original back on top, you can create ethereal glowing effects, which are useful for opticals or (especially) for underwater scenes.

Moving On

Now that you've seen how to use Photoshop's features to enhance your MAX work, you'll take a look at some native 3D Studio MAX plug-ins.

In the next chapter, you'll take a quick look at Harry Denholm's cool MAX Release 1 Material Editor plug-ins, which he's ported to Release 2 for this book. In addition, you'll take a look at Tom Hudson's Greeble plug-in—a plug-in developed exclusively for this book. With it, you can create parametric mechanical details for everything from factory walls to spaceship surfaces.

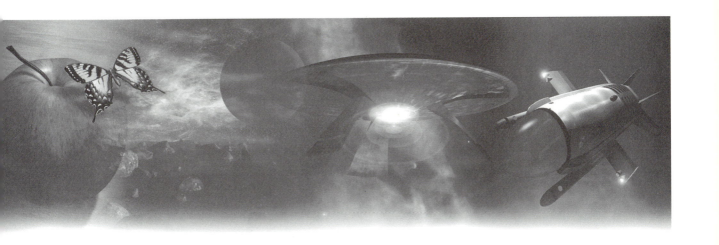

FREE INSIDE!
EXCLUSIVE F/X PLUG-INS
FROM HARRY DENHOLM
AND TOM HUDSON

18

BY JON BELL,
WITH HARRY DENHOLM
AND TOM HUDSON

One of the most exciting aspects of 3D Studio MAX's first year was seeing the enormous number of plug-ins released. MAX's open architecture and the inclusion of the software development kit helped fledgling hackers as well as professional software developers to enhance the core code. In addition, approximately one-third of the source code was available in the SDK, which helped developers build their plug-ins more quickly and easily.

Here is the power of the free market in software development—if a MAX user needed it, a programmer would write it and, in many cases, simply give it away. As of late October 1997 (the shipping date of MAX Release 2), there were more than 400 plug-ins available; half of them are freeware or shareware and are on the developers' Web pages or at other MAX-specific Internet sites.

Another source for these plug-ins is the book that you're now reading. In the \PLUGINS directory on the companion CD-ROM are 20 free 3D Studio MAX Release 2 plug-ins developed by Tom Hudson and Harry Denholm. Tom Hudson is one of the co-developers of 3D Studio/DOS (all versions) and MAX (both Releases 1 and 2). He has created Greeble 1.0, a very cool object modifier that's perfect for adding complex detail to your surfaces.

The other plug-ins on this book's companion CD-ROM come from Harry Denholm and Ishani Graphics. Harry is a Technical Support Technician in Kinetix's Great Britain office, London, England, and is the head of Ishani Graphics. In 1996 and 1997, Harry released almost two dozen free plug-ins—both cool materials and object modifiers. Although his MAX R1 plug-ins were available at Lumens' MAX3D site (www.max3d.com), Harry has generously offered to allow distribution of his recompiled Ishani plug-ins for MAX Release 2 on this book's CD-ROM.

In this chapter, you'll get a quick look at each plug-in. Please note that these plug-ins are provided on an as-is basis, with only the basic documentation included in this chapter. The best way to learn how to use them (especially the materials such as Electolize and Frenetic) is by experimentation. Just load 'em up and go crazy with them!

Installing The Plug-ins

There are 20 free plug-ins in the \PLUGINS directory of the companion CD-ROM:

- Ambient
- Bulge
- Crunch
- Decay
- Electrolize
- Frenetic

- GhostMatte

- Gradynt

- Greeble

- Lossy

- Melt

- Mix

- Outline

- Pinch

- Rock

- Softspot

- Spin

- Stacker

- Stratus

- Wiremapper

Bulge, Decay, Greeble, Melt, Pinch, and Spin are object modifiers; Electrolize, Frenetic, GhostMatte, Gradynt, Mix, Stacker, Softspot, Stratus, and Wiremapper are materials and/or map types. Rock is an Ishani Primitive and re-creates procedural rocks, or boulders. Ambient, Crunch, Lossy, and Outline are Video Post filters.

The installation process for the plug-ins is quick and easy. Here's how:

1. Make sure you don't have a MAX Release 2 session currently active. If you do, the plug-ins won't appear in the program until you quit or until you load a second session.

2. Place the companion CD-ROM in your CD-ROM drive, then open Windows Explorer.

3. Copy GREEBLE.DLM and ISHANI.ZIP from the CD-ROM's \PLUGINS directory to your \3DSMAX2\PLUGINS directory.

4. In your \3DSMAX2\PLUGINS directory, unzip ISHANI.ZIP. (If you're using the DOS command-line version of PKUNZIP, use the -D parameter to create the proper subdirectories.) If you unzip ISHANI.ZIP properly, it will create several subdirectories within your \PLUGINS directory. These directories contain the DL* files for the plug-ins themselves, as well as miscellaneous scene files, additional documentation, registration for enhanced versions of the Mix plug-in, and sample images.

> **Note:** Some of the plug-ins, such as Bulge, require that you have MSVCRT.DLL installed in your Windows \SYSTEM or \SYSTEM32 directory. If you don't have this file, you can download it from the Ishani Web site, the Kinetix forum on CompuServe, or the Microsoft VC support area at www.microsoft.com. If this DLL is not present, some of the Ishani plug-ins will load but not appear. In addition, you will need an unzipping utility, such as WinZIP from Nico Mak Computing or PK-Zip from PK-Ware. If you don't already have a copy of either program, you can download shareware or evaluation versions from the Internet, America Online, or CompuServe. Use your browser's search features (or an Internet search engine, such as www.yahoo.com), and search for "ZIP."

5. Start MAX Release 2. Select File|Configure Paths|Plug Ins, then use the Add feature and the Choose Directory for New Entry browser menu to add each of the Ishani subdirectories to your plug-ins path.

6. Next, quit MAX and restart it. You'll see the new plug-ins appear in either the Material/ Map Browser or the Modify panel (when you click on the More button). You're now ready to use the plug-ins.

First, you'll take a look at Tom Hudson's Greeble; you can then run through Harry Denholm's Ishani plug-ins, which are listed after Greeble in alphabetical order.

What's A Greeble?

In the classic science-fiction films of the 1950s, most spacecraft were depicted as smooth-skinned objects. If they were earthly vessels, they were streamlined, cigar-shaped rockets with swept-back fins, designed for launching from an atmosphere. If they were alien ships, they were usually sleek flying saucers or variants, such as the manta-ray ships of George Pal's 1953 film *The War of the Worlds*.

However, as everyone knows, there's no air in space; a ship designed for deep space travel doesn't need streamlining, so it can be of almost any external configuration necessary. Consequently, a spaceship doesn't need a smooth skin; it can have access panels, antennas, piping, and other gross mechanical details scattered across its surface.

An outgrowth of this design aesthetic started taking hold in the 1960s. TV programs such as Gerry Anderson's *Thunderbirds* and (most especially) films like *2001: A Space Odyssey* presented futuristic vehicles with complex surface details. To depict the vehicles' complicated exteriors, the modelmakers on these productions turned to *kit-bashing*—taking pieces from various commercial model kits and applying them to the surfaces of their original designs. Kit pieces from World War II tank models, railroad cars, battleships, and so on, provided the illusion of intricate hatches, vents, and the like. Subsequent science-fiction films and TV shows, such as the *Alien*, *Star Wars*, and *Star Trek* productions, have continued this approach.

This process must be done artistically, however, with the parts' original intent camouflaged. When done correctly, the application of tiny details helps sell the apparent scale of these vehicles as enormous spacecraft rather than models a few feet long, as shown in Figure 18.1. Done incorrectly, the model simply looks like a brick covered in glue and rolled in model parts—as shown in Figure 18.2.

Since the advent of kit-bashing, effects artists have given a name to these model kit detail parts. British modelmakers such as Martin Bower and Bill Pearson refer to them as "wiggets"; in the United States, such parts are known as "nernies," "greeblies," or "greebles." After consulting our friend Bill George, an effects art director at Industrial Light and Magic, 3D Studio MAX developer Tom Hudson and I settled on the term "greeble" for this book's first plug-in.

Tom's Hudson's Greeble modifier plug-in creates procedural surface details on your MAX mesh objects and/or selected faces. With it, you can dress up an area of your model with random details or even create an entire landscape, such as the surface of the *Star Wars Deathstar* or the industrial wasteland at the beginning of *Bladerunner*.

The Greeble Modifier

If you've already installed the Greeble plug-in, you're ready to play:

1. In 3D Studio MAX, select File|Open and load GREEBLE1.MAX from the \CHAP_18 directory of the companion CD-ROM. Your screen should look like Figure 18.3.

Figure 18.1 An example of model part greebles and styrene sheet plastic details applied to a modeling tile.

Figure 18.2 One of the spacecraft from the campy 1980 Italian film, *Starcrash*. In this case, the model is simply a collection of basic plastic shapes—but instead of applying separate model parts, the effects artists actually *glued* entire model kit "trees" to the surface, then spray-painted the model flat white. Confronted with this effects abomination, one doesn't know whether to laugh or cry.

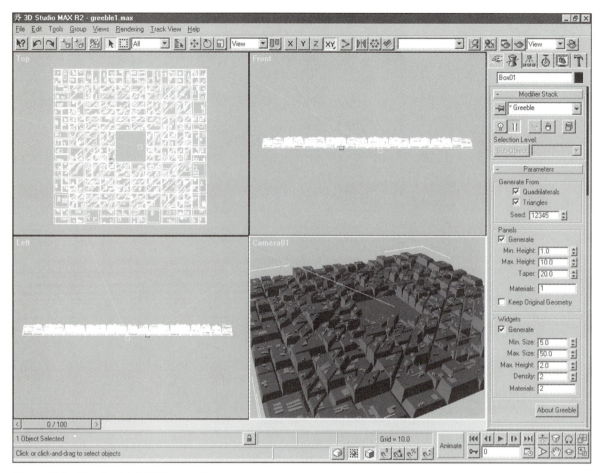

Figure 18.3 The Greeble1.MAX scene file.

GREEBLE1.MAX shows how the Greeble plug-in creates panels from the source object. This is the top of a box object with some of the grids made into explicit triangles. The center has had several edges turned off so it's not a simple quad or triangle; Greeble ignores those faces. The triangular faces are outside this area and are modified. The outer perimeter are the original quads and are also modified.

2. Activate the Camera01 viewport and render the scene. Your rendering should look like Figure 18.4.

To produce this texture effect, I created custom materials that key off the Material ID numbers of the Greeble panels and widgets, or plate details.

3. Open the Material Editor and take a look at the Greeble Green 3 material. This is a Multi/Sub-object material that combines three sets of Blend materials, each using small custom bitmaps. Note that the second material in each Blend type is a face-mapped material, and the mask for each material is also a custom grayscale bitmap (GREEBLE5.JPG). These Blend materials tend to outline and highlight the edges of the Greeble details and make them stand out.

4. Next, load GREEBLE2.MAX from the \CHAP_18 directory. Your screen should look like Figure 18.5.

5. GREEBLE2.MAX shows Greeble applied to various primitives. If you want, render the scene; I've applied the Greeble Green 3 material to these objects as well, as shown in Figure 18.6.

Figure 18.4   The Greeble Blend 3 material applied to the object.

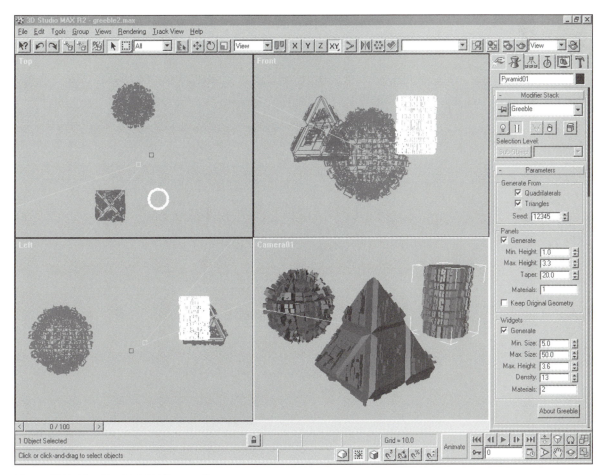

Figure 18.5   The Greeble2.MAX scene file.

Figure 18.6 The Greeble Green 3 material applied to the primitives.

Greeble Controls

The following sections explain the controls for the Greeble plug-in.

Parameters

There are three controls under the Parameters section:

- *Generate From Quads/Triangles*—If these are checked and the source object has quadrilaterals, triangles or both defined, then they're modified.

- *Generate From Triangles*—If checked and the source object has triangular faces defined, they are modified.

- *Seed*—Specifies the initial random number gen-erator value. Change to get different details.

In GREEBLE2.MAX, select the sphere and uncheck Triangles. You'll see the poles return to normal. Turn off Quadrilaterals and the rest of the sphere will no longer be affected.

Panels

- *Generate*—If checked, generates extruded panels from the source geometry. If unchecked, no panels will be extruded.

- *Min. Height and Max. Height (animatable)*—Specifies the height range of the panels in units.

- *Taper (animatable)*—Controls the amount of beveling on the panels, shown as a percent value. Tapering 100 percent will make little pyramids. A taper of 0 will make simple extruded blocks.

- *Materials*—A list of comma-separated numbers indicating which sub-object material IDs to use for panel generation. The values entered are used at random when generating the panels, and at least one number should be entered.

  For example, if the field contains only one number (for example 1), only sub-object material ID 1 will be used for the panels. If the field contains two numbers (1,2), then the Greeble plug-in will generate panels randomly that use sub-object material numbers 1 and 2, in approximately equal numbers. By using the same number more than once in the material list, you can make a certain sub-object material appear more often. For example, entering "1,1,1,2" will create panels that are Material 1 approximately 75 percent of the time and Material 2 approximately 25 percent of the time.

- *Keep Original Geometry*—If checked, the faces that the panels were generated from will remain. (Although this is wasteful, it may come in handy if you collapse the stack, and need to extract the original geometry as an element.) Normally this is unchecked, which means the original triangular or quadrilateral geometry is removed when the panels are generated.

Widgets

These are the detail bits (you might call them "sub-greebles") that are created on top of the panels. If panels are turned off, the widgets are generated on the original geometry. The controls under Widgets are:

- *Generate*—If checked, generates widgets.
- *Min. Size and Max. Size*—Specifies the size of the widgets, shown as a percentage of the panel size.
- *Max. Height*—Specifies the maximum height of the widgets in world units. The widget generator bases the widget height on its size. The longer or wider a widget is, the shorter it is and vice versa.

- *Density*—Specifies the number of widgets to generate on each panel or source face.
- *Materials*—The same as the Materials control under Panels.

Texture Mapping

The Greeble plug-in creates mapping coordinates for all generated elements automatically. If the sub-object materials assigned to the various generated panels or widgets use mapping, the proper mapping coordinates will appear on the modified object.

The Ambient Filter

The Ambient filter is an ambient shading and tinting tool that works in MAX's Video Post menu; its UI is shown in Figure 18.7.

Ambient Controls

The following sections explain the controls for the Ambient filter.

Operation

The three options under Operation control how the shading is done at render time:

- *Averaged Scene Colors*—Takes the average coloration of the scene and enhances it; for example, if there is a large green object near the camera, the image will be tinted a shade of green that is comparable to how much of the frame the object occupies.

- *Highest RGB Value*—Scans the image for the cumulatively brightest point and tints to this color.

- *Tint To Single Color*—Tints the scene image to the color shown in the user-defined swatch to the right.

Tint Settings

These controls set how the tint will be applied to the image:

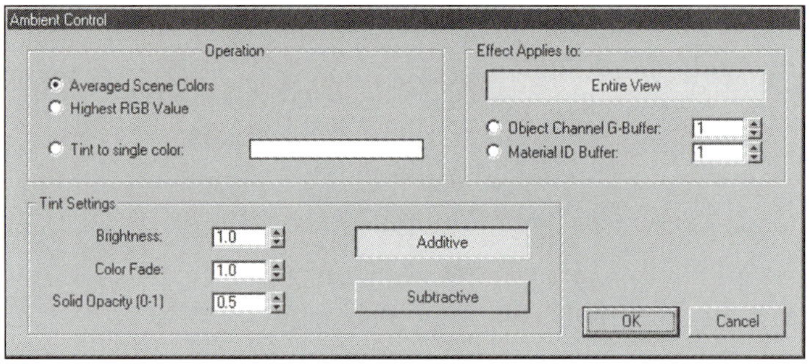

Figure 18.7 The Ambient filter in Video Post.

- *Brightness*—Specifies how bright the tint will be. This control is a color multiplier: 0.0 (no tint) to 10.0 (very bright).

- *Color Fade*—Controls how much to fade the original scene colors before tinting.

- *Solid Opacity*—Controls how brightly the original scene colors will show through the tint.

- *Additive/Subtractive*—Specifies whether the tint will add or subtract the scene colors.

Effect Applies To

The controls in this section specify on which part of the image the tint is to be applied:

- *Entire View*—Applies the tint to the entire scene (default).

- *Object Buffer*

- *Material Buffer*

The Bulge Modifier

Bulge is a Spherify modifier, but it has many functions and controls to create some unique effects—both still and animated. It works on any deformable mesh object and has Gizmo/Apparatus controls, such as Gizmo and Center.

To use Bulge, follow these steps:

1. Select an Editable Mesh object in MAX.

2. Open the Modify Tab panel in MAX, click on More, and choose Bulge, or open the Configure Sets panel and scroll down to Ishani Modifier Tools. When the Bulge modifier is applied to the mesh, you can adjust the parameters and check out the results. An example of Bulge is shown in Figure 18.8.

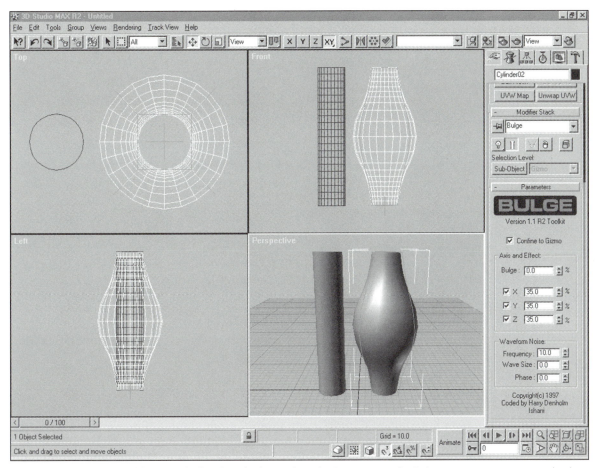

Figure 18.8   A Bulge modifier is applied to the cylinder on the right. By animating the Bulge parameters, you can make the object appear to "breathe."

Bulge Controls

If the Confine To Gizmo option is checked, the effect will only apply to the surfaces inside the Gizmo box. If unchecked, the effect will apply to the entire object.

In addition to the Confine To Gizmo option, there are two main control panels: Axis and Effect and WaveForm Noise, as explained in the following sections.

Axis And Effect

The Axis And Effect Controls define the basic parameters for the bulge algorithm:

* *Bulge*—Controls the size of the bulge to be applied. The values range from -400 to 400 percent. Negative values will implode objects; positive values will explode them.

* *X, Y, and Z*—Separate controls for each axis, which let the user create nonlinear spherification. Each axis has a selector and bulge value. The main bulge operator still works as a universal value.

Waveform Noise

Bulge can apply sine wave noise to the effect by setting these values. Turn Wave Size to 0 to turn off the waveforms—the default is Off:

* *Frequency (1 to 30)*—Specifies the wavelength of the waveform or how compact it will be.

- *Wave Size (0 to 15)*—Controls the intensity of the waves to be applied.

- *Phase*—Sets the phase of the waveform, used for animating the effect.

The Crunch Filter

The Crunch filter is an image color compressor tool that works in MAX's Video Post. Its UI is shown in Figure 18.9.

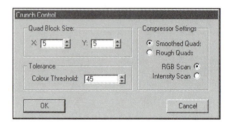

Figure 18.9   The Crunch filter in Video Post.

Crunch Controls

The following sections explain the controls for the Crunch filter.

Quad Block Size And Tolerance

The controls in these two sections specify how the compression is calculated:

- *X and Y*—Defines the size of block that will be used to pick the areas to compress.

- *Color Threshold*—Defines how much a color can "deviate" inside a scanned block. The higher the value, the more "blocky" the compression will become. Setting it to 65535 (the maximum) will give you a full pixelation effect of the size of the X and Y values.

Compressor Settings

These controls set how the operation is calculated:

- *Smoothed Quad and Rough Quad*—Sets the type of compression (either smoothed or rough). Smooth-ed is recommended, although rough is included if you need to simulate bad reception/ signal loss.

- *RGB Scan and Intensity Scan*—RGB Scan takes each component of a quad into consideration, whereas Intensity Scan uses a summed color component method, which may be faster in some cases but gives slightly rougher results.

The Decay Modifier

Decay randomly pushes or pulls sections of a mesh to make it more chaotic or detailed. For example, it creates a roughened rock out of a sphere or dents the surface of a metal object. An example of a "decayed" object is shown in Figure 18.10.

Decay Controls

The following sections explain the controls for the Decay modifier.

Effect

These four controls customize the "look" of the decay:

- *Deform Amount and Surround Amount*—Control by how much the vertices of the host will be decayed. Primary is the control vertex, and Secondary defines how much the vertices around the control vertex will be deformed.

- *Percentage*—Defines the amount of the object to decay. The higher the percentage, the more of the object is decayed.

- *Seed*—Controls the state of the randomization.

Edge Tension

With these two controls, you can limit the decay effect to the protruding edges of an object, such as to roughen just the edges:

- *Angle*—Defines the maximum angle that can occur between faces (in radians) before the decay occurs. For best results, experiment with this value, as the most effective setting can vary from mesh to mesh.

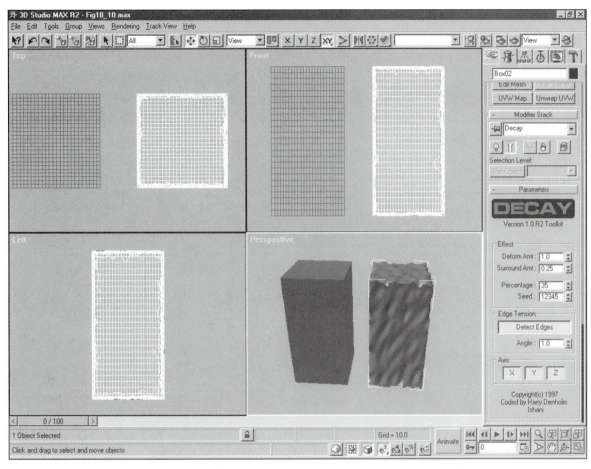

Figure 18.10   Two boxes; the one on the right has Decay applied, with a percentage setting of 35.

Axis

The Axis control defines which of the axis planes will be decayed. For instance, it would be possible for only the Z vertices to be decayed.

The Electrolize Material And Map

Electrolize 2 creates advanced material-based and map-based wipe effects with separately defined "edges" to provide more interesting variations. The effect features edge noise and interference, density controls, and a fully configurable Waveform tool that you can use to apply waves and ripples along the final effect.

Electrolize has a selection of different shapes for the edge, including ShockWave, Radial Sweep, and Encase. It also has opacity controls for the edge and body to create glazes and washes on your materials. Finally, you can use Electrolize to define maps such as Diffuse, Opacity, and Bump maps. Each one of its definable color blocks may also have sub-textures defined. To use the Electrolize map, follow these steps:

1. Open the Material Editor, select an open material slot, and open the Maps rollout.

2. Open a Maps channel, such as Diffuse, and from the Material/Map Browser, select Electrolize. The main control panel appears; its features are outlined in the following sections.

Electrolize Controls

There are control panels for Texture Definitions, Texture Opacity Settings, Edge Settings, Electrolize types and shapes, and WaveForms. As with almost any other feature in MAX, you can animate any of the controls simply by turning on the Animate button and making a change in the Electrolize values on a non-zero frame. (You can even animate the checkbox controls on or off, although this isn't recommended and may cause errors in the final rendering.)

Texture Definitions And Texture Opacity Settings

The Texture Definitions panel contains three defining options for the three parts of the Electrolize effect (this part of the UI is shown in Figure 18.11):

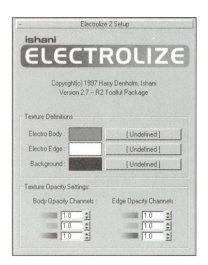

Figure 18.11 The Texture Definitions section of the Electrolize map rollout.

- *Electro Body*—Specifies the main part of the wipe; that is, what will be shown as the phase is increased. The default color is a dusty lilac; the default texture is null.

- *Electro Edge*—Specifies the meeting point between body and background. The default color is white; the default texture is null.

- *Background*—Specifies the texture behind the body and edge. If Sweep Phase is set to 0, the material will be rendered as the background color (Sweep Phase is described in the next section). The default color is black; the default texture is null.

Note that each selection has a user-defined color swatch and texture selector.

The Texture Opacity Settings options control the transparency of the RGB values in your material. There are two sets of controls, one for Body and one for Edge. Each set has three separate RGB values:

- If value is 0, the channel will be totally transparent.

- If value is 1.0, the channel will be normal.

- If value is greater than 1.0, the channel will be brightened.

Edge Settings And Electrolize Type And Shapes:

The Edge Settings section sets up both the style of the edge being generated and its position at the current time (see Figure 18.12):

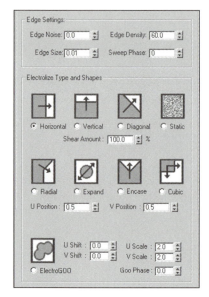

Figure 18.12 The Edge Type section of the Electrolize map panel.

- *Edge Noise (0 to 30.0)*—Applies noise to the edge texture, making it seem rough or sparkly.

- *Edge Size (0 to 1)*—Specifies the relative size of the edge; the greater the size, the more pixels will be applied.

- *Edge Density (0 to 100)*—Specifies how "compact" the edge noise is. A greater value will pack the noise more tightly.

- *Sweep Phase (-1000 to 1000)*—Specifies the phase of the effect, or how complete the wipe is. Usual range is 0 to 150.

Extended range is provided for the use of WaveForm tools and clean effects. Animating this control will create the animation required for wipes. An increase will cause a left-to-right wipe.

Electrolize has different edge forms you can use with your material. (Note that the typical Sweep values are shown here without WaveForms turned on, which can change the values dramatically.) This section of the Electrolize rollout is also shown in Figure 18.12. The settings are as follows:

- *Linear Horizontal (sweep: 0 to 155)*—Sets the basic left-to-right sweep.

- *Linear Vertical (sweep: 0 to 155)*—Sets the basic bottom-to-top sweep.

- *Shear Amount*—Creates slants for the two previous controls. Set to 100.0 to turn it off.

- *Linear Diagonal (sweep: 20 to 215)*—Sets the basic bottom-left-to-top-right sweep.

- *Radial Sweep (sweep: -475 to 475)*—Sets a "clock-hand" sweep, around from the center.

- *Expand (sweep: 0 to 115)*—Sets a sweep that emanates outward from the center.

- *Encase (sweep: 0 to 340)*—Sets a sweep that doubles in from the top to the bottom.

The U and V Position settings adjust where the three controls above start:

- *Random Static (sweep: 0 to 152)*—Creates a random static pattern.

- *ElectroGOO (sweep: -100 to 100)*—Creates an organic "blobby" pattern.

WaveForms

The WaveForms panel is shown in Figure 18.13.
The settings for this panel are:

> **Note:** The sweep control has no actual value; that is, it does not yet correspond to any real space value. This is mainly because the Electrolize shapes and effects can range and differ greatly, especially if using waveforms, so a large range is needed. Typical ranges are described in the next section.

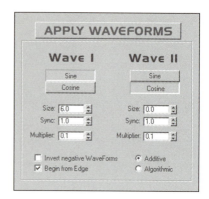

Figure 18.13 The WaveForms panel of the Electrolize map rollout.

- *Apply WaveForms*—Turns the WaveForms effect algorithm on or off.

- *Invert Negative WaveForms*—Reverses any WaveForms that are less than 0 in length. In essence, if this option is on, all waves are drawn forward from the edge.

- *Begin From Edge*—Applies the WaveForm to the edge of the material instead of to the whole material.

There are two WaveForms that are used, and the two sets of three controls under the Sine and Cosine setup options are used to configure them. SIN and COS can be configured separately. At default, only the SIN wave is "turned on"; setting a Size value of 0 will turn the wave off completely. The controls are as follows:

- *Size (0 to 40)*—Sets the wavelength of the WaveForm, or how compact it will be.

- *Sync (0 to 500)*—Specifies the phase of the wave. Use this to animate WaveForms.

- *Multiplier (-1 to 10)*—Specifies how large the crest will be. If the waveform is becoming too pronounced, alter this control to scale it down.

The following two controls are used for wave creation:

- *Additive*—Adds the results of the two waves to create the edge.

- *Algorithmic*—Interpolates the two results for a different effect.

The Frenetic Map

The Frenetic map type is a shader that generates "plasma" noise effects. The effects are customizable, allowing for material texture blends with full animation capabilities. With Frenetic, you can create fire, water, or explosion-type textures.

Frenetic Controls

Below are the settings that enable you to customize the look of the Frenetic material.

Texture Settings

The Texture Settings options define the colors or texture blends. (The textures will be blended and distorted instead of being a flat map.) This section of the rollout is shown in Figure 18.14.

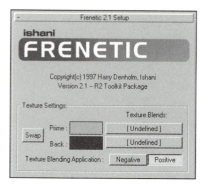

Figure 18.14 The Texture Settings section of the Frenetic map rollout.

Plasma Overlay

The following controls are in the Plasma Overlay section of the rollout (shown in Figure 18.15):

- *Horizontal/Vertical Plasma*—Set the scales of plasma in each axis. You can stretch or pack the plasma effect to any value from 0 to 30.

- *Use Plasma Overlay*—Either displays the standard gradient or displaces it with plasma.

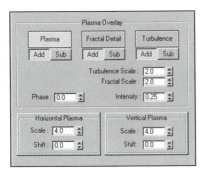

Figure 18.15 The Plasma Overlay section of the Frenetic map rollout.

- *Phase*—Sets the animation frame of the plasma. Animate this to make it flow and glob around.

- *Intensity*—Sets the brightness and contrast of the overlay. You can make more dramatic overlays by increasing these values.

- *Shift X and Y*—Controls the position of the overlay.

Gradient Settings

The controls in this section let you set the parameters for each axis, Horizontal/U and Vertical/V. The Radial and Linear buttons select the type of gradient to use. Figure 18.16 shows the Gradient Settings section of the rollout. The following controls are also in this section:

- *Radial Offset*—Offsets control the center point for the gradients.

- *Effect Falloff*—Makes the gradient less intense. You can make a fade-on effect with this.

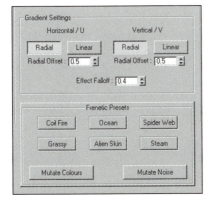

Figure 18.16 The Gradient Settings section of the Frenetic map rollout.

ELECTROLIZE EXAMPLES AND TIPS

Try animating the two waveforms so they pass through each other at different speeds. This will give a good ripple effect that does not look too linear; for example:

Frame 0:	*SIN Sync: 15*	*COS Sync: 1.0*
Frame 100:	*SIN Sync: 3*	*COS Sync: 6*

Make sure that wave creation is set to Additive for the effect to work.

To create a good plasma effect, use waves with the Expand shape and animate both the waves and phase with a wave multiplier of about 0.2.

To create a glowed edge, assign a non-complex color material, such as RGB Tint, to the Electro Edge texture box and assign it a material ID. You can now use the Lens Effects Glow filter in Video Post to pick out the material ID and just glow the edge of your material.

Try putting multiple layers of Electrolize together, such as assigning it to the Electro Body texture box. You can have infinite levels of textures assigned.

The Gradynt Map

Gradynt is an extended gradient map for MAX that allows advanced gradient creation and application. Its UI is shown in Figure 18.17.

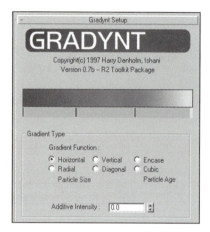

Figure 18.17   The Gradynt map type.

The Gradient Editor

The following sections explain the options under the menus in the Gradient editor.

Keys

Left-click on a key to move it around the keyspace. Left-click just in the keyspace to generate a new key the color of the interpolated value of its two neighbors. Right-click on a key to bring up the Key menu, which has the following options:

- *Edit Settings*—Opens the color assignment dialog.

- *Copy/Paste*—Copies and pastes key color values.

- *Delete Key #x*—Removes the clicked key.

Gradient

Right-click on the gradient display to bring up the gradient menu, which has the following options:

- *Load/Save Gradient*—Loads and saves out all keys and colors to an IG file. (A variety of presets are available when you unzip the ISHANI.ZIP file.)

- *Reset*—Puts the gradient back to the default.

Gradient Functions

Each one of the buttons will apply the gradient in various ways—linearly, radially, or based on particle size or age. The other control (Intensity) will brighten or darken the gradient overall.

The Lossy Filter

The Lossy filter is a simple line-removal compressor that works in MAX's Video Post. Its UI is shown in Figure 18.18.

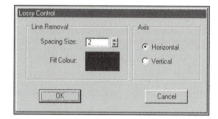

Figure 18.18   The Lossy Video Post filter.

Lossy Controls

The controls for the Lossy filter are as follows:

- *Line Removal*—Configures the type of removal.

- *Spacing Size*—Specifies how far apart the lines are applied.

- *Fill Color*—Specifies the color of the lines.

- *Axis*—Specifies which angle to apply removal:

- *Horizontal/Vertical*—Selects the axis for the lines.

The Melt Modifier

Melt is an object modifier that simulates gradual decay to any geometric mesh. You can specify a viscosity setting that will edit the melt curve. Figure 18.19 shows Melt modifiers applied to a succession of cylinders.

Melt Controls

The controls for the Melt modifier are divided into several sections:

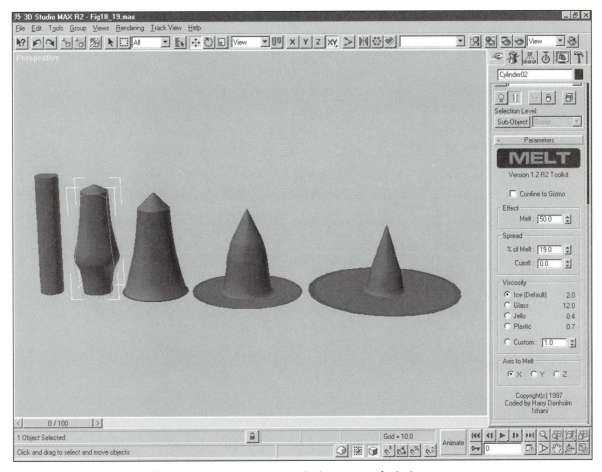

Figure 18.19   The Melt modifier (with increasing settings) applied to a series of cylinders.

- *Effect*—The Effect section contains only one control, Melt, which sets how much, in a percentage of its original form, the object melts.

- *Spread*—As the object melts, it will gradually spread out to a larger surface. The percentage Of Melt control defines how much of the original Melt will be spread out. The CutOff control lets you define a point along the chosen axis where the melt will stop; for example, it would be possible to just melt the top half of a sphere by increasing this value.

- *Viscosity*—These options let you modify the melt curve, ranging from Ice (the default), which is rigid melting, to Jello, which creates a very shallow curve that collapses in on itself.

- *Axis To Melt*—These three controls set the axis along which the melt will occur.

The Mix Modifier

Mix provides a simple but extremely powerful way to blend meshes based on weighted values. It's essentially a "weighted morphing" controller, similar to MAX Release 2's Barycentric morph controller. You can use Mix for facial animation of characters, for example, by setting keyframes of morphs between different face expressions. (For additional information on the Mix Modifier—and to register for later versions—go to www.max3d.com/~ishani.)

Note: *Mix works best on variations of the same object. Although it's possible to use Mix on objects with differing vertex counts, be forewarned that you may simply create a big mess on your screen.*

Mix Controls

The following sections explain the controls for the Mix modifier.

Global Settings Parameters

Use Vertex Selection to cause only the selected vertices on the host mesh to be affected by the mixing effect.

Use a progressive mix to calculate the result in a hierarchical order. For example, it will run down the Channels list and add the objects, so even if Channel 1's value equals 100 percent and Channel 2's value equals 100 percent, Channel 2's object will be the final result.

With a normal mix, the resulting object would be a 100-percent hybrid of both channels. Progressive mixing is smoother, and better for animation purposes.

The Mix Banks

The 10 controllers in the Mix Banks section specify the 10 meshes that can be used to blend into each other. The values in the spinners next to each channel specify the percentage of the object that will be used in the final composition.

To assign an object, click on the blue arrow (which will turn green and point inward), then select another object in the viewport. An example setup is shown in Figure 18.20. You can then turn on the Animate button, and, by adjusting the Mix Bank sliders on different keyframes, create "weighted morphing" between objects.

The Outline Filter

Outline is an outliner filter that keys off either an object or material ID; you apply it in MAX's Video Post. Its UI is shown in Figure 18.21.

Under Effect Application, there are two options that select the target of the effect. The Object Channel and/or the Material Effects Channel options choose which channel to outline with the color shown in the right-hand swatch.

The Pinch And Spin Modifiers

Because the Pinch and Spin modifiers work similarly, and their UIs are virtually identical, they're described together in this section.

Pinch bends an object and compresses the vertices on the inward side of that bend (see Figure 18.22 for an example of this effect).

Spin "twirls" an object around its axis point, basing the twirl on how far away from the center the vertex is; parts farther away from the axis will move quickly, while those nearer the center will move more slowly.

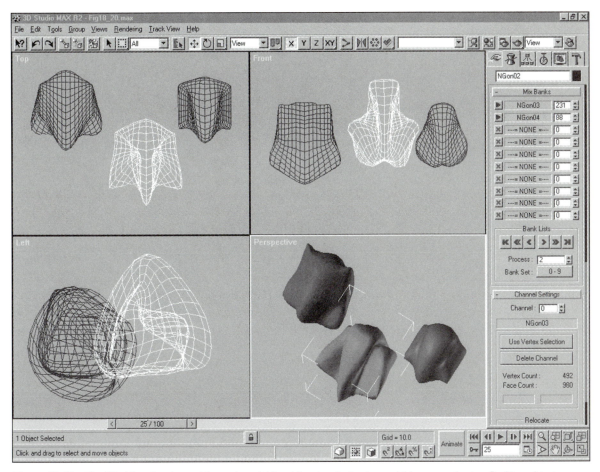

Figure 18.20 The Mix UI and various objects; the middle object is a "mixed morph" between the two flanking objects.

Figure 18.21 The Outline filter.

Pinch And Spin Controls

The following controls are found in both the Pinch and Spin modifiers:

- *X Turn, Y Turn, and Z Turn*—Define how much the effect will appear on each of the axis planes.

- *Multiplier*—A global control for the overall effect.

- *Bias*—Controls how strong the effect is manifested.

- *Confine To Gizmo*—Makes sure that only geometry inside the object's Gizmo object will be affected. The default is Off.

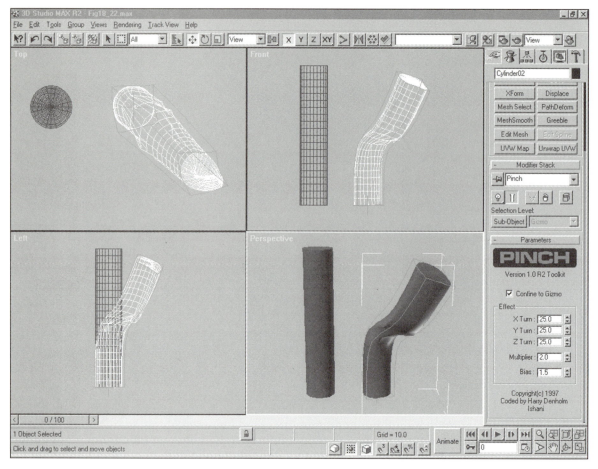

Figure 18.22 The Pinch modifier applied to an object.

The Rock Primitive

The Rock Primitive is a simple "rock" maker. You select it from the Create Panel, under Geometry| Ishani Primitives|Rock. Several examples of these primitives are shown in Figure 18.23.

Primitive Controls

To create the rock primitives, use the following simple controls:

- *Creation Method*—Check either Diameter or Center to create the initial rock primitive.

- *Keyboard Entry*—Use X, Y, and Z spinners to set these values. Radius enables you to type in specific values for creation.

Parameters

The following options are under the Parameters section of the rollout:

Note: Spin works around the axis point defined before the modifier is applied. To change this, you must use MAX's Center Axis To Object control, which is found in the Hierarchy panel.

- *Radius*—Adjust the spinner to increase or decrease the radius of the object.

- *Segments*—Adjust the spinner to increase or decrease the number of segments in the object.

- *Checkboxes*—The Rock primitive contains the following standard MAX Editable Mesh checkboxes: Smoothed, Generate Mapping Coordinates, Hemisphere, and Base To Pivot.

The Softspot Map

Softspot uses waveform mixing to create radial gradients and texture blends. You can define which wave to blend, whether to "pinch" each wave, and the thresholds for both. You can use it to build video walls or bulbs, scaly patterns, and more.

Softspot Controls

Softspot is split into two wave sections with identical controls (the UI is shown in Figure 18.24). You define the parameters for each wave separately and Softspot intertwines them for you.

For each wave, you have the following options, which are in the Gradient Setup section:

- *Phase (0 to 100.0)*—Sets the lateral movement of the wave. Animate this to move the patterns.

- *Iterations (1 to 10.0)*—Specifies how many times the mix is repeated through the material.

- *Thresholds*—Set the amount of drop-off for each gradient. Set both of these to 0 to give a very sharp gradient.

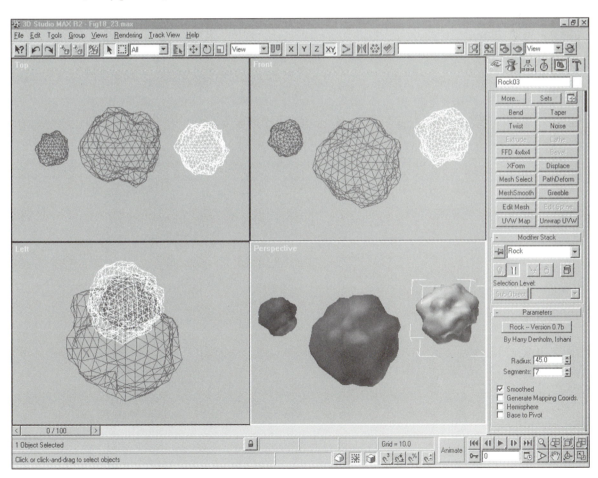

Figure 18.23 The Rock primitives.

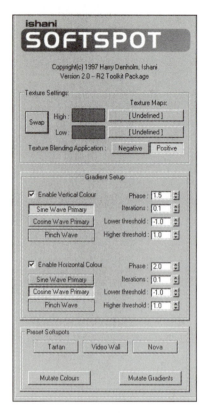

Figure 18.24 The Softspot map controls.

You can choose from either sine or cosine wave-forms and whether or not to pinch them. Pinching makes the wave tighter and more defined.

The Stacker Material

Stacker is a tiling and procedural blocks material that lets you specify the complete layout and appearance of the tiling. (Note that portions of the layering algorithm are based on a 1994 paper by Larry Gritz.)

Stacker Controls

The following sections explain each section of the Stacker rollout and the options it contains.

Blocks Setup

The Blocks Setup panel controls how many blocks are to be generated (horizontally and vertically). It also controls the amount of color variation that is applied per block. Fade Variance controls the level of intensity variation over the blocks. This will not alter the color in any way. The Stacker UI is shown in Figure 18.25.

Background Setup

The background is generated around each block to a value specified by the controls in the Background Setup panel. It also lets you punch holes in the blocks to leave gaps to the background. Jaggies defines how "noisy" the edges should be for the background.

Stacking Layout

The final panel, Stacking Layout, lets you choose how the final array of blocks will be ordered. Line shift can be used to move odd lines around in order to specify how the blocks are layered. You could make brick shapes by setting this to 0.0. Random Shift applies a random factor to the line shifting.

Configuration And Advanced Sections

The Configuration and Advanced sections contain a random seed generator and a button to swap

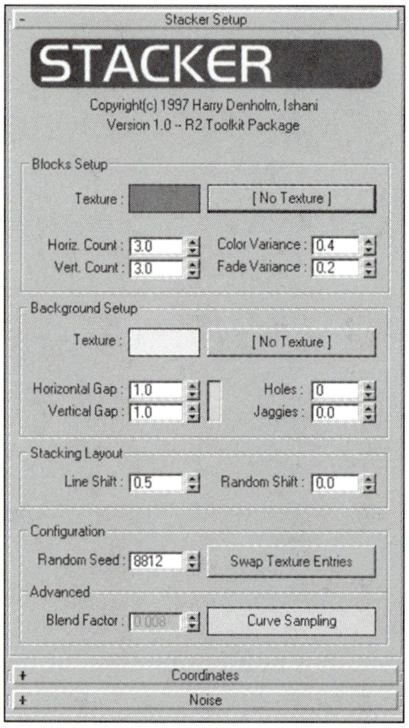

Figure 18.25 The Stacker procedural blocks material controls.

block and background textures. The Advanced section controls the smoothing section of the algorithm. It should normally be set on Curve Sampling, as this produces nice anti-aliasing. Turn this off to specify a linear blend value.

The Stratus Map

Stratus creates proper cloud forms in a 2D plane. It can be used to generate nonlinear noise and fractal patterns to add a bit of realism to a scene. For good effects, assign the same Diffuse and/or Ambient map to a Bump map slot, but soften the clouds. You will get lifelike shading variance at different levels. The Stratus UI is shown in Figure 18.26 (cloud settings).

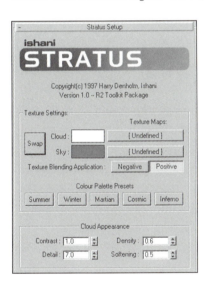

Figure 18.26   The Stratus procedural cloud patterns controls.

Stratus Controls

The following controls are found in the Stratus rollout.

Cloud Appearance

These options let you set the appearance of the clouds:

- *Contrast (0 to 6.0)*—Sets the contrast of the cloud layer.

- *Detail (0 to 30)*—Less is smoother, Higher is more defined. Excessively high values reduce contrast.

- *Softening (0 to 1.0)*—Specifies how smooth the clouds will be. A setting of 1 will be very rough.

- *Density (0 to 2.0)*—Specifies how thick the cloud layer will be.

Fractal Settings:

The Fractal settings define the algorithmic parameters of the clouds (these settings are shown in Figure 18.27):

- *Fractal Scale*—Sets the UV scale of the clouds. Lower values makes clouds that are more "stretched."

- *Fractal Shift*—Sets the UV offset of the cloud layer. Animate this to move them around.

- *Waveform Scale*—Changes the actual shape of the cloud structure.

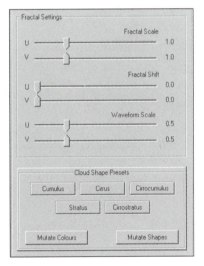

Figure 18.27   The Fractal control settings for the Stratus map type.

The Wiremapper Map

Wiremapper is a map type that simulates the Wire option of a regular MAX material. However, Wiremapper has the advantage of being able to treat the object's wireframe as a bitmap and use it as a Diffuse map, Opacity map, Self-illumination map, and so on.

Wiremapper uses the Barycentric coordinates of an object's faces to find out which lie on each other's paths. In most cases, it creates a flawless wireframe, although certain models will cause trouble.

To get the desired effect, you should experiment—different objects will require different Barycentric codes to be mapped correctly. For example, a sphere is good with Just X selected, whereas a box works with X And Z selected. Proper wire size will also vary for each object, so adjust these settings as needed for the final effect. Figure 18.28 shows the Wiremapper UI.

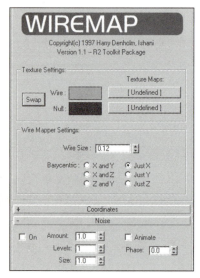

Figure 18.28 The Wiremapper controls.

Wiremapper Controls

The following controls are found in the Wiremapper rollout:

- *Wire Size*—Sets the size of the wire generated. (Duh!)

- *Barycentric codes*—Decide the scanning method to "apply" the wires, as it will differ for each model.

Moving On

This chapter concludes the coverage of the plug-ins included on this book's companion CD-ROM. In the next four chapters, Scot Tumlin, a longtime friend and 3D graphics artist, will assume control of the book. Scot is a frequent contributor to *3D Design* magazine and has experience in 3D Studio/DOS, 3D Studio MAX, Alias PowerAnimator, and Softimage.

Scot will explain how you can use MAX Release 2's expressions and MAXScript to augment your animations. Since the world's finest doctors have assured me that I'm genetically incapable of writing one line of programming code or dealing with the simplest of mathematical formulas, I'll leave you in Scot's capable hands for this section of the book. See you for the afterword!

PART V

TECHIE STUFF

A MATTER
OF EXPRESSION,
PART I

19

BY

SCOT TUMLIN

There was a time when 3D animators required an extensive knowledge of math and programming to create 3D art and animation. Today, 3D software packages sport fancy GUIs and powerful tools as a layer of defense against the underlying code. However, for those animators who didn't doodle in math class, some 3D software packages also allow you control of your scene via mathematical formulas called expressions.

Expressions are mathematical formulas that define a relationship between two or more elements in your scene. Expressions can help you solve a number of animation challenges. You can use them for tedious or repetitive animation, where you don't want to animate a large number of objects "by hand." Another great use for expressions is secondary animation, where a sub-part of an object, like a jet fighter's control surface, will move based on the roll and pitch of the fighter's fuselage.

3D Studio MAX supports expressions in the form of a controller, which contains a formula that you create. You apply the Expression controller to an element in your scene; once the Expression Controller is assigned to an element, the expression takes control. For example, you can use an expression to control the X rotation axis of a given object.

Expressions are not the ultimate solution for every animation problem. Most often, you will use expressions with other animation techniques. With a little bit of work, by the end of this chapter, expressions should become one more weapon in your animation arsenal.

A Simple Expression Demonstration

For your first expression, you'll start with a simple example. You'll then progress through this chapter and the next to more complex geometry, expressions, and transforms.

1. Load 3D Studio MAX, or else save your current MAX scene and reset the program.

2. From the \CHAP_19 directory of this book's companion CD-ROM, load the file SPHERES.MAX. When it loads, you'll see that the scene displays two spheres—Sphere01 (smaller) and Sphere02 (larger). Your objective is to create an expression that rotates Sphere01 (around the Z axis) twice as fast as Sphere02.

Before you continue, you need to switch to Local Axis mode for the Move and Rotate tools. Why? Since you'll apply expressions to specific components of your objects, you need to see the Local axis tripod to determine which axis to use.

3. Click on the Select And Move tool, then change the coordinate system to Local. Finally, make sure that the transform center is set to Use Pivot Point Center. From now on, whenever you use the Select And Move tool, MAX's coordinate system will switch to Local mode and any changes to the model will center at the object's pivot point.

4. Now, repeat the same steps for rotation. Click on the Select and Rotate tool, and change the coordinate system to Local. Also, make sure that the transform center is set to "Use Pivot Point Center". Now, whenever you use the Select and Rotate tool, the coordinate system will switch to Local mode and rotations will be based around the object's pivot point.

THE DSPHERES.MAX FILE

The DSPHERES.MAX file in the \CHAP_19 directory contains the completed expression for this example. Load this file and refer to it if you get into trouble.

It's now time to play detective and answer a few important questions. Which track of which object will receive the expression? Which track of which object will influence the expression? Review the original objective statement, and you should come to the following conclusions:

- First, the Z rotation track of the Sphere01 object (the smaller sphere) will receive the expression.

- Second, the Z rotation track of the Sphere02 object (the larger sphere) will influence the expression.

The next step is to replace the Sphere01 object's Z rotation track with an Expression controller. To access individual axis tracks, we first need to change the default Rotation TCB controller to one that will allow us to get at the axes individually: the Euler XYZ rotation controller.

5. Click on the Sphere01 object to select it, then click on the Track View icon to open the Track View dialog box. You should reduce the Track View clutter by hiding the scene elements you don't need.

6. Click on the Filter icon to open the Track View Filter dialog box, as shown in Figure 19.1.

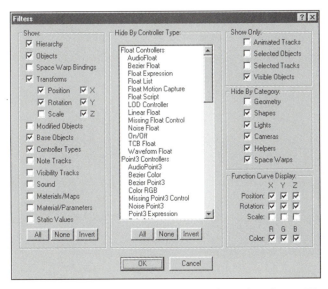

Figure 19.1   3D Studio MAX Release 2's enhanced Track View Filter dialog box.

3D Studio MAX Release 2's Track View filtering has been expanded considerably since Release 1; you can now "weed out" elements in your scene based on a huge number of parameters, including object controllers.

7. Using Figure 19.1 as a guide, turn off all parameters except Hierarchy, Objects, Transforms (Position and Rotation - XYZ), Base Objects, Controller Types, Visible Objects, Hide By Category (All except Geometry), Function Curve Display (Position XYZ, Rotation XYZ and Color RGB). Close the Track View Filter dialog box.

8. In Track View, locate and expand the Sphere01 animation tracks, and select the Rotation TCB track.

9. Click on the Assign Controller button to open the Assign Rotation Controller dialog box. Select Euler XYZ from the list and click on OK to close the dialog box.

10. Now you can access the individual axes. In the Track View, expand the Rotation: Euler XYZ track and select the Z Rotation Bezier: Float track.

11. Click on the Assign Controller icon to open the Assign Float Controller dialog box. Select Float Expression from the list and click on OK to close the dialog box. The Z rotation track changes to Z Rotation: Float Expression. Click on the Properties button to open the Expression controller dialog box. Note the dialog box's title bar lists the name and track of the selected object, as shown in Figure 19.2.

Scalars And Vectors

Now, you need to create a variable that follows the rotation of the Sphere02 object.

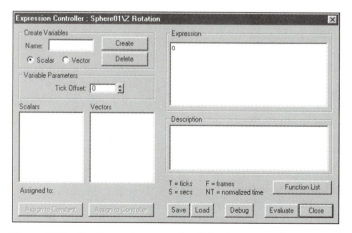

Figure 19.2 The Expression controller dialog box shows the name and track of the selected object.

In the Expression controller dialog box, type the variable **BigZrot** in the Name field.

At this point, you must define the variable as a *scalar* or *vector*. Rotational channels fall into the scalar category because they contain one piece of information—a rotation value. Position channels fall into the vector category because they contain three pieces of information—X, Y, and Z position. You want the **BigZrot** variable to follow the rotational data of the Sphere02 object; thus, you need to define the **BigZrot** variable as a scalar variable.

> **SCALARS AND VECTORS**
>
> To get a list of the possible scalar and vector operators in MAX, go to Help | Online Reference, and do a search on the words Scalar or Vector. You'll find this information under "Expression Controllers."

1. Click on the Scalar button, then click on the Create button. The variable appears in the Scalars column.

2. Click on the Assign To Controller button to open the Track View Pick dialog box. Locate and expand the animation tracks of the Sphere02 object. Click on the Z Rotation: Bezier Float track and click on the OK button. The variable **BigZrot** now equals the value of the Sphere02 object's Z rotation value. The bottom-left corner of the Expression controller dialog box should read Assigned to: Sphere02\Z Rotation as shown in Figure 19.3.

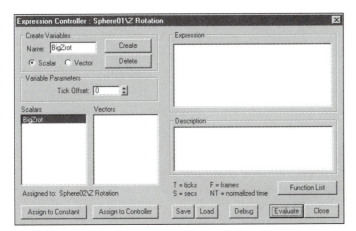

Figure 19.3 The Expression controller dialog box with the **BigZrot** variable assigned.

Do The Math!

At this point, you need a formula that causes the Sphere01 object to rotate at twice the rate of the Sphere02 object. It doesn't take a rocket scientist to realize that multiplying the rotation value by 2 will give the proper result. By multiplying the **BigZrot** variable by 2, you'll get twice the value of the Sphere02 object's Z rotation track.

1. Try it. Enter the following formula in the expression field, as shown in Figure 19.4.

```
BigZrot*2
```

2. Now, click on the Evaluate button, then go to the Top viewport and rotate the Sphere02 object around the Z axis. When the Sphere02 object rotates around the Z axis, the Sphere01 object does the same, only twice as fast.

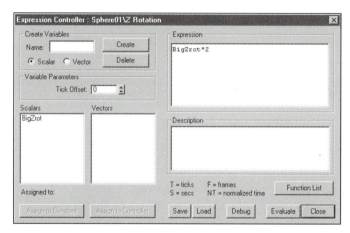

Figure 19.4 A multiplier of two is added to the expression.

Congratulations! You've completed your first expression! If you want, try changing the expression from "*2" to "/2" and observe the results. You can leave the Expression Controller and Track View dialog boxes open while you experiment; remember to click on the Evaluate button after each change you make in the Expression. If you make a syntax error in the Expression, such as mistyping a variable name or improperly expressing a mathematical relationship, the Expression parser will catch it and warn you of your errors.

Reviewing The Procedure

Now, it's time to review the procedure you used to create the sphere expression:

- Set the coordinate system to Local. This displays the Local Axis tripod of a selected object, and helps determine which axis track to use for the expression.

- Determine which object is the target. Use the objective to determine which object in the scene will receive the expression.

- Determine which animation track of the target object will receive the Expression controller. Use the objective and Local Axis tripod to determine which track of the target object to apply the Expression controller.

- Determine which object is the source. Use the objective to determine which object in the scene will influence the target object.

- Determine which animation track of the source object to use. Use the objective and Local Axis tripod to determine which track of the source object will influence the target object.

- Reduce the clutter in the Track View dialog box.

- Replace the target object's track with an Expression controller.

- Edit the Expression controller. Create a variable that follows the proper track of the source object. Use mathematical operators on the variable to get the desired result.

The following examples use this procedure.

Using Expressions To Control A Minisub

This example focuses on one of the best uses for expressions: secondary animation.

For example, let's say you want to create a fighter jet (with multiple control surfaces) that's moving through a canyon. At first this sounds simple enough—you animate the fighter on a path and keyframe its control surfaces. However, what happens when the path through the canyon changes? You can easily animate the jet on a new path, but you'll have to redo the control surfaces. This is where expressions shine. By placing an expression on the control surfaces, you can animate the control surfaces based on the roll and pitch of the fuselage. If the path changes later, the surfaces will still animate properly.

For this example, you'll use a minisub instead of a jet fighter. Your objective is to create an expression that causes the tail fins of the sub to rotate correctly based on the sub's position to simulate control of the sub by an internal human controller.

1. To begin, load the file DF.MAX from the \CHAP_19 directory. An underwater scene appears. This scene features an animated ocean surface, a sandy ocean floor, and the Deep Flight minisub, designed by Hawkes Ocean Technologies, as shown in Figure 19.5. (Note that, unlike the figure, the scene you've loaded is optimized to make it easier for you to work on the expressions for the tail fins.) The objects you don't need to adjust are either hidden, or displayed in bounding box mode.

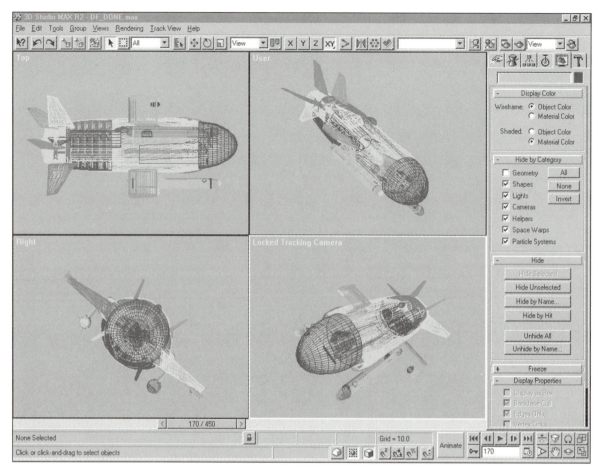

Figure 19.5 The Deep Flight minisub, developed by Hawkes Ocean Technologies (www.deepflight.com).

2. As with the first example, set the coordinate system to Local, then take a look at the animation applied to the sub. Drag the Time Slider and note how the sub moves along a trajectory path. Also, note how the sub rolls and banks during turns.

3. Press the H key to bring up the Select By Name dialog box, then check Display Subtree to display the sub's hierarchy. Note that the Sub Dummy object is the parent of the sub's parts, including the tail fins, named Fin_Left and Fin_Right.

4. Close the Select By Name dialog box, then drag the Time Slider again. Note how the sub Dummy object rolls, causing the sub to roll.

You can use the sub Dummy object to control the roll rate of both tail fins. At this point, you know that each tail fin will get an expression applied to one of its rotation tracks. You also know the sub Dummy object will influence both fins. However, you don't know which tracks of the objects to use.

Which rotation track should you use for the Fin_Left object? You'll figure this out now.

5. Make sure the coordinate system is set to Local. Click on the Fin_Left object; its Local Axis indicator appears, as shown in Figure 19.6.

From a mechanical standpoint, the Fin_Left object rotates around a rod running perpendicular to the

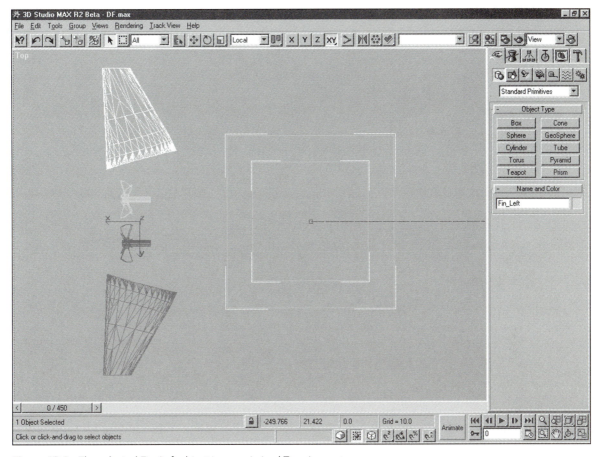

Figure 19.6   The selected Fin_Left object in a maximized Top viewport.

sub's hull. Take a look at the Axis indicator. The Y axis matches the orientation of our imaginary rod. By rotating the Fin_Left object around its Y axis you can reproduce the proper mechanical movement.

6. Click on the sub Dummy object; its Local Axis indicator appears, as shown in Figure 19.7. Note how the sub Dummy object rolls around its Z axis.

7. If necessary, drag the Time Slider and watch the sub Dummy object.

At this point you know where to put the expression, the Fin_Left object's Y rotational track. You also know which object and track will influence the expression—the sub Dummy object's Z rotational track.

Building The Expression

The next step is to build your expression:

1. You'll begin by assigning an Expression controller to the Fin_Left object. Drag the Time Slider to frame 0, then click on the Fin_Left object to select it.

2. Click on the Track View icon to open the Track View dialog box (if necessary, use the Filter tool to reduce clutter). Expand the hierarchy until the Fin_Left object's rotation tracks are visible, as shown in Figure 19.8.

You'll note that I have already replaced the default TCB controller for the Fin rotations with Euler XYZ controllers; again, this lets you access the individual axis tracks.

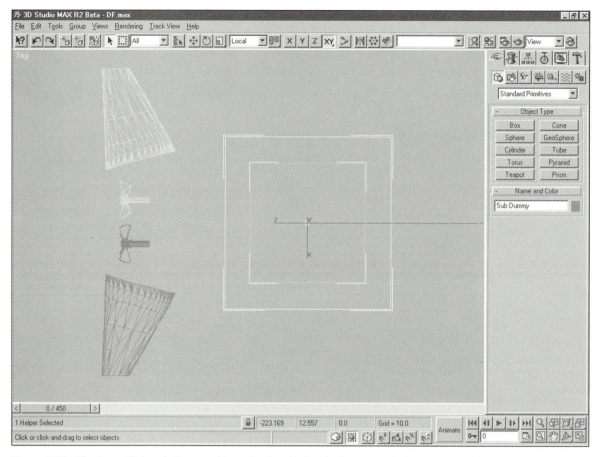

Figure 19.7 The Deep Flight sub Dummy object, showing the Local axis icon, again in a maximized Top view.

3. Click on Y Rotation: Bezier Float; the track name becomes highlighted. Click on the Assign Controller icon; when the Assign Controller dialog box appears, select Float Expression and click on the OK button. The track changes to Y Rotation: Float Expression. You've just assigned an Expression controller to the Fin_Left object's Y rotation track.

4. Click on the Properties button to bring up the Expression controller dialog box. Note that the title of the Expression controller dialog box includes the name of the object and its track, that is, "Fin_Left\Y Rotation."

5. You need a variable that equals the sub Dummy object's Z rotation value, so enter the variable name **SdumZrot** in the name field, make sure that Scalar is active, then click on the Create button; the variable appears in the Scalars column below.

6. Now you have to link the **SdumZrot** variable to the proper track in your scene. If necessary, click on the **SdumZrot** item in the Scalars column, then click on the Assign to Controller button. A new dialog box appears, listing the tracks you could link to this variable.

7. Locate and click on the Sub Dummy object's Z rotation: Bezier Float track, then click on the OK button. The Expression dialog box for this step is shown in Figure 19.9.

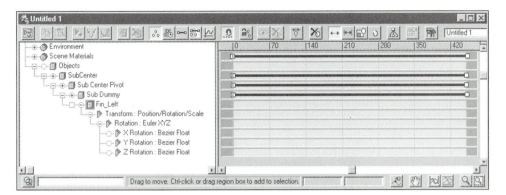

Figure 19.8 The rotation tracks of the selected Fin_Left object.

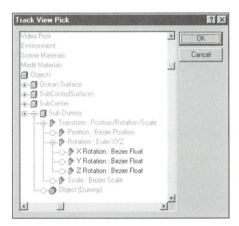

Figure 19.9 The Expression dialog box with the Sub Dummy Z rotation track.

The **SdumZrot** variable now equals the value of the sub dummy object's Z rotation track. When the sub Dummy object's Z rotation value changes, so will the variable **SdumZrot**. You should confirm this now. Here's how:

8. Click on the Debug button; the Expression Debug dialog box appears. The Expression Debug dialog box lists variables already defined. The variable F defines the current frame; it should equal 0 because your Time Slider is on frame 0. The **SdumZrot** variable should also equal 0.

9. Drag the Time Slider and note how the F variable changes indicate the current frame each time you release the mouse button. Also, note the change in the **SdumZrot** variable; it changes as the sub Dummy object rotates.

Rotating The Fins

Now, it's time to create an expression that causes the left fin to rotate the same amount as the sub Dummy object.

Note: *You must type in the functions exactly as they are shown in the Function List. For example, using degtorad in place of degToRad will produce an error. (And of course, you must also type in the names of your variables accurately!)*

1. With the Expression Controller dialog box still open, enter the
    SdumZrot variable in the expression field enclosed in a **degToRad**
    converter.

    ```
    degToRad(SdumZrot)
    ```

This variable is also shown in Figure 19.10.

Note the **degToRad** converter. This causes the Fin_Left object to rotate
properly. Without the converter, the result of the expression produces
large numbers, which creates jerky movement.

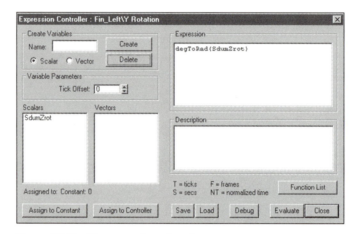

Figure 19.10   The expression takes shape.

2. Drag the Time Slider and note how the Fin_Left object rotates on
    its Y axis as the sub Dummy object rotates. Also, note how the
    Fin_left object rotates the same amount as the sub Dummy ob-
    ject. Finally, at frame 0, the Fin_Left object points up, not
    forward.

3. You can fix this problem with a little subtraction. A value of 90
    degrees would bring the Fin_Left object level with the hull. So,
    edit the expression, subtracting 90 from the **SdumZrot** variable.

    ```
    degToRad(SdumZrot-90)
    ```

4. Click on the Evaluate button. Note how the Fin_Left object ro-
    tates to its proper starting orientation, as shown in Figure 19.11.

5. Now, drag the Time Slider back to frame 255. The Fin_Left object
    rotates, but it's too subtle to notice.

You could add 15 to the expression, but that wouldn't work at frame 0.
Why? Because at frame 0, you want the Fin_Left object's Y rotation
value to equal 0. Adding 15 would cause the Fin_Left object to rotate

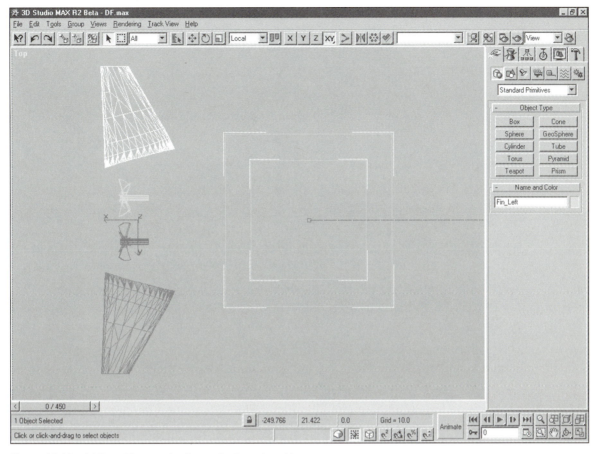

Figure 19.11   Adding -90 resets the fin to a horizontal position.

15 degrees. You could multiply by 15, which would create approximately 15 degrees of rotation during a roll, but still generate a value of 0 at frame 0.

6. To do this, edit the expression, multiplying by 15.

```
degToRad((SdumZrot*15)-90)
```

This expression is also shown in Figure 19.12.

Note the double sets of parentheses. This executes the inner set first, and the outer set last. So the **SdumZrot** variable is multiplied by 15 first, then 90 subtracted from the result.

7. Click in the Evaluate button and drag the Time Slider. Note at frame 0, the Fin_Left object is horizontal (15*0 equals 0).

8. Drag the Time Slider to frame 255 and watch the Fin_Left object rotate.

Oops! The Fin_Left object rotates in the wrong direction.

9. To fix this, you need to make a simple change to the entire expression. Placing a negative sign at the front of the expression creates the opposite rotation, as shown in Figure 19.13. However, you also have to change the -90 to a +90 to account for the negative value.

```
-(degToRad((SdumZrot*15)+90))
```

10. Now play the animation. The Fin_Left object rotates in the proper direction.

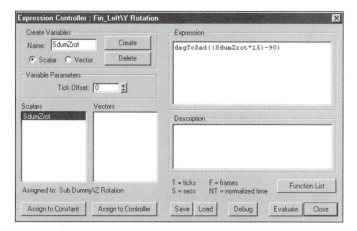

Figure 19.12   Adding *15 to the expression creates more noticeable movement.

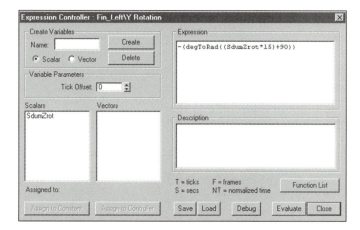

Figure 19.13   Adding a negative sign causes the fin to rotate in the opposite direction.

11.   There is one more adjustment you need to do. First, play the animation a couple of times and examine the timing. The Fin_Left object pivots *during* the rotation (or roll) of the sub. In the real world, the Fin_Left object would pivot first, and produce the subsequent roll movement.

12.   You can fix this by adding a time offset. Enter 9600 into the Tick Offset field. This will cause the Fin_Left rotation to occur 2 seconds (a tick is 1/4800 of a second) before the sub rolls on its side.

13.   Select the **SdumZrot** variable. Change the offset value to 9600.

14.   Click on the Evaluate button and play the animation. The Fin_Left object rotates, and a moment later, the sub rolls on its side.

Now you need to create an expression for the Fin_Right object. (Note: if you continue to roll the submarine beyond 180 degrees, the fins will respond unpredictably. As a later exercise, you may want to modify the expression to limit the rotation of the control surfaces. I'll leave that as homework for you.)

15. Select the Fin_Right object. Close the expression dialog box. From the Track View dialog box, select the Fin_Right object's Y Rotation: Bezier Float track. Click on the Assign Controller icon to open the Assign Float Controller dialog box. Select the Float Expression item and click on the OK button.

16. With the Y Rotation Transform still selected, click on the Properties button. The Expression controller dialog box appears with the title Fin_Right\Y Rotation. Enter 9600 in the Tick offset field.

17. Now, enter a new variable called **SdumZrot2** in the Name field. Click on the Scalar button and click on the Create button. A new variable appears in the Scalar column called **SdumZrot2**.

18. Click on the **SdumZrot2** variable to highlight it. Click on the Assign to Controller button; the Track View pick dialog box appears. Locate and select the Sub Dummy object's Z rotation: Bezier Float track, then click on the OK button to close the Track View Pick dialog box.

19. Using the Fin_Left object as your guide, create a new expression for the Fin_Right object, which is also shown in Figure 19.14.

```
degToRad((SdumZrot2*15)-90)
```

Note the two differences between the expressions for both fin objects. The Fin_right object does not need to reverse direction; thus, a negative sign is not required. Because of this, the -90 does not need changing to +90.

20. Click the Evaluate button and play the animation. Both fins now should work properly.

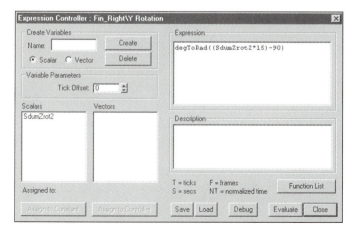

Figure 19.14   The expression for the Fin_Right object.

21. To fine-tune the fins, adjust the 15 value to control the amount of fin rotation. A higher number will cause the fins to rotate more; a lower number produces less fin rotation. As for timing, alter the tick offset value to control the response rate of the sub. A higher value creates a more sluggish response. A lower value creates a quicker, more agile response.

Using Expressions To Rotate The Sub's Propellers

In the real world, the Deep Flight I minisub uses two ducted-fan propellers to push it through the water. The expression you create will use the position animation of the sub to rotate the propellers. The Sub Center object has position animation data applied to its X axis, which runs parallel with the sub's movement. You can use the Sub Center object's X position data to control the sub's propellers.

1. You begin by assigning an Expression controller to the Prop_Left object. Select the Prop_Left object, then click on the Track View icon to open the Track View dialog box. Make sure the Reference Coordinate System is set to Local.

2. Now, examine the Prop_Left object's axis. The Z rotation track represents the prop's shaft. In Track View, select the Z Rotation: Bezier Float track. Click on the Assign Controller icon; when the Assign Float Controller dialog box appears, select Float Expression from the list and click on the OK button to close the dialog box.

3. Click on the Properties window in Track View. In the Expression Controller window, note that the title reads "Prop_Left\Z Rotation." You want to create a variable that equals the value of the Sub Center object's X position track.

4. Type the variable **ScentXpos** in the name field, then click on the Vector radio button. Click on the Create button. The **ScentXpos** variable appears in the Vector column. With the **ScentXpos** variable still highlighted, click on the Assign to Controller button.

5. In Track View, locate and expand the tracks for the Sub Center object. Note how the Position: Bezier Position track does not expand into three distinct X, Y, and Z axes. Your expression will have to extract the X position data from the one track.

6. Select the Position: Bezier Position track and click on the OK button. The **ScentZpos** variable now equals the value of the Sub Center object's position in X, Y, and Z space.

7. Click on the Debug button, and examine the state of the **ScentXpos** variable in the Expression Debug window. The **ScentXpos** variable lists three values separated by commas. The three values represent the X, Y, and Z position data of the sub center object. Of the three values, you only need the X position data. By placing a .x at the end of the variable, you extract only the X position data, as shown in Figure 19.15.

```
degToRad(ScentXpos.x)
```

The expression starts with the Degree to Radian converter, causing the result of the items within the parentheses to be defined as radians. The **ScentXpos** is the variable you created, based on the X, Y, and Z position data of the sub center object. The .x at the end of the variable indicates you want the sub center object's X position data only.

8. Click on Evaluate, then play the animation. The Prop_Left object rotates as the sub moves forward. The rotation of the Prop_Left object is based on distance traveled. If the sub stops

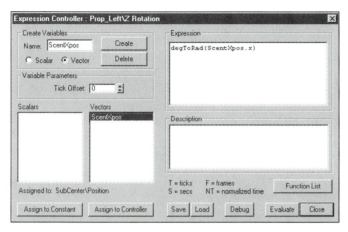

Figure 19.15 The .x extracts only the X position data of the Sub Center object.

to hover, the Prop_Left object will also stop. If the sub accelerates and travels a greater distance between frames, the Prop_Left object will also rotate farther.

9. Now, the Prop_Left object rotates correctly, but it could spin a tad faster. Add a multiplier to increase the overall speed of the Prop_Left object. Edit the expression, adding a *2 after the **ScentXpos.x** variable, as shown in Figure 19.16.

```
degToRad(ScentXpos.x*2)
```

10. Click on the Evaluate button again and play the animation. Now the Prop_Left object spins faster.

Offsetting The Effect

Finally, you should add a little offset to the expression. Since the props push the sub, it makes sense to have the sub appear to react to the

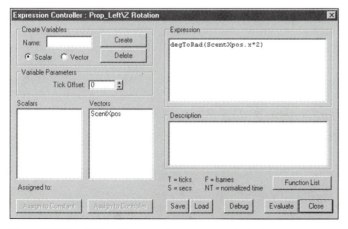

Figure 19.16 Adding *2 causes the props to spin faster.

speed of the props. By adding an offset value, the Prop_Left object will look into the future, compute the sub's speed, and then react to the computation on the current frame.

1. Click on the **ScentXpos** variable in the vector column. Change the Tick Offset to 4800, then click on the Evaluate button and play the animation. The Prop_Left object generates the illusion that it's controlling the speed of the sub.

2. Now, repeat the same steps, creating an expression for the Prop_Right object. First, you need to change the Prop_Right object's Z rotation track to an Expression controller. Select the Prop_Right object, then open the Track View window, if it's not already open.

3. Locate and select the Prop_Right object's Z Rotation: Bezier Float track. Click on the Assign Controller icon to open the Assign Float Controller window. Select Float Expression from the list and click on the OK button. The Z rotation track changes to Z Rotation: Float Expression.

4. Now, create a variable that follows the position data of the sub center object. The Prop_Right object's Z rotation track should be highlighted; if not, select it now. Click on the Properties button to open the Expression controller window. Enter 4800 into the offset field.

5. Type a new variable called **ScentXpos2** in the name field. Click on the Vector button, then click on the Create button to create the new variable. It should then appear in the Vector column. The **ScentZpos2** variable should also be highlighted; if not, click on it now.

6. Click on the Assign to Controller button. Locate and select the sub center object's Position: Bezier Position track, then click on OK to close the Track View pick window.

7. Finally, you use the Prop_Left expression as your template to create a similar expression. Enter the same expression used for the Prop_Left object, as shown in Figure 19.17.

```
degToRad(ScentXpos2.x*2)
```

8. Finally, play the animation. Oops—both propellers turn in the same direction (the real sub uses counter-rotating propellers to minimize the torque effects). You can fix that with a negative value. Edit the expression, adding a minus sign to the expression.

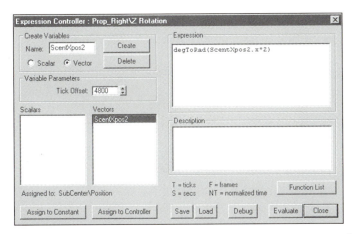

Figure 19.17   Use the Prop_Left object's expression as a starting point for the Prop_Right expression.

```
-(degToRad(ScentXpos2.x*2))
```

9.   Now if you play the animation, the props move correctly.

Again, you can tweak the expressions to change the performance of the sub. Increasing the tick offset value increases the delay between the speed of the props changing and the speed of the sub increasing. Increasing the 2 value causes the general speed of the propellers to increase.

Moving On

In this chapter, you learned how to create expressions for objects in your scene, using simple spheres, and then the complex Deep Flight minisub.

In the next chapter, you'll see how you can link expressions to not just geometric transforms of your objects, but to their materials as well. In keeping with some of the science fiction themes present in this book and its predecessor, you'll witness (and create) a flying saucer landing. With expressions, you'll control not just the saucer's landing gear, but its engine glow, too.

Keep watching the skies....

A Matter
Of Expression,
Part II

20

By

Scot Tumlin

Expressions are formulas that define relationships between elements in your scene. They're great for handling tedious and secondary animation. However, there are times when you need more power.

In the previous chapter, you created expressions that manipulated geometry. This chapter shows you how to use expressions to control materials and lights. In homage to the science-fiction theme of the previous *3D Studio MAX f/x* book, the two examples in this chapter use a flying saucer UFO object. The first example shows you how to change a material's properties. You'll create an expression that changes a material's Offset value as the saucer moves. This will produce the illusion that the saucer's "magnetic pulse drive" (or whatever) is actually propelling the craft.

The second example shows you how to move a light in your scene. You'll create an expression that causes two omni lights to orbit the saucer as it moves, producing an interactive lighting effect.

Using Expressions To Manipulate Materials

One of the powerful features of MAX is that it gives you the ability to animate a number of material parameters over time. The first expression example in this chapter takes advantage of this feature.

Your objective is to create an expression that alters the Offset track of a Cellular map used in the Glowing Engine material. The offset track slides a texture along its assigned surface. This material is applied to the bottom of a flying saucer model that you'll load from the companion CD-ROM. The Glowing Engine material imparts a visible means of (fantasy) propulsion to the craft.

In this example, the Saucer Hull object's Z position axis will manipulate the Offset track. You'll use the expression creation procedure (covered in the previous chapter) to create the material expression:

1. Load 3D Studio MAX, or save your current MAX scene and reset the program.

2. Load SAUCER.MAX from the \CHAP_20 directory of the companion CD-ROM. You'll see a scene with a typical flying saucer UFO.

Now, it's detective time. Which track of which object will receive the expression? Which track of which object will influence the expression? Review the original objective statement and you should come to the following conclusions:

- First, the Offset track of the Glowing Engine material will receive the expression.

- Second, the Z position track of the Saucer Hull object will influence the expression.

The next step is to assign an Expression controller to the Glowing Engine material's Offset track.

3. Click on the Track View icon to open the Track View window. Reduce the Track View clutter by hiding the scene elements you don't need.

4. Click on the Filter icon to open the Track View Filter window, which is shown in Figure 20.1. 3D Studio MAX Release 2's Track View filtering has been expanded considerably since Release 1; you can now "weed out" elements in your scene based on a huge number of parameters, including Object Controllers.

THE DSAUCER.MAX FILE

The DSAUCER.MAX file in the companion CD-ROM's \CHAP_20 directory contains the completed expression for this example. Load this file and refer to it if you get into trouble.

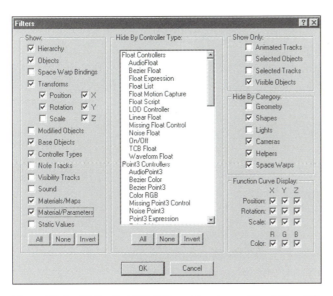

Figure 20.1 3D Studio MAX Release 2's enhanced Track View Filter window.

5. Using Figure 20.1 as your guide, turn on (check) the following parameters: Hierarchy, Objects, Transforms (Position, Rotation, Scale, X, Y, and Z), Base Objects, Controller Types, Materials/ Maps, Materials/Parameters, Visible Objects (under Show Only), Hide By Category (all except Geometry and Lights), Function Curve Display (Position XYZ, Rotation XYZ, and Color RGB). The remaining parameters should be unchecked.

6. Close the Track View Filter window.

7. Locate and expand the Medit Materials track in the Track View window. Locate and expand the Glowing Engine material. Two tracks appear: Parameters and Maps.

8. Expand the Maps track, then expand the Diffuse: Noise Glow (Cellular) track. Next, expand the Coordinates track. The Offset:

Track appears, as shown in Figure 20.2. Cellular shaders contain an offset parameter. The offset track shown corresponds to the offset parameter of Glowing engine material.

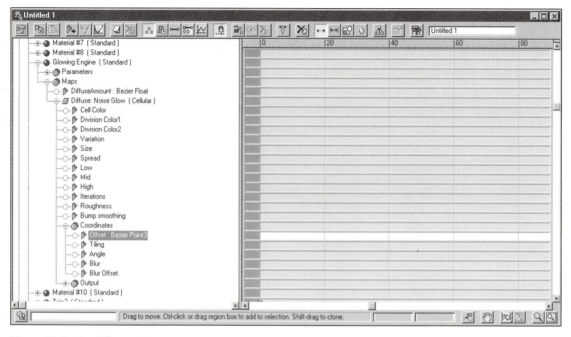

Figure 20.2 The Offset track.

9. Click on the Offset track, then click on the Assign Controller icon to open the Assign Point3 Controller window.

10. Select Point3 Expression and click on the OK button to close the window. The Offset track changes to Offset: Point3 Expression. A point3 expression contains three numbers separated by commas. The three numbers represent X, Y, and Z values. Some parameters like Offset use a point3 value.

11. Click on the Properties button to open the Expression Controller window. Note that the window's title bar includes the name and track of the selected object, as shown in Figure 20.3.

Creating A Vector

Now you need to create a variable that contains the position of the Saucer Hull object.

1. Type "HullPos" in the Name field in the Expression Controller window.

At this point, you'll need to define the variable as a *vector*. Position channels fall into the vector category because they contain three pieces

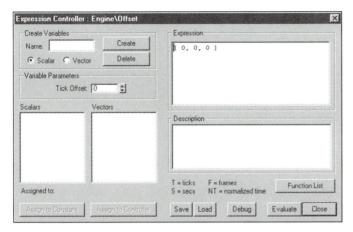

Figure 20.3   The Expression Controller window shows the name and track of the selected object.

of information: X, Y, and Z position locations. The **HullPos** variable should contain the positional data of the Saucer Hull object; thus, you'll need to define the **HullPos** variable as a vector variable.

2. Click on the Vector button and then click on the Create button. The variable appears in the Vector column.

3. Click on the Assign To Controller button to open the Track View Pick window. Then, locate and expand the tracks for the Saucer Hull object.

4. Click on the Position: Bezier Position track and click on the OK button. The **HullPos** variable now equals the Saucer Hull object's X, Y, Z position value. The lower-left corner of the Expression Controller window should read "Assigned to: Saucer Hull\Position", as shown in Figure 20.4.

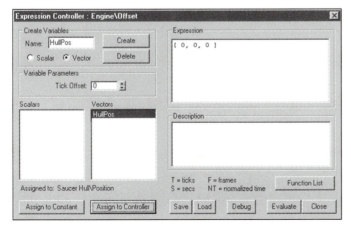

Figure 20.4   The Expression Controller window with the **HullPos** variable assigned.

Do The Math! (Again)

Now you need a formula that causes the Offset track to change as the saucer rises. Your expression will be based on the Saucer Hull object's Z track. Before you can write the expression, you'll need to know what values the Z track is generating:

1. Click on the Debug button in the Expression Controller window.

2. The Expression Debug window lists a number of defined variables, including **F**, which denotes the current frame. Drag the Time Slider and observe the **HullPos** variable. The Z values range from 0 at frame 0 to approximately 1300 at frame 100.

Now you know the range of values the Z track generates. Next, you'll need to enter an expression that captures the value of the Z track.

3. Try it. Enter "[0, HullPos.z, 0]" in the Expression field, as shown in Figure 20.5.

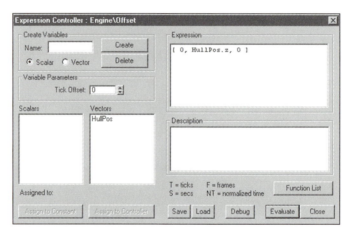

Figure 20.5 The expression tracks the Z position of the Saucer Hull object.

The Offset track uses a point3 variable. The Offset track accepts three values: X, Y, and Z. Placing the **HullPos** variable in the Y section of the vector affects the Y Offset value of the material. The **.z** at the end of the **HullPos** variable pulls just the Z data out of the Hull positional vector, leaving the X and Y data behind.

Consequently, the expression should place the Saucer Hull object's Z position in the Y offset. Now, test to see if this is true.

4. Click on the Debug button to open the Expression Debug window. Drag the Time Slider to frame 0. The bottom of the Expression Debug window lists the expression's current value. At frame 0, the expression value should be [0,0,0].

5. Drag the Time Slider to frame 100. At frame 100, the expression value should be approximately [0,1300,0]. Look up at the list of variables in the Expression Debug window. At frame 100, the **HullPos** variable is approximately [.8, 0,1300]. Note that the Y value of the expression equals the Z value of the Saucer Hull object. The expression does track the Saucer Hull object properly.

6. You can render out your own 100-frame animation, or you can view SAUCER1.AVI from the \CHAP_20 directory of the companion CD-ROM. You'll see that the Glowing Engine material changes as the saucer rises.

Slowing Down The Effect

In the previous example, the expression returns a value of 0 at frame 0. At frame 100, the expression returns a value of approximately 1300. Therefore, the Offset value increases as the saucer rises.

You can use multiplication by less than a unit value to slow down the effect:

1. If necessary, open the Track View window and locate the Offset track.

2. Click on the Offset track to select it, then click on the Properties icon to open the Expression window.

3. Next, change the expression as follows (the expression is shown in Figure 20.6):

```
[ 0, HullPos.z*0.15, 0 ]
```

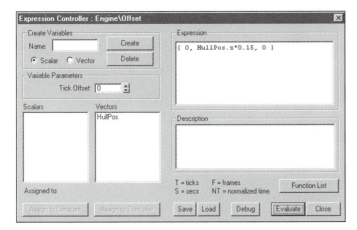

Figure 20.6   The expression produces 15 percent of the Saucer Hull object's Z position value.

THE DORBIT.MAX FILE

DORBIT.MAX, which is in the \CHAP_20 directory of the companion CD-ROM, contains the completed expression for this example. Load this file and refer to it if you get into trouble.

4. Click on the Evaluate button to record the change in the expression field, then click on the Debug button to open the Expression Debug window.

5. Drag the Time Slider to frame 100. Note the result in the lower section of the Expression Debug window. The expression equals 15 percent of the **HullPos** variable.

6. As with the previous example, you can render this sequence or view SAUCER2.AVI from the \CHAP_20 directory to see the results.

Now the Offset effect moves slower. Here are some things to try:

• Experiment with different values ranging from .01 to .90.

• Try applying the expression to the X and Z Offset values.

Orbiting An Omni Light Around The Saucer

For your next trick, you'll create an expression that moves two Omni lights based on the position of the Saucer Hull object. The lights will rise with the saucer while orbiting the saucer's hull. The Saucer Hull object's X, Y, and Z tracks will affect the X, Y, Z position of the Omni lights.

Again, follow this procedure to create your expression:

1. Load 3D Studio MAX, or save your current MAX scene and reset the program.

2. Load ORBIT.MAX from the \CHAP_20 directory of the companion CD-ROM. You'll see a scene with the flying saucer surrounded by two Omni lights.

It's detective time again. Which track of which object will receive the expression? Which track of which object will influence the expression? Review the original objective statement and you should come to the following conclusions:

• First, the position track of the two Omni lights will receive the expression.

• Second, the position track of the Saucer Hull object will influence the expression.

Let's start with the Omni01 light. First, you need to assign an Expression controller to the Omni01 Position: Bezier position track.

3. Click on the Track View icon to open the Track View window. Reduce the Track View clutter by hiding the scene elements you don't need, as in the earlier example.

4. Click on the Filter icon to open the Track View Filter window, which is shown in Figure 20.1.

5. Using Figure 20.1 as your guide, turn on (check) the following parameters: Hierarchy, Objects, Transforms (Position, Rotation, Scale X, Y, and Z), Base Objects, Controller Types, Materials/ Maps, Materials/Parameters, Visible Objects (under Show Only), Hide By Category (all except Geometry and Lights), Function Curve Display (Position XYZ, Rotation XYZ, and Color RGB). The remaining parameters, in the Filter window, should be un-checked.

6. Close the Track View Filter window.

7. Next, in Track View, locate and expand the Omni01 track, as shown in Figure 20.7.

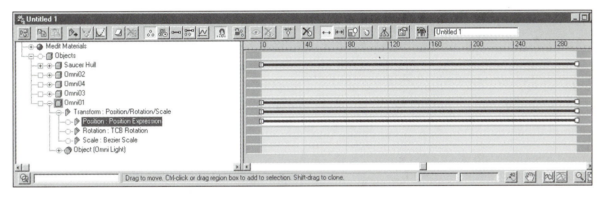

Figure 20.7   The Omni01 light's animation tracks.

8. Click on the Position: Bezier position track, then click on the Assign Controller icon to open the Assign Position Controller window.

9. Select Position Expression and click on the OK button to close the window. The position track changes to Position: Position Expression.

10. Click on the Properties button to open the Expression Controller window. Note that the window's title bar includes the name and track of the selected object, as shown in Figure 20.8.

Creating A Vector

As with the first example in this chapter, now you'll need to create a variable that reproduces the position of the Saucer Hull object:

1. In the Expression Controller window, type "HullPos" in the Name field. Again, the **HullPos** variable will return the value of the Saucer Hull X, Y, Z position. Thus, the **HullPos** variable is a *vector*.

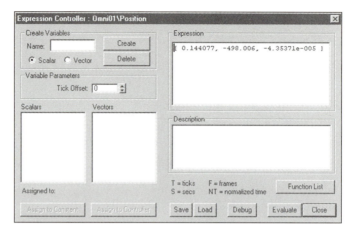

Figure 20.8 The Expression Controller window shows the name and track of the selected object. The values on your screen may differ.

2. Click on the Vector button and then click on the Create button. The variable appears in the Vector column.

3. Click on the Assign To Controller button to open the Track View Pick window. Locate and expand the tracks of the Saucer Hull object.

4. Next, click on the Position: Bezier Position track and click on the OK button. The **HullPos** variable now equals the Saucer Hull object's X, Y, Z position value. The lower-left corner of the Expression Controller window should read "Assigned to: Saucer Hull\Position", as shown in Figure 20.9.

Do The Math! (Yet Again...)

Now, you need a formula that causes the Omni01 light's position track to change as the saucer moves. Your expression will be based on the Saucer Hull object's X, Y, and Z axes.

First, you'll create an expression that places the Omni01 light in the center of the Saucer Hull object:

1. Enter the following formula in the Expression field, as shown in Figure 20.10.

   ```
   ([HullPos.x,HullPos.y,HullPos.z])
   ```

   Then click on the Evaluate button.

Examine the Top and Right viewport windows. Note how the Omni01 light jumps to the center of the Saucer Hull object. Drag the Time Slider and the Omni01 light will move with the saucer. Both objects are using the same X, Y, Z position data, thus, they both appear in the same location in 3D space.

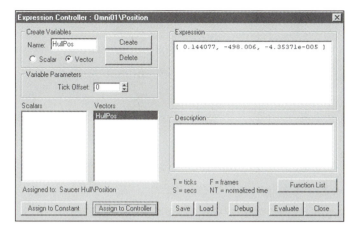

Figure 20.9 The Expression Controller window with the **HullPos** variable assigned.

Take a look at the expression in Figure 20.10. The expression generates a vector. And as stated earlier, a vector contains three pieces of information: X, Y, and Z positional data. The expression in Figure 20.10 is broken down into three sections separated by commas:

- The first section, **HullPos**.x, gets the X position value of the Saucer Hull object.

- The second section, **HullPos**.y, gets the Y position value of the Saucer Hull object.

- Finally, the third position, **HullPos**.z, gets the Z position value of the Saucer Hull object.

So, if the Saucer Hull object were at XYZ coordinates 5, 10, 20, the expression in Figure 20.10 would generate ([5,10,20]). Keep this format in mind as you proceed with the example.

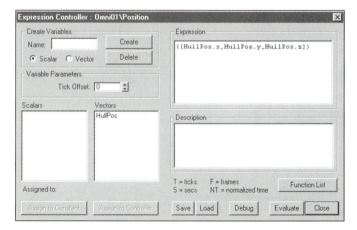

Figure 20.10 The expression places the Omni01 light in the center of the Saucer Hull object.

Now you'll make the Omni01 light move around the Saucer Hull object.

2. You can use the *cosine* and *sine* functions to create a circular path around the Saucer Hull object. Both functions will get the Omni01 light orbiting properly.

3. The Omni01 light's orbit should take it around the saucer in a horizontal plane, that is, around its "equator." So, edit the expression as shown here and in Figure 20.11:

```
([(500*cos(360*S)),(500*sin(360*S)),0])
```

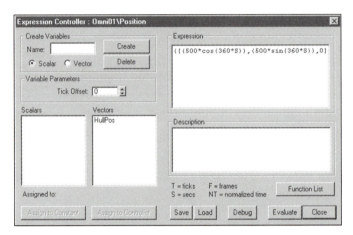

Figure 20.11 This expression causes the Omni01 object to orbit the origin (0,0,0).

4. Next, click on the Evaluate button and then drag the Time Slider. The Omni01 light orbits the saucer.

Take a look at the expression in Figure 20.11. It replaces the **HullPos**.x, .y, and .z with a Cosine function, Sine function, and 0 value, respectively. It may appear confusing at first, but look at the location of the commas. The commas still define a valid vector. They separate the expression into three distinct sections:

• The first section, (500*cos(360*S)), does a number of things, starting with the innermost parenthesis. First, 360 is multiplied by the seconds variable. The **S** (seconds) variable is predefined by MAX. Beginning at 0, the **S** variable increments, 1/30th of a second, on every frame. This causes the Omni light to complete one revolution every 30 frames. Next, the cosine is computed, and the cosine result multiplied by 500. The 500 value denotes a radius. The larger the value, the longer the radius. Taken together, the first section of the expression causes the Omni01 light to oscillate from East to West and back to East (as indicated in the Top viewport window).

- The second section uses the same basic concept, except the Sine function is used in place of the Cosine function. The second section causes the Omni01 light to oscillate North to South (Top viewport window). When combined, the first and second sections of the expression create a horizontal circular orbit path.

- The last section contains a zero, causing the orbit to maintain planar, or no up-down movement. Why? Because the last section of a vector appies to the Z axis. In your scene, the Z axis defines altitude. Placing a 0 in the third section of the vector allows no movement on the Z axis, or no up/down movement. Placing a 0 in the third position also locates the center of the orbit at the World 0,0,0 coordinates.

5. Drag the Time Slider and observe the Omni01 light in the Top viewport window.

Oops! The Omni01 light orbits around the center of the universe, not the center of the saucer.

6. Edit the expression as shown here and in Figure 20.12:

```
([HullPos.x +(500*cos(360*S)),HullPos.y
  +(500*sin(360*S)),0])
```

Take a look at the expression in Figure 20.12. What you did was add the **HullPos**.x and **HullPos**.y values to the first two sections of the expression. Again, note the two commas and how they separate the portions of the expression. Now the Omni01 light moves around the saucer, not the center of the universe.

7. Try this again. Drag the Time Slider and observe the Omni01 light in the Top viewport window. Now it moves properly

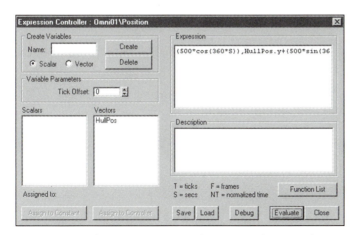

Figure 20.12   The expression causes the Omni01 object to orbit around the saucer.

around the saucer, but examine the Omni01 light in the Right or Front viewport window. The Omni01 light does not rise up with the saucer.

You need to add a value to the Z section of the expression. Basically, the Omni01 light should use the Saucer Hull object's Z position. The best way to get this value is to pull just the Z position data from the **HullPos** variable.

8. Edit the expression with the following values, which are also shown in Figure 20.13. Note: you can use the Enter key to place long expressions on multiple lines:

```
([HullPos.x +(500*cos(360*S)),HullPos.y +
(500*sin(360*S)),HullPos.z])
```

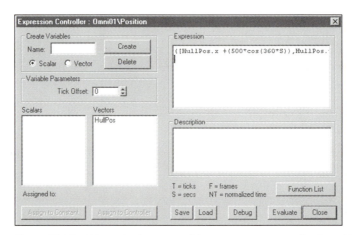

Figure 20.13 Editing the Z section of the expression causes the Omni01 light to rise with the saucer.

Now when the saucer rises, the Omni01 light rises properly. Spend a few moments looking at the light position from different angles in the various viewports.

On To The Second Light

The first light moved around the saucer's edge like the earth moving around the sun. The second Omni light will move over and under the saucer like bubblegum stuck to a tire tread.

Start by assigning an Expression controller to the Omni02 light's position track:

1. Close the Expression window but leave the Track View window open. Locate and expand the Omni02 tracks.

2. Click on the Position: Bezier position track, then click on the Assign Controller icon to open the Assign Position Controller window. Select Position Expression and click on the OK button to close the window. The position track changes to Position: Position Expression.

3. Click on the Properties button to open the Expression Controller window. Note that the window's title bar includes the name and track of the selected object.

Creating Another Vector Variable

As with the first Omni light, you need to create a variable that reproduces the position of the Saucer Hull object:

1. In the Expression Controller window, type "HullPos2" in the Name field.

The **HullPos2** variable will return the value of the Saucer Hull X, Y, Z position. Thus, the **HullPos2** variable is a vector.

2. Click on the Vector button and then click on the Create button. The variable appears in the Vector column.

3. Click on the Assign To Controller button to open the Track View Pick window. Locate and expand the tracks for the Saucer Hull object. Click on the Position: Bezier Position track and click on the OK button.

The **HullPos2** variable now equals the Saucer Hull object's X, Y, Z position value. The lower-left corner of the Expression Controller window should read "Assigned to: Saucer Hull\Position", as shown in Figure 20.14.

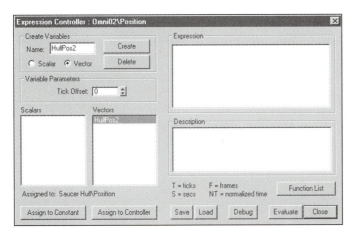

Figure 20.14   The **HullPos2** variable assigned to the Saucer Hull Position track.

Do The Math! (For The Last Time...)

Now you need a formula that causes the Omni02 light's position track to change as the saucer moves:

1. To make your life a little easier, you can retype the expression you created for the Omni01 light, as shown earlier in Figure 20.13. Edit the expression by changing the **HullPos** variable to **HullPos2**, as shown in Figure 20.15:

   ```
   ([HullPos2.x + (500*cos(360*S)),HullPos2.y,HullPos2.z
     +(500*sin(360*S))])
   ```

2. Drag the Time Slider; you'll see the Omni02 light jump to the same location as the Omni01 light. This makes sense because both lights share the same expression. However, your objective for the Omni02 light differs from the Omni01 light.

Now you can create an expression that causes the Omni02 light to move over the top of the saucer. Rearranging the expression in Figure 20.15 should do the trick.

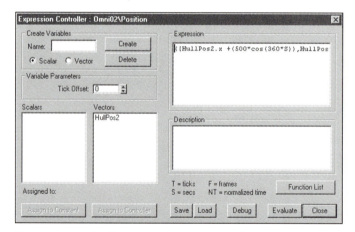

Figure 20.15   The changes made to the expression used for the Omni01 light.

3. Take a look at the expression in Figure 20.15. Note the two commas that separate the expression into three sections.

The first section (to the left of the first comma) causes the Omni02 light to oscillate between the front and rear of the Saucer Hull object. The second section of the expression (between the first and second commas) causes the Omni02 light to oscillate between the left and right sides of the Saucer Hull object.

When they are combined, the first two sections of the expression create an orbit path around the Saucer Hull object. The third and final section of the expression (after the second comma) produces the Z position location of the Saucer Hull object. When the Saucer Hull object rises, so does the Omni02 light.

A New Objective

Your objective for the Omni02 light is to create an orbit path over the top of the Saucer Hull object. You'll need an expression that does two things.

First, the Omni02 light must oscillate between the front and rear of the Saucer Hull object. Second, the Omni02 light must oscillate between the top and bottom of the Saucer Hull object. When both oscillations are combined, you'll get an orbit path over the top of the Saucer Hull object.

The first section of the expression in Figure 20.15 solves your first problem. The second section of the expression doesn't solve either problem. The third section reproduces the Z position of the Saucer Hull object.

At this point, you know changes must be made to the second and third sections of the expression. So, you'll change the second section of the expression, making it mimic the Y position of the Saucer Hull object:

1. Edit the expression with the value shown here:

   ```
   ([HullPos2.x +(500*cos(360*S)),HullPos2.y,HullPos2.z])
   ```

2. Drag the Time Slider and observe the movement of the Omni02 light in the Top, Right, and Front viewport windows. The Omni02 light oscillates between the front and rear of the Saucer Hull object. So far, so good.

3. You need a way to get the Omni02 light to move *over and under* the Saucer Hull object. Up-down movement is controlled by the third section of the expression, the Z axis. Thus, you need to place an expression in this section of the expression. Edit the expression with the value shown as follows:

   ```
   ([HullPos2.x +(500*cos(360*S)),HullPos2.y,HullPos2.z
     +(500*sin(360*S))])
   ```

4. Drag the Time Slider and observe the Omni02 light. The Omni02 light now moves over the Saucer Hull object properly.

Take a look at the expression in Step 3. Basically, you swapped the second and third sections of the expression. The combination of the first and third sections creates the vertical orbit over the Saucer Hull object. Both Omni lights now orbit the saucer as it moves through space.

Now, as for tweaking the expressions.... Note that changing the 500 radius value changes the distance of the light from the saucer. Using a lower value creates a tighter orbit. Using different values for the X and Z portions of the expression creates an elliptical path.

As you can see, expressions can provide you with a great deal of control over the elements in your 3D scene. Any element in your scene that has an animation track can accept an expression. To create your own, just follow the procedure used in this chapter and the last. Start with simple examples and work your way to more complex formulas. Use the Expression Debug window; it shows you what values your variables are returning.

Finally, for some additional homework, try the following:

- Create an expression that changes the color of a texture.
- Create an expression that changes the brightness of a light.

Moving On

This chapter concludes our look at MAX's expressions. Coming up in the next two chapters is more "techie stuff." In Chapters 21 and 22, you'll learn about the powerful MAXScript feature of 3D Studio MAX Release 2. With MAXScript, you can create scripts to animate complex scene elements—everything from flying saucer landing gear to dancing butterflies.

A LOOK AT MAXSCRIPT, PART I

21

BY

SCOT TUMLIN

In this chapter, you'll take a look at a new Release 2 feature, MAXScript. You'll learn how to use scripts to add "behaviors" to objects in your scene.

MAXScript enables you to create animation *scripts*. Like a computer program, a script consists of a series of instructions that affect elements in your scene.

Expressions and MAXScript are similar in that both of them control elements in your scene. However, MAXScript also provides access to the core functions of 3D Studio MAX. Most, if not all, of the tools available via the user interface are available via MAXScript. If you can do it with a series of mouse clicks, you can do it with MAXScript. In addition, most expressions can carry out one or two instructions at best. However, a MAXScript can execute hundreds of instructions. With MAXScript, you don't have to be an expert in Visual C++. You can create the plug-in you've always wanted!

This chapter and the next will expose you to the power of MAXScript. As you progress through the tutorials, you'll create landing gear (for this chapter's flying saucer) that automatically extends and retracts. In the next chapter, you'll see how to create realistic flying motions for butterflies, including "flocking" behavior. In short, you will code!

MAXScript And Other Programming Languages

MAXScript is a programming language, like Basic, Pascal, C, or C++. The structure of MAXScript is similar to Basic or C. Programming languages are used to create a list of instructions that the computer will carry out. The computer speaks one language: assembly (or machine) language. The sole purpose of a programming language is to convert your instructions into assembly language.

There are two ways to convert your instructions into assembly language. The first is to use a non-interpreted language like C. A non-interpreted language reads your entire list of instructions and tries to convert the list into assembly language.

The second way is to use an interpreted language like MAXScript. An interpreted language reads one instruction at a time and converts it to assembly language. The benefit of a non-interpreted language is faster execution, but the cost is lack of interactivity during conversion from instructions to assembly language. The programmers who wrote MAX used a non-interpreted language, C++. The benefit of an interpreted language is interactivity, but the cost is lack of speed. Artists want to see the result of their actions more quickly.

A good analogy is pre-rendered animation versus realtime animation. Pre-rendered animation looks great, but you don't know what you'll get until the rendering completes. Realtime animation doesn't look as good, but you'll see the result instantly.

A Simple Script Demonstration

Back in Chapter 20, you created a simple expression that rotated a sphere based on the movement of another sphere. Your first script example will reproduce the same rotation animation. You'll start by loading the necessary geometry file:

1. Load 3D Studio MAX, or save your current MAX scene and reset the program.

2. Load SPHERES.MAX from the \CHAP_21 directory of the companion CD-ROM. You'll see that the scene displays two spheres—Sphere01 (smaller) and Sphere02 (larger). Your goal is to create a script that rotates Sphere01 (around the Z axis) twice as fast as Sphere02.

3. Switch the coordinate system to Local. Click on the Select And Move tool and change the coordinate system to Local. Finally, set the transform center to Use Pivot Point Center, the default.

4. Repeat the same steps for rotation. Click on the Select And Rotate tool, change the coordinate system to Local, and set the transform center to Use Pivot Point Center.

5. Click on the Utilities panel to display the currently loaded utilities.

6. Click on the MAXScript button; the lower section of the panel reveals the MAXScript UI.

7. Click on the Open Listener button; the MAXScript Listener window appears. The Listener window gives you immediate feedback from your script instructions. Let's try it. Type "$Sphere01" in the Listener window as shown in Listing 21.1 and press Enter.

Listing 21.1   Your first line of code!

```
$Sphere01
```

Note how your text appears in black. The command you entered asked for information about the Sphere01 object. Once the code is entered, the Listener returns the result of your instruction in blue text. The returned data lists the location of the Sphere01 object in 3D space. You can use the Listener window to experiment with and debug your scripts.

THE ROTATE.MS SCRIPT

ROTATE.MS, in the \CHAP_21 directory of the companion CD-ROM, contains the complete script for this example. Load this script and refer to it if you get into trouble.

DSPHERES.MAX, which is also in the \CHAP_21 directory, shows the result of the script. Load this geometry file and refer to it if you get into trouble.

Note: *MAXScript is a utility and it appears on the Utilities tab. You may have to install MAXScript on the Utility panel. Please refer to your documentation and install MAXScript before proceeding. When it's installed, the MAXScript plug-in should appear in the Utilities panel.*

The goal of this script is to emulate the expression you created in Chapter 20. Basically, the Sphere01 object should rotate twice as far on the Z axis as the Sphere02 object. The expression in Listing 21.2 was used in Chapter 20 to get the desired result. The script you'll create will use the same mathematical formula.

Listing 21.2   The expression used in Chapter 20.

```
BigZrot*2
```

8. Click on the Open Script button; the Choose Editor window appears. Load ROTATE.MS (a script file) from the \CHAP_21 directory of the companion CD-ROM. A new window that contains the ROTATE.MS program appears. The following ROTATE.MS script appears in Listing 21.3.

Listing 21.3   The ROTATE.MS script.

```
animate on
for t = 0 to 200 by 1 do at time t
(
  bigzrot = $Sphere02.rotation.z_rotation *2
  $Sphere01.rotation.z_rotation = bigzrot
)
animate off
```

The Rotate Script, Line By Line

Now you'll take a good look at the script.

The script begins with the **animate on** command. The **animate on** command turns on animation recording. All actions that create movement will be recorded until the **animate off** command is reached. The **animate on** command is MAXScript's equivalent to the Animate button.

The second line is a **for/loop** command. The **for/loop** command is used to repeat a series of commands a given number of times. The line begins with **for**, which denotes a **for/loop** command. The "t" is an index variable that changes value as the **for/loop** command executes.

The equal (=) sign defines the range of values that "t" will assume. In this example, the **0 to 200** portion of the line defines the range. Thus, "t" will start at 0 and end at 200.

The **by 1** portion tells the command how to increment through the 0 to 200 range. The 1 tells the command to move from 0 to 200 in increments of 1. So "t" starts as 0, then "t" becomes 1, then "t" become 2, and so on. If the by value was .5, "t" would start as 0, then become .5, then become 1, and so on.

The **do** portion of the **for/loop** statement completes the **for/loop** command. However, an optional portion is added to the end of the **for/ loop** command. The **at time t** portion defines the **t** variable as time. So the entire line advances the time, starting at frame 0 and ending at frame 200.

The next line contains an open parenthesis. This line defines the start of the series of commands that should be executed during each cycle of the **for/loop** command. The sixth line contains a close parenthesis that sets the end of the commands in the **for/loop**.

The fourth line defines the **bigzrot** variable. This line is the equivalent to the expression in Chapter 20. The purpose of this line is to tell the program what value the **bigzrot** variable should contain. The line contains two portions separated by an equal sign. The left portion is the name of the variable you want to define. The variable will hold some value. In this case, the variable name is **bigzrot**.

The right portion defines the value of the **bigzrot** variable. The right side will define the value. In this case, the value should equal two times the Sphere02 object's Z rotation value. The right portion starts with **$Sphere02**, which states, "The **bigzrot** variable should equal some parameter of the object Sphere02."

The **.rotation** narrows it down a bit by stating, "The **bigzrot** variable should equal some rotation element of the Sphere02 object." The **.z_rotation** narrows it down completely, stating, "The **bigzrot** variable should equal the Z rotation track of the Sphere02 object." Finally, the *** 2** portion takes the Z rotation value and multiplies it by 2.

At this point, the program can calculate the value of the **bigzrot** variable from the known value of the Z rotation track of Sphere02. Now you need to get this value to the Sphere01 object. The fifth line assigns the value of the **bigzrot** variable to the Sphere01 object's Z rotation track. The fifth line is also separated by an equal sign. The left portion defines which track of the Sphere01 object to use. The syntax is the same as the right section of the fourth line. The **$Sphere01** denotes which object, which in this case is Sphere01. The **.rotation** narrows it down to one of the rotation tracks. The **.z_rotation** defines the exact rotation track. Simply stated, this line assigns the value of the **bigzrot** variable in the Sphere01 object's Z rotation track.

The sixth line contains a closed parenthesis. As described earlier, this denotes the ending of the lines that should be repeated via the **for/loop** line.

The last line turns off the Animate Record feature.

The Rotate Script: A Walk-through

Now, you'll do a mental run through the script and see what happens. Assume that the Sphere02 object's Z rotation value is set to 15 before the script is executed:

- The first line is executed and the Animate button is turned on. Any transform commands that are found will create animation tracks until an Animate Off command is executed.

- The second line is executed, storing the value 0 in the **t** variable. The **t** variable refers to the current frame. When the **t** variable increments, the current frame increments.

- The third line is executed (the open parenthesis), and the computer knows to execute all series of commands that are listed until a solo closed parenthesis is found.

- The fourth line executes a number of tasks. First, the Sphere02 object's Z rotation value at frame 0 is stored (15). Next, this value is multiplied by 2 (15*2=30). Finally, the result of the multiplication is stored in the **bigzrot** variable (**bigzrot**=30). So at this point, the **bigzrot** variable holds a value of 30.

- The fifth line is executed and the Sphere01 object's Z rotation value is set to equal the **bigzrot** variable. So at this point, the Sphere01 object's Z rotation track equals 30. This is twice the value of the Sphere02 object's Z rotation track, which is the objective in this exercise.

- The sixth line (the closed parenthesis) is executed and the program does a number of important tasks. First, the program checks to see if "t" equals 200. If it does, the program continues on to line seven. If "t" does not yet equal 200, then it loops back to the fourth line. At this point in our hypothetical example, "t" still equals 0, so the program loops back up to line four. Next, the "t" value is incremented from 0 to 1, that is, time is advanced to frame 1.

- Finally, lines four and five are executed again. This repeats until "t" equals 200. When "t" equals 200, the program does not loop up to line four; instead, it continues to line seven. Line seven is executed and the Animate Record feature is turned off.

The Rotate Script For Real

Enough talk! Now you'll run the script and see what happens:

1. Drag the Time Slider to frame 0. Select Evaluate All from the File menu in the ROTATE.MS window. The script executes and the text "OK" appears in the Listener window. The OK text indicates that the computer found no errors in your script.

2. Take a look at the Sphere01 object. Note the white outline indicating that a keyframe was stored at frame 0. Open the Track View window. Locate and expand the Sphere01 object. Note the keyframes stored on each frame of the rotation tracks from frame 0 to 200. Close the Track View window.

3. Now you'll move the Sphere02 object and see how the Sphere01 object responds. Select the Rotate tool. Click on the Z axis indicator. Click on the Sphere02 object in the top viewport window. Rotate the Sphere02 object around the Z axis; the Sphere01 object doesn't move.

What happened? The Track View shows that keyframes were recorded for all 201 frames.

4. Take a look at the script. The Sphere01 object should rotate twice as far as the Sphere02 object. Unfortunately, the Sphere02 object didn't move during the execution of the script. So the value taken from the Sphere02 object remained the same.

You just experienced the major difference between expressions and scripts. Once assigned, an expression constantly monitors your scene looking for changes. Recall the two-sphere example in Chapter 20. The Sphere01 object responded once the expression was assigned. When you rotated the Sphere02 object, the Sphere01 object rotated twice as far.

Until the script is executed, it doesn't monitor your scene. Once executed, the script looks for changes in your scene and responds accordingly. As you saw earlier, rotating the Sphere02 object didn't affect the Sphere01 object. For this example to work, you must first animate the Sphere02 object.

5. Minimize the ROTATE.MS and Listener windows. Drag the Time Slider to frame 0, if necessary, then click on the Animate button to turn on animation recording. Drag the Time Slider to frame 200. Rotate the Sphere02 (larger) object around the Z axis. Click on the Animate button to turn off animation recording. Scrub the Time Slider a few times to confirm that the Sphere02 object is animated.

6. Execute the script again. Maximize the ROTATE.MS window. Select Evaluate All from the ROTATE.MS window's File menu. The script executes again. Minimize the ROTATE.MS window. Drag the Time Slider. Now the Sphere01 object rotates properly.

So why did it work this time? Again, look at the script. The fourth line gets the current Z rotation value of the Sphere02 object. The key word here is *current*. As the Z rotation value of the Sphere02 object changes, so does the value captured. The fourth line is repeated 201 times, once for each frame in the animation. At a given frame, the fourth line asks, "What is the current Z rotation value of the Sphere02 object?" The Sphere02 object is changing on every frame, so the answer changes also.

The two-sphere example here and in the expressions chapter, shows how to reach the same animation goal by using expressions and MAXScript. It would make more sense to use an expression for this example. However, you have more control if you use scripts; note how the **for/loop** defined the range of animation. Changing the 0 to 50 and the 200 to 100 would only create keyframes for frames 50 to 100. An expression starts on the first frame and ends on the last frame. Changing the **by** value to 5 would create keyframes on every fifth frame.

A script can execute a number of instructions. In the previous example, you repeated two lines of code. You could have just as easily repeated two hundred lines of code. An expression can handle a few instructions; one script can alter multiple parameters of multiple objects. In the previous example, you changed one parameter—the Z rotation track. You could have altered numerous parameters, including scale, rotation, movement, visibility, material, and color. You could do the same with expressions, but you would have to use one for each animation track.

Controlling Landing Gear With MAXScript

Now it's time to move on to a more complex example. For your next trick, you'll create a script that controls a flying saucer's landing gear. The script will control the extension and retraction of the landing gear based on the altitude of the saucer. When the saucer descends past a certain altitude, the gear will extend. When the saucer rises past a certain altitude, the gear will retract.

You'll start by loading the necessary geometry file:

THE GEAR.MS SCRIPT

GEAR.MS, in the \CHAP_21 directory of the companion CD-ROM, contains the completed script for this example. Load this script and refer to it if you get into trouble. DGEAR.MAX, also in the \CHAP_21 directory, shows the result of the script. Load this geometry file and refer to it if you get into trouble.

1. Load 3D Studio MAX, or save your current MAX scene and reset the program. To clear the listener window, click on its title bar. Press Ctrl-A to select all text in the listener window. Press the Delete key to remove the text.

2. Load GEAR.MAX from the \CHAP_21 directory of the companion CD-ROM. You'll see a flying saucer, a ground plane, and a Target Camera.

3. Drag the Time Slider and observe the animation. The saucer moves along the Z axis. It descends between frames 0 and 100 and rests between frames 100 and 150. Finally, the saucer rises between frame 150 and 250.

The Saucer object is the parent of a number of parts. It uses three legs that extend when it lands. Each leg consists of two objects: a leg and a pad; the leg is the parent of the pad.

4. Click on the Select By Name button, then check Display Subtree. Note the three sets of legs, LandingLeg01, LandingLeg02, and LandingLeg03. During extension or retraction, the three legs rotate around their X axes.

At this point, you have enough information to create the script. You'll get the current altitude from the Saucer object's Z axis. Based on the current altitude, you'll rotate the three LandingLeg objects about their X axes.

5. Click on the Utilities panel to display the currently loaded utilities, then click on the MAXScript button. The lower section of the panel reveals the MAXScript UI.

6. Click on the Open Listener button—the MAXScript Listener window appears—then click on the New Script button. An untitled script window appears.

The first line of your script is a remark announcing the purpose of the script. Remarks are highly useful; they explain what the script is doing step-by-step. They also help others understand your code. Any text that begins with two hyphens(- -) is considered a remark. MAXScript ignores remarks and moves on to the next line of code.

7. Enter the remark line as it appears in Listing 21.4, ending it with a carriage return (press Enter):

Listing 21.4 The first line of code (a remark).

```
-- landing gear rotation script
```

CLEARING THE LISTENER WINDOW

At times, you may want to clear the Listener window. Click on it to activate it, press Ctrl+A to select all the text in the window, and press the Delete key. This deletes all the text and clears the Listener window.

Defining Variables

Now that you know what the script does, you'll define some variables:

1. Press Enter to skip a line. Enter the variable-definitions code as it appears in Listing 21.5.

Listing 21.5   The variable-definitions section of your script.

```
-- Now define a few variables
check_obj = $Saucer
gear_obj = $LandingLeg01
start_frame = 0
end_frame = 250
start_alt = 1500
end_alt = 250
extend_angle = 50
retract_angle = 0
diff = extend_angle - retract_angle
divider = (start_alt - end_alt)/diff
```

Take a look at the variable-definitions code. The first line is a remark explaining the purpose of this section of code. The next eight lines define a series of variables. Note how all eight lines follow the same format. The left side of the equal sign is the variable. The right side of the equal sign is the value the variable should take. A space on both sides of the equal sign is not required, but it makes for easier reading.

The script uses two objects from the scene: Saucer and LandingLeg01. You'll get the current altitude from the Saucer object. The LandingLeg01 object will rotate based on the altitude of the first object. You'll rotate the LandingLeg01 object first. So you need two variables: one for the Saucer object and one for the LandingLeg01 object. The second line stores the Saucer object in the **check_obj** variable. The **check_obj** variable represents the saucer object. Altering the **check_obj** variable, alters the saucer object. The third line stores the value of the LandingLeg01 object in the **gear_obj** variable. Again, the **gear_obj** variable represents the LandingLeg01 object.

Next, you need to create a number of variables that store important values. The script needs to know when to start and stop recording frames. The next two lines set these limits. The **start_frame** variable tells the script to start recording on frame 0. The **end_frame** variable tells the script when to stop recording: on frame 250.

The script also needs to know at what altitude the gear should begin to extend. The sixth line stores this value in the **start_alt** variable; the gear begins to extend at 1500. Then, the script needs to know when the gear should reach full extension. The seventh line stores this value in the **end_alt** variable. So the gear reaches full extension at an altitude of 250. Your script could use fixed numbers instead of the above variables. But if you later want to change the ending altitude you would have to search the entire script for the 250 value. It's easier to define a variable in the beginning of your script, like **end_alt**. Following lines refer to the **end_alt** variable, not a fixed number repeated throughout the script. Changing the end_alt value requires a change on one line, not throughout the script. This is the power of using variables.

Next, the script needs to know how far to rotate the target object. The **extend_angle** variable defines the target object's extend angle; the Gear object reaches full extension at an angle of 50. The **retract_angle** variable defines the target object's retract angle; the Gear object reaches full retraction at an angle of 0.

Finally, the script needs to compute values based on the variables already created. The first variable, **diff**, holds the difference between the extend and retract angle of the landing leg01 object. So far, this variable equals 50 (50 - 0 = 50). The second variable, **divider**, breaks the difference between the two altitudes into 50 "chunks." The role of these two variables will become evident later in the chapter. With your variables defined, it's time to move to the meat of the script.

Rotating The Landing Gear

Next, you'll create the code that rotates the landing gear. Your script will carry out the following tasks:

1. Turn on the Animate button.

2. Repeat the following tasks over a user defined range of frames.

3. Check the current altitude of the Saucer object and compare it to the start and end altitude variables.

4. Extend the landing gear if the Saucer object's altitude falls under the start altitude.

5. Retract the landing gear if the Saucer object's altitude is above the start altitude.

Step #1: Turning On Animation

Now you'll turn on the Animate button with your script:

1. Add the **animate on** command to the end of your script. Your script should resemble Listing 21.6.

Listing 21.6   The **animate on** command is added.

```
-- landing gear rotation script

 -- Now define a few variables
check_obj = $Saucer
gear_obj = $LandingLeg01
start_frame = 0
end_frame = 250
start_alt = 1500
end_alt = 250
extend_angle = 50
retract_angle = 0
diff = extend_angle - retract_angle
divider = (start_alt - end_alt)/diff

 -- turn on the Animate button
animate on
```

Step #2: Creating A Loop

Now, you'll create a for loop that repeats based on the **start_frame** and **end_frame** variables:

1. Take a look at the **for/loop** command in Listing 21.7.

Listing 21.7   The **for/ loop** command.

```
for t in start_frame to end_frame by 1 do at
time t
```

Note the **start_frame** and **end_frame** variables used in the command. Remember, you defined these two variables at the beginning of the script. The **start_frame** variable equals 0, and the **end_frame** variable equals 250.

2. You can replace the variables with their actual values to make the command easier to understand. Take a look at Listing 21.8.

Listing 21.8   The **for /loop** command exposed.

```
for t in 0 to 250 by 1 do at time t
```

3. The **for /loop** command in Listing 21.8 will start at frame 0 and repeat until frame 250 is reached. The value is stored in the **t** variable. So on frame 0, "t" equals 0. On frame 250, "t" equals 250. The **by 1** portion of the command tells the script to count using units of 1. The **at time** t portion defines the value stored in "t" as time. Add the **for /loop** command in Listing 21.7 to your script. Your script should resemble Listing 21.9. Note the open parenthesis on the last line.

Listing 21.9   The **for loop** command added to your script.

```
-- landing gear rotation script
-- Now define a few variables
check_obj = $Saucer
gear_obj = $LandingLeg01
start_frame = 0
end_frame = 250
start_alt = 1500
end_alt = 250
extend_angle = 50
retract_angle = 0
```

```
diff = extend_angle - retract_angle
divider = (start_alt - end_alt)/diff

 -- turn on the Animate button
animate on

 -- rotate the landing gear
for t in start_frame to end_frame by 1 do at
time t
(
```

Step #3: Comparing Altitude

Now you'll compare the Saucer object's current altitude with the **start_alt** and **end_alt** variables:

1. You'll use an **if/then** command to execute the comparison. The format of an **if/then** command appears in Listing 21.10.

Listing 21.10 The format of an **if/then** statement.

```
if 2 + 2 = 4 then
(
  print "hi"
  print "how are you"
  print "bye"
)
```

The **if/then** command begins by checking for a condition. If the condition is met, then a series of commands, which are enclosed in parentheses, are executed. If the condition is not met, then the commands within the parentheses are skipped.

The first line in Listing 21.10 asks, "Does two plus two equal four?" Because two plus two *does* equal four, the **if/then** statement would return a true state. If two plus two did not equal four, the **if/then** statement would return a false state.

If a true state is set, the commands between parentheses are executed. If a false statement is set, the commands between parentheses are skipped. The code in Listing 21.10 would return a true state and the print commands would execute.

2. So, you need an **if/then** statement to ask the question, "Is the current altitude of the Sau-

cer object between the start and end altitude variables?" Take a look at the **if/then** statement shown in Listing 21.11.

Listing 21.11 An **if/then** statement checking the altitude of the saucer object.

```
if check_obj.pos.z <= start_alt and
check_obj.pos.z > end_alt then
```

A number of variables in Listing 21.11 should look familiar. You defined the **check_obj** variable at the beginning of your script. The **check_obj** variable currently stores the Saucer object's value. The **.pos.z** portion of the variable "pulls" just the Z position from the Saucer object. Thus, the **check_obj.pos.z** variable equals the Saucer object's current Z position.

The **start_alt** variable stores the value 1500. The **end_alt** variable stores the value 250. As with the for loop command, you can replace the variables with their actual values to make the command easier to understand. The **if/then** command shown in Listing 21.12 replaces the variables with their actual values.

Listing 21.12 The **if/then** statement exposed.

```
if check_obj.pos.z <= 1500 and
check_obj.pos.z > 250 then
```

The **check_obj.pos.z** variable remains because it changes over time. Remember, this is the current value of the Saucer object's Z position. When the saucer moves up or down, the value of the **check_obj.pos.z** variable changes.

Most often, you'll create **if/then** statements that check for one condition. The **if/then** command in Listing 21.12 checks for two conditions. The give-away? The **and** in the middle of the command. The **and** portion separates the **if/then** command into two conditions. The first condition asks, "Is the

Saucer object's Z position less than or equal to 1500?" The second condition asks, "Is the Saucer object's Z position greater than 250?"

If both conditions are false, the script skips the commands enclosed in the **if/then** statement. If one condition is true and the other false, again, the script skips the commands enclosed in the **if/then** statement. If both conditions are true, the script executes the commands enclosed in the **if/then** statement.

3. Add the **if/then** command to your script. At this point, your script should resemble the code shown in Listing 21.13.

Listing 21.13   Your script—so far.

```
-- landing gear rotation script
-- Now define a few variables
check_obj = $Saucer
gear_obj = $LandingLeg01
start_frame = 0
end_frame = 250
start_alt = 1500
end_alt = 250
extend_angle = 50
retract_angle = 0
diff = extend_angle - retract_angle
divider = (start_alt - end_alt)/diff

 -- turn on the Animate button
animate on

 -- rotate the landing gear
for t in start_frame to end_frame by 1 do at
time t
(
  if check_obj.pos.z <= start_alt and
check_obj.pos.z > end_alt then
```

Step #4: Rotating The Gear

Next, you need to come up with a formula that rotates the landing gear based on the Saucer object's altitude:

1. Take a look at the code shown in Listing 21.14.

Listing 21.14   The formula that produces the proper rotation value.

```
calc = -(((check_obj.pos.z - end_alt)/
divider)- extend_angle)
```

The code in Listing 21.14 looks just like the variable definitions you created earlier. The left side of the equal sign defines the name of a variable. In Listing 21.14, the variable is called **calc**. The right side of the equal sign computes a value that's stored in the **calc** variable.

2. Replace the variables with actual numbers. For this exercise, assume the saucer has descended to an altitude of 1500. Listing 21.15 show, the formula with actual numbers.

Listing 21.15   The formula with actual numbers.

```
calc = -(((1500 - 250)/25)-50)
```

The 1500 value is based on the current altitude of the Saucer object. The 250 value is based on the **end_alt** variable, which is set to 250. The 25 value is based on the value of **start_alt** minus the value of **end_alt**, which equals 1250. This value is divided by 50, producing the result 25. The 50 value is based on the **extend_angle** variable, which is set to 50.

The innermost parentheses are executed first. So, 250 is subtracted from 1500, producing 1250. This value is divided by 25, producing 50. This value subtracts 50 and the result is 0. The negative sign after the equal sign produces the final result, which is -0. So, when the Saucer object descends to an altitude of 1500, the landing gear rotates -0 degrees. Because 1500 is the starting altitude, the -0 result is exactly what you want.

3. Repeat this process for a lower altitude. Let's assume the Saucer object has descended to an altitude of 625 units. The formula will be as follows (see Listing 21.16):

Listing 21.16 The formula when the Saucer object is at an altitude of 625 units.

```
calc = -(((625 - 250)/25)-50)
```

In this formula, 250 is subtracted from 625, producing 375. This value is divided by 25, producing 15. This value subtracts 50 and the result is -35. The negative sign after the equal sign produces the final result, which is 35. Therefore, when the Saucer object descends to an altitude of 625, the landing gear rotates 35 degrees, from its starting position.

4. You'll repeat this process one final time. Assume the Saucer object has descended to an altitude of 250, which is the end altitude limit. The formula will now be as shown in Listing 21.17.

Listing 21.17 The formula when the Saucer object is at an altitude of 250 units.

```
calc = -(((250 - 250)/25)-50)
```

Now, 250 is subtracted from 250, producing 0. This value is divided by 25, producing 0. This value subtracts 50 and the result is -50. The negative sign after the equal sign produces the final result, 50. So when the Saucer object descends to an altitude of 250, the landing gear rotates 50 degrees. Note that full extension for the gear is 50 degrees; thus the gear extends fully when the **end_alt** limit is reached.

5. The result of this calculation is stored in the **calc** variable. Now, you need to store the **calc** value in the LandingLeg01 object, as shown in Listing 21.18.

Listing 21.18 Storing the **calc** value in the LandingLeg01 object.

```
gear_obj.rotation.x_rotation = calc
```

You defined the **gear_obj** variable so that it equals the LandingLeg01 object. The **gear_obj.rotation.x_rotation** "points" to the LandingLeg01 object's X rotation track. The code in Listing 21.18 stores the **calc** variable's value in the LandingLeg01 object's X rotation track.

6. Next, add the code that causes the LandingLeg01 object to rotate based on the altitude of the Saucer object. Your script should resemble Listing 21.19. Note the use of indentation to organize code within for/ loops and if/then statements.

Listing 21.19 Your current script.

```
-- landing gear rotation script
-- Now define a few variables
check_obj = $Saucer
gear_obj = $LandingLeg01
start_frame = 0
end_frame = 250
start_alt = 1500
end_alt = 250
extend_angle = 50
retract_angle = 0
diff = extend_angle - retract_angle
divider = (start_alt - end_alt)/diff

  -- turn on the Animate button
animate on

  -- rotate the landing gear
for t in start_frame to end_frame by 1 do at
time t
(
  if check_obj.pos.z <= start_alt and
check_obj.pos.z end_alt then
  (
    calc = -(((check_obj.pos.z - end_alt)/
divider)-extend_angle)

  gear_obj.rotation.x_rotation = calc )
)
```

"Exceeding Ship Design Parameters, Captain!"

At this point, you've told the script what to do if the Saucer object is between both altitude limits.

However, you have not told the script what to do when the Saucer Object is *above* the altitude limits. To do so, follow these steps:

1. Basically, you need to check to see if the Saucer object is above the value of the **start_alt** variable. If it is, set the LandingLeg01 object to its retracted position. Take a look at Listing 21.20.

Listing 21.20 Is the Saucer object above the start_alt value?

```
if check_obj.pos.z > start_alt then
(
  gear_obj.rotation.x_rotation =
retract_angle
)
```

The **if/then** statement in Listing 21.20 asks, "Is the Saucer object's Z position greater than the value stored in the **start_alt** variable?" This statement would return a true state if the Saucer object's Z position was 1501 or greater. If a true state is reached, the retract angle is stored in the LandingLeg01 object's X rotation track.

2. Add this portion of code to complete your script. Your script should resemble Listing 21.21. Note the matching open and closed parentheses.

Listing 21.21 Your finished script.

```
-- landing gear rotation script
-- Now define a few variables
check_obj = $Saucer
gear_obj = $LandingLeg01
start_frame = 0
end_frame = 250
start_alt = 1500
end_alt = 250
extend_angle = 50
retract_angle = 0
diff = extend_angle - retract_angle
divider = (start_alt - end_alt)/diff

  -- turn on the Animate button
animate on
```

```
  -- rotate the landing gear
for t in start_frame to end_frame by 1 do at
time t
(
  if check_obj.pos.z <= start_alt and
check_obj.pos.z > end_alt then
  (
    calc = -(((check_obj.pos.z - end_alt)/
divider)-extend_angle)

  gear_obj.rotation.x_rotation = calc
  )

  if check_obj.pos.z > start_alt then
  (
  gear_obj.rotation.x_rotation =
retract_angle
  )
)
```

3. Save the script and give it a try. Make sure GEAR.MAX is loaded from the companion CD-ROM's \CHAP_21 directory. Click on the Script window and press Ctrl+E to execute the script. If you entered everything correctly, the Listener window will report OK.

4. Drag the Time Slider and observe the Saucer object. As the Saucer Object descends, the LandingLeg01 object extends.

Extending The Remaining Landing Gear

Next, you'll extend the remaining LandingLeg objects:

1. Change "gear_obj = $LandingLeg01" to "gear_obj = $LandingLeg02". Execute the script again.

2. Drag the Time Slider and observe the results. Now, two of the three legs extend.

3. Finally, change "gear_obj = $LandingLeg02" to "gear_obj = $LandingLeg03" and repeat the process. Now, all three legs extend properly.

The variable-definition section defines the important values your script needs to function. You can change the variables at the beginning of the script to suit your needs. For example, change the **end_alt** variable to define a new end altitude limit. The **check_obj** variable should change to reflect the axis used to define altitude.

So, if you use this script in another scene that uses a Y position to define altitude, change the **check_obj** variable to **check_obj.pos.y**. The **gear_obj** variable should change to reflect the axis used for pivoting. For example, if the landing gear of another object pivots on the Z axis, you would change the **gear_obj** variable to **gear_obj.rotation.z**.

Moving On

In the next chapter, you'll continue your look at MAXScript by investigating behavioral motion. With MAXScript, you can set up a script that makes a butterfly flutter around your screen with natural movements. With a little tweaking, you can also use this script to create flocking behavior—and produce anything from fluttering butterflies to schooling fish.

22

A LOOK AT MAXSCRIPT, PART II

BY

SCOT TUMLIN

In this chapter, you will create two scripts that will explore motion path animation, random number generation, and the Bend modifier.

The first script will animate a butterfly along a motion path. The script will randomly slide and bank the butterfly; it will also create a hoplike flight path for the butterfly. Finally, the script will control a Bend modifier assigned to the butterfly's wings.

The second script will cause a second butterfly to follow the first. The second script randomly slides the second butterfly based on the movement of the first butterfly. It will also cause the second butterfly to follow the first at a preset distance.

The Flap Script

Let's get to it! To make your butterfly zip around, do the following:

1. Start 3D Studio MAX, or save your current MAX scene and reset the program.

2. Click on the Utilities panel to access your 3D Studio MAX utilities.

3. Click on the MAXScript button. The Utilities panel expands, displaying the MAXScript tools.

4. Click on the Open Listener button to open the Listener window.

5. Click on the New Script button to open a new script window.

6. Load BFLY.MAX from the \CHAP_22 directory of the companion CD-ROM. You'll see that the scene displays a butterfly.

Move the Time Slider. The butterfly moves along a predefined motion path. Next, you'll create a list of tasks for the script:

- Add random movement to the left/right of the motion path.

- Add random bank to the butterfly's flight.

- Make the butterfly hop as it moves along the path.

- Flap the butterfly's wings based on ascent and descent.

Creating The Variables

Now that you know the script's features, you'll create the necessary variables. Your script will animate a butterfly over time; thus, you'll need variables for the start and end frames. Your script will apply animation to an object selected from your scene, so you'll need a variable that stores data from the selected object. The butterfly is a child of a Dummy object and the Dummy object is assigned to the path. Because the butterfly is a child of the Dummy object, the butterfly follows the Dummy object along the path.

1. Take a look at the code in Listing 22.1. The four variables store the frame and object values you'll need to get the script started.

2. Enter the code as it appears in Listing 22.1 to the beginning of your script.

Listing 22.1 The start of the script, with initial variables defined.

```
-- first we define some variables
  start_frame = 1
  end_frame = 300
  pick_obj = $ButterflyBody
```

USE CTRL+D!

Use Ctrl+D to color-code your scripts for easier viewing and debugging.

The first line in Listing 22.1 is a remark that explains the purpose of this section of code. The second and third lines tell the script when to begin recording animation and when to stop recording animation. The fourth line tells the script to animate the ButterflyBody object. Usually, only these three variables are required. Most, if not all, animation scripts need to know three things:

- When to start animating.

- When to stop animating.

- What object in the scene to animate.

Creating Left/Right Deviation From The Motion Path

Now you can tackle left/right deviation, the first task of this script. This is an animation script, so you'll need to turn on the Animate button and create a **for loop**.

1. Add the **animate on** command to your script and create a **for loop**. Your code should resemble Listing 22.2.

Listing 22.2 The **animate on** and **for loop** commands added.

```
-- first we define some variables
  start_frame = 1
  end_frame = 300
  pick_obj = $ButterflyBody

-- now we animate
animate on
(
  for t in start_frame to end_frame by 1 do at time t
  (
```

The **animate on** command turns on the Animate button. This should be old news by now. Note the open parenthesis under the **animate on** command; this defines the start of the commands that will create animation.

Note: *This book's margins cause some commands to appear on two or more lines. In the Listener window, the italicized commands actually fit on one line.*

The **for loop** command stores the current frame number in the variable t. The **start_frame** variable defines the frame to begin recording, frame 1. The **end_frame** variable defines the frame to end recording, frame 300. The **by 1** portion of the command increments by 1. The **do at time t** portion tells the script that the **t** variable is time. Note the parenthesis under the **for loop** command. The parenthesis defines the start of the commands that will repeat 300 times.

Now, you'll create the code that randomly moves the butterfly to the left and right of the path. The key word is "random." The script should create a random number. MAXScript has a command called **random** that generates a random number within a given range. Listing 22.3 shows the format of the **random** command:

Listing 22.3   MAXScript's **random** command.

```
R = (random 1 10)
```

2. Take a look at the random command in Listing 22.3. When this command is executed, the **R** variable takes on a value between 1 and 10, inclusive. Execute the command a second time and the **R** value will change to another number.

3. Give it a try: Type the code in Listing 22.3 in the Listener window and press Enter. The Listener window returns a value in blue text. Note that the number falls within the range of 1 and 10, inclusive.

4. Delete the answer, press Enter a few more times, and note how the result is different.

So how can you use this command? Your objective is to randomly move the butterfly to the left and right of the path. You can replace the 1 and 10 (Listing 22.3) with numbers that define the limit of left/right travel away from the path. You could enter fixed values, but it makes more sense to create a new variable that you can always change later.

Listing 22.4   MAXScript's **random** command added to the butterfly script.

```
-- first we define some variables
   start_frame = 1
   end_frame = 300
   pick_obj = $ButterflyBody

   lr_max = 250

-- animation code here
 animate on
 (
```

```
for t in start_frame to end_frame by 1 do at time t
(
  lr_dev = (random -lr_max lr_max)

  print lr_dev
)
)
```

The code in Listing 22.4 includes the **random** command and a few other changes. Note the **lr_max** variable added at the sixth line. This variable stores the maximum number of units the butterfly is allowed to move from the path. The **lr_max** variable is currently set to 250 units. Also, the **random** command was added after the **for loop** command. The line reads

```
lr_dev = (random -lr_max lr_max)
```

If you replace the **lr_max** variable with its actual value, you'll get

```
lr_dev = (random -250 250)
```

Compare this to the **random** command discussed earlier in Listing 22.3. The **random** command generates a value between -250 and 250. The result is stored in the **lr_dev** variable.

You'll see if this really works.

> ### THE PRINT COMMAND
>
> You can use the **print** command to debug your scripts. Adding a **print** command to your script sends information to the Listener window. The command is simple to use. Type "print" followed by the variable you want to observe/debug. For example, "print t" sends the value of the **t** variable to the Listener window. Once you have debugged your scripts, remove the print command.

5. Add the **lr_max** variable and **random** command to your script. Also, add the two parentheses at the end of the script. Finally, add the **print** command to send output to the listener window. Your script should resemble the code shown in Listing 22.4.

6. Select the script window and press Ctrl+E to execute the script. Take a look at your scene—nothing happens because you haven't assigned animation to objects in your scene. Take a look at the Listener window. A series of numbers should appear; 300 to be exact. Note how the numbers range from -250 to 250. You are looking at the value of the **lr_dev** variable on each frame of your animation.

7. At this point, you can assign the value of the **lr_dev** variable to your butterfly. Add the code necessary to store the **lr_dev** variable in the X position of the ButterflyBody object. Your script should resemble Listing 22.5.

Listing 22.5   The random result assigned to the Butterfly.

```
-- first we define some variables
  start_frame = 1
```

```
    end_frame = 300
    pick_obj = $ButterflyBody

    lr_max = 250

-- animation code here
  animate on
  (
    for t in start_frame to end_frame by 1 do
  at time t
    (
      lr_dev = (random -lr_max lr_max)

      in coordsys world pick_obj.pos.x = lr_dev


    )
  )
```

The **print** command is replaced with a new line. The new line starts with "in coordsys world". This portion of the line defines MAX's coordinate system to world. The remaining portion of the line, "pick_obj.pos.x = lr_dev", stores the random value from the **lr_dev** variable in the Butterfly object's X position. You'll see what happens.

8. Click inside the script window and press Ctrl+E to execute the script. Move the Time Slider and observe the butterfly in the Top viewport window (see Figure 22.1). You can also right-click on the ButterflyBody object and turn on Display Trajectory.

As the figure indicates, the Butterfly object's X position does randomly change, but the butterfly is centered around the origin (Figure 22.1). The butterfly should be centered around the Dummy object assigned to the path. Take a look at the code in Listing 22.6.

Listing 22.6   Now the butterfly centers around the Dummy object.

```
-- first we define some variables
    start_frame = 1
    end_frame = 300
    pick_obj = $ButterflyBody
    path_obj = $Bdummy
    lr_max = 250
```

```
-- animation code here
  animate on
  (
    for t in start_frame to end_frame by 1 do
  at time t
    (
      lr_dev = (random -lr_max lr_max)

      in coordsys world pick_obj.pos.x =
  path_obj.pos.x + lr_dev

    )
  )
```

Note the change in the last line. You still use the world coordinate system, but the latter portion of the line has changed. The **lr_dev** variable was added to the path object's X position. This creates the offset you need. A new variable definition was also added in line 6. The new variable, **path_obj**, stores the values for the object assigned to the path, Bdummy. Add the changes to your script and give it a try!

9. Move the Time Slider to frame 0. If necessary, center the ButterflyBody object with the Bdummy object. Highlight the script window and press Ctrl+E to execute the script. Move the Time Slider and observe the result in the top viewport window. Now the butterfly moves around the Dummy object.

So what happened? The new code adds the random value to the Dummy object's X position. For example, if the random value is 100 and the Dummy object's X position is 50, the Butterfly object's X position would equal 150. This puts the Butterfly object's X position 100 units to the right of the Dummy object, which is your goal (Figure 22.2). Figure 22.1 shows the result of the old code. The butterfly's X position equaled 100, which is 100 units to the right of the origin; this is not your goal. Figure 22.2 shows the result of the new code; now, the butterfly randomly moves to the left and right of the Dummy object. Because the script generates random numbers, the butterfly's movement

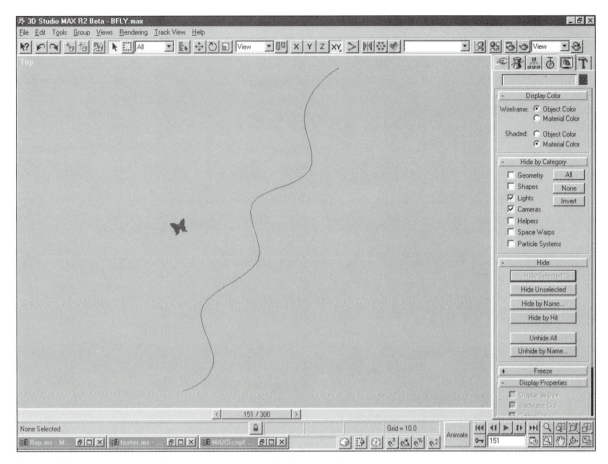

Figure 22.1 Oops—the butterfly is not centered over the Dummy object.

will be different every time. You can also experiment with smaller random values to get smoother, more subtle movement.

Adding Random Bank To The Butterfly's Motion

You'll now move on to the next task: adding random bank to the butterfly's flight. Again, you'll generate a random value and add it to the Butterfly object's Y rotation track. First, you'll need a new variable that stores the Butterfly object's initial Y rotation value. Next, you'll need a variable to store the maximum bank angle. You must also generate a random value and store it in a temporary variable. Finally, you'll add the random value to the Butterfly object's Y rotation track.

1. Take a look at the code in Listing 22.7.

Listing 22.7 The result of the new code—the butterfly banks.

```
-- first we define some variables
  start_frame = 1
  end_frame = 300
  pick_obj = $ButterflyBody
  path_obj = $Bdummy
  lr_max = 250

      init_angle = at time 0
pick_obj.rotation.y_rotation

  bank_max = 25


-- animation code here
 animate on
 (
  for t in start_frame to end_frame by 1 do
at time t
  (
   lr_dev = (random -lr_max lr_max)
```

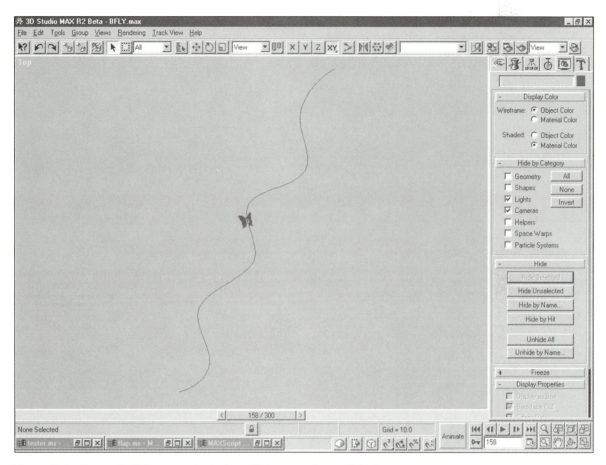

Figure 22.2 The result of the new code; the butterfly is centered around the Dummy object

```
   in coordsys world pick_obj.pos.x =
path_obj.pos.x + lr_dev


   bank_dev = (random -bank_max bank_max)


   about pivot pick_obj.rotation.y_rotation =
init_angle + bank_dev


 )
 )
```

A new variable called **init_angle** appears at line 8. The **init_angle** variable stores the value of the Butterfly object's Y rotation track at frame 0. The **at time 0** portion of the line looks at frame 0. The remainder of the line tells the script to look at the Butterfly object's Y rotation track. The script starts at frame 1, so you can use frame 0 to adjust your objects. Another new variable, called **bank_max**, is added at line 10. This variable stores a value of 25, the maximum bank rotation allowed.

Two additional lines are added at the end of the script. The first generates a random value based on the **bank_max** variable. Basically, the line generates a value from -25 to 25 and stores the value in the **bank_dev** variable. The second line adds the random value stored in **bank_dev** to the Butterfly object's initial Y rotation value. The sum replaces the last value in the Butterfly object's Y rotation track.

2. Add the new code to your script. Your script should then resemble the preceding code in Listing 22.7. Highlight the script window and press Ctrl+E to execute the script. Move the

Time Slider and observe the top viewport window. Now, the butterfly randomly rotates around its Y axis.

3. Switch to the Camera01 object and move the Time Slider, to get a better look (see Figure 22.3).

Getting The Butterfly To Hop

Now, you'll solve the third task—you'll create the hop movement for the butterfly. The butterfly should climb and dive as it moves along the path. The easiest way to produce this type of oscillating movement is to use a sine function. A sine function produces a wavelike path.

Imagine a curve that starts with a value of 0. Over time, this value increments to 1, decrements to -1,

and increments back to 0. Imagine this cycle looping over and over. A sine function produces this type of curve. The same curve would cause the butterfly to climb and dive in a smooth motion. You'll create some code that uses a sine function to alter the altitude of the butterfly. Take a look at the code in Listing 22.8.

Listing 22.8   The script with a sine command added.

```
-- first we define some variables
   start_frame = 1
   end_frame = 300
   pick_obj = $ButterflyBody
   path_obj = $Bdummy
   lr_max = 250
   init_angle = at time 0
pick_obj.rotation.y_rotation
   bank_max = 25
```

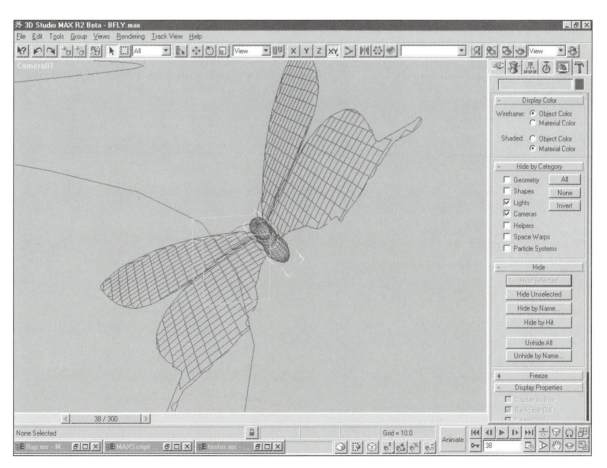

Figure 22.3 Now the butterfly rotates around its Y axis.

```
-- animation code here
 animate on
 (
   for t in start_frame to end_frame by 1 do
at time t
   (
    lr_dev = (random -lr_max lr_max)

    in coordsys world pick_obj.pos.x =
path_obj.pos.x + lr_dev


    bank_dev = (random -bank_max  bank_max)

    about pivot pick_obj.rotation.y_rotation =
init_angle + bank_dev


   vpath = sin t

   print vpath


   )
 )
```

The last two lines were added to the script. The first computes a sine function based on the current frame number and stores this value in the **vpath** variable. The second line prints the current value of the **vpath** variable to the Listener window.

1. Add the two new lines to your script and execute it. Then, take a look in the Listener window. Imagine that the value shown is the butterfly's altitude in relation to the motion path. At frame 0, the butterfly's altitude is 0; the butterfly is on the path. At frame 90, the butterfly rises to an altitude of 1 above the path. At frame 270, the butterfly drops to -1 under the path. The remaining frames increment the butterfly back toward the path.

So the sine function is returning a smooth, wave-like path. However, the 1 to -1 range is too small. To fix this problem, you'll use a multiplier. Take a look at the code in Listing 22.9.

Listing 22.9   Adding a multiplier to the sine command.

```
vpath = (sin t) * 300
```

The line in Listing 22.9 adds a multiplier to the sine function. The sine function is multiplied by 300, which creates a higher value.

2. Add the multiplier to your script and execute the script. Take a look at the Listener window. Instead of 1 to -1, the range is 300 to -300.

3. Take another look at the numbers in the Listener window. The wave takes too long to complete. The butterfly rises to 300 units above the path at frame 90, and drops to -300 units at frame 270. You need a way to control the frequency of the sine wave. A higher frequency produces more wave cycles. Take a look at the following code in Listing 22.10.

Listing 22.10   Increasing the frequency of the sine wave.

```
vpath = sin (t * 5) * 300
```

The **t** variable is multiplied by 5. By multiplying the **t** value by 5, a wave with more frequency is created.

4. Change your script to reflect Listing 22.9 and execute the code again. Take a look at the values generated in the Listener window. Again, imagine that the result in the Listener window is the altitude of the butterfly. At frame 18, the butterfly climbs to 300 units above the motion path. The last set of values in the Listener window didn't reach 300 units until frame 90. This indicates a higher frequency.

Take one more look at the numbers generated in the Listener window. The sine function produces a path that travels above and below the motion path. The butterfly needs a hoplike motion so its path doesn't travel below the motion path (see Figure 22.4).

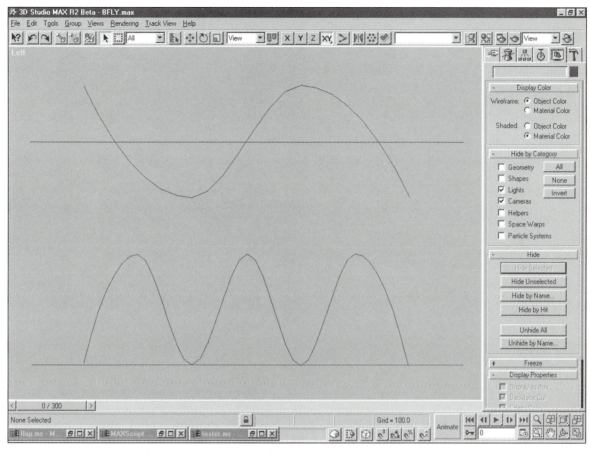

Figure 22.4 A comparison of sine path and the hop path.

The top path in Figure 22.4 shows the result of a sine function. The path travels above and below the motion (horizontal) path. The bottom path produces a hoplike motion, which is your goal. Remember, a standalone sine function starts at 0, increases to 1, descends to -1, and returns to 0. If you could convert the negative values to positive values, you would produce a hoplike motion. You'll make this change using the ABS function.

5. Take a look at the following line of code in Listing 22.11.

Listing 22.11 Comparison of sine path and "hop" path.

```
vpath = abs(sin (t*5) * 300)
```

Compare the code in Listing 22.11 with the code in Listing 22.10. Note the new **abs** function in Listing 22.11. The **abs** function converts negative values to positive values.

6. Change your code to match Listing 22.11 and execute the script. Observe the results in the Listener window. Now, the negative values are positive.

Again, imagine that the result in the Listener window is the altitude of the butterfly. The butterfly starts on the motion path at frame 0. At frame 18, the butterfly rises to 300 units above the motion path. At frame 36, the butterfly drops to the altitude of the motion path. Now, the **abs** function kicks in and returns positive values. So, instead of dropping below the motion path, the butterfly rises, creating the hop. You'll incorporate the sine function in the next script. Your script should resemble Listing 22.12.

Listing 22.12 The script with sine function incorporated.

```
-- first we define some variables
   start_frame = 1
   end_frame = 300
   pick_obj = $ButterflyBody
   path_obj = $Bdummy
   lr_max = 250

   init_angle = at time 0
pick_obj.rotation.y_rotation

   bank_max = 25
   alt_max = 300
   freq = 5

-- animation code here
 animate on
 (
   for t in start_frame to end_frame by 1 do
at time t
   (
   lr_dev = (random -lr_max lr_max)

   in coordsys world pick_obj.pos.x =
path_obj.pos.x + lr_dev


   bank_dev = (random -bank_max bank_max)


   about pivot pick_obj.rotation.y_rotation =
init_angle + bank_dev

   vpath = abs(sin (t*freq) * alt_max)

   in coordsys world pick_obj.pos.z =
path_obj.pos.z + vpath


   )
 )
```

Examine the changes made to the script. First, two new variables are added to the variable definition section. The first variable, **alt_max**, sets the maximum altitude of the butterfly to 300. The second variable, **freq**, sets the initial frequency for the sine function to 5. You'll substitute these defined variables for the numeric values you used to develop your script.

Both variables are used at the end of the script. The line

```
vpath = abs(sin (t*freq) * alt_max)
```

starts by multiplying the **t** variable by 5, the current value of the **freq** variable. Next, a sine wave is created from the result. The sine wave is multiplied by 300, the current value of the **alt_max** variable. The result is stored in the **vpath** variable.

The next line:

```
in coordsys world pick_obj.pos.z =
path_obj.pos.z + vpath
```

applies the **vpath** value to the Butterfly object's Z position track. First, the coordinate system is set to world. Next, the **vpath** value is added to the Z value of the path object Bdummy. The result is stored in the Butterfly object's Z position track.

7. You'll see what happens. Execute the script and move the Time Slider. Observe the butterfly in the left viewport window (see Figure 22.5). The butterfly hops along the path, while banking and sliding. Three tasks down, one to go!

Making The Butterfly's Wings Flap Based On Rise/Fall

Next, you'll perform the fourth task, flapping the butterfly's wings based on ascent and descent. The butterfly in the scene has four wings. A bend modifier is assigned to each wing. The code you add will change the bend modifier's angle. As the butterfly rises, the max bend angle value allowed will increase, creating a more dramatic flap. As the butterfly descends, the max bend angle value allowed will decrease, creating a subtle flap. You'll use another sine function to create the flap motion. You'll add the code that is necessary to bend one of the butterfly's wings.

1. Take a look at the code in Listing 22.13.

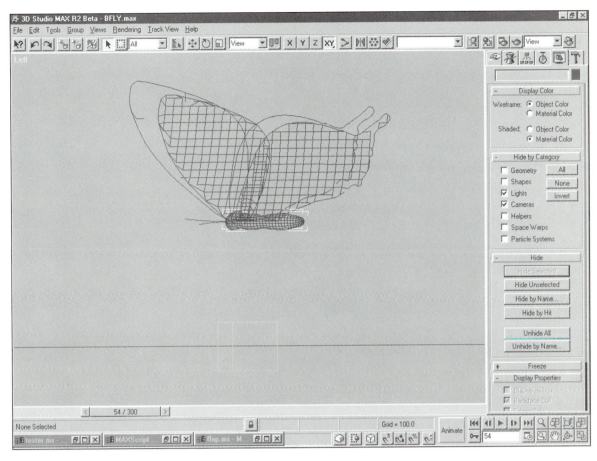

Figure 22.5 Now the butterfly "hops."

Listing 22.13 Note the use of remarks to make the code easier to understand and debug by you and others.

```
-- first we define some variables
   start_frame = 1
   end_frame = 300
   pick_obj = $ButterflyBody
   path_obj = $Bdummy
   lr_max = 250
   init_angle = at time 0
pick_obj.rotation.y_rotation
   bank_max = 25
   alt_max = 300
   freq = 5
   flap_obj = $LowerWingLeft
   flap_max = 60
   flap_freq = 30


-- animation code here
 animate on
(
 for t in start_frame to end_frame by 1 do
at time t
  (
   -- left/right movement
   lr_dev = (random -lr_max lr_max)

   in coordsys world pick_obj.pos.x =
path_obj.pos.x + lr_dev

   -- bank movement
   bank_dev = (random -bank_max bank_max)


   about pivot pick_obj.rotation.y_rotation =
init_angle + bank_dev

   -- hop movement
   vpath = abs(sin (t*freq) * alt_max)

   in coordsys world pick_obj.pos.z =
path_obj.pos.z + vpath
```

```
-- flap movement
  pump = (sin(t*flap_freq)*flap_max)
  flap_obj.bend.angle = pump


 )
)
```

The **flap_obj** variable on line 12 tells the script which object will bend. Currently, the LowerWingLeft object is stored in the **flap_obj** variable. The **flap_max** variable defines the maximum allowed bend angle, which is currently set to 60 degrees. The **flap_freq** variable sets the frequency for the sine function used to bend the wings. With the variables set, you can create the code that bends the wings.

The wings should bend above and below the butterfly's body. This requires a smooth transition between positive and negative values. As demonstrated earlier, a sine function produces a smooth curve. The line

```
pump = (sin(t*flap_freq)*flap_max)
```

in Listing 22.13 starts by multiplying the **t** variable with the **flap_freq** variable. The result is multiplied by the **flap_max** variable. The sine of the result is stored in the **pump** variable.

The next line stores the value of the **pump** variable in a bend modifier. The bend modifier is assigned to LowerWingLeft object. The **flap_obj** portion of the second line stores the name of the object you want to bend. The **.bend** portion of the second line tells the script to focus on the bend modifier assigned to the LowerWingLeft object. The **.angle** portion of the line tells the script to focus on the angle parameter of the bend modifier. You can use this syntax to focus on any track of an object in the scene.

2. Add the new lines to your script, execute the script, and observe the results in the Camera01 window. Note that the LowerWingLeft object bends as the butterfly moves along the path (Figure 22.6).

The next step is to control the bend based on ascent and descent. One way to determine if the butterfly is climbing or diving is to compare its current altitude with its previous altitude. If the current altitude is greater, the butterfly is climbing. If the current altitude is less than the previous altitude, the butterfly is diving. When the butterfly is climbing, set the **bend_max** variable to a higher value. This creates a more dramatic flapping motion. When the butterfly is diving, set the **bend_max** variable to a lower value. This creates a more subtle flapping motion. Take a look at the code in Listing 22.14.

Listing 22.14 Creating a more subtle flapping motion.

```
-- first we define some variables
    start_frame = 1
    end_frame = 300
    pick_obj = $ButterflyBody
    path_obj = $Bdummy
    lr_max = 250
    init_angle = at time 0
pick_obj.rotation.y_rotation
    bank_max = 25
    alt_max = 300
    freq = 5
    flap_obj = $LowerWingLeft
    flap_max = 60
    flap_freq = 30
    last_alt = 0

-- animation code here
 animate on
 (
  for t in start_frame to end_frame by 1 do
at time t
  (
    -- left/right movement
    lr_dev = (random -lr_max lr_max)

    in coordsys world pick_obj.pos.x =
path_obj.pos.x + lr_dev

    -- bank movement
    bank_dev = (random -bank_max bank_max)

    about pivot pick_obj.rotation.y_rotation =
init_angle + bank_dev
```

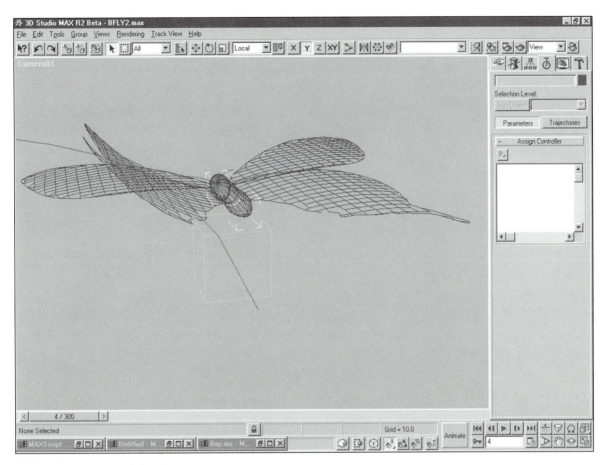

Figure 22.6   The butterfly bends its wing.

```
   -- hop movement
   vpath = abs(sin (t*freq) * alt_max)

   in coordsys world pick_obj.pos.z =
path_obj.pos.z + vpath

   -- flap movement
   now_alt = pick_obj.pos.z
   if now_alt > last_alt then
   (
    flap_max = 60
   )
   else
   (
    flap_max = 10
   )

   pump = (sin(t*flap_freq)*flap_max)
   flap_obj.bend.angle = pump last_alt =
now_alt

   )
  )
```

The **last_alt** variable appears on frame 15. The **last_alt** variable stores the altitude that the Butterfly object was on the previous frame. This variable is compared to the altitude of the Butterfly object at the current frame. The comparison determines whether the butterfly is rising or falling.

The bottom of the script adds a few more lines. The first:

```
now_alt = pick_obj.pos.z
```

stores the altitude of the **pick_obj** at the current frame in the **now_alt** variable. The next line is an **if/then** statement that asks, "Is the **now_alt** variable greater than the **last_alt** variable?" If this statement is true, then the next three lines are executed. If this statement is false, then the three lines that follow the **else** command are executed.

Both sections of the **if/then** statement alter the value of the **flap_max** variable. When the butterfly is rising, the **if/then** statement gets a true condition and the **flap_max** variable is set to 60. When the butterfly is falling, the **if/then** statement gets a false condition and the **flap_max** variable is set to 10.

The last line stores the value of the **now_alt** variable in the **last_alt** variable. How does this line alter the code? Assume that the script is on frame 1 and that the butterfly's altitude is 10. The **now_alt** line is executed and the **now_alt** variable equals 10, the butterfly's altitude. The **if/then** line asks if the **now_alt** variable is greater than the **last_alt** variable, defined as 0 for a starting value. Because 10 is greater than 0, a true condition is returned. The **flap_max** variable is set to 60, and the program moves to the last line. The last line is executed, and the **last_alt** variable equals 10, the current value of the **now_alt** variable.

The **for loop** is executed, and the script moves to frame 2. The butterfly's altitude is now 20. The **now_alt** line is executed, and the **now_alt** variable equals 20, the butterfly's current altitude. The **if/then** line asks if the **now_alt** variable is greater than the **last_alt** variable. The **last_alt** variable still equals 10. Because 20 is greater than 10, a true condition is returned. Again, the **flap_max** variable is set to 60, and the program moves to the last line. The last line is executed, and the **last_alt** variable is set to 20, the current value of the **now_alt** variable. This repeats until the last frame is processed.

The **last_alt** variable always represents the Butterfly object's altitude during the previous frame.

3. Add the new lines to your script, execute the script, and observe the results. As the butterfly rises, the flapping is more dramatic (Figure 22.7a). As the butterfly falls, the flapping is more subtle (Figure 22.7b). Change the **flap_obj** variable to the next wing object and repeat the process. Repeat the process two more times, animating the remaining wing objects.

Customizing The FLAP.MS Script

That wraps up this script. To customize the script, you have a number of parameters to experiment with. First, your scene must contain the following elements:

- A motion path

- An object assigned to the path like the Bdummy object

- An object that is a child of the object assigned to the path, like the ButterflyBody object (i.e., ButterflyBody)

- One or more wing objects like the LowerWindLeft object (i.e., LowerWingLeft)

You can modify the FLAP.MS script to bend all four wings at one time. Your variable defintion section of your script would look like this:

```
-- first we define some variables
    start_frame = 1                  -- store
start frame
    end_frame = 300                  -- store
end frame
    pick_obj = $ButterflyBody        -- object
to animate
    path_obj = $Bdummy               -- object
on path
    lr_max = 250          -- max # units to left
or right of path
init_angle = at time 0
pick_obj.rotation.y_rotation          -- init
angle of pick_obj at frame 0
    bank_max = 15                     -- max #
degrees to roll
    alt_max = 300                     -- max #
units above and below path
    freq = 2                          -- freq of
the sin wave
    flap_obj = $LowerWingLeft         -- object
to flap
    flap_obj2= $LowerWingRight
    flap_obj3 = $UpperWing Left
    flap_obj4 = $UpperWingRight
    flap_max = 60                     -- max #
degrees to flap
    flap_freq = 30                    -- how
often should I flap
    last_alt = 0                      -- alt fm
prev. frame
```

Figure 22.7a A dramatic flap when the butterfly rises.

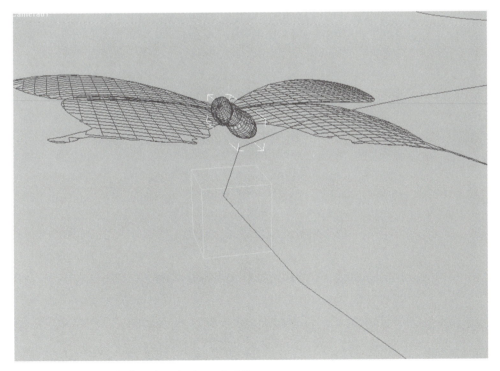

Figure 22.7b A subtle flap when the butterfly falls.

The bend code would look like this:

```
pump = (sin(t*flap_freq)*flap_max)   -- create a sine wave
for the bend
  flap_obj.bend.angle = pump          -- apply the sine wave
to the bend modifier
        flap_obj2.bend.angle = pump
        flap_obj3.bend.angle = pump
        flap_obj4.bend.angle = pump
```

Changing the **start_frame** and **end_frame** variables defines the range of frames to animate. The **pick_obj** variable defines the object you want animated along the path. The **path_obj** variable defines the object assigned to the motion path. The **flap_obj** variable defines the object that should flap during animation.

The **lr_max** variable defines the maximum distance allowed to slide the butterfly to the left and right of the motion path. A higher value causes the butterfly to move farther away from the path. The **init_angle** variable stores the initial angle of the Butterfly object. This value is used as an offset for the random bank code. This variable should always point to frame 0, and the **start_frame** variable should never start at frame 0. This gives you the opportunity to adjust your objects on frame 0.

The **bank_max** variable defines the maximum angle allowed for banking. The higher the number, the more "roll" allowed. The **alt_max** variable defines how high the butterfly can rise. The higher the number, the higher the butterfly can rise. The **freq** variable defines how often the butterfly will hop during the animation sequence. Use a higher number to get more hops during the course of your animation. The **flap_max** variable defines the maximum angle allowed. A higher number produces dramatic flapping motion. Finally, the **flap_freq** variable defines how often the wings should flap. Use a higher number to get more flap cycles completed before the animation ends.

4. When done, save the file and the script.

Adding A Second Butterfly

Next, you'll create a script that moves a second but-terfly based on the movement of the first butterfly.

To create the second butterfly, follow these steps:

1. Start 3D Studio MAX, or save your current MAX scene and reset the program.

2. Click on the Utilities panel to access your 3D Studio MAX utilities.

3. Click on the MAXScript button. The Utilities panel expands, displaying the MAXScript tools.

4. Click on the Open Listener button to open the Listener window.

5. Click on the New Script button to open a new script window.

6. Load BTRACK.MAX from the \CHAP_22 directory of the companion CD-ROM. You'll see that the scene displays two butterflies.

The second butterfly is a copy of the first and uses the same hierarchy; its part names end with 2 (i.e., ButterflyBody2). The parent object of the second butterfly is Bdummy2. The ButterflyBody2 object is a child of the Bdummy2 object, and the remaining body parts are children of ButterflyBody2. The Bdummy_stable object was added to the scene to act as a target object without path rotation. The Bdummy_stable object moves along the path without rotating.

Move the Time Slider. The first butterfly moves along a path with animation created by the FLAP.MS script. You'll create a list of tasks for this script to apply to the second butterfly:

- Add random movement to the left/right of the first butterfly.

- Pivot the second butterfly based on its left/right movement.

- Make the second butterfly follow the first.

- Add random bank to the butterfly's flight.

- Make the butterfly hop as it moves along the path.

- Flap the butterfly's wings based on ascent and descent.

Solving Tasks 4, 5, And 6

Among the tasks listed, numbers 4, 5, and 6 match the tasks of the first script. You'll use the same code to get the same results.

1. Take a look at the script in Listing 22.15. The code resembles the script you created for the first butterfly. You'll start with this script and add the code needed to complete tasks 1, 2, and 3.

2. First, load TASK456.MS from the \CHAP_22 directory of the companion CD-ROM. The script will resemble Listing 22.15.

Listing 22.15   The task456.ms script.

```
-- first we define some variables
start_frame = 1
end_frame = 300
pick_obj = $Bdummy2
trk_obj = $Bdummy_stable
hop_obj = $ButterflyBody2
bank_max = 30

init_angle = at time 0
hop_obj.rotation.y_rotation

alt_max = 400
freq = 2
flap_obj = $LowerWingLeft2
flap_max = 60
flap_freq = 30
last_alt = 0

-- animation code here
animate on

(
for t in start_frame to end_frame by 1 do
at time t
(

-- compute random bank deviation
bank_dev = (random -bank_max
bank_max)

about pivot
hop_obj.rotation.y_rotation =
init_angle + bank_dev

-- compute hop deviation
vpath = abs(sin ((t+30)*freq) * alt_max)

in coordsys world hop_obj.pos.z
=pick_obj.pos.z + vpath
```

```
-- compute flap
now_alt = hop_obj.pos.z
if now_alt > last_alt then
(
 flap_max = 60
)
else
(
 flap_max = 10
)

 pump = (sin(t*flap_freq)*flap_max)
 flap_obj.bend.angle = pump
 last_alt = now_alt


 )
)
```

Examine the variables section in Listing 22.15. The **pick_obj** variable stores values for the object that will receive the animation, Bdummy2. The **trk_obj** variable stores values for the object that the second butterfly tracks, Bdummy_stable. The **hop_obj** variable stores values for the object that will rise and fall, ButterflyBody2. The **inital_angle** variable stores the initial Y rotation value of the **hop_obj** at frame 0. Finally, the **flap_obj** variable stores the name of the object to bend, LowerLeftWing2.

The ButterflyBody2 object values are stored in the **hop_obj** variable. So, the random bank portion of the script replaces the Z position of the **pick_obj** with the **hop_obj**. The second butterfly doesn't move along a motion path, so the hop portion of the code replaces the **path_obj** variable with the **hop_obj** variable. The **pick_obj**, Bdummy2, does not change altitude, so the flap portion of the script stores the altitude of the **hop_obj** in the **now_alt** variable.

You'll see what happens in a second.

3. Execute the script and observe your scene. The second butterfly banks randomly, rises and falls, and bends its LowerWingLeft2 child object.

4. Edit the **flap_obj** variable, changing the LowerWingLeft2 to LowerWingRight2. Run the script again and bend the LowerWingRight2 object. Repeat these two steps for the two upper wings. Now, all four wings should bend (see Figure 22.8).

Creating Random Left/Right Movement For The Second Butterfly

Tasks 4, 5, and 6 are completed. Now, you'll work on the first task, random left/right movement. The first butterfly based its random left/right movement on the motion path. The second butterfly will use the X position of the first butterfly.

1. Take a look at the code in Listing 22.16.

Listing 22.16 The code needed to generate random left/right movement for the second butterfly.

```
-- first we define some variables
    start_frame = 1
end_frame = 300
pick_obj = $Bdummy2
  trk_obj = $Bdummy_stable
  hop_obj = $ButterflyBody2
  bank_max = 30

init_angle = at time 0
hop_obj.rotation.y_rotation

  alt_max = 300
  freq = 2
  flap_obj = $LowerWingLeft2
  flap_max = 60
  flap_freq = 30
  last_alt = 0

  speed = 250

-- animation code here
animate on

(
 for t in start_frame to end_frame by 1 do
at time t
 (
```

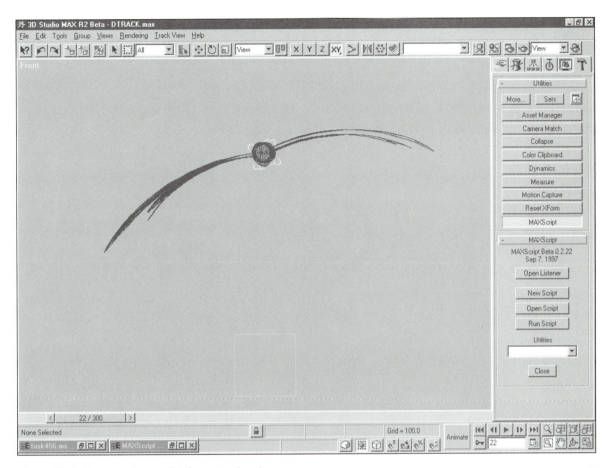

Figure 22.8 The second butterfly's four wings bending.

```
  -- left/right deviation from b1
  tx = trk_obj.pos.x
  direction = (random -1 1)


      pick_obj.pos.x = (direction * speed)
+ tx

  -- compute random bank deviation
bank_dev = (random -bank_max bank_max)

    about pivot hop_obj.rotation.y_rotation =
init_angle + bank_dev

  -- compute hop deviation
  vpath = abs(sin ((t+30)*freq) * alt_max)

  in coordsys world hop_obj.pos.z =
pick_obj.pos.z + vpath

  -- compute flap
  now_alt = hop_obj.pos.z
  if now_alt > last_alt then
```

```
(
 flap_max = 60
)
else
(
 flap_max = 10
)

pump = (sin(t*flap_freq)*flap_max)
flap_obj.bend.angle = pump
last_alt = now_alt


  )
)
```

A new variable, **speed**, is added to the variable definition section. The **speed** variable determines how far the second butterfly should slide. The random slide code is added just after the **for loop** command. The first line stores the current X position of the Bdummy_stable object in the **tx** variable. The next line stores a random number from -1 to 1 in the **direction** variable. A negative value indicates a left direction; a positive value indicates a right direction. The fifth line multiplies the **direction** variable and the **speed** variable.

The result of the random function generates a negative slide to the left or a positive slide to the right. The result is added to the **tx** variable, which centers the second butterfly to the first butterfly. If the result is not added to the **tx** variable, the second butterfly would be centered around the origin at 0,0,0. The sum is stored in the Bdummy2 object's X position track.

2. Add the code to your script. Your script should resemble Listing 22.16. Execute the script and observe the result. The second butterfly randomly slides to the left and right of the first butterfly (Figure 22.9).

Getting The Second Butterfly To Pivot

Now you'll tackle the second task: pivoting the second butterfly based on its left/right movement.

1. Take a look at the code in Listing 22.17.

Listing 22.17 This script causes the second butterfly to slide.

```
-- first we define some variables
    start_frame = 1
  end_frame = 300
  pick_obj = $Bdummy2
  trk_obj = $Bdummy_stable
  hop_obj = $ButterflyBody2
bank_max = 30
```

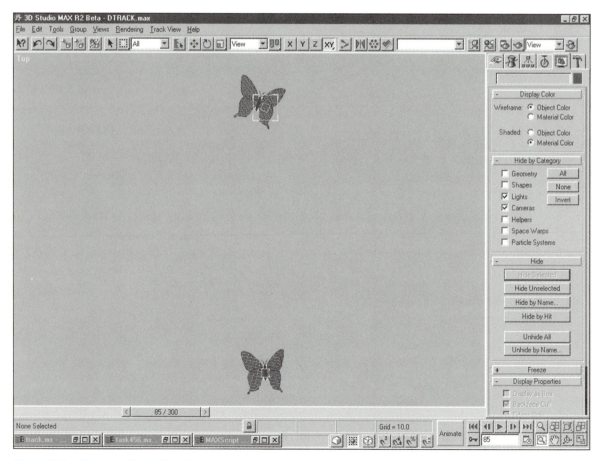

Figure 22.9 The second butterfly sliding along.

```
  init_angle = at time 0
hop_obj.rotation.y_rotation

   alt_max = 300
      freq = 2
      flap_obj = $LowerWingLeft2
      flap_max = 60
      flap_freq = 30
 ast_alt = 0

 speed = 250
 max_pivot = 15

 -- animation code here
 animate on


 (
  for t in start_frame to end_frame by 1 do
 at time t
   (

    -- left/right deviation from b1
    tx = trk_obj.pos.x
    direction = (random -1 1)

         pick_obj.pos.x = (direction * speed) +
 tx

      -- pivot b2 based on direction above
      pick_obj.rotation.z_rotation = direction *
 max_pivot


    -- compute random bank deviation
    bank_dev = (random -bank_max
    bank_max)

    about pivot
    hop_obj.rotation.y_rotation = init_angle +
 bank_dev

    -- compute hop deviation
    vpath = abs(sin ((t+30)*freq) * alt_max)

    in coordsys world hop_obj.pos.z =
 pick_obj.pos.z + vpath

    -- compute flap
    now_alt = hop_obj.pos.z
    if now_alt > last_alt then
    (
     flap_max = 60
```

```
   )
   else
   (
    flap_max = 10
   )

   pump = (sin(t*flap_freq)*flap_max)
   flap_obj.bend.angle = pump
   last_alt = now_alt


  )
 )
```

The first butterfly pivots via the motion path. The second butterfly pivots based on its sliding direction. When the second butterfly slides left, it pivots left. The new variable, **max_pivot**, is added to the variable definition list. The **max_pivot** variable defines the maximum allowed pivot for the ButterflyBody2 object. The pivot portion of the code appears after the random slide portion. The second shaded line of code multiplies the direction variable by the **max_pivot** variable, so if the direction variable generates a negative number, the multiplication generates a negative pivot value. Because a negative value causes a slide to the left, the same negative value causes a pivot to the left.

2. Add the new code. Your script should resemble Listing 22.17. Execute the script and observe the results; the butterfly slides and pivots in the same direction (Figure 22.10).

Making The Second Butterfly Follow The First

Now, you'll solve the final task: making the second butterfly follow the first. The second butterfly should keep a defined distance as it follows the first. The first butterfly moves along the Y axis. The second butterfly's Y position is based on the first butterfly's Y position.

1. Take a look at the code in Listing 22.18.

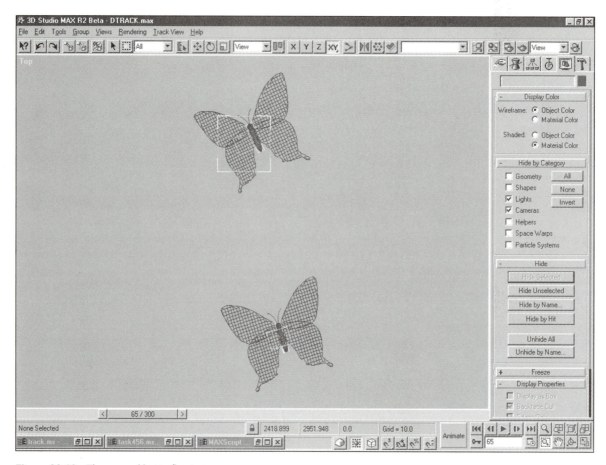

Figure 22.10 The second butterfly pivots.

Listing 22.18 The follow-at-a-distance code is added to the script.

```
-- first we define some variables
  start_frame = 1
end_frame = 300
pick_obj = $Bdummy2
trk_obj = $Bdummy_stable
hop_obj = $ButterflyBody2
bank_max = 30

init_angle = at time 0
hop_obj.rotation.y_rotation

  alt_max = 300
freq = 2
flap_obj = $LowerWingLeft2
flap_max = 60
flap_freq = 30
last_alt = 0

  speed = 250

max_pivot = 15
Shy = 1200


-- animation code here
animate on

(
  for t in start_frame to end_frame by 1 do
at time t
  (

    -- left/right deviation from b1
    tx = trk_obj.pos.x
    direction = (random -1 1)

      pick_obj.pos.x = (direction * speed) +
tx

    -- pivot b2 based on direction above
```

```
    pick_obj.rotation.z_rotation = direction *
max_pivot

    -- keep distance from b1
    ty = trk_obj.pos.y
    pick_obj.pos.y = ty - shy - (random 0
speed)

    -- compute random bank deviation
    bank_dev = (random -bank_max
    bank_max)

    about pivot
    hop_obj.rotation.y_rotation = init_angle +
bank_dev

    -- compute hop deviation
    vpath = abs(sin ((t+30)*freq) * alt_max)


    in coordsys world hop_obj.pos.z =
pick_obj.pos.z + vpath

    -- compute flap
    now_alt - hop_obj.pos.z
    if now_alt > last_alt then
    (
      flap_max = 60
    )
    else
    (
      flap_max = 10
    )

    pump = (sin(t*flap_freq)*flap_max)
    flap_obj.bend.angle = pump
    last_alt = now_alt


  )
)
```

The final variable, **shy**, is added to the variable definition section of the script. The **shy** variable defines the distance between the two butterflies on the Y axis. The higher the value, the more "shy" the second butterfly is. The following portion of code appears after the pivot portion. The **ty** variable stores the current Y position of the first butterfly. The next line generates a random number from 0 to the **speed** variable. The **speed** variable defines the

maximum range the second butterfly can move, so the **random** function returns a random speed value from 0 through 250.

The random result is subtracted from the **shy** variable. This keeps the butterfly within the allowed distance. Finally, this result is subtracted from the **ty** variable, which causes the second butterfly to keep pace with the first butterfly.

2. Add this code to your script. Your script should resemble Listing 22.18. Execute the code and observe the results. The second butterfly follows the first (see Figure 22.11). Your track script is complete.

Customizing The TRACK.MS Script

Refer to "Customizing The FLAP.MS Script" earlier in this chapter to customize the variables not mentioned in this section.

The following lists each variable used in the above scripts with a brief explanation:

- **pick_obj**—Defines the object that follows the first butterfly.

- **trk_obj**—The object in the scene that the **pick_obj** should follow.

- **hop_obj**—The object that should rise and fall based on the **pick_obj**.

- **flap_obj**—Defines the object that should flap during animation.

- **max_pivot**—Defines the maximum allowed pivot angle. Increasing this variable causes the **pick_obj** to pivot more during sliding.

- **speed**—Defines the maximum distance the **pick_obj** can move. Increasing this number moves the **pick_obj** further.

- **shy**—Defines the maximum distance between the two butterflies. Increasing the **shy** value increases the gap between the two butterflies.

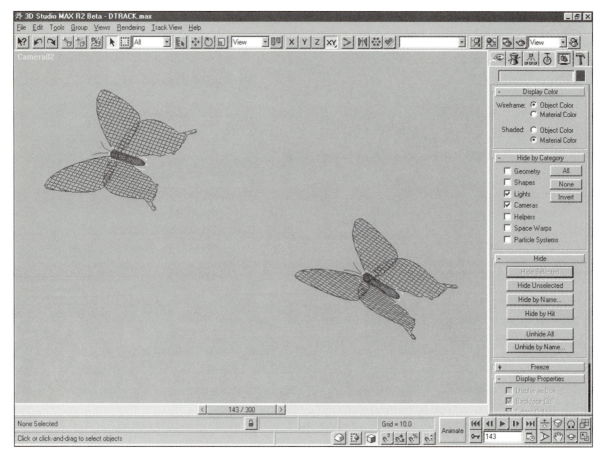

Figure 22.11   The second butterfly follows the first.

Moving On

In the previous four chapters, you took an in-depth look at expressions and scripting with 3D Studio MAX. Both tools add additional levels of control to your scene elements.

This wraps up the "techie" section of this book and, basically, the book itself. You'll find a wealth of MAX and other special-effects information in the appendices.

AFTERWORD

As I mentioned in the introduction (and reiterated in the conclusion) of my first 3D Studio MAX f/x book, I've always been interested in and enjoy what *isn't*, rather than what *is*. I think this is true of most artists, inventors, explorers, scientists, writers, composers, dreamers—people involved in creating and synthesizing something new out of existing materials; people who ask "what if...?"

Although some people might think that many artists enjoy the world of the imagination more so than the so-called "real world," I don't see a disparity between the two. Your imagination—the worlds it creates, the visions it makes into reality—is as tangible and as much a "real" part of you as the color of your eyes and the sound of your voice. The landscape of your imagination is a part of your "real" world, too.

In that sense, computer graphics artists have it perhaps more easy than other artists. Painters can capture real-world or imaginary scenes on canvas, and photographers and filmmakers can capture moving simulations of reality. With a computer and the right graphics software, you can have the best of both worlds. You can create the stylized reality of painting, and combine it with the kinetic movement of filmmaking—and you can do it on your own. You don't need teams of in-house programmers, art critics, or a committee of bean counters to help you envision, create, and visit computer-generated realities.

Ultimately, I hope that this book and the examples contained here have stimulated your creativity, and that you'll go off to not just duplicate the effects contained here, but to expand on them, and show the rest of the world things that we haven't seen before.

Jon A. Bell
April, 1998

3D STUDIO
MAX R2.5
F/X AND DESIGN

APPENDIX A:
ABOUT THE CD-ROM

SETTING UP YOUR MAP PATHS

Most of the maps you need for the tutorials are contained in their respective chapter directories and in the \MAPS directory of your companion CD-ROM.

To make sure you have access to all the maps on the CD-ROM, load 3D Studio MAX Release 2, select File|Configure Paths, and manually add the companion CD-ROM \MAPS directory to your map paths. If you get a "Missing Map" error message when trying to load or render one of the CD-ROM's .MAX files, make sure you've got your map paths set up correctly.

This book includes a standard ISO-9660-format CD-ROM, located in a sleeve on the inside back cover. The CD-ROM contains all of the example animations and images contained in the book, as well as scene files, models, material libraries, and Photoshop 4.0 ATN batch files (used to create effects described in Chapter 17.) The CD-ROM also includes more than 300MB of original texture maps, distributed royalty free and available immediately for your personal use.

Demonstration animations for the chapter tutorials are on the CD-ROM as AVI files rendered at 320×240 resolution. Various figures from each chapter are included in the \FIGURES subdirectories within each chapter's directory. As you follow along with the instructions in each chapter, you will be either viewing or loading pertinent images and mesh and/or scene files from the CD-ROM.

Important: You do not need to install the MAX files from the companion CD-ROM onto your hard drive. If you load the MAX files directly into 3D Studio MAX, the program will automatically add the proper CD-ROM directories to the MAX Map Paths list. Because of the size of the demo animation files, however, you may want to copy them into your 3DSMAX\IMAGES directory and play them back from your hard drive to get better playback speed.

The Directories

The companion CD-ROM contains the following directories:

- \ARTBEATS contains 53 digitized explosion images, courtesy of Artbeats Software (www.artbeats.com).

- \CHAP_03 through \CHAP_22 correspond to the tutorials presented in Chapters 3 through 22. They contain the MAX scene files, textures, and other files required for each chapter's tutorial.

- \DIGIMATN contains demo versions of the Digimation plug-ins Bones Pro, Clay Studio Pro, Shag: Fur, Lightning, Sandblaster, Tree Factory, and Splash! In addition, there are several demonstration .AVIs and image files to preview. Each demo is a self-installing executable file; to install, copy it to a temporary directory on your hard drive, then double-click on the file in Windows Explorer, or use the Start|Run feature of Windows 95 or Windows NT. The file will launch and install the demo on your hard drive; just follow the instructions on your screen.

- \INFOGRAF contains two subdirectories: \PLUGINS and MODELS. The \PLUGINS directory contains compressed (ZIP format) demonstration versions of REM Infografica's MetaREYES, DirtyREYES,

ClothREYES, JetaREYES, and CartoonREYES. To use these plug-ins, copy them to a temporary directory on your hard drive, then use an uncompression utility, such as PK-Zip from PK-Ware, or WinZIP, from Niko-Mak Computing, to unzip the files. Then, double-click on each program's SETUP.EXE file in Windows Explorer, or use the Start|Run feature of Windows 95 or Windows NT. The file will launch and install the demo on your hard drive; just follow the instructions on your screen. The \MODELS directory contains another subdirectory called \KAMOV; in it, you'll find an incredibly detailed version of a Russian Kamov-type helicopter, complete with texture maps. These plug-ins and the model were kindly furnished by REM Infografica, a leading distributor and creator of MAX plug-ins and models. (For more information on its products, contact it online at www.infografica.com.)

- \MAPS contains all the maps used in the book, along with additional maps.

- \MATLIBS contains the MAXFX2.MAT Material Library, which includes all of the materials used in the book's .MAX scene files, as well as some cool additional materials. (Note that you can learn a lot about creating cool materials—especially the new Raytrace materials and maps—by loading some of these pre-built versions, then examining their settings.)

- \PLUGINS contains duplicates of the plug-ins from \CHAP_18 (for those of you who need a reminder of where all this stuff is). This directory contains Tom Hudson's Greeble 1.0 plug-in, and Harry Denholm's Ishani plug-ins (about 20 in all!).

- \PYROMANI contains several image sequences adapted from Visual Concept Engineering's Pyromania CD-ROM series (used by permission from VCE). I've processed the original versions of these images in Photoshop 4.0, and they're suitable for many colorful optical effects. (You can order the originals from VCE and from various 3D software dealers; for more information, see Appendix B and check the various Internet URLs.)

- \SCENES contains two files: the Deep Flight I minisubmarine, built by Scot Tumlin and book author/editor Jon A. Bell, and the Japanese *anime*-style robot featured in Chapter 3, built exclusively for this book. (Feel free to animate him using MAX's inverse kinematics.)

If you have any questions about this book or the CD-ROM contents, feel free to email me at 74124.276@compuserve.com.

THE FIGURES

All the tutorial screen shots presented in this book use the 3D Studio MAX defaults that are present when you first install the program. If you have altered your keyboard hotkey assignments or other user-customizable features of the user interface, you may find that some of the instructions presented here do not correspond precisely with your 3D Studio MAX Release 2 desktop layout.

If you wish, you can change most of your default screen settings back to their defaults by using the File|Preferences Panel. Please see your MAX manuals for further information on configuring your program layout.

APPENDIX B:
3D STUDIO MAX
RESOURCES

At the time I wrote the first *3D Studio MAX f/x* book in 1996, I was beta-testing MAX Release 1, and (of course), there were virtually no online resources devoted specifically to MAX. Consequently, I felt compelled to print a huge amount of information in the appendices of the first book, such as product names, and their respective manufacturers, addresses, and phone numbers.

Since then, the MAX world has expanded tremendously, and the best source for up-to-date information on MAX-related books, plug-ins, training videos, MAX-compliant hardware, and the like, is through the extensive network of online MAX resources. By following only a few of the URLs listed here, you can link to dozens—perhaps hundreds—of Internet sites (both Web pages and newsgroups) that offer a wealth of MAX information. (If you have trouble locating a specific newsgroup or Web page, use a Search engine such as Alta Vista or Yahoo and type "3D STUDIO MAX" to see what's out there.) The newsgroups feature ongoing discussion and debate about their particular topics and can be a good resource if you have questions about 3D Studio/DOS, 3D Studio MAX, and related software and hardware.

The number-one place to find MAX information on the Internet is Kinetix's own Web site at www.ktx.com, of course. Other excellent sources of information include:

- www.3dartist.com—The Web site for *3D Artist Magazine*; also features links to many MAX-related hardware and software vendors as well as The MAX Page, a MAX-specific resources page. Note that this one URL provides links to a huge number of companies that provide MAX-related software and hardware.

- www.3dcafe.com—Another excellent source for 3D models and plug-ins.

- www.3dsite.com—A great source for 3D models and freeware and shareware plug-ins.

- www.max3d.com—News, links, tutorials, and plug-in information.

- www.amazon.com—Billed as "the world's largest bookstore," Amazon offers secure online purchases of a huge variety of books, numbering in the millions. Use its search features to look for books on 3D Studio MAX and other computer graphics topics.

If you subscribe to the CompuServe Information Service, you'll find the Kinetix forum, one of the best sources for 3D Studio MAX information. Technical support personnel from Kinetix subsidiary frequent the forum regularly and are available to answer questions. In addition, third-party vendors who provide supplemental tools for 3D Studio also have a strong presence on the forum. Programmers, animators, and hardware experts are always available to help you with your 3D Studio needs. (At press time, Kinetix was considering moving much of its support from CompuServe to its Web site; check the www.ktx.com Web site for further updates.)

To find the forum, just type "Go Kinetix" at any CompuServe prompt; for your 3D Studio/DOS needs, type "Go Ammedia."

APPENDIX C:
SPECIAL EFFECTS,
ANIMATION,
AND FILMMAKING
RESOURCES

The following books, magazines, and Web sites may be useful to 3D Studio MAX graphics artists, animators, and filmmakers.

Books

Animation, A Reference Guide
Thomas W. Hoffer
Hardcover, $59.95
Greenwood Publications Group, 1982
ISBN 0313210950

Animation: From Script to Screen
Shamus Culhane
Reprint Edition
Paperback, $14.95
St. Martin's Press, 1990
ISBN 0312050526
An ex-Disney animator describes the animation process.

Animals in Motion
Eadweard Muybridge
Hardcover, $24.95
Dover Publications, 1989
ISBN 0486202038

The Muybridge books (see *The Human Figure in Motion*, which follows) have long been considered indispensable reference works for artists and animators studying motion. Muybridge's photographic motion studies, done in the late 1880s, are still invaluable today.

The Complete Book of Scriptwriting
J. Michael Straczynski
Revised
Hardcover, $19.95
Writer's Digest Books, 1996
ISBN 0898795125

J. Michael Straczynski is also the Executive Producer of the TV series *Babylon 5*, which relies almost exclusively on computer-generated imagery for its special effects.

Contemporary Animator
John Halas
Hardcover, $54.95
Focal Press, 1991
ISBN 0240512804

Experimental Animation: Origins of a New Art
Robert Russet and Cecile Starr
Reprint Edition
Hardcover, $14.95
Da Capo Press, 1988
ISBN 0306803143

The Grammar of the Film Language
Daniel Arijon
Reprint Edition
Paperback, $24.95
Samuel French Trade, 1991
ISBN 187950507X

The Human Figure in Motion
Eadweard Muybridge
Hardcover, $24.95
Dover Publications, 1989
ISBN 0486202046

The Illusion of Life: Disney Animation
Frank Thomas and Ollie Johnston
Revised
Hardcover, $60.00
Hyperion, 1995
ISBN 0786860707

Many people regard this as the definitive work on classical animation; computer animators should also study it.

Magazines

American Cinematographer

ASC Holding Corporation

1782 N. Orange Dr., Hollywood, CA 90028

800-448-0145

$5.00 per issue, subscription $35/year, monthly

American Cinematographer often has articles on special visual effects for both film and TV.

Animation

30101 Agoura Court, Suite 110

Agoura Hills, CA 91301

818-991-2884

$4.95, subscription $58/year, monthly

Cinefantastique

7240 W. Roosevelt Rd., Forest Park, IL 60130

708-366-5566

$5.95, subscription $48/year, monthly

This science fiction media magazine often features articles on special effects in film and TV.

Cinefex

Box 20027, Riverside, CA 92516

$8.50, subscription $26/quarterly

The definitive resource for the special effects aficionado. Although it's expensive, it's worth every penny—and it's one of the few magazines in which I read every word, of every issue. Should be required reading for anyone interested in the visual effects field and computer graphics.

Cinescape

Cinescape Group, Inc.

1920 Lombard, IL 60148

708-268-2498

$4.99, $29.95/year, monthly

Starlog

Starlog Group

475 Park Avenue South

New York, NY 10016

800-8775549

$4.99, $39.97/year, monthly

Web Sites

http://www.3dcafe.com
3D Café, source for 3D models and textures.

http://www.aint-it-cool-news
Ain't It Cool News; a movie gossip Web site.

http://www.bftr.com
Banned From The Ranch, a hot special effects house in Santa Monica, California.

http://www.bio-vision.com
Biovision motion capture.

http://www.blur.com
Blur Studios, a special effects house in Santa Monica, California; Blur creates its effects using 3D Studio MAX.

http://www.digitaldirectory.com/animation.html
The Digital Directory.

http://www.dd.com
Digital Domain.

http://www.disney.com
Walt Disney Pictures.

http://www.ktx.com
Kinetix.

http://www.rga.com

R/GA Digital Studios.

http://www.rhythm.com

Rhythm & Hues Studios.

http://www.vfxhq.com

Visual Effects Headquarters, site specializing in discussing special effects.

http://www.viewpoint.com

Viewpoint DataLabs.

http://www.viewpoint.com/avalon

Viewpoint DataLabs: Avalon public domain 3D models and textures site.

INDEX

3

D

N

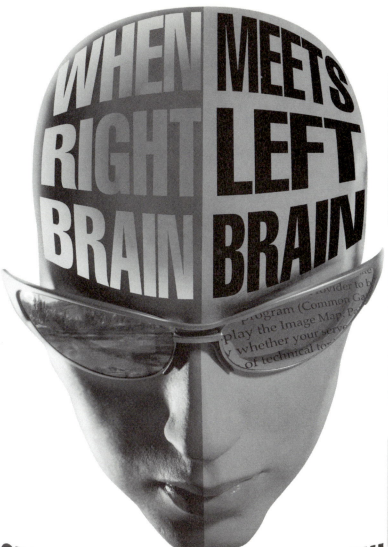

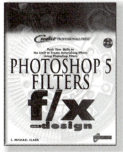

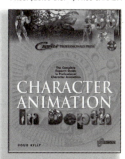

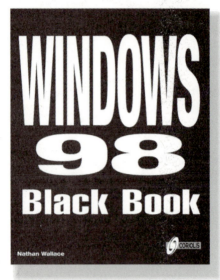